Deep Network Design for Medical Image Computing
Principles and Applications

THE ELSEVIER AND MICCAI SOCIETY BOOK SERIES

Advisory Board

Titles

Balocco, A., et al., Computing and Visualization for Intravascular Imaging and Computer Assisted Stenting, 9780128110188.

Dalca, A.V., et al., Imaging Genetics, 9780128139684.

Depeursinge, A., et al., Biomedical Texture Analysis, 9780128121337.

Munsell, B., et al., Connectomics, 9780128138380.

Pennec, X., et al., Riemannian Geometric Statistics in Medical Image Analysis, 9780128147252.

Trucco, E., et al., Computational Retinal Image Analysis, 9780081028162.

Wu, G., and Sabuncu, M., Machine Learning and Medical Imaging, 9780128040768.

Zhou S.K., Medical Image Recognition, Segmentation and Parsing, 9780128025819.

Zhou, S.K., et al., Deep Learning for Medical Image Analysis, 9780128104088.

Zhou, S.K., et al., Handbook of Medical Image Computing and Computer Assisted Intervention, 9780128161760.

MICCAI

Deep Network Design for Medical Image Computing
Principles and Applications

Haofu Liao

S. Kevin Zhou

Jiebo Luo

ACADEMIC PRESS

An imprint of Elsevier

Academic Press is an imprint of Elsevier
125 London Wall, London EC2Y 5AS, United Kingdom
525 B Street, Suite 1650, San Diego, CA 92101, United States
50 Hampshire Street, 5th Floor, Cambridge, MA 02139, United States
The Boulevard, Langford Lane, Kidlington, Oxford OX5 1GB, United Kingdom

ISBN: 978-0-12-824383-1

For information on all Academic Press publications
visit our website at https://www.elsevier.com/books-and-journals

Publisher: Mara E. Conner
Acquisitions Editor: Tim Pitts
Editorial Project Manager: Emily Thomson
Production Project Manager: Surya Narayanan
Jayachandran
Cover Designer: Christian J. Bilbow

Typeset by VTeX

Working together
to grow libraries in
developing countries

www.elsevier.com • www.bookaid.org

To our families for their enduring support

Contents

List of figures

Acknowledgments

We would like to thank our collaborators for their contributions to the research works involved in the case studies of this book. Specifically, we thank Yuncheng Li for his comments on the research work in Section 3.2. We thank Yucheng Tang for his analysis and summary of some experimental results, and Gareth Funka-Lea for his fruitful comments and inspiration for the research work in Section 4.2. We thank Addisu Mesfin for providing sample data and clinical consulting on the research work in Section 5.2. We thank Wei-An Lin, Jiarui Zhang, and Jingdan Zhang for their participation in data collection and for providing fruitful comments and corrections to the research work in Section 6.2. We thank Zhimin Huo and William J. Sehnert for providing CBCT data, fruitful comments, and detailed feedback on the research work in Section 7.2. We thank Wei-An Lin for his significant contributions in co-leading the project, and Cheng Peng, Xiaohang Sun, Jingdan Zhang, and Rama Chellappa for their analysis, comments, and support of the research work in Section 7.3. We thank Wei-An Lin and Jianbo Yuan for their comments on the research work in Section 8.2. We thank Cheng Peng for his significant contributions in co-leading the project, and Gina Wong and Rama Chellappa for their analysis, comments, and support of the research work in Section 9.2.

CHAPTER

Introduction

1

CONTENTS

1.1 Medical image computing

Medical imaging [2] leverages physical principles such as light, sound, electromagnetic radiation, nuclear magnetic resonance, and radioactivity to create visual representations or images of human (or animal) body often in a noninvasive fashion or sometimes via an invasive procedure. The most common imaging modalities in clinical medicine include X-ray radiography, ultrasound, computed tomography (CT), magnetic resonance imaging (MRI), and digital pathology. Because imaging data account for about 90% of all healthcare data [10], they form one of the most important sources of evidence for clinical decision-making such as clinical diagnosis and medical intervention.

Medical image computing (MIC) concerns the development of computational and mathematical methods for addressing problems pertaining to medical imaging. The MIC field can be broadly divided into two categories,[1] medical image reconstruction and medical image analysis. The former is about forming an image from acquired signals or generating an image with enhanced quality; the latter is about analyzing of an image to derive results meaningful for clinical decision-making. Below we present several key MIC technologies [3,18,1,23] arising from the various medical imaging applications.

---

[1] There is an argument in the literature that MIC is only about medical image analysis in a narrow sense. We include both reconstruction and analysis in our book as we believe that computing is relevant and key to both.

1.1.1 Medical image reconstruction

A medical imaging device such as a CT or MRI scanner acquires signals that are not necessary images already. The goal of *medical image reconstruction* [20] is to compute a visual representation (i.e., an image) from acquired signals.

Denoting the acquired signals by x and the image of the object to be reconstructed by y, often the imaging principle is succinctly expressed by a linear system

$$x = A\,y, \tag{1.1}$$

where A is a system matrix or a transformation operator. For CT, A is a Radon transform; for MRI, A is a Fourier transform.

If x is sufficiently sampled, then reconstruction is straightforward by invoking the corresponding inverse transform. The challenge arises when x is not sufficiently sampled. Reconstruction of high quality images from these restricted acquisitions has important clinical implications. For instance, because iodine dose is often of concern in CT, it is preferred to reduce the radiation exposure to a patient via special acquisitions (such as low dose acquisition) and limited sampling (such as sparse views and limited angles); both, however, induce more imaging noise and artifacts. In MRI, the speed of imaging is important as an MRI scanner is loud and uncomfortable to stay inside. Fast MRI is thus introduced by sampling less signals than usual.

In this book, we broadly include the topic of *medical image enhancement* as a part of medical image reconstruction, which aims to adjust the intensities of an image so that the resultant image is more suitable for display or further analysis. Typically, both the input and output of an enhancement method are images, which differ from those of the aforementioned reconstruction method. But as we will also show in the book, it may be helpful to include the image reconstruction as part of the enhancement procedure to further improve the quality of the resultant images.

Enhancement methods include denoising [7], superresolution [17], CT metal artifact reduction [14], motion artifact removal [4], MRI bias field correction [9], image harmonization [6], and so on. Recently, much research has focused on modality translation and synthesis, which can be considered as image enhancement steps.

1.1.2 Medical image analysis

There are many medical image analysis technologies commonly found in the literature.

Medical image segmentation [19] assigns labels to known pixels so that the pixels with the same label form a segmented object. Segmentation has numerous applications in clinical quantification, therapy, and surgical planning.

Medical image registration [8] aligns the spatial coordinates of one or more images into a common coordinate system. Registration finds its wide applications in population analysis, longitudinal analysis, and multimodal fusion, and is also commonly used for image segmentation via label transfer.

Computer aided detection (CADe) and diagnosis (CADx) [5] are two technologies directly related to clinical diagnosis. CADe aims to localize or find a bounding box that contains an object (typically a lesion) of interest. CADx aims to further classify the localized lesion as benign/malignant or one of multiple lesion types.

Other analysis technologies include landmark detection [15,13], image or view recognition [21,16], automatic report generation [11,22], etc.

1.1.3 Medical image computing as functional approximation

In mathematics, the above MIC technologies can be regarded as function approximation methods, which approximate a true mapping F that takes an image (or multiple images in a multimodal scenario) as input and outputs a specific y,

$$y = F(x). \tag{1.2}$$

The definition of y varies depending on the technology, which itself depends on the application or task. In CADe, y denotes a bounding box; in image registration, y is a deformation field; in image segmentation, y is a label mask image; in image enhancement, y is a quality-enhanced image typically of the same size as the input image x; and in image reconstruction, x is the acquired signal and y is the reconstructed image.

Given a medical image analysis task, there are two common computational frameworks to address it. The first framework is optimization-based,

$$\hat{y} = \arg\min_y L(y, x) + R(y), \tag{1.3}$$

where L is a loss function that measures the inconsistency between y and the observed x, and R is a regularizer or prior belief. For example, in a total variation image reconstruction, $L(y, x) = \|x - A\,y\|_2$ and $R(y) = \|\nabla y\|$. Therefore, in the optimization-based framework, the function approximation is via an *implicit function* that is embedded in the optimization problem.

The second framework is learning-based. Take supervised learning as an example. Assume that a training dataset $\{(x_n, y_n); n = 1, \ldots, N\}$ is available and that the function is parameterized by θ, a learning-based framework aims to minimize a loss function defined as

$$L(\theta) = \frac{1}{N} \sum_{n=1}^{N} L(F_\theta(x_n), y_n) + R(F_\theta(x_n)) + R'(\theta), \tag{1.4}$$

where $L(F_\theta(x), y)$ is a item-wise loss function that penalizes the prediction error, $R(F_\theta(x))$ reflects the prior belief about the output, and $R'(\theta)$ is a regularization term about the function parameters.

There are many ways to approximate F; however, deep learning (DL) [12], a branch of machine learning (ML), is currently one of the most powerful methods for function approximation. Since its renaissance, deep learning has been widely used in various medical imaging tasks and has achieved substantial success in many medical imaging applications. A deep neural network is parameterized by θ, which includes the number of layers, the number of nodes of each layer, the connecting weights, the choices of activation functions, etc. The neural network that is found to approximate F can be written as $F(x) = \phi_{\hat{\theta}}(x)$, where $\hat{\theta}$ comprises the parameters that minimize the above-defined loss function. Although the neural network $\phi_{\hat{\theta}}(x)$ does represent a type of model, it is generally thought of as a "black box" since it does not represent a designed model based on well-understood physical or mathematical principles.

1.2 Deep learning design principles

The concept of deep learning originated from the machine learning community and was initially applied to solve computer vision problems. Since then deep learning has been largely developed in the context of machine learning and computer vision. As a result, there are many deep learning techniques that we could use to solve machine learning and computer vision problems.

MIC is closely related to machine learning and computer vision. In fact, many MIC problems can be formulated in the framework of machine learning and computer vision. Thus, deep learning techniques developed from these two fields may be adapted to address MIC problems. This book introduces deep learning techniques following this regime. That is, for each MIC topic, we associate it with the relevant tasks or approaches in machine learning and computer vision. Then, based on this connection, we present the corresponding deep learning techniques and show how they may be applied to address the MIC topic.

More importantly, we also note that there is specialty and expertise in medicine, and thus the design is not limited to deep learning techniques themselves. Instead, this book also shows how to build deep learning solutions to address challenges that are specific to MIC and to introduce medical domain knowledge that facilitates the problem-solving process.

1.2.1 Computer vision techniques for medical image computing

Over the years, researchers from the computer vision community have well-formulated the basic computer vision problems. For each problem, there have been well-established deep learning architectures and corresponding objectives to train the models. This book introduces how we may learn from the existing solutions of computer vision to address similar problems in MIC.

Connection to computer vision tasks.   Many basic tasks of medical image computing are from computer vision, such as image classification, image segmentation, object detection, image enhancement, etc. Therefore, for those tasks, we formulate problems in the same settings as for computer vision. We provide analogies so that readers may easily map specific problems in MIC to the corresponding computer vision tasks. Moreover, certain tasks in computer vision can be categorized into several subtasks with dedicated solutions. For example, image segmentation may have two variants, semantic and instance segmentation. For MIC, we also follow such a differentiation and show which MIC problems would fall into one category or the other.

Deep neural network architectures.   Designing deep neural network architectures is critical in deep learning. It defines the function (Eq. (1.2)) searching space which largely impacts the performance of a deep learning model. Fortunately, there have been many efforts made in computer vision to address the design of deep neural networks. For MIC, in many cases, we do not need to reinvent the wheel but just adopt the well-performing architectures. Therefore, we introduce the possible choices of network architectures for each MIC topic. In particular, we focus on the seminal architectures in computer vision and provide related works that leveraged those architectures to address MIC problems.

Objective functions.   For objective functions, we mostly introduce those used for supervised learning, as denoted in Eq. (1.4). This is because most of the existing MIC and computer vision problems are formulated under the supervised learning paradigm. The choices of objective functions are often task-dependent, and once we have established the task connections between MIC and computer vision, we could readily apply objective functions from computer vision to MIC.

1.2.2 Machine learning techniques for medical image computing

Computer vision defines the tasks we may use to address MIC problems, and machine learning defines how we may train models for a given task. With the development of deep learning, we have been equipped with various methods to train deep learning models. This flexibility allows us to develop models for MIC under different problem settings.

For example, if we have different types of labels for a given MIC problem, we may choose to leverage all the labels and train the model under a multitask learning setting. If we aim to improve the aesthetic quality of translated images, we may choose to apply adversarial learning. If we do not have paired images for training image enhancement models, we may apply unpaired learning techniques. In this book, we will consider solving MIC problems under these different scenarios and introduce the corresponding learning methods to demonstrate the practical use of deep learning for MIC.

1.2.3 Medical domain knowledge

When designing deep learning solutions, we should also acknowledge the difference between MIC and generic computer vision/machine learning. It is not only about modifying the existing methods in computer vision or machine learning so that they can work with the corresponding MIC problems. It is also crucial to identify and leverage domain knowledge in medicine so that the overall solution better addresses MIC problems. Specifically, this book will mostly cover the following topics when introducing medical domain knowledge.

Volumetric image processing. Many MIC problems involve volumetric images such as CT and MR images. In contrast, it is very rare to see volumetric images used when solving general computer vision problems. As a result, deep learning techniques were initially designed to only work with 2D images; when it comes to volumetric images they may not be directly applicable. Direct application may be incapable of understanding 3D context and/or incur high computational cost. This book will introduce deep learning solutions in MIC with specific designs to address volumetric images.

Medical physics. Medical physics is the foundation of medical imaging. It provides theories for medical image reconstruction. Therefore, when addressing many medical image reconstruction problems, it could be quite helpful to take medical physics into consideration. For example, we may consider Radon transformation for CT image reconstruction and Fourier transformation for MR image reconstruction. Meanwhile, existing image enhancement approaches for natural images are mostly agnostic of the image reconstruction process because the imaging information is unknown or lost, and the deep learning models work only within the image domain. In this book, we introduce how to apply deep learning solutions from computer vision to address medical image reconstruction problems. More importantly, we show how to put them under the context of medical physics and propose specialized designs for medical image reconstruction.

Problem-specific knowledge. Moreover, for many MIC problems, we may also consider exploring problem-specific knowledge when designing deep learning solutions. For example, in skin lesion recognition, we may consider the occurrence of skin lesions in different body locations and leverage this information for better recognition of skin lesions. In vertebrae localization, we may exploit the fact that vertebrae in a spine column are sequentially ordered and introduce special deep neural networks such as recurrent neural networks to better learn to produce inherently sequential outputs. In this book, we will focus on several case studies where problem-specific knowledge may be considered and present designs to incorporate the knowledge.

1.3 Chapter organization

Since these design principles are in fact motivated by real tasks, they are best illustrated in real applications. Thus, we naturally organize the book in the following order. Chapter 2 introduces deep learning basics. It is then followed by various chapters on four representative analysis tasks, including skin disease and lesion recognition (Chapter 3), vertebrae location and identification from CT (Chapter 4), cardiac structure contouring from intracardiac echocardiography (Chapter 5), and 2D–3D registration for image-guided intervention (Chapter 6), as well as three representative reconstruction tasks, including CT artifact reduction with supervised (Chapter 7) and unsupervised (Chapter 8) settings and synthesis of novel X-ray view (Chapter 9).

Table 1.1 The organization of book chapters with their corresponding design principles.

Chapter	Problems	Technologies	Imaging modalities	Deep learning modules	Medical domain knowledge	Generative model for medicine
3	Skin disease / lesion recognition	Classification	Dermatology image	2D CNN, transfer learning multitask learning	Correlation between lesion types and body locations	–
4	Vertebrae location and identification	Detection	CT	Multitask 3D CNN, recurrent NN	Sequential order of spinal columns	–
5	Cardiac structure contouring	Segmentation	Ultrasound	3D UNet, 2D UNet	Cardiac priors from CT, ultrasound catheter positions	GAN for cross-modality 3D inpainting
6	Image-guided intervention	Registration	CT & X-ray	Multiview Siamese UNet	Digitally reconstructed radiographs, X-ray points-of-interest triangulation	–
7	Supervised artifact reduction	Reconstruction	CT	Mask pyramid network, Radon inverse layer	Radon transformation for tomography	Multiscale feature LSGAN, focus loss
8	Unsupervised artifact reduction	Reconstruction	CT	Artifact disentanglement network	Artifact-free & -affected group, artifact disentanglement	Latent space manipulation
9	Novel view synthesis	Synthesis	X-ray	3D UNet, Residual dense network	Differentiable CT forward- and backprojection, X-ray imaging simulation	GAN for realistic X-ray synthesis

Table 1.1 contains a list of chapters together with specifications about tasks, imaging modalities, and applicable deep learning techniques.

References

[1] Isaac Bankman, Handbook of Medical Image Processing and Analysis, Elsevier, 2008.

[2] Jacob Beutel, Harold L. Kundel, Richard L. Van Metter, Handbook of Medical Imaging, vol. 1, SPEI Press, 2000.

[3] Jacob Beutel, Milan Sonka, Harold L. Kundel, Richard L. Van Metter, J. Michael Fitzpatrick, Handbook of Medical Imaging: Medical Image Processing and Analysis, vol. 2, SPIE Press, 2000.

[4] Jonathan D. Blumenthal, Alex Zijdenbos, Elizabeth Molloy, Jay N. Giedd, Motion artifact in magnetic resonance imaging: implications for automated analysis, NeuroImage 16 (1) (2002) 89–92.

[5] Heang-Ping Chan, Lubomir M. Hadjiiski, Ravi K. Samala, Computer-aided diagnosis in the era of deep learning, Medical Physics 47 (5) (2020) e218–e227.

[6] Blake E. Dewey, Can Zhao, Jacob C. Reinhold, Aaron Carass, Kathryn C. Fitzgerald, Elias S. Sotirchos, Shiv Saidha, Jiwon Oh, Dzung L. Pham, Peter A. Calabresi, et al., DeepHarmony: a deep learning approach to contrast harmonization across scanner changes, Magnetic Resonance Imaging 64 (2019) 160–170.

[7] Manoj Diwakar, Manoj Kumar, A review on CT image noise and its denoising, Biomedical Signal Processing and Control 42 (2018) 73–88.

[8] Yabo Fu, Yang Lei, Tonghe Wang, Walter J. Curran, Tian Liu, Xiaofeng Yang, Deep learning in medical image registration: a review, Physics in Medicine and Biology (2020).

[9] Mélanie Gaillochet, Kerem Can Tezcan, Ender Konukoglu, Joint reconstruction and bias field correction for undersampled MR imaging, in: International Conference on Medical Image Computing and Computer-Assisted Intervention, Springer, 2020, pp. 44–52.

[10] GE Healthcare, Beyond imaging: the paradox of AI and medical imaging innovation, https://www.gehealthcare.com/article/beyond-imagingthe-paradox-of-ai-and-medical-imaging-innovation, 2018.

[11] Baoyu Jing, Pengtao Xie, Eric Xing, On the automatic generation of medical imaging reports, in: Proceedings of the 56th Annual Meeting of the Association for Computational Linguistics (Volume 1: Long Papers), 2018, pp. 2577–2586.

[12] Yann LeCun, Yoshua Bengio, Geoffrey Hinton, Deep learning, Nature 521 (7553) (2015) 436.

[13] Weijian Li, Yuhang Lu, Kang Zheng, Haofu Liao, Chihung Lin, Jiebo Luo, Chi-Tung Cheng, Jing Xiao, Le Lu, Chang-Fu Kuo, Shun Miao, Structured landmark detection via topology-adapting deep graph learning, in: Andrea Vedaldi, Horst Bischof, Thomas Brox, Jan-Michael Frahm (Eds.), Computer Vision – ECCV 2020 – 16th European Conference, Glasgow, UK, August 23–28, 2020, Proceedings, Part IX, in: Lecture Notes in Computer Science, vol. 12354, Springer, 2020, pp. 266–283.

[14] Wei-An Lin, Haofu Liao, Cheng Peng, Xiaohang Sun, Jingdan Zhang, Jiebo Luo, Rama Chellappa, Shaohua Kevin Zhou, DuDoNet: dual domain network for CT metal artifact reduction, in: IEEE Conference on Computer Vision and Pattern Recognition, CVPR 2019, Long Beach, CA, USA, June 16–20, 2019, Computer Vision Foundation / IEEE, 2019, pp. 10512–10521.

[15] David Liu, S. Kevin Zhou, Dominik Bernhardt, Dorin Comaniciu, Search strategies for multiple landmark detection by submodular maximization, in: 2010 IEEE Computer Society Conference on Computer Vision and Pattern Recognition, IEEE, 2010, pp. 2831–2838.

[16] Hui Luo, Jiebo Luo, Robust online orientation correction for radiographs in PACS environments, IEEE Transactions on Medical Imaging 25 (10) (2006) 1370–1379.

[17] Dwarikanath Mahapatra, Behzad Bozorgtabar, Rahil Garnavi, Image super-resolution using progressive generative adversarial networks for medical image analysis, Computerized Medical Imaging and Graphics 71 (2019) 30–39.

[18] Jerry L. Prince, Jonathan M. Links, Medical Imaging Signals and Systems, Pearson Prentice Hall, Upper Saddle River, 2006.

[19] Nima Tajbakhsh, Laura Jeyaseelan, Qian Li, Jeffrey N. Chiang, Zhihao Wu, Xiaowei Ding, Embracing imperfect datasets: a review of deep learning solutions for medical image segmentation, Medical Image Analysis (2020) 101693.

[20] Ge Wang, Yi Zhang, Xiaojing Ye, Xuanqin Mou, Machine Learning for Tomographic Imaging, IOP Publishing, 2019.

[21] Zhoubing Xu, Yuankai Huo, JinHyeong Park, Bennett Landman, Andy Milkowski, Sasa Grbic, S. Kevin Zhou, Less is more: simultaneous view classification and landmark detection for abdominal ultrasound images, in: International Conference on Medical Image Computing and Computer Assisted Intervention, Springer, 2018, pp. 711–719.

[22] Jianbo Yuan, Haofu Liao, Rui Luo, Jiebo Luo, Automatic radiology report generation based on multi-view image fusion and medical concept enrichment, in: Dinggang Shen, Tianming Liu, Terry M. Peters, Lawrence H. Staib, Caroline Essert, Sean Zhou, Pew-Thian Yap, Ali R. Khan (Eds.), Medical Image Computing and Computer Assisted Intervention – MICCAI 2019 – 22nd International Conference, Shenzhen, China, October 13–17, 2019, Proceedings, Part VI, in: Lecture Notes in Computer Science, vol. 11769, Springer, 2019, pp. 721–729.

[23] S. Kevin Zhou, Daniel Rueckert, Gabor Fichtinger, Handbook of Medical Image Computing and Computer Assisted Intervention, Academic Press, 2019.

Deep learning basics

CONTENTS

2.1 Convolutional neural networks

Convolutional neural network (CNN) is one of the most popular neural networks used in deep learning. The first successful CNN model was proposed by Lecun et al. [22] in 1998 for hand-written digit recognition. Despite this early success, however, CNNs were not widely used until the booming of deep learning, especially when Krizhevsky et al. [21] proposed a CNN named AlexNet which won the first place in the ILSVRC [33] competition from ImageNet. The successes of AlexNet and its successors, such as VGGNet [36], Inception [39], and ResNet [17], etc., are mostly due to three factors [35]: 1) the availability of large dataset, 2) the advances in GPUs and the corresponding high performance libraries for scientific computing, and 3) the developments in training deep neural networks.

    The core building block of a CNN is the convolutional layer. Let $\mathcal{W} = \{\mathbf{W}_1, \mathbf{W}_2, \ldots, \mathbf{W}_K\}$ be a set of kernels and $\mathcal{B} = \{b_1, b_2, \ldots, b_K\}$ be a set of biases. Then, for an input $\mathbf{X}^{l-1}$, the computation of the lth convolution layer with the kth kernel can be written as

$$\mathbf{X}_k^l = f(\mathbf{W}_k * \mathbf{X}^{l-1} + b_k), \qquad (2.1)$$

where $*$ denotes a convolution operation, and f is an activation function. Eq. (2.1) is repeated for each kernel, which results in a K-dimensional feature map, i.e., $\mathbf{X}^l = \{\mathbf{X}_1^l, \mathbf{X}_2^l, \ldots, \mathbf{X}_K^l\}$. Fig. 2.2(a) illustrates a typical 2D convolution operation

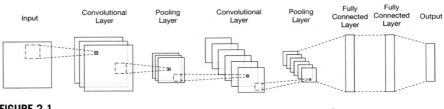

FIGURE 2.1

An example CNN structure.

with a kernel convolving with an image. The convolution operates in a sliding window manner. At each window location, it computes the dot-product between the entries of the kernel and the corresponding pixels in the image. The pixels form an image patch with the same size as the kernel.

The convolutional layers in CNNs are effective in extracting features from images as they can exploit the spatially-local correlation of neighborhood pixels. And because convolutional layers are sparsely connected, when compared with standard feedforward neural networks with similar depth, CNNs have significantly fewer parameters. This not only makes CNNs more computationally efficient but also more easily trainable.

As shown in Fig. 2.1, a typical convolutional neural network usually has several convolutional layers with periodically inserted pooling layers in-between. The convolutional layers are used to extract hierarchical feature representations and pooling layers serve to reduce the spatial size of the feature representations which then reduces the amount of parameters and computation in CNNs. At the end of CNNs, there are usually several fully-connected layers which act as a classifier for the extracted feature representations.

2.1.1 3D convolutional neural networks

Standard CNNs have 2D convolutional layers for feature extraction, and they work very well in 2D image processing. However, when it comes to volumetric image processing, 2D convolutional layers may not be a good choice.

A straightforward approach to volumetric image processing is to think of the volume slices as the color channels in 2D images, and thus 2D convolution operation can be directly applied. As illustrated in Fig. 2.2(a), the 2D slices on the left form the input of size $H \times W \times C$. For a 2D color image, C equals to 3, and for a volumetric image, C equals to the length of the third dimension. For 2D convolution, the kernel is 3D with size $M \times N \times C$ where the third dimension spans across all the channels, i.e., the third dimension equals to C. This encodes the features across the channel dimension and maps the result back to a 2D feature map. However, for 3D images, such encoding strategy is not appropriate as the spatial information along the third dimension will be lost when all the information of that dimension is aggregated onto a 2D feature map.

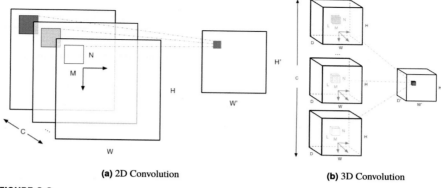

(a) 2D Convolution   **(b)** 3D Convolution

FIGURE 2.2

Comparison of 2D convolution and 3D convolution.

Instead, a better solution would be using 3D convolutional layers for volumetric images. Fig. 2.2(b) illustrates a 3D convolution operation. The input on the left is 4D of size $W \times H \times D \times C$ (shown as a sequence of 3D volumes), i.e., three spatial dimensions plus a channel dimension. For a volumetric image, it only has one channel, i.e., $C = 1$. For intermediate 3D convolutional layers, the inputs are 3D feature maps with the channel dimension representing the features of a 3D region, i.e., C equals the number of features. Similarly, the kernel of a 3D convolution is 4D of size $M \times N \times L \times C$ (displayed as a sequence of small 3D volumes). When the kernel moves in a sliding window manner along the three dimensional directions, 3D local spatial information will be mapped to the corresponding 3D location in the feature map. This gives a better 3D feature representation than the compromised solution with 2D convolutional layers.

One limitation of 3D CNNs is their high computational cost, due to the use of 3D convolution. Therefore, they are relatively less exploited by the medical image computing community. One of the first papers using 3D CNNs was proposed Dou et al. [12] in 2016 for detecting cerebral microbleeds from MR images. In their paper, the authors only trained and fed their 3D CNN with small MR samples, and in this way they avoided the expensive 3D convolution for the entire image. Following their idea, 3D CNNs have been applied to other problems such as heart segmentation [23], intervertebral disc localization and detection [7], brain segmentation [6], gland segmentation [8], etc.

2.2 Recurrent neural networks

Recurrent neural network (RNN) is another important type of neural network. It differs from conventional feedforward neural networks in that it contains feed-back connections and internal states. These components allow RNN to process a sequence of inputs and keep track of contextual information of inputs at different time steps.

Given a sequence of T inputs $\{\mathbf{x}_1, \mathbf{x}_2, \ldots, \mathbf{x}_T\}$ and an initial hidden state $\mathbf{h}_0$ at time step 0, the simplest form of RNN can be written as follows:

$$\mathbf{h}_t = f(\mathbf{W}\mathbf{x}_t + \mathbf{V}\mathbf{h}_{t-1} + \mathbf{b}), \tag{2.2}$$

where f is a nonlinear activation function, $\mathbf{b}$ is the bias, $\mathbf{W}$ and $\mathbf{V}$ are the weights for the inputs and hidden states, respectively. RNN can be regarded as a program with an internal state. At each time step t, RNN uses its current state $\mathbf{h}_{t-1}$ to process the input $\mathbf{x}_t$ and updates the state to $\mathbf{h}_t$ for future computation. In this way, RNN can exploit the relation among the inputs at different time steps, which makes it good at processing sequences.

Due to this capability of processing sequences, RNNs have been widely applied to address problems requiring sequence modeling. They are initially introduced to address nature language processing problems, such as text generation [26,27,37], machine translation [3,38,24], speech recognition [16], and image captioning [40,11,41]. RNNs have also gained attention from the medical image computing community, and have been used for cardiac image analysis [20,31], blood vessel segmentation [14], and tissue segmentation [1], etc.

2.2.1 Long short-term memory

Neural networks often suffer from being too deep due to the well-known vanishing gradient problem. When the input sequence is long, RNN is effectively deep in time. Therefore, it also suffers from processing long sequences for the same reason. To address this problem, Hochreiter et al. [19] proposed a novel RNN architecture called long short-term memory (LSTM) in 1997, which not only addresses the vanishing gradient problem but also models better the long range dependencies of input sequence.

Depending on the hidden state connectivities and activation functions, LSTM can have several variations. A widely used LSTM is given as follows [15]:

$$\begin{pmatrix} \mathbf{i}_t \\ \mathbf{f}_t \\ \mathbf{o}_t \\ \mathbf{g}_t \end{pmatrix} = \begin{pmatrix} \sigma \\ \sigma \\ \sigma \\ \tanh \end{pmatrix} T_{2n,4n} \begin{pmatrix} \mathbf{h}_t^{l-1} \\ \mathbf{h}_{t-1}^l \end{pmatrix}, \tag{2.3}$$

$$\mathbf{c}_t^l = \mathbf{f}_t \odot \mathbf{c}_{t-1}^l + \mathbf{i}_t \odot \mathbf{g}_t, \tag{2.4}$$

$$\mathbf{h}_t^l = \mathbf{o}_t \odot \tanh(\mathbf{c}_t^l). \tag{2.5}$$

Here, $\mathbf{i}$, $\mathbf{f}$, $\mathbf{o}$, $\mathbf{g}$, $\mathbf{c}$, and $\mathbf{h}$ are the input gate, forget gate, output gate, input modulation gate, cell, and hidden state, respectively; $T_{2n,4n}$ denotes an affine transformation that maps hidden states at previous time step $\mathbf{h}_{t-1}^l$ and previous layer $\mathbf{h}_t^{l-1}$ to the corresponding gate outputs. The results of $T_{2n,4n}$ are applied element-wise via σ or tanh, where σ denotes the sigmoid function.

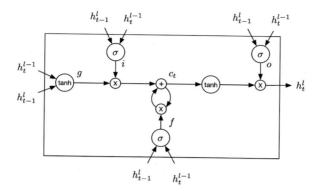

FIGURE 2.3

The architecture of an LSTM memory cell [42].

The architecture of an LSTM cell is given in Fig. 2.3. The $\mathbf{h}_t^{l-1}$ from previous layer and $\mathbf{h}_{t-1}^{l}$ from previous time step will first be modulated by the modulation gate g. Then, the information from g will be filtered by the input gate i, i.e., the input gate i decides which input should be kept. The filtered input will be part of c_t. The other part of c_t will be from c_{t-1} which is filtered by the forget gate f, i.e., the forget gate f decides which information from c_{t-1} should be erased. The two parts will be added up to produce current cell state c_t. Finally, the hidden state h_t^l for current time step and layer is computed by modulating with a tanh function and applying output gate o.

2.2.2 Bidirectional RNN

Standard RNNs usually assume that information from future inputs is not available at the current time step. However, for some applications, such an assumption is not always necessary. For example, in machine translation where the task is to translate a sentence from one language to another, we are not limited to only seeing the words that have already been translated but also future words to be translated. Thus, Schuster et al. [34] proposed a new RNN structure, called bidirectional RNN, which can make use of the information from future time steps.

The architecture of a bidirectional RNN is simple. As shown in Fig. 2.4, a bidirectional RNN can be constructed by stacking two RNN cells of different directions: one from left to right and the other from right to left. At each time step t, the input x_t will be fed into both RNN cells, which encode the information from the past and future, respectively. Then, the final result y_t is computed by combining the outputs of the two RNN cells. Formally put, let x_t be the input at time step t, $\mathbf{h}_{t-1}$ and $\mathbf{h}_{t+1}$ be the hidden states at time $t-1$ and $t+1$, respectively. The corresponding equations for computing a bidirectional RNN can be written as

$$\overrightarrow{\mathbf{h}_t} = f(\overrightarrow{\mathbf{W}}\mathbf{x}_t + \overrightarrow{\mathbf{V}}\mathbf{h}_{t-1} + \overrightarrow{\mathbf{b}}), \qquad (2.6)$$

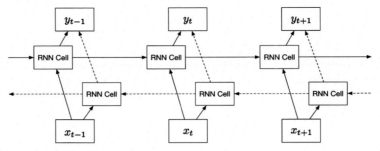

FIGURE 2.4

Bidirectional RNN.

$$\overleftarrow{\mathbf{h}_t} = f(\overleftarrow{\mathbf{W}}\mathbf{x}_t + \overleftarrow{\mathbf{V}}\mathbf{h}_{t+1} + \overleftarrow{\mathbf{b}}), \tag{2.7}$$

$$\mathbf{y}_t = g(\mathbf{U}\mathbf{h}_t + \mathbf{c}) = g(\mathbf{U}[\overrightarrow{\mathbf{h}_t}; \overleftarrow{\mathbf{h}_t}] + \mathbf{c}), \tag{2.8}$$

where $\overrightarrow{\mathbf{W}}$, $\overrightarrow{\mathbf{V}}$, $\overleftarrow{\mathbf{W}}$, $\overleftarrow{\mathbf{V}}$, and $\mathbf{U}$ are the weights of the LSTM cells; $\overrightarrow{\mathbf{b}}$, $\overleftarrow{\mathbf{b}}$, and $\mathbf{c}$ are the biases of the LSTM cells; f and g are the activation functions.

2.3 Deep image-to-image networks

Deep image-to-image networks (DI2INs) refer to the neural networks whose input and output have the same spatial dimensions. The input to a DI2IN is usually an image. The output is a translated representation of the input, and its content spatially aligns with the input. The exact form of the output is task dependent. For a segmentation task, the output is a segmentation mask. For an image superresolution task, the output is a higher-resolution version of the input. Given this definition, many medical image computing problems fall into this category, and DI2INs play an important role to address these problems. In this section, we introduce basic concepts of DI2IN. We will revisit DI2IN multiple times in later chapters when discussing specific solutions to medical image computing problems.

2.3.1 Retaining spatial resolutions

Typically, DI2IN are constructed with convolutional layers and thus can be regarded as a special type of CNN (while by definition it may not be limited to CNNs). However, conventional CNNs consist of pooling layers and strided convolutions; both reduce the spatial resolution of the extracted feature maps. While this is intended for hierarchical feature extraction, it conflicts with the goal of DI2INs for retaining spatial resolution of inputs. A simple solution to address this problem is to avoid pooling layers or strided convolutions in the network architecture. However, this will significantly increase computational costs which prohibit training deep neural networks.

Moreover, without pooling or strided convolution operations, receipt fields of convolutional layers will only increase slowly which results in poor feature extractions.

To better retain the spatial resolutions, an alternative solution is to add operations that reverse the downsampling effect of pooling and strided convolutions. There are two common choices for this idea. One is to introduce deconvolution layers which operate as the backward of the strided convolution and thus increase the spatial resolution of the input. The limitation of deconvolution layers is that they will introduce checkerboard artifacts [30]. This is usually fine for segmentation tasks but creates problems for tasks such as artifact reduction where the fidelity of the outputs is critical. Another way is to introduce upsampling operators followed by convolutional layers. The common upsampling operations, such as bilinear interpolation, do not have the checkerboard artifact problem and hence is better in preserving fidelity. The only compromise is that this solution is slightly more expensive than deconvolutions.

2.3.2 Fully convolutional networks

Conventional CNNs also have fully connected (FC) layers at the end. This is required for classification tasks to map extracted features to classification predictions. However, for DI2INs, it becomes infeasible with FC layers since the outputs of FC layers have fixed dimensions, which again conflicts with the requirement of DI2INs. To address this problem, we could simply remove FC layers from CNNs and, for the last convolution layer, we set the output feature dimension to the expected dimension of the task. For example, we set the output dimension to three if we expect the output to be an image.

Alternatively, we may choose not to throw away FC layers. In particular, CNN models for classification usually perform well on feature extraction and may serve as backbones for downstream tasks. In this case, we may reuse those CNN models and transform them into DI2INs. To this end, we transform FC layers into convolutional layers with "1 × 1" kernels [25]. In this way, the transformed network is identical to the original CNN model, but outputs feature maps instead of fixed-sized feature vectors. With this design, we could then add deconvolution layers at the end to retain the spatial dimensions of the input (as we have introduced earlier). Such network architectures without FC layers are called "fully convolution networks (FCNs)." In fact, all DI2INs can be as regarded as FCNs.

2.3.3 Encoder–decoder networks

The original FCN architecture was modified from CNN models and thus has a relatively weak decoding part. That is, the CNN model extracts strong visual features, but the generation of outputs is only achieved via a few deconvolution layers. For a better generation of outputs, we may employ an encoder–decoder design for DI2INs. Specifically, we introduce a dedicated network called decoder to decode outputs from the extracted features. The encoder design is similar to CNN architectures for classification and consists of a set of encoding blocks (e.g., convolutional layers followed by pooling layers) to extract features with relatively higher semantics. The decoder design is usually symmetric to the encoder and has the same number of decoding blocks (as the encoding counterparts in the encoder). With this design, encoder–decoder networks provide stronger generation of the output, which is important to DI2INs where generation quality is usually a major performance metric.

Moreover, the encoder–decoder design is usually combined with skip connections for better decoding of the visual features. The original skip connection idea was introduced by He et al. [18] which combined visual features from earlier layers to later ones to facilitate the learning of deep CNNs. Inspired by this idea, skip connections are also employed in encoder–decoder networks. The most famous one is U-Net [32] which introduces skip connections between the encoder and decoder. In this way, lower level visual features can also be leveraged by the decoder for better generation of outputs.

2.4 Deep generative networks

In recent years, there is a surge of research interest in deep generative models (DGMs). For medical image computing, DGMs have been widely applied to address medical image reconstruction problems. The straightforward way of introducing DGMs for medical image reconstruction is to directly apply basic models, such as variational autoencoders (VAEs) or generative adversarial networks (GANs). But as we will see later in this book, it is also beneficial to leverage external knowledge in medicine to improve the performance and/or advance the functionalities of DGMs for better medical image reconstruction. In this section, we introduce different ways in literature to demonstrate how DGMs may interact with external knowledge.

Before moving on to knowledge-involved models, we first briefly introduce the two seminal DGMs, VAEs and GANs. VAE proposes a practical estimator of the variational lower bound by introducing a reparameterization trick, such that the approximation of the posterior is tractable and efficient. Based on this technique, VAE can be readily implemented by formulating the approximated posterior as the encoder and the likelihood as the decoder. Note that the encoder (also known as the inference model) is trained jointly with the decoder (also known as the generative model) in VAEs. This allows a mapping from the data space to the latent space and is very useful for many problems such as feature learning and image-conditioned generation.

GANs propose to bypass the intractable probabilistic computation by approximating a sampling network for the data distribution. The sampling network is trained in an adversarial fashion where a generator is trained to generate data samples as "real" as possible, while a discriminator is trained to distinguish "real" samples from generated samples. Most importantly, the authors proved that when the global optimum is achieved, the approximated data distribution is identical to the real data distribution if unlimited capacity is given to the generator and discriminator. However, unlike VAEs, GANs do not originally provide an inference mechanism which makes them incapable of giving an abstract interpretation of data samples.

2.4.1 Basic models

In this section, we introduce some basic variants of VAEs or GANs. We focus on basic increments to VAEs or GANs where new functionalities are enabled to allow better knowledge interaction. We only select those models that are considered as building blocks of many other models/applications.

cGAN. The conditional GAN (cGAN) [28] came right after the original GAN paper to enable the control over the generation. Given a noise z and a conditional input y, e.g., categorical labels, the model controls the generation by allowing the generator to see both the data sample (generated or real) and the corresponding conditional input y at the same time. In this way, the discriminator can learn to figure out any discordance between the generator outputs and the conditional inputs. This forces generator to output data samples that correspond to the conditional input and hence imposes the control. The objective function for cGAN can then be given as

$$\min_{G} \max_{D} V(D, G) = \mathbb{E}_{\mathbf{x} \sim p(\mathbf{x})}[\log D(\mathbf{x}|y)] + \mathbb{E}_{z \sim p(z)}[\log(1 - D(G(z|y)))]. \quad (2.9)$$

The control in cGAN, however, is implicitly induced and hence is not always guaranteed. In the extreme case, the discriminator can choose to ignore the conditional input with the objective still being optimized.

InfoGAN. In terms of functionalities, a conventional GAN typically has two limitations: 1) it does not have an inference mechanism; 2) its generation cannot be controlled. InfoGAN [9] is proposed to address these two issues. It provides an unsupervised disentanglement over the latent variables and an inference network for the disentangled component of the latent variables. InfoGAN achieves this by maximizing the mutual information between a controlling latent code c, i.e., the latent variables to be disentangled, and the generator output $G(z, c)$ where G denotes the generator and z denotes other latent variables. Intuitively, this means that we want z to be easily inferred from the generator's output $G(z, c)$. Formally, this means adding a mutual information term to the original GAN objective,

$$\min_{G,Q} \max_{D} V_{\text{InfoGAN}}(D, G, Q) = V(D, G) - \lambda L_I(G, Q). \quad (2.10)$$

Here, D denotes the discriminator, Q denotes the inference network for c, $V(D, G)$ denotes the original GAN objective, and $L_I(G, Q)$ denotes the variational mutual information term.

ALI/BiGAN. Although InfoGAN provides an inference mechanism to GANs to certain extent, it cannot perform inference to the whole latent vector which limits its ability to infer a full latent representation for data samples. This can be addressed using ALI [13] and BiGAN [10]. Note that ALI and BiGAN are identical models independently proposed by Dumoulin et al. and Donahue et al. In this idea, they introduce an encoder network E to perform the inference, i.e., mapping a data sample $\mathbf{x}$ to its latent space $E(\mathbf{x})$. Then, having the discriminator to distinguish between the

real data plus inferred representation pair, i.e., $(\mathbf{x}, E(\mathbf{x}))$ and the generated data plus
the real latent coding pair, i.e., $(G(z), z)$. This idea can be formally written as

$$\min_{G,E} \max_D V(D, E, G) = \mathbb{E}_{\mathbf{x}\sim p(\mathbf{x})}[\log D(\mathbf{x}, E(\mathbf{x}))] + \mathbb{E}_{z\sim p(z)}[\log(1 - D(G(z), z))].$$
(2.11)

This method offered a simple, yet useful function to GANs. Especially, when the
generation is conditioned on an input image, the encoder can directly convert the
image to a generator recognizable latent code to facilitate the control.

ACGAN.   Another approach to controlled generation using side information is
proposed by ACGAN [29]. Unlike the cGAN approach, the control in ACGAN in explicitly enforced. It uses an auxiliary classifier to infer the conditional input from the
generated outputs. Therefore, the generator has to output data samples that consistent
with the conditional inputs. Note that the auxiliary classifier may share parameters
with the discriminator in a multitask learning [5] fashion and the objective functions
in this case can be written as

$$L_{\text{adv}} = \mathbb{E}_{\mathbf{x}\sim p(\mathbf{x})}[\log D(\mathbf{x})] + \mathbb{E}_{z\sim p(z)}[\log(1 - D(G(z, y)))],$$
(2.12)
$$L_{\text{cls}} = \mathbb{E}_{\mathbf{x}\sim p(\mathbf{x})}[\log p(y|D(\mathbf{x}))] + \mathbb{E}_{z\sim p(z)}[\log p(y|D(G(z, y)))],$$
(2.13)

where D is trained to maximize $L_{\text{cls}} + L_{\text{adv}}$ while G is trained to maximize $L_{\text{cls}} -
L_{\text{adv}}$.

DAGAN.   One of the disadvantages of cGAN and ACGAN is that they require
the side information (conditional input) to be seen during the training. However, in
some cases, such as data augmentation, this may not be satisfied. Instead, it may
require the side information to contain some features that can be interpreted by the
generator. To tackle this situation, DAGAN [2] can be an option. Let $\mathbf{x}_i$ and $\mathbf{x}_j$ be
two distinct real data samples. DAGAN uses an encoder E to encode the embedded
features of $\mathbf{x}_i$. The encoding is necessary as it extracts the side information that is
recognizable to the generator G, i.e., only part of the information from $\mathbf{x}_i$ is used
as the side information. Then G combines the latent code from $E(\mathbf{x}_i)$ and the noise
z to generate the data sample. The discriminator D distinguishes between the real
pair $(\mathbf{x}_i, \mathbf{x}_j)$ and fake pair $(G(E(\mathbf{x}_i), z)), \mathbf{x}_j)$. Here, $\mathbf{x}_j$ is to make sure the generated
sample is different from $\mathbf{x}_i$ to avoid an identity mapping. The objective function for
DAGAN can be given as

$$\min_{G,E} \max_D V(D, E, G) = \mathbb{E}_{\mathbf{x}\sim p(\mathbf{x})}[\log D(\mathbf{x}_i, G(E(\mathbf{x}_i), z))]$$
$$+ \mathbb{E}_{z\sim p(z)}[\log(1 - D(\mathbf{x}_i, \mathbf{x}_j))].$$
(2.14)

ML-VAE.   In the general case of data augmentation, for a given set of data samples with the same topic, we want to generate more data samples of that topic. This,
however, cannot be well addressed by DAGAN as it can only take a look at one data
sample at a time. When the given data sample is not generalized well by DAGAN,
the data augmentation is failed. One possible solution to this situation is to allow the

generator to have a look at the entire set of available samples of that topic. Thus, the generator can get a better chance to understand more aspects of the topic and generate better about the samples. This is exactly what ML-VAE [4] attempts to achieve. Let G be a group of samples of the same topic. ML-VAE assumes that the data samples between groups are independent and data samples with in a group are dependent. The objective function of the VAE can be rewritten as

$$
\begin{aligned}
\text{ELBO}(G; \theta, \phi_c, \phi_s) = &\sum_{i \in G} \mathbb{E}_{q_{\phi_c}(C_G | \mathbf{X}_G)} [\mathbb{E}_{q_{\phi_s}(S_i | X_i)} [\log p_\theta (X_i | C_G, S_i)]] \\
&- \sum_{i \in G} D_{\text{KL}}(q_{\phi_s}(S_i | X_i) \| p(S_i)) - D_{\text{KL}}(q_{\phi_c}(C_G | \mathbf{X}_G) \| p(C_G)),
\end{aligned}
$$

(2.15)

where θ is the parameters of the generative model, ϕ_c is the topic parameters of the inference model, ϕ_s is the variance parameters of the inference model, C_G is the latent code for the group, S_i is the latent code for the ith sample in the group, $\mathbf{X_G}$ is all the samples in the group, X_i is the ith data sample, q_{ϕ_c} is the topic part of the inference model, q_{ϕ_s} is the variance part of the inference model, and p_θ is the generative model.

References

[1] Simon Andermatt, Simon Pezold, Philippe Cattin, Multi-dimensional gated recurrent units for the segmentation of biomedical 3D-data, in: International Workshop on Large-Scale Annotation of Biomedical Data and Expert Label Synthesis, Springer, 2016, pp. 142–151.

[2] Antreas Antoniou, Amos Storkey, Harrison Edwards, Data augmentation generative adversarial networks, arXiv preprint, arXiv:1711.04340, 2017.

[3] Michael Auli, Michel Galley, Chris Quirk, Geoffrey Zweig, Joint language and translation modeling with recurrent neural networks, in: EMNLP, vol. 3, 2013.

[4] Diane Bouchacourt, Ryota Tomioka, Sebastian Nowozin, Multi-level variational autoencoder: learning disentangled representations from grouped observations, arXiv preprint, arXiv:1705.08841, 2017.

[5] Rich Caruana, Multitask learning, in: Learning to Learn, Springer, 1998, pp. 95–133.

[6] Hao Chen, Qi Dou, Lequan Yu, Pheng-Ann Heng, VoxResNet: deep voxelwise residual networks for volumetric brain segmentation, arXiv preprint, arXiv:1608.05895, 2016.

[7] Hao Chen, Qi Dou, Xi Wang, Jing Qin, Jack C.Y. Cheng, Pheng-Ann Heng, 3D fully convolutional networks for intervertebral disc localization and segmentation, in: International Conference on Medical Imaging and Virtual Reality, Springer, 2016, pp. 375–382.

[8] Hao Chen, Xiaojuan Qi, Lequan Yu, Pheng-Ann Heng, DCAN: deep contour-aware networks for accurate gland segmentation, in: Proceedings of the IEEE Conference on Computer Vision and Pattern Recognition, 2016, pp. 2487–2496.

[9] Xi Chen, Yan Duan, Rein Houthooft, John Schulman, Ilya Sutskever, Pieter Abbeel, InfoGAN: interpretable representation learning by information maximizing generative adversarial nets, in: Daniel D. Lee, Masashi Sugiyama, Ulrike von Luxburg, Isabelle Guyon, Roman Garnett (Eds.), Advances in Neu-

ral Information Processing Systems 29: Annual Conference on Neural Information Processing Systems 2016, December 5–10, 2016, Barcelona, Spain, 2016, pp. 2172–2180, http://papers.nips.cc/paper/6399-infogan-interpretable-representation-learning-by-information-maximizing-generative-adversarial-nets.

[10] Jeff Donahue, Philipp Krähenbühl, Trevor Darrell, Adversarial feature learning, arXiv: 1605.09782, 2016.

[11] Jeffrey Donahue, Lisa Anne Hendricks, Sergio Guadarrama, Marcus Rohrbach, Subhashini Venugopalan, Kate Saenko, Trevor Darrell, Long-term recurrent convolutional networks for visual recognition and description, in: Proceedings of the IEEE Conference on Computer Vision and Pattern Recognition, 2015, pp. 2625–2634.

[12] Qi Dou, Hao Chen, Lequan Yu, Lei Zhao, Jing Qin, Defeng Wang, Vincent C.T. Mok, Lin Shi, Pheng-Ann Heng, Automatic detection of cerebral microbleeds from MR images via 3D convolutional neural networks, IEEE Transactions on Medical Imaging 35 (5) (2016) 1182–1195.

[13] Vincent Dumoulin, Ishmael Belghazi, Ben Poole, Olivier Mastropietro, Alex Lamb, Martin Arjovsky, Aaron Courville, Adversarially learned inference, arXiv preprint, arXiv: 1606.00704, 2016.

[14] Huazhu Fu, Yanwu Xu, Stephen Lin, Damon Wing Kee Wong, Jiang Liu, DeepVessel: retinal vessel segmentation via deep learning and conditional random field, in: International Conference on Medical Image Computing and Computer-Assisted Intervention, Springer, 2016, pp. 132–139.

[15] Alex Graves, Generating sequences with recurrent neural networks, arXiv preprint, arXiv:1308.0850, 2013.

[16] Alex Graves, Navdeep Jaitly, Towards end-to-end speech recognition with recurrent neural networks, in: ICML, vol. 14, 2014, pp. 1764–1772.

[17] Kaiming He, Xiangyu Zhang, Shaoqing Ren, Jian Sun, Deep residual learning for image recognition, in: Proceedings of the IEEE Conference on Computer Vision and Pattern Recognition, 2016, pp. 770–778.

[18] Kaiming He, Xiangyu Zhang, Shaoqing Ren, Jian Sun, Identity mappings in deep residual networks, in: European Conference on Computer Vision (ECCV), Springer, 2016, pp. 630–645.

[19] Sepp Hochreiter, Jürgen Schmidhuber, Long short-term memory, Neural Computation 9 (8) (1997) 1735–1780.

[20] Bin Kong, Yiqiang Zhan, Min Shin, Thomas Denny, Shaoting Zhang, Recognizing end-diastole and end-systole frames via deep temporal regression network, in: International Conference on Medical Image Computing and Computer-Assisted Intervention, Springer, 2016, pp. 264–272.

[21] Alex Krizhevsky, Ilya Sutskever, Geoffrey E. Hinton, ImageNet classification with deep convolutional neural networks, in: F. Pereira, C.J.C. Burges, L. Bottou, K.Q. Weinberger (Eds.), Advances in Neural Information Processing Systems 25, Curran Associates, Inc., 2012, pp. 1097–1105.

[22] Yann LeCun, Léon Bottou, Yoshua Bengio, Patrick Haffner, Gradient-based learning applied to document recognition, Proceedings of the IEEE 86 (11) (1998) 2278–2324.

[23] Jinpeng Li, Rongzhao Zhang, Lin Shi, Defeng Wang, Automatic whole-heart segmentation in congenital heart disease using deeply-supervised 3D FCN, in: International Workshop on Reconstruction and Analysis of Moving Body Organs, Springer, 2016, pp. 111–118.

[24] Shujie Liu, Nan Yang, Mu Li, Ming Zhou, A recursive recurrent neural network for statistical machine translation, 2014.

[25] Jonathan Long, Evan Shelhamer, Trevor Darrell, Fully convolutional networks for semantic segmentation, in: Proceedings of the IEEE Conference on Computer Vision and Pattern Recognition, 2015, pp. 3431–3440.

[26] Tomas Mikolov, Martin Karafiát, Lukas Burget, Jan Cernocký, Sanjeev Khudanpur, Recurrent neural network based language model, in: Interspeech, vol. 2, 2010, p. 3.

[27] Tomáš Mikolov, Stefan Kombrink, Lukáš Burget, Jan Černocký, Sanjeev Khudanpur, Extensions of recurrent neural network language model, in: Acoustics, Speech and Signal Processing (ICASSP), 2011 IEEE International Conference on, IEEE, 2011, pp. 5528–5531.

[28] Mehdi Mirza, Simon Osindero, Conditional generative adversarial nets, arXiv preprint, arXiv:1411.1784, 2014.

[29] Augustus Odena, Christopher Olah, Jonathon Shlens, Conditional image synthesis with auxiliary classifier GANs, 2017, pp. 2642–2651.

[30] Augustus Odena, Vincent Dumoulin, Chris Olah, Deconvolution and checkerboard artifacts, Distill 1 (10) (2016) e3.

[31] Rudra P.K. Poudel, Pablo Lamata, Giovanni Montana, Recurrent fully convolutional neural networks for multi-slice MRI cardiac segmentation, arXiv preprint, arXiv:1608.03974, 2016.

[32] Olaf Ronneberger, Philipp Fischer, Thomas Brox, U-Net: convolutional networks for biomedical image segmentation, in: International Conference on Medical Image Computing and Computer-Assisted Intervention, 2015.

[33] Olga Russakovsky, Jia Deng, Hao Su, Jonathan Krause, Sanjeev Satheesh, Sean Ma, Zhiheng Huang, Andrej Karpathy, Aditya Khosla, Michael S. Bernstein, Alexander C. Berg, Fei-Fei Li, ImageNet large scale visual recognition challenge, International Journal of Computer Vision 115 (3) (2015) 211–252.

[34] Mike Schuster, Kuldip K. Paliwal, Bidirectional recurrent neural networks, IEEE Transactions on Signal Processing 45 (11) (1997) 2673–2681.

[35] Dinggang Shen, Guorong Wu, Heung-Il Suk, Deep learning in medical image analysis, Annual Review of Biomedical Engineering (2017).

[36] Karen Simonyan, Andrew Zisserman, Very deep convolutional networks for large-scale image recognition, CoRR, arXiv:1409.1556 [abs], 2014.

[37] Ilya Sutskever, James Martens, Geoffrey E. Hinton, Generating text with recurrent neural networks, in: Proceedings of the 28th International Conference on Machine Learning (ICML-11), 2011, pp. 1017–1024.

[38] Ilya Sutskever, Oriol Vinyals, Quoc V. Le, Sequence to sequence learning with neural networks, in: Advances in Neural Information Processing Systems, 2014, pp. 3104–3112.

[39] Christian Szegedy, Wei Liu, Yangqing Jia, Pierre Sermanet, Scott Reed, Dragomir Anguelov, Dumitru Erhan, Vincent Vanhoucke, Andrew Rabinovich, Going deeper with convolutions, in: Proceedings of the IEEE Conference on Computer Vision and Pattern Recognition, 2015, pp. 1–9.

[40] Kelvin Xu, Jimmy Ba, Ryan Kiros, Kyunghyun Cho, Aaron C. Courville, Ruslan Salakhutdinov, Richard S. Zemel, Yoshua Bengio, Show, attend and tell: neural image caption generation with visual attention, in: ICML, vol. 14, 2015, pp. 77–81.

[41] Quanzeng You, Hailin Jin, Zhaowen Wang, Chen Fang, Jiebo Luo, Image captioning with semantic attention, in: Proceedings of the IEEE Conference on Computer Vision and Pattern Recognition, 2016, pp. 4651–4659.

[42] Wojciech Zaremba, Ilya Sutskever, Oriol Vinyals, Recurrent neural network regularization, arXiv preprint, arXiv:1409.2329, 2014.

Deep network design for medical image analysis and selected applications

Classification: lesion and disease recognition

3

CONTENTS

Image *classification* is the task of recognizing the content of images and assigning class labels accordingly. In medicine, it often means giving diagnostic labels, determining the type of lesions, or grading the severity of a disorder in medical images. For many medical problems, such as the classification of skin diseases, nodular chest X-ray, Alzheimer's disease, and vertebrae, where the classification requires a considerable level of expertise or is error-prone, a computerized solution is desired for more objective and reliable results.

Traditionally, one can use human-engineered feature extraction algorithms in combination with a classifier to complete this task. This approach is applicable to some simple problems, such as the identification of melanoma from benign skin tumors, where the visual features are regular and predictable. However, when the classification task involves more diversified subjects, such as the classification of all skin diseases, feature engineering becomes infeasible. Moreover, hand-crafted feature engineering often involves complicated image preprocessing so that more discriminative and robust features can be extracted. A diverse data distribution will likely break the image preprocessing pipeline.

In contrast, deep learning has its advantages in automating the classification of medical images. First, deep learning models are often trained in an end-to-end fashion which obviates the need for complicated image preprocessing. Meanwhile, due to the ability to learn hierarchical feature representations, deep learning methods are surprisingly better at learning intrinsic structures from images. When transfer learning is applied [20], the visual knowledge previously learned (usually from a large-scale of natural images) by deep classification models can also be transferred to address the current medical problem under investigation. This not only can provide a more robust model but also make the training on a smaller medical dataset possible.

In this chapter, we introduce how to design deep neural networks for medical image classification. We begin with Section 3.1 by introducing several design principles, including 1) the choice of deep neural networks (Section 3.1.1), 2) the choice of classification tasks and objectives (Section 3.1.2), 3) what is and when to apply transfer learning (Section 3.1.3), and 4) what is and when to apply multitask learning (Section 3.1.4). Next, in Sections 3.2 and 3.3, we provide two case studies and show how these design principles are applied to address the skin lesion and disease recognition problems. Specifically, in Section 3.2, we introduce two classification scenarios, multiclass and multilabel classification. We investigate if one classification scenario could be better than the other when it comes to skin lesion and disease recognition [33]. In Section 3.3, we position the skin lesion recognition problem under a multitask learning scenario and investigate the benefit of leveraging additional tasks for skin lesion recognition [32].

3.1 Design principles
3.1.1 Choice of deep neural networks

Image classification is one of the earliest and most studied tasks in deep learning. Thus, for medical image classification, especially 2D medical image classification, instead of designing neural networks by ourselves, we may consider directly applying the existing models. Some early works include AlexNet [31], VGGNet [50], and GoogleNet [52]. Compared to non-deep learning approaches, these models show exceptional performance on the ImageNet classification task [46]. Therefore, they had been soon after adopted to solve medical problems such as skin disease/lesion classification [15,37], pathological chest X-ray classification [3,4,10], mitosis detection [36,56,49], and nucleus classification [19,21]. Despite the popularity, these early deep neural networks, however, are outdated and do not retain competitive performance compared with the later models.

The current mainstream deep neural networks are ResNet [23] based models, where ResNet proposes the residual connection idea to make the training of very deep neural networks possible. Following ResNet, ResNext [60] introduces group convolutions, DenseNet [26] expands the residual connection to dense connections, and SENet [25] adds squeeze-excitation blocks. Although these subsequent works improve ResNet in different ways, ResNet is still currently the most widely used deep neural network due to its simplicity and high performance.

Meanwhile, in computationally limited scenarios, such as medical image computing on mobile devices, it may be desired to deploy light-weighted deep neural networks. Therefore, later works, such as MobileNet [24] and ShuffleNet [66], propose to replace the expensive convolutional components with cheaper ones, such as separable convolutions and shuffle group convolution, while reduce the compromise in accuracy.

More recently, the deep neural network designs for image classification have rapidly shifted to two new directions. One is network architecture search (NAS), where instead of hand designing the desired network architecture we develop methods to search from the possible design space and output the best performing network after searching. Well-known models from this direction are EfficientNet [53] and RegNetY [40], both of which show better than ResNet performance while being more efficient in computation.

Another direction is the use of transformer-based models for image classification. At a high-level, this change comes from the motivation that the attention mechanism of transformer has more desired computer vision property than convolution. The recent advances such ViT/DeiT [14,54], T2T-ViT [63], and Swin [35] have indeed shown that transformer based models can outperform the state-of-the-art convolution based models.

3.1.2 Choice of classification tasks and objectives

Generally speaking, medical image classification is the task of assigning categorical labels to medical images. However, depending on the specific medical problem, there could be three different ways of assigning the labels, namely, multiclass classification, multilabel classification, and multiinstance classification, with each requiring different classification objectives.

Multiclass classification. The simplest and most common form of image classification is multiclass classification. That is, we assume each medical image can only have a single label. For example, in chest radiograph classification, we may consider predicting if the patient has pneumonia or not. Hence, each chest radiograph may only have one binary label denoting "pneumonia" or "normal." A common choice of the loss function for multiclass classification is the negative log-likelihood loss. Let z_j be the neural network's jth output, i.e., the logit for the jth class. The probability of classifying the image as the jth class can be given with a softmax function

$$a_j = \frac{e^{z_j}}{\sum_k e^{z_k}}.$$

$$(3.1)$$

Assuming that the ground-truth label of the image is y, the negative log-likelihood loss can be simply written as

$$\mathcal{L} = -\log(a_y). \tag{3.2}$$

Multilabel classification.   In some other cases, a medical image could have multiple labels. For example, a skin disease may present in different lesion characteristics and hence we may assign multiple lesion labels to the same dermatology image. For multilabel classification, we usually choose binary cross-entropy loss. Let us denote the ground truth of an image $\mathbf{X}$ as a binary vector $\mathbf{Y} = [y_1, y_2, \dots, y_L]^T$ where L is the maximum number of labels an image can have and y_j is given as

$$y_j = \begin{cases} 1, & \text{if the } j\text{th label is associated with } \mathbf{X}, \\ 0, & \text{otherwise.} \end{cases} \tag{3.3}$$

Similarly, let z_j be the neural network's jth output, i.e., the logit for the jth label. The probability of assigning the jth label to the image can be given with a sigmoid function

$$a_j = \sigma(z_j) = \frac{1}{1 + e^{-z_j}}. \tag{3.4}$$

And the corresponding binary cross-entropy loss is

$$\mathcal{L} = -\sum_{j=1}^{L} y_j \log a_j + (1 - y_j) \log(1 - a_j). \tag{3.5}$$

Multiinstance classification.   Finally, we may also collect multiple images from the same entity and classify them at the entity level, not the image level. We call such classification multiinstance classification. A typical application of multiinstance classification in medicine is the classification of histological images. Histological images usually have very high resolution and, therefore, it is impractical to input a histological image entirely to the deep neural network. A common solution is to crop a bag of image patches (i.e., instances) from the histological image and assign a categorical label to the bag, which essentially becomes a multiinstance classification problem. In deep learning, the critical part for multiinstance classification is the aggregation of features from the instances. Let $\mathbf{X} = \{\mathbf{X}_1, \mathbf{X}_2, \dots, \mathbf{X}_K\}$ denote a bag of K instances and $\mathbf{h}_k$ denote the features of the kth instance $\mathbf{x}_k$. We aim to derive an aggregated feature $\mathbf{z}$ from $\{\mathbf{h}_1, \mathbf{h}_2, \dots, \mathbf{h}_K\}$ to represent $\mathbf{X}$. In general, there are three ways for aggregating the features [27], namely max pooling

$$\mathbf{z}_m = \max_k \{\mathbf{h}_{km}\}, \tag{3.6}$$

average pooling,

$$\mathbf{z} = \frac{1}{K} \sum_k \mathbf{h}_k, \tag{3.7}$$

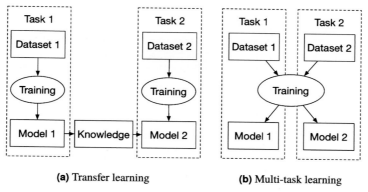

(a) Transfer learning   **(b)** Multi-task learning

FIGURE 3.1

Comparison of single task learning, transfer learning and multitask learning.

and attention-based pooling,

$$\mathbf{z} = \sum_k \alpha_k \mathbf{h}_k,\tag{3.8}$$

where $\mathbf{z}_m$ denotes the mth feature of $\mathbf{z}$, $\mathbf{h}_{km}$ denotes the mth feature of $\mathbf{h}_k$ and α_k denotes the attention weight for $\mathbf{h}_k$. After the aggregation, $\mathbf{z}$ can be sent to a fully connected layer to compute the classification logits for the bag. For the classification loss, we may either choose the negative log-likelihood loss as in Eq. (3.2) if the bag can only have a single label or choose the binary cross-entropy loss as in Eq. (3.5) if the bag can have multiple labels.

3.1.3 Transfer learning

Labeling medical images is expensive. It requires a considerable level of medical knowledge and is usually done by medical professionals. As a result, the medical datasets we can get are usually small. On the other hand, deep neural networks are large models with tens to hundreds of millions of parameters. Therefore, to avoid overfitting, it requires a large dataset to train a deep neural network from scratch. Fortunately, one way to address this gap in dataset size is through transfer learning. Transfer learning, as illustrated in Fig. 3.1(a), is a technique that improves the learning of a new task through the transferring of the knowledge learned from an exiting task [62]. The goal of transfer learning is at least to speed up the training of the new task with less amount of data, but it may also improve the training and result in a better model.

In deep learning, transfer learning typically has two forms: 1) converting the learned network to a feature extractor, or 2) fine-tuning the parameters of the learned network. These two scenarios of applying transfer learning are based on the observation that the features extracted from lower-level layers of the networks trained for different tasks are usually look similar. Hence, it may be beneficial if one takes part or even all of the trained components from one model and applies it to another.

A learned network can be converted into a feature extractor by removing the last fully connected layer. The last fully connected layer in a neural network is usually used as a classifier. By removing the last fully connected layer, the output of the remaining network would be the feature vectors it uses for classification. Then, the rest of the neural network can be fixed as a feature extractor for the new task. Note that it is also possible to use the outputs from other layers as the features for the new task. For example, the feature outputs from the last convolutional layer keep the spatial information of the input image. Hence, they may be the desired features for some tasks such as image segmentation.

Fine-tuning is another way of transfer learning. In fine-tuning, the network for the new task is trained based on an existing model. At the beginning, the parameters of the network are initialized from a trained model. Then, the parameters will be slightly adjusted during training to fit the new task. Fine-tuning the parameters is flexible. Parameters of lower-level layers can be fixed during the training if they are general enough to represent the new task. On the other hand, if parameters of the higher-level layers are too specific to the existing model, then they can be randomly initialized and trained from scratch.

It is important to choose a good model for fine-tuning. A typical choice is to take a state-of-the-art CNN model pretrained on a large image dataset, such as ImageNet [46], MSCOCO [34], etc., and fine-tune the pretrained model for the new task. There are lots of resources where the training checkpoints of those pretrained models can be found. For example, Caffe [29] has a model zoo that allows people to share their trained models.

3.1.4 Multitask learning

For diagnostic purposes, the same medical image may come with different types of labels. For example, an X-ray image reading may result in a diagnostic report and disease label. A dermatology image may have a disease label and lesion label. These diagnostic-related labels are usually correlated and combined to help healthcare professionals to make final diagnostic decisions. Therefore, when building a deep learning model, it may also be beneficial to leverage the different types of labels to improve the classification performance. To this end, we could consider training the model with multitask learning.

Multitask learning (MTL), illustrated in Fig. 3.1(b), is an approach to improve the learning of one task by simultaneously training the task together with other related tasks. During MTL, the domain information of other tasks can be inductively transferred to the main task, which improves the generalization of the learning [6]. MTL is typically applied to neural networks by sharing the hidden layers for different tasks and using backpropagation to learn the tasks in parallel.

Suppose we are given a set of T tasks with the training data of tth task denoted as $\{(\mathbf{y}_i^t, \mathbf{x}_i^t)\}$, where $\mathbf{y}_i^t$ and $\mathbf{x}_i^t$ are the input and label of the ith data, respectively. Then, the T tasks can be trained simultaneously using the following multitask loss:

$$\arg\min_{\{\mathbf{W}^t\}_1^T} \sum_{t=1}^{T} \sum_{i=1}^{N} \alpha^t \ell^t (\mathbf{y}_i^t, f(\mathbf{x}_i^t, \mathbf{W}^t)) + \Phi(\mathbf{W}^t). \qquad (3.9)$$

Here, α^t is the importance coefficient of loss function ℓ^t; α^t is used to weigh each loss so that the learning of different tasks proceeds at a similar pace. This is important if different types of loss function are used, e.g., classification loss and regression loss. Further, f^t is the effective neural network of task t. Some of the hidden layers of f^t will be shared across different tasks and the parameters of those hidden layers will be learned jointly. Finally, Φ is the regularization function for the network parameters $\mathbf{W}^t$.

Learning different tasks simultaneously is not trivial. One problem is how to control the over-fittings introduced by some tasks when their learning converge way before other tasks. One way to solve this problem is to tweak the importance coefficients so that different tasks converge at a similar pace. However, tweaking the importance coefficients is empirical and requires trial-and-error which complicates the design of MTL networks. To address this problem, Zhang et al. [67] followed the idea of [6] and proposed an early stopping technique for multitask deep convolutional network.

The other problem that arises when training multitask neural networks is how to decide the parameter sharing. In MTL, different tasks will share hidden layers, but which and how many hidden layers to share is usually user-defined. A typical design strategy is to share lower layers as they usually encode more general features and split at the top layers for different tasks. This strategy requires multiple trials of different sharing settings, which makes the already complicated DNN design even more complicated. Hence, Yang et al. [61] proposed an algorithm to automatically learn the extent to which the parameters should be shared.

MTL has been applied to deep learning methods for many medical problems. For example, Zhang et al. [65] proposed a deep MTL model to annotate gene expression patterns. Suk et al. [51] used MTL to perform feature selection in a hierarchical fashion for Alzheimer's disease diagnosis. Moeskops et al. [38] combined the training in an MTL fashion for medical image segmentation. Chen et al. [8] leveraged MTL to improve the training of a joint model for vertebrae localization and identification.

3.2 Case study: skin disease classification versus skin lesion characterization

The diagnosis of skin diseases is challenging. To diagnose a skin disease, a variety of visual clues may be used such as the individual lesional morphology, the body

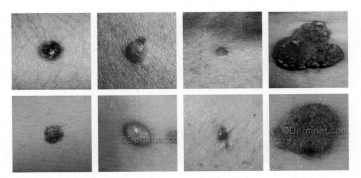

FIGURE 3.2

Some visually similar skin diseases. First row (left to right): malignant melanoma, dermatofibroma, basal cell carcinoma, and seborrheic keratosis. Second row (left to right): compound nevus, intradermal nevus, benign keratosis, and Bowen's disease.

site distribution, color, scaling, and arrangement of lesions. When the individual elements are analyzed separately, the recognition process can be quite complex [11]. For example, the well-studied skin cancer, melanoma, has four major clinical diagnosis methods: ABCD rules, pattern analysis, Menzies method, and 7-point checklist. To use these methods and achieve a satisfactory diagnostic accuracy, a high level of expertise is required as the differentiation of skin lesions demands a great deal of experience [58].

In recent years, deep convolutional neural networks become very popular in feature learning and object classification. The use of high-performance GPUs makes it possible to train a network on a large-scale dataset so as to yield better performance. Many studies [48,28,52,50] from the ImageNet Large Scale Visual Recognition Challenge (ILSVRC) [46] have shown that the state-of-the-art CNN architectures are able to surpass humans in many computer vision tasks. Therefore, we propose to construct a skin disease classifier with CNNs.

However, training CNNs directly using diagnosis labels may not be viable. First, for some diseases, their lesions are so similar that they cannot be distinguished visually. Fig. 3.2 shows the dermatology images of eight different skin diseases. We can see that the two diseases in each column have very similar visual appearances. Thus, it is very difficult to make a judgment between the two diseases with only visual information. Second, many skin diseases are not so common that only a few images are available for training. Table 3.1 shows the dataset statistics of the dermatology atlases we used in this study. We can see that there are tens of hundreds of skin diseases. However, most of them contain very few images. Third, skin disease diagnosis is a complex procedure that often involves many other modalities, such as palpation, smell, temperature changes, and microscopy examinations [11].

On the other hand, lesion characteristics, which inherently describe the visual aspects of skin diseases, arguably should be considered as the ideal ground truth for training. For example, the two images in the first column of Fig. 3.2 can both be labeled with hyperpigmented and nodular lesion tags. Compared with using the sometimes ambiguous disease diagnosis labels for these two images, the use of the lesion tags can give a more consistent and precise description of the dermatology images.

In this study, we investigate the performance of CNNs trained with disease and lesion labels, respectively. We collected 75,665 skin disease images from six different publicly available dermatology atlases. We then train a multiclass CNN for disease-targeted classification and another multilabel CNN for lesion-targeted classification. Our experimental results show that the top-1 and top-5 accuracies for the disease-targeted classification are 27.6% and 57.9% with a mean average precision (mAP) of 0.42. While for the lesion-targeted skin disease classification, a much higher mAP of 0.70 is achieved.

3.2.1 Background

Much work has been proposed for computer-aided skin disease classification. However, most of them use human-engineered feature extraction algorithms and restrict the problem to certain skin diseases, such as melanoma [2,59,18,47,5]. Some other works [12,55,1] use CNNs for unsupervised feature learning from histopathology images and only focus on the detection of mitosis, an indicator of cancer. Recently, Esteva et al. [16] proposed a disease-targeted skin disease classification method using CNN. They used the dermatology images from the Dermnet atlas, one of the six atlases used in this study, and reported that their CNN achieved 60.0% top-1 accuracy and 80.3% top-3 accuracy. However, they performed the CNN training and testing on the same dataset without cross-validation which makes their results unpersuasive.

3.2.2 Dataset

We collect dermatology photos from the following dermatology atlas websites: 1) **AtlasDerm**, 2) **Danderm**, 3) **Derma**, 4) **DermIS**, 5) **Dermnet**, and 6) **DermQuest** [57]. These atlases are maintained by professional dermatology resource providers. They are used by dermatologists for training and teaching purpose. All of the dermatology atlases have diagnosis labels for their images. For each dermatology image, only one disease diagnosis label is assigned. We use these diagnosis labels as the ground truth to train the disease-targeted skin disease classifier.

However, each of the atlases maintains its own skin disease taxonomy and naming convention for the diagnosis labels. It means that different atlases may have different labels for the same diagnosis and some diagnosis may have several variations. To address this problem, we adapt the skin disease taxonomy used by the DermQuest atlas and merge the diagnosis labels from other atlases into it. We choose the DermQuest atlas because of the completeness and professionalism of its dermatology resources. In most of the cases, the labels for the same diagnoses may have similar naming conventions. Therefore, we merge them according to the word or string similarity of two diagnosis labels. We use the string pattern matching algorithm described

Table 3.1 Dataset statistics.

Atlas	# of Images	# of Diagnoses
AtlasDerm	8766	478
Danderm	1869	97
Derma	13,189	1195
DermIS	6588	651
Dermnet	21,861	488
DermQuest	22,082	657
Total	**75,665**	**2113**

in [43], where the string similarity is measured by $S = \frac{2M}{T}$. Here, M is the number of matches and T is the total number of characters in both strings. The statistics of the merged atlases is given in Table 3.1. Note that the total number of diagnoses in our dataset is 2113 which is significantly higher than for any of the atlases. This is because we use a conservative merging strategy such that we merge two diagnosis labels only when their string similarity is very high ($S > 0.8$). Thus, we can make sure no two diagnosis labels are incorrectly merged. For those redundant diagnosis labels, they only contain a few dermatology images. We discard them by choosing a threshold that filters out less frequent diagnosis labels.

For the disease-targeted skin disease classification, we choose the AtlasDerm, Danderm, Derma, DermIS, and Dermnet datasets as the training set and the DermQuest dataset as the test set. Due to the inconsistency of the taxonomy and naming convention between the atlases, most of the diagnosis labels have only a few images. As our goal is to investigate the feasibility of using CNNs for disease-targeted skin disease classification, we remove these noisy diagnosis labels and only keep those labels that have more than 300 images. As a result of the label refinement and cleaning, we have 18,096 images in the training set and 14,739 images in the test set. The total number of diagnosis labels is 38.

For the skin lesions, only the DermQuest dataset contains the lesion tags. Unlike the diagnosis, which is unique for each image, multiple lesion tags may be associated with a dermatology image. There are a total of 134 lesion tags for the 22,082 dermatology images from DermQuest. However, most lesion tags have only a few images and some of the lesion tags are duplicated. After merging and removing infrequent lesion tags, we retain 23 lesion tags.

Since only the DermQuest dataset has the lesion tags, we use images from the DermQuest dataset to perform training and testing. The total number of dermatology images that have lesion tags is 14,799. As the training and test sets are sampled from the same dataset, to avoid overfitting, we use 5-fold cross-validation in our experiment. We first split our dataset into 5 evenly sized, nonoverlapping "folds." Next, we rotate each fold as the test set and use the remaining folds as the training set.

3.2.3 **Methodology**

We use CNNs for both the disease-targeted and lesion-targeted skin disease classifications. For the disease-targeted classification, a multiclass image classifier is trained
and for the lesion-targeted classification, we train a multilabel image classifier. Our
CNN architecture is based on the AlexNet [31] and we modify it according to our
needs. The AlexNet architecture was one of the early wining entry of the ILSVRC
challenges which is considered sufficient for this study. Readers may refer to the latest
winning entry (MSRA [23] as of ILSVRC 2015) for better performance. Implementation details of training and testing the CNNs are given in the following sections.

Disease-targeted skin disease classification.   For the disease-targeted skin disease
classification, each dermatology image is associated with only one disease diagnosis.
Hence, we train a multiclass classifier using CNN. We fine-tune the CNN with the
BVLC AlexNet model [29] which is pretrained from the ImageNet dataset [46]. Since
the number of classes we are predicting is different with the ImageNet images, we
replace the last fully connected layer (1000 dimensions) with a new fully connected
layer where the number of outputs is set to the number of skin diagnoses in our
dataset. We also increase the learning rate of the weights and bias of this layer as the
parameters of the newly added layer is randomly initialized. For the loss function, we
use the softmax function [39] and connect a new softmax layer to the newly added
fully connected layer. Formally put, let z_j^L be the weighted input of the jth neuron of
the softmax layer, where L is the total number of the layers in the CNN (For AlexNet,
$L = 9$). Thus, the jth activation of the softmax layer is

$$a_j^L = \frac{e^{z_j^L}}{\sum_k e^{z_k^L}}. \tag{3.10}$$

And the corresponding softmax loss is

$$E = -\frac{1}{N} \sum_{n=1}^{N} \log(a_{y^n}^L), \tag{3.11}$$

where N is the number of images in a minibatch, y^n is the ground truth of the nth
image, and $a_{y^n}^L$ is the y^nth activation of the softmax layer. In the test phase, we choose
the label j that yields the largest activation a_j^L as the prediction, i.e.,

$$\hat{y} = \arg\max_j a_j^L. \tag{3.12}$$

Lesion-targeted skin disease classification.   As we mentioned earlier, multiple
lesion tags may be associated with a dermatology image. Therefore, to classify skin
lesions, we need to train a multilabel CNN. Similar to disease-targeted skin disease
classification, we fine-tune the multilabel CNN with the BVLC AlexNet model. To

train a multilabel CNN, two data layers are required. One data layer loads the dermatology images, and the other data layer loads the corresponding lesion tags. Given an image $\mathbf{X}_n$ from the first data layer, its corresponding lesion tags from the second data layer are represented as a binary vector $\mathbf{Y}_n = [y_1^n, y_2^n, \ldots, y_Q^n]^T$ where Q is the number of lesions in our data set and $y_j^n, j \in \{1, 2, \ldots, Q\}$ is given as

$$y_j^n = \begin{cases} 1, & \text{if the } j\text{th label is associated with } \mathbf{X}_n, \\ 0, & \text{otherwise.} \end{cases} \tag{3.13}$$

We replace the last fully connected layer of the AlexNet with a new fully connected layer to accommodate the lesion tag vector. The learning rate of the parameters of this layer is also increased so that the CNN can learn features of the dermatology images instead of those images from ImageNet. For the multilabel CNN, we use the binary cross-entropy [39] as the loss function and replace the softmax layer with a sigmoid cross-entropy layer. Let z_j^L be the weighted input, then the jth activation of the sigmoid layer can be written as

$$a_j^L = \sigma(z_j^L) = \frac{1}{1 + e^{-z_j^L}}. \tag{3.14}$$

And the corresponding cross-entropy loss is

$$E = -\frac{1}{N} \sum_{n=1}^{N} \sum_{j=1}^{Q} y_j^n \log a_j^L + (1 - y_j^n) \log (1 - a_j^L). \tag{3.15}$$

For a given image $\mathbf{X}$, the output of the multilabel CNN is a confidence vector $\mathbf{C} = [a_1^L, a_2^L, \ldots, a_Q^L]^T$. Here, a_j^L is the jth activation of the sigmoid cross-entropy layer. It denotes the confidence of $\mathbf{X}$ being related to the lesion tag j. In the test phase, we use a threshold function $t(\mathbf{X})$ to determine the lesion tags of the input image $\mathbf{X}$, i.e., $\hat{\mathbf{Y}} = [\hat{y}_1, \hat{y}_2, \ldots, \hat{y}_Q]^T$ where

$$\hat{y}_j = \begin{cases} 1, & a_j^L > t(\mathbf{X}), \\ 0, & \text{otherwise,} \end{cases} \quad j \in \{1, 2, \ldots, Q\}. \tag{3.16}$$

For the choice of the threshold function $t(\mathbf{X})$, we adapt the method recommended in [64] which picks a linear function of the confidence vector by maximizing the multilabel accuracy on the training set.

3.2.4 Experiments

In this section, we investigate the performance of the CNNs trained for the disease-targeted and lesion-targeted skin disease classifications, respectively. For both the disease-targeted and lesion-targeted classifications, we fine-tune CNNs from ImageNet pretrained models. However, note that the ImageNet pretrained models are trained from images containing mostly artifacts, animals, and plants. This is very different from our skin disease cases. To investigate the features learned only from skin diseases and avoid using useless features, we also train the CNNs from scratch.

We conduct all the experiments using the Caffe deep learning framework [29] and run the programs with a GeForce GTX 970 GPU. For the hyperparameters, we follow the settings used by the AlexNet, i.e., batch size $= 256$, momentum $= 0.9$, and weight decay $= 5.0 \times e^{-4}$. We use 0.001 and 0.01 learning rate for fine-tuning and training from scratch, respectively.

Performance of disease-targeted classification.　To evaluate the performance of the disease-targeted skin disease classifier, we use the top-1 and top-5 accuracies, mAP score, and the confusion matrix as the metrics. Following the notations in Section 3.2.3, let $\mathbf{C}_n$ be the output of the multiclass CNN when the input is $\mathbf{X}_n$ and $\mathbf{T}_n^k$ be the labels of the k largest elements in $\mathbf{C}_n$. The top-k accuracy of the multiclass CNN on the test set is given as

$$A_{\text{top-}k} = \frac{\sum_{n=1}^{N} Z_n^k}{N}, \tag{3.17}$$

where Z_n^k is

$$Z_n^k = \begin{cases} 1, & y^n \in \mathbf{T}_n^k, \\ 0, & \text{otherwise}, \end{cases} \tag{3.18}$$

and N is the total number of images in the test set. For the mAP, we adapt the definition described in [70],

$$\text{mAP} = \frac{1}{N} \sum_{i=1}^{N} \sum_{j=1}^{Q} p_i(j) \Delta r_i(j), \tag{3.19}$$

where $p_i(j)$ and $r_i(j)$ denote the precision and recall of the ith image at fraction j, $\Delta r_i(j)$ denotes the change in recall from $j - 1$ to j, and Q is the total number of possible lesions. Finally, for the confusion matrix $\mathbf{M}$, its elements are given as

$$\mathbf{M}(i, j) = \frac{\sum_{n=1}^{N} I(y^n = i) I(\hat{y}^n = j)}{N_i}, \tag{3.20}$$

where y^n is the ground truth, $\hat{y}^n$ is the prediction, and N_i is the number of images whose ground truth is i.

Table 3.2 shows the accuracies and mAP of the disease-targeted skin disease classifiers with the CNNs trained from scratch or using fine-tuning. It is interesting to note that the CNN trained using transfer learning performs better than the CNN trained from scratch only on skin diseases. It suggests that the more general features learned from the richer set of ImageNet images can still benefit the more specific classification of the skin diseases. And training from scratch did not necessarily help the CNN learn more useful features related to the skin diseases. However, even for the CNN

Table 3.2 Accuracies and mAP of the disease-targeted classification.

Learning Type	Top-1 Accuracy	Top-5 Accuracy	mAP
Fine-tuning	27.6%	57.9%	0.42
Scratch	21.1%	48.9%	0.35

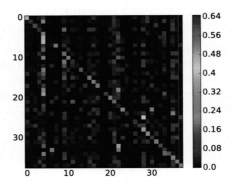

FIGURE 3.3

The confusion matrix of the disease-targeted skin disease classifier with fine-tuned CNN.

trained with fine-tuning, the accuracies and mAP are not satisfactory. Only 27.6% top-1 accuracy, 57.9% top-5 accuracy, and 0.42 mAP score are achieved.

The confusion matrix computed for the fine-tuned CNN is given in Fig. 3.3. The row indices correspond to the actual diagnosis labels and the column indices denote the predicted diagnosis labels. Each cell is computed using Eq. (3.20) which is the percentage of the prediction j among images with ground truth i. A good multiclass classifier should have high diagonal values. We find in Fig. 3.3 that there are some off-diagonal cells with relatively high values. This is because some skin diseases are visually similar, and the CNNs trained with diagnosis labels still cannot distinguish among them. For example, the off-diagonal cell at row 8 and column 22 has a value of 0.60. Here, label 8 represents "compound nevus" and label 22 stands for "malignant melanoma." It means about 60% of the "compound nevus" images are incorrectly labeled as "malignant melanoma." If we look at the two images in the first column of Fig. 3.2, we can see that these two diseases look so similar in appearance that not surprisingly the disease-targeted classifier fails to distinguish them.

Performance of lesion-targeted classification. As we use a multilabel classifier for the lesion-targeted skin disease classification, the evaluation metrics used in this experiment are different from those used in the previous section. To evaluate the performance of the classifier on each label, we use the label-based precision, recall, and F-measure. And to evaluate the overall performance, we use the macro-average of the precision, recall and F-measure. In addition, the mAP is also used as an evaluation metric of the overall performance.

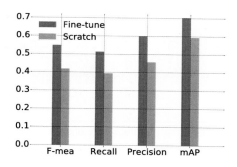

FIGURE 3.4

The precision, recalls, F-measures, and mAP scores of the disease-targeted skin disease classifier fine-tuned CNN.

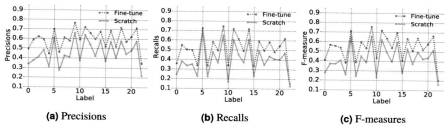

(a) Precisions   (b) Recalls   (c) F-measures

FIGURE 3.5

Label-based precisions, recalls, and F-measures.

Let Y_i be the set of images whose ground truth contains lesion i and Z_i be the set of images whose prediction contains lesion i. Then, the label-based and the macro-averaged precision, recall, and F-measure can be defined as

$$P_i = \frac{|Y_i \cap Z_i|}{|Z_i|}, \quad P_{\text{macro}} = \frac{1}{Q}\sum_{i=1}^{Q} P_i,$$

$$R_i = \frac{|Y_i \cap Z_i|}{|Y_i|}, \quad R_{\text{macro}} = \frac{1}{Q}\sum_{i=1}^{Q} R_i, \qquad (3.21)$$

$$F_i = \frac{2|Y_i||Z_i|}{|Y_i| + |Z_i|}, \quad F_{\text{macro}} = \frac{1}{Q}\sum_{i=1}^{Q} F_i,$$

where Q is the total number of possible lesion tags.

Fig. 3.4 shows the overall performance of the lesion-targeted skin disease classifiers. The macro-average of the F-measure is around 0.55 and the mean average precision is about 0.70. This is quite good for a multilabel problem. The label-based precisions, recalls, and F-measures are given in Fig. 3.5. We can see that for the

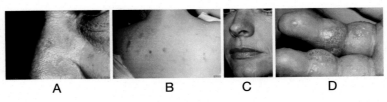

A   B   C   D

FIGURE 3.6

Failure cases. Ground truth (left to right): atrophy, excoriation, hypopigmented, vesicle. Top prediction (left to right): erythematous, erythematous, ulceration, edema.

lesion-targeted skin disease classification, the fine-tuned CNN performs better than the CNN trained from scratch which is consistent with our observation in Table 3.2. It means for the lesion-targeted skin disease classification problem, it is still beneficial to initialize with weights from ImageNet pretrained models. We also see that the label-based metrics are mostly above 0.5 in the fine-tuning case. Some exceptions are atrophy (0), erythemato-squamous (4), excoriation (6), oozing (15), and vesicle (22). The failures are mostly due to: 1) the lesiona not visually salient or masked by other larger lesions, or 2) sloppy labeling of the ground truth.

Some failure cases are shown in Fig. 3.6. Image *A* is labeled as atrophy. However, the atrophic characteristic is not so obvious and it is more like an erythematous lesion. For image *B*, the ground truth is excoriation which is the little white scars on the back. However, the red erythematous lesion is more apparent. So the CNN incorrectly classified it as a erythematous lesion. Similar case can be found in image *D*. For image *C*, the ground truth is actually incorrect.

Fig. 3.7 shows the image retrievals using the lesion-targeted classifier. Here, we take the output of the second to last fully connected layer (4096 dimensions) as the feature vector. For each query image from the test set, we compare its features with all the images in the training set and outputs the 5-nearest neighbors (in euclidean distance) as the retrievals. The retrieved images with green solid frames match at least one lesion tag of the query image. And those images with red dashed frames have no common lesion tags with the query image. We can see that the retrieved images are visually and semantically similar to the query images.

3.2.5 Discussion

In this study, we have shown that, for skin disease classification using CNNs, lesion tags rather than the diagnosis tags should be considered as the target for automated analysis. To achieve better diagnosis results, computer-aided skin disease diagnosis systems could use lesion-targeted CNNs as the cornerstone component to facilitate the final disease diagnosis in conjunction with other evidence. We have built a large-scale dermatology dataset from six professional photosharing dermatology atlases. We have trained and tested the disease-targeted and lesion-targeted classifiers using CNNs. Both fine-tuning and training from scratch were investigated in training the CNN models. We found that, for skin disease images, CNNs fine-tuned from

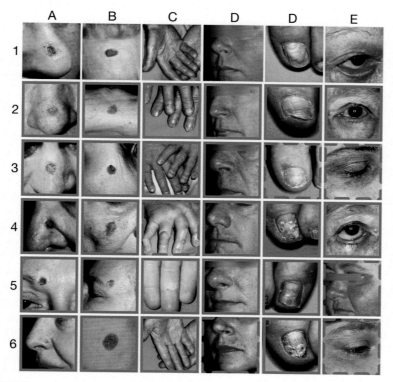

FIGURE 3.7

Images retrieved by the lesion-targeted classifier. Row 1: the query images from the test set. Row 2-6: the retrieved images from the training set. Dotted borders annotate errors. Ground truth of the test images from column A to D: "crust, ulceration," "hyperpigmented, tumor," "scales," "erythematous, telangiectasis," "nail hyperpigmentation, onycholysis," and "edema, erythematous."

pretrained models perform better than those trained from scratch. For the disease-targeted classification, it can only achieve 27.6% top-1 accuracy and 57.9% top-5 accuracy as well as 0.42 MAP. The corresponding confusion matrix contains some high off-diagonal values which indicates that some skin diseases cannot be distinguished using diagnosis labels. For the lesion-targeted classification, a 0.70 MAP score is achieved, which is remarkable for a multilabel classification problem. Image retrieval results also confirm that CNNs trained using lesion tags learn the dermatology features very well.

3.3 Case study: skin lesion classification with multitask learning

Instead of treating the skin lesion classification as a stand-alone problem and training a CNN model using skin lesion labels only, we further propose to jointly optimize the skin lesion classification with a related auxiliary task, body location classification. The motivation behind this design is to make use of the body site predilection of skin diseases [11] as it has long been recognized by dermatologists that many skin diseases and their corresponding skin lesions are correlated with their body site manifestation. For example, a skin lesion caused by sun exposure is only present in sun-exposed areas of the body (face, neck, hands, arms) [7]. Therefore, a CNN architecture that can exploit the domain-specific information contained in the body locations should be intuitively helpful in improving the performance of our skin lesion classification model.

In this study, we present a multitask learning framework for universal skin lesion (all lesion types) classification using deep convolutional neural networks. In order to learn a wide variety of visual aspect of skin lesions, we first collect 21,657 images from DermQuest (http://www.dermquest.com), a public skin disease atlas contributed by dermatologists around the world. We then formulate our model into a dual-task based learning problem with specialized loss functions for each task. Next, to boost the performance, we fit our model into the state-of-the-art deep residual network (ResNet) [23] which is the winning entry of ILSVRC 2015 [46] and MS COCO 2015 [34].

To our best knowledge, this is the first attempt to target the universal skin lesion classification problem systematically using a deep multitask learning framework. We show that the jointly learned representations from body locations indeed facilitate the learning for skin lesion classification. Using the state-of-the-art CNN architecture and combining the results from different models we can achieve as high as a 0.80 mean average precision (mAP) in classifying skin lesions.

3.3.1 Background

Most of the existing works [2,59,18] only focus on one or a few skin diseases and solve the problem using conventional machine learning approach, i.e., extracting manually engineered features from segmented lesion patches and classifying with a linear classifier such as SVM. While in our study, we target a more challenging problem where all skin diseases are considered.

Many CNN related approaches have been proposed to solve dermatology problems in recent years. Some works [12,55,1] used CNNs as an unsupervised feature extractor and detect mitosis, an indicator of cancer, from histopathology images. Esteva et al. [15] presented a CNN architecture for diagnosis-targeted skin disease classification. They trained their model with a contemporary CNN architecture using a large-scale dataset (23,000 images). Similar to our study, they also tried to classify skin diseases in a broader range. What sets us apart from their work is instead of training with diagnosis labels and making diagnostic decision directly, our work classifies skin diseases by their lesional characteristics. According to Section 3.2, skin lesion is proven to be a more appropriate subject for skin disease classification as many diagnoses cannot be distinguished visually. Recently, [30] also proposed a CNN based model to classify skin lesions for nondermoscopic images. However, the authors only managed to build their model on a prior art CNN architecture with a relatively small dataset (1300 images).

Multitask learning (MTL) [6] is an approach to learning a main task together with other related tasks in parallel with the goal of a better generalization performance. Learning multiple tasks jointly has been proven to be very effective in many computer vision problems, such as attribute classification [22], face detection [42], face alignment [68], and object detection [45]. However, we find no multitask learning based algorithm has been developed for dermatology related problems.

3.3.2 Dataset

All the dermatology images used in this study are collected from DermQuest. We choose DermQuest against other dermatology atlases is because it has the most detailed annotations and descriptions for each of the dermatology image and it is the only public dermatology atlas that contains both skin lesion and body location labels. Most of the dermatology images from DermQuest are contributed by individual dermatologists. When contributing an image, they are required to input the descriptions (diagnosis, primary lesions, body location, pathophysiology, etc.) by their own. As the terminology used by dermatologists are not unified, they may use different terms and morphologies when describing a dermatology image which results in an inconsistency of DermQuest images.

Due to the inconsistency, there are 180 lesion types in total in the DermQuest atlas, which is larger than any of the existing lesion morphology lists. Therefore, with the help of a dermatologist, we refined the list of lesion types to make sure they reasonably and consistently represent the lesional characteristics of the images in DermQuest. We refine and merge lesions based on the lesion morphology described in [11] with some modifications: 1) we removed those infrequent lesion types (less than 10 images) as they do not have enough images for our model to learn some meaningful features, 2) for some popular (greater than 1000 images) sublesion types, such as hyperpigmented papule lesion under the papule family, we do not merge them as there are enough images in the dataset so that our model can distinguish them from other sublesions under the same family, and 3) some of the lesion types have common visual characteristics, such atrophy, erosion and ulcer, we also merge them together.

After the refinement, we finally come up with a lesion morphology list with 25 lesions types for the DermQuest images. Note that there might be multiple lesion labels associated with an image as a skin disease usually manifests different lesional characteristics at a time.

For the body location labels, the terminology used is more consistent. We do not modify too much except we removed those infrequent labels as we did for the lesions. We also merged some body locations that are too specific to not be mixed with its

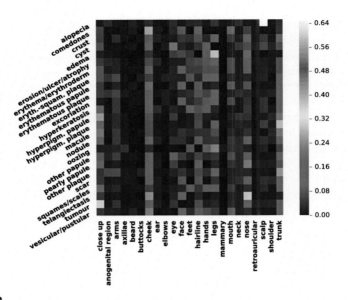

FIGURE 3.8

The correlation matrix between skin lesion and body location. Each row denotes a skin lesion and each column denotes a body location. A cell at (i, j) denotes the proportion of the images with both label i and label j among all the i images (best viewed in color).

nearby regions in an image. For example, an image labeled with nails usually contains parts of the fingers. Thus, it is actually hard to tell whether it should be labeled with nails or fingers. Hence, we directly merge them into the "hands" category. There are 23 body locations in the final list.

We also investigate the correlation between skin lesions and body locations among images in DermQuest. The correlation map is shown in Fig. 3.8. Here, each row denotes a skin lesion and each column denotes a body location. Let N_i denote the total number of images in our dataset that has lesion i and M_j denote the total number of images that has body location j. Then, the cell at (i, j) can be computed by

$$R_{ij} = \frac{N_i \cap M_j}{N_i}. \tag{3.22}$$

Thus, if a skin lesion frequently appears on certain body location, we will see a high very value of R_{ij}. Notice that we have 23 body location types. Thus, if a skin lesion has no specific predilection of body locations, then cells in the corresponding row should all have values close to $1/23$, i.e., dark blue in the color bar. For example, the cells in row "erythema/erythroderm" are almost in blue, which means "erythema/erythroderm" has little body location predilection. This is consistent with our knowledge that "erythema/erythroderm" is a very commonly seen lesion that can exists anywhere in the body. We can also see that "alopecia" is highly correlated with "scale." It makes sense as "alopecia" is a lesion that related with hair loss.

3.3.3 Methodology

Deep multitask learning.   To jointly optimize the main (skin lesion classification) and auxiliary (body location classification) tasks, we formulate our problem as follows. Let $(\mathbf{X}_i, \mathbf{u}_i, v_i), i \in \{1, \dots N\}$ denotes the ith data in the training set, where $\mathbf{X}_i$ is the ith image and $\mathbf{u}_i$ and $v_i \in \{1, \dots, Q\}$ are the ith labels for the skin lesion and body location, respectively. As multiple lesion types may be associated with a dermatology image, the lesion label $\mathbf{u}_i = [u_1^i, u_2^i, \dots, u_P^i]$ is a binary vector with

$$u_j^i = \begin{cases} 1, & \text{if the } j\text{th lesion is associated with } \mathbf{X}_i, \\ 0, & \text{otherwise.} \end{cases} \qquad (3.23)$$

Here, P and Q denotes the number of skin lesions and body locations in our dataset. Our goal is to minimize the objective function

$$\mathcal{L}(\mathbf{W}) = \frac{1}{N} \sum_{i=1}^{N} \ell_{les}(\mathbf{X}_i, \mathbf{u}_i; \mathbf{W}) + \frac{1}{N} \sum_{i=1}^{N} \ell_{loc}(\mathbf{X}_i, v_i; \mathbf{W}) + \Phi(\mathbf{W}) \qquad (3.24)$$

in which $\Phi(\cdot)$ is a regularization term, $\ell_{les}(\cdot)$ is the loss function for skin lesions, and $\ell_{loc}(\cdot)$ is the loss function for body locations.

Since there might be multiple lesions associated with an input image, we use a sigmoid cross-entropy function for the skin lesion loss so that each lesion can be optimized independently. Let $s_j(\mathbf{X}_i; \mathbf{W}), j \in \{1, \dots, P\}$ denotes the jth output of the last fully connected (FC) layer for the skin lesions. Then the jth activation of the sigmoid layer can be written as

$$a_j(\mathbf{X}_i; \mathbf{W}) = \frac{1}{1 + e^{-s_j(\mathbf{X}_i; \mathbf{W})}} \qquad (3.25)$$

and the corresponding cross-entropy loss is

$$\ell_{les}(\mathbf{X}_i, \mathbf{u}_i; \mathbf{W}) = -\sum_{j=1}^{P} u_j^i \log a_j(\mathbf{X}_i; \mathbf{W}) + (1 - u_j^i) \log (1 - a_j(\mathbf{X}_i; \mathbf{W})).$$

For the body locations, it is a many-to-one classification problem. Thus, we use a softmax loss function so that only one label will be optimized each time. Let $t_j(\mathbf{X}_i; \mathbf{W}), j \in \{1, \dots, Q\}$ denotes the jth output of the last FC layer for the body locations. Then the jth activation of the softmax layer can be written as

$$b_j(\mathbf{X}_i; \mathbf{W}) = \frac{e^{t_j(\mathbf{X}_i; \mathbf{W})}}{\sum_k e^{t_k(\mathbf{X}_i; \mathbf{W})}} \qquad (3.26)$$

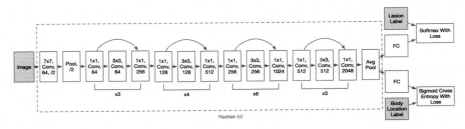

FIGURE 3.9

The network structure of the proposed method. "Conv" denotes the convolutional layer, "Pool" denotes the pooling layer, and "FC" denotes the fully connected layer. The three dark blocks are the data layers for images, skin lesions, and body locations, respectively. The net architecture inside the dotted area is identical to the ResNet-50 network.

and the corresponding softmax loss is

$$\ell_{loc}(\mathbf{X}_i, v_i; \mathbf{W}) = -\log(b_{v_i}(\mathbf{X}_i; \mathbf{W})). \tag{3.27}$$

Finally, for the regularization term, we use the L_2 norm

$$\Phi(\mathbf{W}) = \gamma \|\mathbf{W}\|_2, \tag{3.28}$$

where the regularization parameter γ controls the trade-off between the regularization term and the loss functions.

Implementation. The architecture of the proposed method is given in Fig. 3.9. We build our CNN architecture on top of ResNet-50 (50 layers). Though it is possible to use a deeper ResNet to get a marginal performance gain, ResNet-50 is considered sufficient for this proof-of-concept study. To facilitate our goal in MTL, three data layers are used. One data layer is for the images and the other two data layers are for the lesion labels and body location labels, respectively. We then remove the finally FC layer in the original ResNet and add two sibling FC layers, one for the skin lesions and the other for the body locations. After the FC layers, we add a sigmoid cross entropy loss layer for the skin lesion classification and a softmax layer for the body location classification.

We use the Caffe deep learning framework [29] for all of our experiments and run the programs with a GeForce GTX 1070 GPU. As transfer learning has shown to be more effective in image classification problems [44], instead of training from scratch, we initialize our network from the ImageNet [13] pretrained ResNet-50 model. As a dermatology image may be taken from different distances, the scale of certain skin lesions may vary. Thus, following the practice in [50], we scale each image with its shorter side length randomly selected from [256, 480]. This process is called scale jittering. Then we follow the ImageNet practice in which a 224 × 224 crop is randomly sampled from the mean subtracted images or their horizontal flips. In the testing phase, we perform the standard 10-crops testing using the strategy from [31].

For the hyperparameters, we use SGD with a mini-batch size of 20 and set the momentum to 0.9 and the weight decay (the regularization parameter) to 0.0001. The initial learning rate is 0.001 and is reduced by 0.1 when error plateaus. It is worth mentioning that the two newly added FC layers have bigger learning rate multipliers (10 for the weights and 20 for the bias) so that their effective learning rate is actually 0.01. We use higher learning rate for these two layers is because their weights are randomly initialized. The model is trained for up to 12×10^4 iterations. Note that this is a relatively large number for fine-tuning. This is because the scale jittering greatly augmented our dataset and it takes longer time for the training to converge. During the training, we do not see any overfitting from the validation set.

3.3.4 Experiments

In this section, we investigate the performance of the proposed method on both the skin lesion classification and body location classification tasks. In all of our experiments, we use data collected from DermQuest. In total, there are 21,657 images that contain both the skin lesion and body location labels. To avoid overfitting, 5-folds cross-validation is used for each experiment.

Performance of skin lesion classification.   For skin lesion classification, since it is a multilabel classification problem, we use mean average precision (mAP) as the evaluation metrics following the practice in VOC [17] and ILSVRC. In this study, we use two different mAPs: 1) class-wise mAP, where we treat the sorted evaluations of all images on certain class as a ranking and compute the mAP over the classes and 2) image-wise mAP, where we treat the sorted evaluations of all classes on certain image as a ranking and compute the mAP over the images.

Formally put, the two metrics can be computed using the following formulas:

$$\text{mAP-class} = \frac{1}{P} \sum_{i=1}^{P} \sum_{j=1}^{N} p_i(j) \Delta r_i(j), \tag{3.29}$$

$$\text{mAP-image} = \frac{1}{N} \sum_{i=1}^{N} \sum_{j=1}^{P} q_i(j) \Delta s_i(j). \tag{3.30}$$

Here, N is the total number of images, P is the total number of classes, $p_i(j)$ is the precision of the ranking for class i at cut-off j, and $\Delta r_i(j)$ is the difference of the recall (of the ranking for class i) from cut-off $j - 1$ to j; $q_i(j)$ and $\Delta s_i(j)$ can be defined similarly to $p_i(j)$ and $\Delta r_i(j)$.

We compare our proposed method with two stand-alone architectures (single task) based on AlexNet and ResNet-50, respectively. For the hyperparameters of AlexNet, we use the settings from [31], i.e., batch size = 256, momentum = 0.9, and weight decay = 0.0005. For the stand-alone ResNet-50, we use the same hyperparameter settings as our proposed method. Both the two architectures are fine-tuned from ImageNet pretrained models with learning rate set to 0.01.

Table 3.3 Skin lesion classification results. "AlexNet" and "ResNet" are trained using skin lesion labels only. "MTL" is the proposed method. An ensemble of "ResNet" and "MTL" is given under "Ensemble."

Lesion Type	Average Precision			
	AlexNet	**ResNet**	**MTL**	**Ensemble**
alopecia	0.763	0.845	0.843	**0.855**
comedones	0.687	0.817	**0.861**	0.858
crust	0.677	0.783	0.794	**0.807**
cyst	0.461	0.625	0.698	**0.702**
edema	0.633	0.707	0.751	**0.758**
erosion/ulcer/atrophy	0.774	0.850	0.867	**0.873**
erythema/erythroderm	0.742	0.820	**0.844**	0.843
eryth.-squam. plaque	0.496	0.658	0.683	**0.690**
erythematous papule	0.767	0.846	0.857	**0.861**
erythematous plaque	0.538	0.670	0.704	**0.708**
excoriation	0.467	0.605	0.635	**0.651**
hyperkeratosis	0.643	0.772	0.796	**0.802**
hyperpig. papule	0.589	0.690	**0.738**	0.730
hyperpig. plaque	0.473	0.637	**0.675**	**0.675**
macule	0.619	0.742	**0.780**	0.777
nodule	0.704	0.793	0.813	**0.820**
oozing	0.497	0.595	**0.674**	0.663
other papule	0.344	0.559	0.600	**0.603**
pearly papule	0.716	0.849	0.875	**0.879**
other plaque	0.331	0.553	0.549	**0.562**
scar	0.521	0.690	**0.728**	0.726
squames/scales	0.591	0.704	**0.748**	0.746
telangiectasis	0.655	0.821	0.837	**0.848**
tumor	0.598	0.728	0.768	**0.770**
vesicular/pustular	0.664	0.792	0.814	**0.823**
mAP-class	0.598	0.726	0.757	**0.761**
mAP-image	0.704	0.778	0.792	**0.798**

The classification results are shown in Table 3.3. Here, "AlexNet" and "ReNet" are the two stand-alone architectures, "MTL" is our proposed method, and "Ensemble" contains the ensemble results of "ResNet" and "MTL." First, we can see "ResNet" outperforms "AlexNet" by a big leap which shows that the use of the state-of-the-art CNN architecture helps a lot in boosting the performance. Then, we also observe a decent performance improvement against "ResNet" when using our proposed method. It means the joint optimization with body location classification can really benefit the learning of the lesional characteristics. Finally, we find that the high-

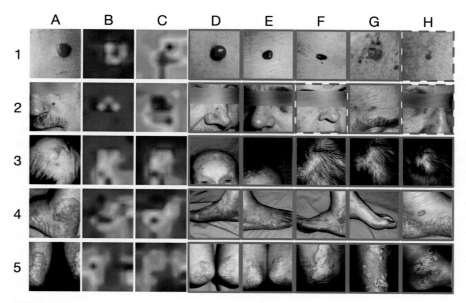

FIGURE 3.10

Image retrieval: (A) the query images; (B) image attention of the primary lesion; (C) image attention of the body location; (D)–(H) retrieved images. Retrieved image with red dotted border means it has no common lesion labels with the query image. Primary lesions of 1–5: nodule, erosion/ulcer/atrophy, alopecia, erythematous squamous plaque, squames/scales.

est mAP can be achieved with an ensemble of "ResNet" and "MTL," i.e., choosing the best evaluation scores of the two models for each image.

We further analyze the performance difference of each class between "ResNet" and "MTL." We find that, in general, if a skin lesion has a strong correlation with a body location, it will also have a better performance gain when using "MTL." Typical examples are "comedone," "edema," "hyperpigmented papule," "oozing," and "tumor." They all have a strong correlation with certain body locations and we see they also have at least a 4% improvement when using "MTL." However, there are some exceptions. For example, we do not see any improvement from "alopecia" even though it has a very strong correlation with "scalp." One possible reason is that the strong correlation between "alopecia" and "scalp" makes "scalp" bias too much to "alopecia" such that some variations will not be learned. We will further verify this hypothesis in the later discussion.

Image retrieval and image attention.   Fig. 3.10 shows the image retrieval and attention of the proposed method. For image retrieval, we take the output of the last pooling layer (pool5) of the ResNet as the feature vector. For each query image from the test set, we compare its features with all the images in the training set and outputs the 5-nearest neighbors (in euclidean distance) as the retrieval. If a retrieved image matches at least one label of the query image, we annotate it with a green solid frame. Otherwise, we annotate it with a red dotted frame. We can see that the retrieved images are visually very similar to the query image.

For image attention, we adapt the method in [69]. We first fetch the output of the final convolution layer (res5c) and get a set of 2048 7×7 activation maps. Next, we calculate the weighted average of the activation maps using the learned weights from the final FC layer. As the weights of an FC layer is a $K \times 2048$ matrix where K is the number of outputs of the FC layer, we will get K attention spots. We select the attention map that corresponding to the ground truth of the input image as the final image attention. As there are two FC layers in our architecture, we obtain two attention maps (one for the skin lesion and the other for the body location) for each input image.

In Fig. 3.10, Column B contains the image attention for the primary skin lesions and Column C contains the image attention for the body locations. In general, the image attention for skin lesions should focus more on the lesion area and the image attention for body locations should focus more on the body parts. For Rows 1–2 and 4–5, it is almost the case and we can see our trained model knows where it should pay attention to. However, for Row 3 ("alopecia"), the skin lesion attention map and the body location attention map look very similar. It means for a "scalp" image, the skin lesion classifier and the body location classifier are trained to make similar decisions. That is when the skin lesion classifier sees an image with scalp, it will almost always output an "alopecia" label. This is too biased and it explained why we did not see a performance boost for the "alopecia" label.

Performance of body location classification.   We also compare the performance of our method with its stand-alone counterpart in classifying body locations. To this end, we fine-tune another ResNet-50 model with body location labels only. For the evaluation metrics, the standard top-1 and top-3 accuracies are used as body location classification is a multiclass classification problem. The evaluation results are given in Fig. 3.11. We can also see a performance improvement from "ResNet" to "MTL." This is somewhat counterintuitive as the classification of a body location should have nothing to do with the skin lesions. However, as we restrict the images to be derma-tological images, a slight performance gain is reasonable.

3.3.5 Discussion

We have developed a deep multitask learning framework for universal skin lesion classification. The proposed method learns skin lesion classification and body location classification in parallel based on the state-of-the-art CNN architecture. To be able to learn a wide variety of lesional characteristics and classify all kinds of lesion types, we have also collected and built a large-scale skin lesion dataset using images from DermQuest. The experimental results have shown that 1) training using the state-of-the-art CNN architecture on a large scale of skin lesion dataset leads to a universal skin lesion classification system with good performance, 2) it is indeed beneficial to use the body location classification as an auxiliary task and train a

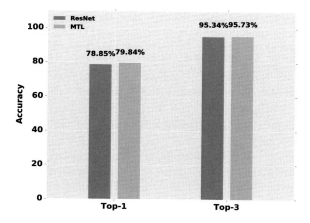

FIGURE 3.11

Body location classification results. "ResNet" is trained using body location only and "MTL" is the proposed multitask learning method.

deep multitask learning based model to achieve improved skin lesion classification, 3) an ensemble of the proposed method and its stand-alone counterpart can achieve an image-wise mAP as high as 0.80, 4) the performance of body location classification is also improved under the deep multitask learning framework, and 5) it is also confirmed by the obtained image retrieval and attention that the trained model not only learns the lesional features very well but also knows generally where to pay attention to.

3.4 Summary

We have introduced several design principles for medical image classification and provided two case studies to show how DNNs can be used to assist the classification of skin lesions and diseases.

For the choices of neural networks, we investigate both AlexNet and ResNet for skin lesion classification and show that the mainstream network ResNet significantly outperformed the early model AlexNet. The investigation indicates that using deeper and more recent neural networks designed for natural image classification also benefits medical image classification. We refer readers to Section 3.1.1 for more DNN models of choices when designing their models for medical image classification.

For the choices of classification tasks and objectives, we apply multiclass classification to address the skin disease classification problem and apply multilabel classification to address the skin lesion characterization problem. We show how the learning objectives are constructed to address these two different dermatology-related classification tasks. By comparing these two classification approaches, we illustrate what a practically useful approach is to achieve robust skin disease diagnosis.

We also apply transfer learning by fine-tuning the ImageNet pretrained models for skin disease diagnosis. We show that the fine-tuned model outperforms the model trained from scratch. It means that the knowledge learned from natural image classification is transferable to the task of skin disease and lesion classification. However, transfer learning does not always work for medical problems. We refer readers to some further readings [41,9] to understand better how to apply transfer learning to medical image computing.

Finally, we present a multitask learning approach to skin lesion classification. We provide a detailed neural network design as well as the objective function design for a deep learning based multitask classification model. We demonstrate that introducing body part classification as an auxiliary task is helpful in training a better skin lesion classification model.

References

[1] John Arevalo, Angel Cruz-Roa, Viviana Arias, Eduardo Romero, Fabio A. González, An unsupervised feature learning framework for basal cell carcinoma image analysis, Artificial Intelligence in Medicine (2015).

[2] JoseLuisGarcía Arroyo, BegoñaGarcía Zapirain, Automated detection of melanoma in dermoscopic images, in: Jacob Scharcanski, M. Emre Celebi (Eds.), Computer Vision Techniques for the Diagnosis of Skin Cancer, in: Series in BioEngineering, Springer, Berlin–Heidelberg, 2014, pp. 139–192.

[3] Yaniv Bar, Idit Diamant, Lior Wolf, Hayit Greenspan, Deep learning with non-medical training used for chest pathology identification, in: SPIE Medical Imaging, International Society for Optics and Photonics, 2015, p. 94140V.

[4] Yaniv Bar, Idit Diamant, Lior Wolf, Sivan Lieberman, Eli Konen, Hayit Greenspan, Chest pathology identification using deep feature selection with non-medical training, Computer Methods in Biomechanics and Biomedical Engineering: Imaging & Visualization (2016) 1–5.

[5] Catarina Barata, Jorge S. Marques, Teresa Mendonça, Bag-of-features classification model for the diagnose of melanoma in dermoscopy images using color and texture descriptors, in: Mohamed Kamel, Aurélio Campilho (Eds.), Image Analysis and Recognition, in: Lecture Notes in Computer Science, vol. 7950, Springer, Berlin–Heidelberg, 2013, pp. 547–555.

[6] Rich Caruana, Multitask learning, in: Learning to Learn, Springer, 1998, pp. 95–133.

[7] Russell L. Cecil, Lee Goldman, Andrew I. Schafer, Goldman's Cecil Medicine, 23th ed., Elsevier/Saunders, Philadelphia, 2012.

[8] Hao Chen, Chiyao Shen, Jing Qin, Dong Ni, Lin Shi, Jack C.Y. Cheng, Pheng-Ann Heng, Automatic localization and identification of vertebrae in spine CT via a joint learning model with deep neural networks, in: International Conference on Medical Image Computing and Computer-Assisted Intervention, Springer, 2015, pp. 515–522.

[9] Sihong Chen, Kai Ma, Yefeng Zheng, Med3D: transfer learning for 3D medical image analysis, CoRR, arXiv:1904.00625 [abs], 2019.

[10] Mark Cicero, Alexander Bilbily, Errol Colak, Tim Dowdell, Bruce Gray, Kuhan Perampaladas, Joseph Barfett, Training and validating a deep convolutional neural network for computer-aided detection and classification of abnormalities on frontal chest radiographs, Investigative Radiology 52 (5) (2017) 281–287.

[11] N.H. Cox, I.H. Coulson, Diagnosis of skin disease, in: Rook's Textbook of Dermatology, 7th edn., Blackwell Science, Oxford, 2004, p. 5.

[12] Angel Cruz-Roa, Ajay Basavanhally, Fabio González, Hannah Gilmore, Michael Feldman, Shridar Ganesan, Natalie Shih, John Tomaszewski, Anant Madabhushi, Automatic detection of invasive ductal carcinoma in whole slide images with convolutional neural networks, in: SPIE Medical Imaging, International Society for Optics and Photonics, 2014, p. 904103.

[13] Jia Deng, Wei Dong, Richard Socher, Li-Jia Li, Kai Li, Fei-Fei Li, ImageNet: a large-scale hierarchical image database, in: 2009 IEEE Computer Society Conference on Computer Vision and Pattern Recognition (CVPR 2009), June 20–25, 2009, Miami, Florida, USA, 2009, pp. 248–255.

[14] Alexey Dosovitskiy, Lucas Beyer, Alexander Kolesnikov, Dirk Weissenborn, Xiaohua Zhai, Thomas Unterthiner, Mostafa Dehghani, Matthias Minderer, Georg Heigold, Sylvain Gelly, et al., An image is worth 16×16 words: transformers for image recognition at scale, arXiv preprint, arXiv:2010.11929, 2020.

[15] Andre Esteva, Brett Kuprel, Roberto A. Novoa, Justin Ko, Susan M. Swetter, Helen M. Blau, Sebastian Thrun, Dermatologist-level classification of skin cancer with deep neural networks, Nature 542 (7639) (2017) 115–118.

[16] Andre Esteva, Brett Kuprel, Sebastian Thrun, Deep Networks for Early Stage Skin Disease and Skin Cancer Classification, 2015.

[17] Mark Everingham, Luc Van Gool, Christopher K.I. Williams, John M. Winn, Andrew Zisserman, The Pascal visual object classes (VOC) challenge, International Journal of Computer Vision 88 (2) (2010) 303–338.

[18] Gabriella Fabbrocini, ValerioDe Vita, Sara Cacciapuoti, GiuseppeDi Leo, Consolatina Liguori, Alfredo Paolillo, Antonio Pietrosanto, Paolo Sommella, Automatic diagnosis of melanoma based on the 7-point checklist, in: Jacob Scharcanski, M. Emre Celebi (Eds.), Computer Vision Techniques for the Diagnosis of Skin Cancer, in: Series in BioEngineering, Springer, Berlin–Heidelberg, 2014, pp. 71–107.

[19] Zhimin Gao, Lei Wang, Luping Zhou, Jianjia Zhang, HEp-2 cell image classification with deep convolutional neural networks, IEEE Journal of Biomedical and Health Informatics 21 (2) (2017) 416–428.

[20] Ian Goodfellow, Yoshua Bengio, Aaron Courville, Deep Learning, MIT Press, 2016.

[21] Xian-Hua Han, Jianmei Lei, Yen-Wei Chen, HEp-2 cell classification using K-support spatial pooling in deep CNNs, in: International Workshop on Large-Scale Annotation of Biomedical Data and Expert Label Synthesis, Springer, 2016, pp. 3–11.

[22] Emily M. Hand, Rama Chellappa, Attributes for improved attributes: a multitask network for attribute classification, CoRR, arXiv:1604.07360 [abs], 2016.

[23] Kaiming He, Xiangyu Zhang, Shaoqing Ren, Jian Sun, Deep residual learning for image recognition, in: Proceedings of the IEEE Conference on Computer Vision and Pattern Recognition, 2016, pp. 770–778.

[24] Andrew G. Howard, Menglong Zhu, Bo Chen, Dmitry Kalenichenko, Weijun Wang, Tobias Weyand, Marco Andreetto, Hartwig Adam, Mobilenets: efficient convolutional neural networks for mobile vision applications, arXiv preprint, arXiv:1704.04861, 2017.

[25] Jie Hu, Li Shen, Gang Sun, Squeeze-and-excitation networks, in: Proceedings of the IEEE Conference on Computer Vision and Pattern Recognition, 2018, pp. 7132–7141.

[26] Gao Huang, Zhuang Liu, Laurens Van Der Maaten, Kilian Q. Weinberger, Densely connected convolutional networks, in: Proceedings of the IEEE Conference on Computer Vision and Pattern Recognition, 2017, pp. 4700–4708.

[27] Maximilian Ilse, Jakub Tomczak, Max Welling, Attention-based deep multiple instance learning, in: International Conference on Machine Learning, PMLR, 2018, pp. 2127–2136.

[28] Sergey Ioffe, Christian Szegedy, Batch normalization: accelerating deep network training by reducing internal covariate shift, in: International Conference on Machine Learning, 2015, pp. 448–456.

[29] Yangqing Jia, Evan Shelhamer, Jeff Donahue, Sergey Karayev, Jonathan Long, Ross B. Girshick, Sergio Guadarrama, Trevor Darrell, Caffe: convolutional architecture for fast feature embedding, in: Proceedings of the ACM International Conference on Multimedia, MM'14, Orlando, FL, USA, November 03–07, 2014, 2014, pp. 675–678.

[30] Jeremy Kawahara, Aïcha BenTaieb, Ghassan Hamarneh, Deep features to classify skin lesions, in: 13th IEEE International Symposium on Biomedical Imaging, ISBI 2016, Prague, Czech Republic, April 13–16, 2016, 2016, pp. 1397–1400.

[31] Alex Krizhevsky, Ilya Sutskever, Geoffrey E. Hinton, ImageNet classification with deep convolutional neural networks, in: F. Pereira, C.J.C. Burges, L. Bottou, K.Q. Weinberger (Eds.), Advances in Neural Information Processing Systems 25, Curran Associates, Inc., 2012, pp. 1097–1105.

[32] Haofu Liao, Jiebo Luo, A deep multi-task learning approach to skin lesion classification, in: The Workshops of the Thirty-First AAAI Conference on Artificial Intelligence, February 4–9, 2017, San Francisco, California, USA, in: AAAI Technical Report, vol. WS-17, AAAI Press, 2017.

[33] Haofu Liao, Yuncheng Li, Jiebo Luo, Skin disease classification versus skin lesion characterization: achieving robust diagnosis using multi-label deep neural networks, in: 23rd International Conference on Pattern Recognition, ICPR 2016, Cancún, Mexico, December 4–8, 2016, IEEE, 2016, pp. 355–360.

[34] Tsung-Yi Lin, Michael Maire, Serge J. Belongie, James Hays, Pietro Perona, Deva Ramanan, Piotr Dollár, C. Lawrence Zitnick, Microsoft COCO: common objects in context, in: Computer Vision – ECCV 2014 – 13th European Conference, Zurich, Switzerland, September 6–12, 2014, Proceedings, Part V, 2014, pp. 740–755.

[35] Ze Liu, Yutong Lin, Yue Cao, Han Hu, Yixuan Wei, Zheng Zhang, Stephen Lin, Baining Guo, Swin transformer: hierarchical vision transformer using shifted windows, arXiv preprint, arXiv:2103.14030, 2021.

[36] Christopher D. Malon, Eric Cosatto, et al., Classification of mitotic figures with convolutional neural networks and seeded blob features, Journal of Pathology Informatics 4 (1) (2013) 9.

[37] Afonso Menegola, Michel Fornaciali, Ramon Pires, Sandra Avila, Eduardo Valle, Towards automated melanoma screening: exploring transfer learning schemes, arXiv preprint, arXiv:1609.01228, 2016.

[38] Pim Moeskops, Jelmer M. Wolterink, Bas H.M. van der Velden, Kenneth G.A. Gilhuijs, Tim Leiner, Max A. Viergever, Ivana Išgum, Deep learning for multi-task medical image segmentation in multiple modalities, in: International Conference on Medical Image Computing and Computer-Assisted Intervention, Springer, 2016, pp. 478–486.

[39] Michael A. Nielsen, Neural Networks and Deep Learning, Determination Press, 2015.

[40] Ilija Radosavovic, Raj Prateek Kosaraju, Ross Girshick, Kaiming He, Piotr Dollár, Designing network design spaces, in: Proceedings of the IEEE/CVF Conference on Computer Vision and Pattern Recognition, 2020, pp. 10428–10436.

[41] Maithra Raghu, Chiyuan Zhang, Jon M. Kleinberg, Samy Bengio, Transfusion: understanding transfer learning for medical imaging, in: Hanna M. Wallach, Hugo Larochelle, Alina Beygelzimer, Florence d'Alché-Buc, Emily B. Fox, Roman Garnett (Eds.), Advances in Neural Information Processing Systems 32: Annual Conference on Neural Information Processing Systems 2019, NeurIPS 2019, December 8–14, 2019, Vancouver, BC, Canada, 2019, pp. 3342–3352.

[42] Rajeev Ranjan, Vishal M. Patel, Rama Chellappa, HyperFace: a deep multi-task learning framework for face detection, landmark localization, pose estimation, and gender recognition, CoRR, arXiv:1603.01249 [abs], 2016.

[43] John W. Ratcliff, David E. Metzener, Pattern matching: the gestalt approach, Dr. Dobb's Journal 13 (7) (1988) 46.

[44] Ali Sharif Razavian, Hossein Azizpour, Josephine Sullivan, Stefan Carlsson, CNN features off-the-shelf: an astounding baseline for recognition, in: IEEE Conference on Computer Vision and Pattern Recognition, CVPR Workshops 2014, Columbus, OH, USA, June 23–28, 2014, 2014, pp. 512–519.

[45] Shaoqing Ren, Kaiming He, Ross B. Girshick, Jian Sun, Faster R-CNN: towards real-time object detection with region proposal networks, in: Advances in Neural Information Processing Systems 28: Annual Conference on Neural Information Processing Systems 2015, December 7–12, 2015, Montreal, Quebec, Canada, 2015.

[46] Olga Russakovsky, Jia Deng, Hao Su, Jonathan Krause, Sanjeev Satheesh, Sean Ma, Zhiheng Huang, Andrej Karpathy, Aditya Khosla, Michael S. Bernstein, Alexander C. Berg, Fei-Fei Li, ImageNet large scale visual recognition challenge, International Journal of Computer Vision 115 (3) (2015) 211–252.

[47] Aurora Sáez, Begoña Acha, Carmen Serrano, Pattern analysis in dermoscopic images, in: Jacob Scharcanski, M. Emre Celebi (Eds.), Computer Vision Techniques for the Diagnosis of Skin Cancer, in: Series in BioEngineering, Springer, Berlin–Heidelberg, 2014, pp. 23–48.

[48] Pierre Sermanet, David Eigen, Xiang Zhang, Michaël Mathieu, Rob Fergus, Yann LeCun, Overfeat: integrated recognition, localization and detection using convolutional networks, arXiv preprint, arXiv:1312.6229, 2013.

[49] Anat Shkolyar, Amit Gefen, Dafna Benayahu, Hayit Greenspan, Automatic detection of cell divisions (mitosis) in live-imaging microscopy images using Convolutional Neural Networks, in: Engineering in Medicine and Biology Society (EMBC), 2015 37th Annual International Conference of the IEEE, IEEE, 2015, pp. 743–746.

[50] Karen Simonyan, Andrew Zisserman, Very deep convolutional networks for large-scale image recognition, CoRR, arXiv:1409.1556 [abs], 2014.

[51] Heung-Il Suk, Seong-Whan Lee, Dinggang Shen, Alzheimer's Disease Neuroimaging Initiative, et al., Deep sparse multi-task learning for feature selection in Alzheimer's disease diagnosis, Brain Structure and Function 221 (5) (2016) 2569–2587.

[52] Christian Szegedy, Wei Liu, Yangqing Jia, Pierre Sermanet, Scott Reed, Dragomir Anguelov, Dumitru Erhan, Vincent Vanhoucke, Andrew Rabinovich, Going deeper with convolutions, in: Proceedings of the IEEE Conference on Computer Vision and Pattern Recognition, 2015, pp. 1–9.

[53] Mingxing Tan, Quoc Le, Efficientnet: rethinking model scaling for convolutional neural networks, in: International Conference on Machine Learning, PMLR, 2019, pp. 6105–6114.

[54] Hugo Touvron, Matthieu Cord, Matthijs Douze, Francisco Massa, Alexandre Sablayrolles, Hervé Jégou, Training data-efficient image transformers & distillation through attention, arXiv preprint, arXiv:2012.12877, 2020.

[55] Haibo Wang, Angel Cruz-Roa, Ajay Basavanhally, Hannah Gilmore, Natalie Shih, Mike Feldman, John Tomaszewski, Fabio Gonzalez, Anant Madabhushi, Cascaded ensemble of convolutional neural networks and handcrafted features for mitosis detection, in: SPIE Medical Imaging, International Society for Optics and Photonics, 2014, p. 90410B.

[56] Haibo Wang, Angel Cruz-Roa, Ajay Basavanhally, Hannah Gilmore, Natalie Shih, Mike Feldman, John Tomaszewski, Fabio Gonzalez, Anant Madabhushi, Mitosis detection in breast cancer pathology images by combining handcrafted and convolutional neural network features, Journal of Medical Imaging 1 (3) (2014) 034003.

[57] Website addresses for AtlasDerm, Danderm, Derma, DermIS, Dermnet and DermQuest, http://www.atlasdermatologico.com.br, http://www.danderm-pdv.is.kkh.dk, http://www.derma.pw, http://www.dermis.net, http://www.dermnet.com, http://www.dermquest.com, 2016.

[58] John D. Whited, James M. Grichnik, Does this patient have a mole or a melanoma?, JAMA 279 (9) (1998) 696–701.

[59] Fengying Xie, Yefen Wu, Zhiguo Jiang, Rusong Meng, Dermoscopy image processing for Chinese, in: Jacob Scharcanski, M. Emre Celebi (Eds.), Computer Vision Techniques for the Diagnosis of Skin Cancer, in: Series in BioEngineering, Springer, Berlin–Heidelberg, 2014, pp. 109–137.

[60] Saining Xie, Ross Girshick, Piotr Dollár, Zhuowen Tu, Kaiming He, Aggregated residual transformations for deep neural networks, in: Proceedings of the IEEE Conference on Computer Vision and Pattern Recognition, 2017, pp. 1492–1500.

[61] Yongxin Yang, Timothy Hospedales, Deep multi-task representation learning: a tensor factorisation approach, arXiv preprint, arXiv:1605.06391, 2016.

[62] Jason Yosinski, Jeff Clune, Yoshua Bengio, Hod Lipson, How transferable are features in deep neural networks?, in: Advances in Neural Information Processing Systems, 2014, pp. 3320–3328.

[63] Li Yuan, Yunpeng Chen, Tao Wang, Weihao Yu, Yujun Shi, Zihang Jiang, Francis E.H. Tay, Jiashi Feng, Shuicheng Yan, Tokens-to-token ViT: training vision transformers from scratch on ImageNet, arXiv preprint, arXiv:2101.11986, 2021.

[64] Min-Ling Zhang, Zhi-Hua Zhou, Multilabel neural networks with applications to functional genomics and text categorization, IEEE Transactions on Knowledge and Data Engineering 18 (10) (2006) 1338–1351.

[65] Wenlu Zhang, Rongjian Li, Tao Zeng, Qian Sun, Sudhir Kumar, Jieping Ye, Shuiwang Ji, Deep model based transfer and multi-task learning for biological image analysis, IEEE Transactions on Big Data (2016).

[66] Xiangyu Zhang, Xinyu Zhou, Mengxiao Lin, Jian Sun, Shufflenet: an extremely efficient convolutional neural network for mobile devices, in: Proceedings of the IEEE Conference on Computer Vision and Pattern Recognition, 2018, pp. 6848–6856.

[67] Zhanpeng Zhang, Ping Luo, Chen Change Loy, Xiaoou Tang, Facial landmark detection by deep multi-task learning, in: European Conference on Computer Vision, Springer, 2014, pp. 94–108.

[68] Zhanpeng Zhang, Ping Luo, Chen Change Loy, Xiaoou Tang, Learning deep representation for face alignment with auxiliary attributes, IEEE Transactions on Pattern Analysis and Machine Intelligence 38 (5) (2016) 918–930.

[69] Bolei Zhou, Aditya Khosla, Àgata Lapedriza, Aude Oliva, Antonio Torralba, Learning deep features for discriminative localization, CoRR, arXiv:1512.04150 [abs], 2015.

[70] Mu Zhu, Recall, Precision and Average Precision, Department of Statistics and Actuarial Science, University of Waterloo, 2004, p. 2.

Detection: vertebrae localization and identification

CONTENTS

Medical object/landmark *detection* is the task of localizing and identifying anatomical regions of interest in medical images. In general, there are two types of detection tasks: 1) anatomical landmark detection and 2) anatomical object detection. Anatomical landmark detection aims to localize anatomically-meaningful points, such as bone joints or artery bifurcation points, in the human body. As those points are usually unique and positioned in a relatively fixed location, anatomical landmark detection methods are usually leveraged to help healthcare professionals for the navigation, measurement, and monitoring of the human body. Anatomical object detection aims to localize and identify the anatomical objects, such as lesions, nodules, or cells, in the human body. Unlike the anatomical landmarks, anatomical objects are nonunique and appear in unpredictive locations in the human body. For example, a brain tumor may appear in any location of the brain and there could be multiple brain tumors that coexist. Therefore, anatomical object detection methods are usually used to facilitate the diagnosis and monitor the progression of diseases.

While the localization and identification of anatomical landmarks and objects are critical in many biomedical applications, it is time-consuming and error-prone to obtain them manually. To annotate the anatomical landmarks, it usually requires the healthcare professionals to browse through a significant amount of slices/scans of the medical images. For anatomical objects, it is even worse since there could be many instances in each slice/scan and their locations could be anywhere, which may lead to considerably more labor effort. Furthermore, some anatomical landmarks/objects are visually similar or challenging to identify, which require more expertise for the interpretation of medical images or result in lower annotation quality.

Automatic and reliable detection of the anatomical objects/landmarks has been a long-standing goal in medical image computing. As with other medical image analysis tasks, traditional approaches [69,39,31,5,56] to medical object/landmark detection rely on handcrafted image features and hence are less robust to the variations of medical images. To address this limitation, deep neural networks have been widely applied to the existing solutions [48,52,16,46,62,26] for medical object/landmark detection. Compared to the handcrafted feature extraction approaches, deep neural networks extract more robust image features and have shown surpassing human-level performance on image classification [23].

Since medical object/landmark detection can be addressed via image classification patch-by-patch in a sliding window manner, deep neural networks have first been leveraged to improve the sliding-window based detection models [52,63,16], where efforts have been made to convert the natural image classification networks to effectively recognize anatomical objects/landmarks from medical image patches. Meanwhile, there has been a rapid development of natural image object detectors [50,14,37] which equipped with specialized network designs, such as region proposal network [50] and feature pyramid network [36], for more effective object detection. Therefore, some other approaches [62,26] propose to develop upon existing natural image object detectors for medical object detection. Finally, inspired by the deep learning solutions for human pose detection [60,47] and the advanced image-to-image networks such as U-Net [51], deep image-to-image models have been proposed for anatomical landmark detection [46,64].

This chapter introduces how to design deep neural networks for medical object/landmark detection. In Section 4.1, we first present three families of deep learning models for medical object/landmark detection. We discuss the benefits of these models and provide scenarios for which these models could be applied. Next, we distinguish between medical object detection and medical landmark detection. We give formal definitions of the two tasks and introduce several variations of the objective functions for each task. In Section 4.2, we provide a case study on medical landmark detection [35] to show how the introduced design principles could be applied in practice. Specifically, we introduce a sliding-window based model for vertebrae labeling in CT images and propose a solution to incorporate both the short- and long-term context information for better modeling of the spinal column structure.

4.1 Design principles
4.1.1 Choice of deep neural networks
Sliding-window based models.   Early deep learning approaches to medical object/landmark detection are sliding-window based, where the objects/landmarks are detected voxel-by-voxel, slice-by-slice, or patch-by-patch in a sliding window manner. As medical object/landmark detection often involves 3D images such as CT or

MR images, the major deciding factor for the design of these methods is the memory and computation efficiency so that 3D images can be reasonable effectively processed under the hardware constraints.

A straightforward approach is to directly apply 2D CNNs slice by slice and have classifiers to decide if the slice contains the target objects/landmarks or not. For example, Yang et al. [63] proposed a 2D approach to landmark detection on distal femur surface. They applied CNNs to classify each of the 2D images along the x, y, and z axes, and a landmark candidate was detected when the three orthogonal slices, along the x, y, and z axes, respectively, contained the landmark. De Vos et al. [15] proposed a similar idea for 3D chest anatomy localization in CT images. But instead of detecting landmark points, they applied a postprocessing method to derive 3D bounding boxes from the slice classification results. While these 2D based solutions are efficient in terms of memory and computation, they have an obvious limitation, i.e., they process each image slice independently without the critical 3D context information.

Therefore, to help 2D CNNs incorporate the 3D information, other researchers propose a 2.5D approach to medical object detection. In this approach, the input to 2D CNNs is not a single image slice but a triplet of three orthogonal slices, which provide more context information along the x, y, and z axes, and the classification is not to decide if the slice contains the object but rather to decide if the intersection of the three orthogonal slices belongs to the object. Based on this idea, Prasoon et al. [48] introduced a triplanar CNN for knee cartilage segmentation. In their approach, however, the three orthogonal slices were separately sent to three different CNNs and only the classification layer would jointly see the features of the three slices. To better extract features of the three orthogonal slices and better exploit the 3D context, Roth et al. [52] proposed to regard the three orthogonal slices as the three channels of the image (similar to the RGB channels). In this way, a single 2D CNN could jointly extract features of the orthogonal slices which provided a better opportunity to learn the correlations between the three slices and formed the 3D understanding. Although the 2.5D based approaches can learn better the 3D context, with only the orthogonal slices they cannot fully understand the 3D spatial and shape relations of the anatomy since the important volumetric information is missing.

To truly leverage the 3D information, 3D CNNs have to be considered. A naive approach with 3D CNNs is to take 3D patches as the input and process the full 3D image patch by patch in a sliding window manner. With reduced size of the 3D patches, such a 3D sliding window based approach is feasible but is still computationally expensive since there could be millions of voxels in the 3D images (and hence millions of 3D patches will be processed). One compromise solution is to apply heuristics to select candidate 3D patches [11] which can significantly reduce the computational cost. But the overall performance of the model will be limited by the 3D candidate selection method which is usually less robust to the variation of the input images. To address this issue, Dou et al. [16] proposed to introduce 3D FCN [43] for more efficient sliding window patch processing. Compared with the naive approach, 3D FCN avoids the duplicated feature extraction for overlapped 3D patches and hence can be hundreds of times faster than the naive approach. In Dou et al.'s approach, the 3D FCN performed patch-level detection of lesions where a positive detection indicated that the patch contained a lesion. Although the 3D FCN is efficient, such a patch-level classification requires a dense sliding window (i.e., the effective sampling stride should be short), which is still relatively expensive. To further reduce the computational cost, in Section 4.2, we introduce a multitask FCN for vertebrae localization, which, in addition to classifying the 3D patches (i.e., if the patch contains the centroid of the vertebrae), also directly regresses to the exact centroid locations. In this way, the vertebrae localization can be achieved via the regression predictions and, as a result, dense sliding window is not required.

Two- and single-stage object detectors.   An alternative solution to medical object detection is to build upon the existing models for natural image object detection, which can be organized into two main categories: two- and singe-stage object detectors [41].

The most well known two-stage object detector is the region based CNN or R-CNN. R-CNN was first introduced by Girshick et al. [18] and has then been developed into several variations [17,50,14,22] with improved performance. In R-CNN, the object detection is divided into two stages. In the first stage, region proposals are generated, which can be regarded as the candidates of the final objects. In the second stage, the features of each region proposal will be sent to a classifier to decide the category of the objects and a regressor to refine the object bounding boxes. Such a two-stage approach has proven to be very effective in natural image object detection [41], and thus has also been adapted to address medical object detection problems.

When the medical problem is a 2D problem, R-CNN can be directly applied. For example, Liu et al. [40] used R-CNN to detect colitis from 2D abdominal CT slices and Zhang et al. [70] introduced R-CNN into a smartphone-based system for early childhood caries diagnosis. However, when the input image was 3D, extra steps may be required in order to apply R-CNN. There are two possible choices. First, we may consider converting the 3D image to 2D and then leverage R-CNN to address the converted 2D problem. For example, Wang et al. [61] proposed to detect degenerative osteophytes from PET/CT images using R-CNN. In their approach, they first converted the 3D object detection problem to 2D by generating unwrapped cortical shell maps from the PET/CT images. Then, they applied R-CNN to detect the degenerative osteophytes from the 2D unwrapped maps. Second, we may also consider modifying the R-CNN so that it can be applied to better address the 3D problem. Liao et al. [34] converted the 2D region proposal network (RPN) in faster R-CNN [50] to a 3D version so that it could generate 3D region proposals directly for pulmonary nodule detection. Yan et al. [62] proposed to improve the R-FCN [14] (a variant of R-CNN) with designs to incorporate the 3D information along the axial direction for better lesion detection from CT images.

While two-stage approaches are effective in terms of accuracy, they are generally less efficient in terms of computational cost. Therefore, many single-stage approaches have been proposed [42,49,37] for faster object detection. Compared with their two-stage counterparts, singe-stage object detectors do not have the region proposal generation stage, postclassification or feature resampling. Instead, the object detection is achieved end-to-end with a single network, which yields significant speed-up. Due to this efficiency in computation and the end-to-end trainability property, single-stage object detectors have since been applied to solve medical object detection problems. Jaeger et al. [26] proposed a Retina-UNet for medical object detection based on the popular single-stage object detector RetinaNet [37]. They converted the feature pyramid network [36] in RetinaNet to a U-Net like architecture so that the proposed method can perform semantic segmentation in addition to the medical object detection. Meanwhile, they also showed that the proposed method can be feasibly converted to a 3D version and hence can detect objects in 3D directly. Zlocha et al. [71] further improved RetinaNet with optimized anchor configuration for better detection of the small lesions. Similar to the Retina-UNet, their model also had the lesion segmentation branch. But instead of using GT annotations, they proposed to leverage RECIST labels to generate pseudo and weak segmentation labels for training.

Image-to-image based models.   So far, we have introduced the sliding-window based models and the two-stage/single-stage object detectors. The sliding-window based models are reasonably effective, however, as the sliding-windows are operated locally, these models do not have the ability to incorporate the important global context information, which limits the further improvement of these models. The two-stage/single-stage object detectors are designed for object detection problems. When it comes to landmark detection, some of the designs for object detectors may not be necessary and the network architecture design can be simplified. Therefore, to incorporate the global information and better address the landmark detection problem, image-to-image based models may be considered.

As its name suggests, image-to-image based models take an image as the input and output a transformed version of the image. In medical landmark detection, the input is usually the entire medical image, and hence all the information (both local and global) from the image can be potentially observed and leveraged by the image-to-image model. The output is a landmark heatmap with each channel indicates the location of a landmark. In this way, it obviates the need for location regression which is less accurate while commonly exists in object detectors.

Image-to-image based models are first proposed to address the natural image landmark detection problems. One of the earliest image-to-image approach to landmark detection was proposed by Tompson et al. [60]. They used an FCN-like network to generate likelihood heatmaps for human pose estimation. However, the likelihood heatmap did not consider the fuzziness in landmark annotation, which may inappropriately penalize the model for suboptimal predictions. To address this issue, Pfister et al. [47] proposed to use Gaussian heatmaps to represent landmarks. The Gaussian blobs allowed lower responses near the landmark which hence addressed better the annotation fuzziness.

Due to their effectiveness in natural image landmark detection, image-to-image models have soon been adapted to address anatomical landmark detection problems.

Inspired by Pfister et al. [47], Payer et al. [46] explored several possible image-to-image network architectures with Gaussian heatmap and applied them to both 2D and 3D anatomical landmark detection problems. They showed that, by simply using a U-Net-like image-to-image architecture, the model could achieve significant improvement over previous solutions. Following a similar idea, Yang et al. [64] proposed a 3D U-Net like image-to-image model for vertebra labeling. They also introduced a message passing scheme [60] to enhance the Gaussian heatmaps via a graphical model.

4.1.2 Choice of detection tasks and objectives

Object detection.   Object detection is the task of localizing and recognizing objects in image. In medical image analysis, it often means finding small anatomical objects such as lesions or nodules, but may also cover the detection of organs or other types of anatomical regions of interest. Unlike object localization which only localizes a single object, object detection aims to localize all possible objects of interest in the image. The detection of an object is usually achieved by providing a bounding box (either 2D or 3D) that tightly encloses the object but could also be simply providing the coordinates of the object's centroid. In this section, we assume the detection is for the bounding boxes of the object but the idea applies to the centroid detection as well.

Formally, let $\mathbf{x}$ be an image with M objects of interest $\mathbf{y} = \{\mathbf{y}_i\}_{i=1}^{M}$. Each object $\mathbf{y}_i$ can be represented as $\mathbf{y}_i = \{\mathbf{b}_i, c_i\}$, where $\mathbf{b}_i$ denotes the object's bounding box (or centroid) and $c_i \in \{1, \ldots, K\}$ denotes the category label of the object. Let $\hat{\mathbf{y}} = \{\hat{\mathbf{b}}_i, \hat{\mathbf{p}}_i\}_{i=1}^{N}$ be the model's N object detection predictions, where $\hat{\mathbf{b}}_i$ denotes the bounding box of the ith prediction and $\hat{\mathbf{p}}_i$ denotes the predicted categorical probabilities of the object. The objective function for object detection can be generally written as

$$\mathcal{L}(\mathbf{y}, \hat{\mathbf{y}}) = \sum_{i=1}^{N} \mathcal{L}_{\text{cls}}(c_{\sigma(i)}, \hat{\mathbf{p}}_i) + \lambda \mathbb{1}(c_{\sigma(i)} \neq \varnothing) \mathcal{L}_{\text{loc}}(\mathbf{b}_{\sigma(i)}, \hat{\mathbf{b}}_i), \qquad (4.1)$$

where $\mathcal{L}_{\text{cls}}$ is the classification loss, $\mathcal{L}_{\text{loc}}$ is the localization loss, $\sigma(i)$ is the index mapping between the M ground-truth labels and N predictions, and λ is the weight that balances the classification and localization. Note that when the ground-truth label for the ith prediction is the background (i.e., $c_{\sigma(i)} = \varnothing$), the ground-truth bounding box is undefined. Hence, we apply an indicator function $\mathbb{1}(\cdot)$ to ignore this case when computing the localization loss.

There are multiple choices for the classification loss. The most common one is the negative log-likelihood loss

$$\mathcal{L}_{\text{cls}}(c_{\sigma(i)}, \hat{\mathbf{p}}_i) = -\log \hat{\mathbf{p}}_i(c_{\sigma(i)}), \qquad (4.2)$$

where we aim to classify the object into one of the K categories (e.g., types of glands in histology images). However, the classification in object detection is usually a highly imbalanced classification problem. This is because the background is usually dominant in the image and only a small portion of the image contains objects. For example, in lung nodule detection, the majority of the image are healthy tissues and only several countable locations have lung nodules. To address this issue, we may consider the α-balanced version of the negative log-likelihood loss

$$\mathcal{L}_{\text{cls}}(c_{\sigma(i)}, \hat{\mathbf{p}}_i) = -\alpha_{c_{\sigma(i)}} \log \hat{\mathbf{p}}_i(c_{\sigma(i)}), \tag{4.3}$$

where $\alpha_{c_{\sigma(i)}}$ is the weight that balances the different categories. Typically, we set higher α values for categories that are less frequent. A better way to address the class imbalance issue for object detection is to apply the focal loss [37],

$$\mathcal{L}_{\text{cls}}(c_{\sigma(i)}, \hat{\mathbf{p}}_i) = -\alpha_{c_{\sigma(i)}} (1 - \hat{\mathbf{p}}_i(c_{\sigma(i)}))^\gamma \log \hat{\mathbf{p}}_i(c_{\sigma(i)}). \tag{4.4}$$

This loss assigns more weights to the less confident predictions. Since the less confident predictions usually comes from the less frequent categories, this loss handles imbalanced classification better in practice.

For the localization loss, one popular choice is simply the L_1 loss

$$\mathcal{L}_{\text{loc}}(\mathbf{b}_{\sigma(i)}, \hat{\mathbf{b}}_i) = \sum_t \|b^t_{\sigma(i)} - \hat{b}^t_i\|_1, \tag{4.5}$$

Here, $b^t_{\sigma(i)}$ and $\hat{b}^t_i$ denote the object's localization ground truth and prediction, respectively. The exact definition is approach specific. For example, if we aim to localize the object's centroids, then $\mathbf{b} = \{b^x, b^y\}$ denotes the coordinates of the centroid. Besides, they may also denote the bound box's center coordinates, width and height [9] or the offsets of these values [17]. Another choice for the localization loss is the smooth L_1 loss

$$\mathcal{L}_{\text{loc}}(\mathbf{b}_{\sigma(i)}, \hat{\mathbf{b}}_i) = \sum_t \text{smooth}_{L_1}(b^t_{\sigma(i)}, \hat{b}^t_i), \tag{4.6}$$

where the smooth L_1 function is defined as

$$\text{smooth}_{L_1}(x) = \begin{cases} 0.5x^2, & \text{if } |x| < 1, \\ |x| - 0.5, & \text{otherwise.} \end{cases} \tag{4.7}$$

Compared with the L_1 loss, it addresses better the fuzziness of the localization labeling and penalizes less when the prediction is close to the ground truth. Finally, the localization loss is sometimes optional. Especially, when the localization is for the centroids of objects, the classification probability map may be directly used to produce the object's centroids [16,52].

Landmark detection.   Landmark detection is the task of localizing landmarks from image. Similar to object detection, this task also aims to provide the location of points of interest (i.e., landmarks) in the image. However, unlike object detection where there could be multiple objects with the same type, in landmark detection, there could only be at most one landmark with the same type (i.e., the landmarks are unique). For example, in vertebrae localization, each vertebra is unique in the human body and there is no two vertebrae with the same name. Similarly, in hand landmark detection, the hand landmarks, such as fingertips and joints, are unique for each person. While the landmark detection problem can be directly addressed by object detection approaches (since it can be regarded as a special case of object detection), existing landmark detection approaches leverage this uniqueness of landmarks in problem definition and address it with specialized architecture designs and objective functions.

Given an image $\mathbf{X}$, there are in total K landmarks we aim to detect from $\mathbf{X}$. Let $\mathbf{y} = \{\mathbf{y}_i\}_{i=1}^K$ be the K ground-truth labels for the K landmarks. Each landmark label is defined as $\mathbf{y}_i = \{c_i, \mathbf{t}_i\}$, where $c_i \in \{0, 1\}$ is a binary label indicating if the landmark is present in the image and $\mathbf{t}_i$ describes the coordinates of the landmark. There are typically two choices for landmark detection losses, point and heatmap regression. The point regression loss is similar to the object detection loss. Let $\hat{\mathbf{y}}_i = \{\hat{p}_i, \hat{\mathbf{t}}_i\}$ be the model's prediction for the ith landmark, where $\hat{p}_i$ denotes the predicted probability for the existence of the landmark and $\hat{\mathbf{t}}_i$ denotes the predicted coordinates of the landmark. The point regression loss can be written as

$$\mathcal{L}(\mathbf{y}, \hat{\mathbf{y}}) = \sum_{i=1}^K \mathcal{L}_{\text{cls}}(c_i, \hat{p}_i) + \lambda \mathbb{1}(c_i = 1)\mathcal{L}_{\text{loc}}(\mathbf{t}_i, \hat{\mathbf{t}}_i), \qquad (4.8)$$

where $\mathcal{L}_{\text{cls}}$ is a classification loss, and we could simply use a binary cross entropy loss for $\mathcal{L}_{\text{cls}}$

$$\mathcal{L}_{\text{cls}}(c_i, \hat{p}_i) = -c_i \log \hat{p}_i - (1 - c_i) \log (1 - \hat{p}_i). \qquad (4.9)$$

Further, $\mathcal{L}_{\text{loc}}$ is the localization loss, and we could use the L_1 loss or the smooth L_1 loss for $\mathcal{L}_{\text{loc}}$ as defined in Eqs. (4.5) and (4.6), respectively. Note that unlike object detection, we do not need the index mapping $\sigma(\cdot)$ between the ground truth and prediction. This is because there are always K ground-truth landmarks and K landmark predictions for each image, which results in a one-to-one mapping.

Alternatively, we could formulate the landmark detection problem as a heatmap regression problem. For the K landmarks, we create K ground-truth heatmaps $\mathbf{M} = \{\mathbf{M}_i\}_{i=1}^K$. Each heatmap $\mathbf{M}_i$ has the same dimensions as the input image $\mathbf{X}$ and $\mathbf{M}_i(\mathbf{s}) \in [0, 1]$ indicates the probability of the ith landmark is located at position $\mathbf{s}$ of $\mathbf{X}$. Similarly, let $\hat{\mathbf{M}}$ denote the predicted heatmaps by the model. The heatmap regression loss can be written as

$$\mathcal{L}(\mathbf{M}, \hat{\mathbf{M}}) = \sum_{i=1}^K \sum_{\mathbf{s}} \|\mathbf{M}_i(\mathbf{s}) - \hat{\mathbf{M}}_i(\mathbf{s})\|^2. \qquad (4.10)$$

A common choice for the ground-truth heatmap is the Gaussian heatmap [47], where $\mathbf{M}_i(\mathbf{s})$ is defined as

$$\mathbf{M}_i(\mathbf{s}) = \frac{1}{Z}\exp\left(-\frac{1}{2\sigma^d}\sum_j^d (s^j - t_i^j)^2\right). \tag{4.11}$$

Here, s^j and t_i^j are the coordinates of $\mathbf{s}$ and landmark location $\mathbf{t}_i$ at dimension j; Z is a normalization term so that $\mathbf{M}_i(\mathbf{s}) \in [0, 1]$.

4.2 Case study: vertebrae localization and identification

Medical imaging techniques have been widely used in the diagnosis and treatment of spinal disorders. They provide physicians the essential tools for evaluating spinal pathologies and facilitate the spinal surgery by enabling noninvasive visualization for surgical planning and procedure. When evaluating spinal health, 3D imaging techniques, such as magnetic resonance imaging (MRI) and computed tomography (CT), are usually the first choices of healthcare providers as they give better views of the spinal anatomy. However, identifying individual vertebra from 3D images, which is usually an initial step of reviewing and analyzing spinal images, is nontrivial and time-consuming [6].

Computational methods can be used to automate the quantitative analysis of spinal images and therefore enhance physicians' ability to provide spinal healthcare. In this context, we investigate the automation of localizing and identifying individual vertebrae from CT scans, which can substantially benefit the daily work of radiologists and many subsequent tasks in spinal image analysis. On the one hand, the localization and identification results of individual vertebrae can be leveraged by many other computerized spinal analysis tasks, such as vertebral body/intervertebral disc segmentation [4,3], 3D spine reconstruction [33,58], spinal image registration [45,53], and so on. On the other hand, it may be a crucial component of many computer-aided diagnosis and intervention systems for spinal health [67,2,61,38,28,32].

However, designing a computerized vertebrae identification and localization system is quite challenging. Unlike other classification problems where the objects are often visually distinct, identifying individual vertebrae is challenging (demonstrated in Fig. 4.1) as neighboring vertebrae usually share similar morphological appearance. When the quality of the CT scan is low or only a narrow field-of-view is shown, it is really challenging to distinguish two neighboring vertebrae due to the similarity in appearance. Moreover, because of pathologies, the anatomical structure of a vertebrae column is also not always regular and predictable and it gets even more complicated if a patient has surgical implants around the vertebrae, which often reduces the contrast of the vertebrae boundaries. Although the state-of-the-art methods have already achieved acceptable performance on a challenging 3D spine dataset [20,19], we argue that to further improve the vertebrae identification and localization performance,

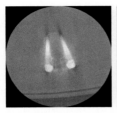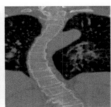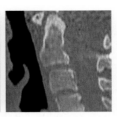

FIGURE 4.1

The variability of spinal CT scans. Warping is performed for sagittal and coronal slices. Shown from left to right are the CT scan slices with surgical implants, blurry vertebrae boundaries, abnormal curvature, and narrow field-of-view.

a computerized system should 1) use a 3D feature extraction scheme such that it can better leverage the *short-range contextual information,* e.g., the presence of nearby organs of the target vertebrae; 2) process the 3D spinal image in a sequential manner with the ability of encoding the *long-range contextual information,* e.g., the fixed spatial order of the vertebrae;, and 3) learn the vertebrae identification and localization simultaneously and share the domain information of the two tasks during the training.

To this end, we propose a novel method which jointly learns vertebrae identification and localization by combining 3D convolutional and recurrent neural networks. We first develop a 3D fully convolutional neural network (FCN) to extract features of CT images in a sliding window fashion. The proposed 3D FCN employs 3D convolutional layers as its core components. 3D convolutional layers can encode 3D contextual information of the receptive field, which gives a better feature representation of the 3D spinal image than their 2D counterparts. To further improve the feature extraction, the proposed 3D FCN is trained in a multitask learning (MTL) manner [17] that leverages both the vertebrae centroid and name information simultaneously. The extracted features of the spinal images, however, only encode the short-range contextual information of each sampling area. Due to the special anatomical structure of spine column, vertebrae in spinal images have a fixed spatial order which provides important long-range contextual information. To incorporate this domain-specific information into our model, we further propose to use a recurrent neural network (RNN) to encode the long-range contextual information that persists in the spinal images. Specifically, we develop a bidirectional MTL RNNs to jointly learn the long-range contextual information from two directions (from cervical vertebrae to sacral vertebrae and the other way around) for both the identification and localization tasks.

Note that RNN-enabled architectures have been used by existing works for key frame detection from medical videos [12,29] or for biomedical image segmentation [13,7]. Video-based problems are handled at *frame-level* with conventional CNNs and RNNs are used to capture the temporal relations between frames. Segmentation-based problems are solved at *pixel-level* by image-to-image networks (e.g., U-Net or FCN) and RNNs are used to refine the results. While, in this context, we focus on regressing the vertebrae locations as well as predicting their corresponding types. Neither of the existing RNN-related approaches can directly address this task. Instead, we argue that for our problem CT images should be processed at *sample-level* for location regression and vertebrae classification. Hence, we propose a novel framework which first uses a 3D FCN to jointly scan the CT images for vertebrae locations and types at sample-level and then uses an RNN to capture the structural relations between samples. To facilitate the unique sample-level approach, the FCN is developed through a two-stage design: in the first stage a 3D CNN is trained using CT image samples and in the second stage the trained CNN is converted to FCN for fast sample scanning from CT images. The RNN accordingly is deployed to adapt the sample feature sequences. As a result, the formulated approach can incorporate both the short- and long-range information for better structural understanding other than learning the spatial-temporal relations or the pixel-level contextual information.

The contributions of this work are summarized as follows:

- We propose a novel multitask 3D CNN for landmark detection. The proposed architecture encodes better feature representations by jointly learning classification and regression with 3D convolutions, which can benefit many landmark detection problems that use 3D medical images.
- We improve the general 3D FCN framework by introducing RNNs to incorporate the long-range contextual information in 3D images. This RNN based approach can be useful for many other similar problems in 3D medical image processing where the target objects usually have similar anatomic structures and thus contextual information is critical.
- The proposed approach outperforms the state-of-the-art on a challenging dataset by a significant margin.

4.2.1 Background

Many methods have been proposed to identify and localize vertebrae automatically. Some early systems [44,54,27,68] usually require prior knowledge or have constraints about the content of the spinal images, making them less robust to more general cases in spinal imaging. In 2012, Glocker et al. [20] proposed a more general method that works for arbitrary field-of-view CT scans. However, their work makes assumptions about the shape and appearance of vertebrae, which may not be satisfied on pathological or abnormal spinal images. To address the limitations, [19] further proposed a method that transforms sparse centroid annotations into dense probabilistic labels so that the modeling of shape and appearance can be avoided. However, these methods are based on handcrafted feature extraction methods which cannot encode more general visual characteristics of spinal images and as a result they fail to handle more complicated pathological cases when surgical implants exist. Chen et al. [10] recently proposed to use convolutional neural networks (CNNs) to extract more robust features and their work achieved a superior performance on the same dataset

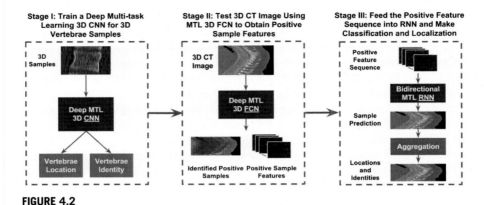

FIGURE 4.2

Overall architecture of the proposed method for vertebrae identification and localization.

as [20,19]. In their work, they use 2D CNNs to encode the features of 3D CT volumes. Although it has been shown that for some segmentation tasks, applying 2D CNNs to 3D data can give reasonably good results, the segmentation itself can sometimes be addressed slice by slice which favors 2D operations [21,8]. However, as denoted Dou et al. [16] and also demonstrated in this work, 2D CNNs do not work well in detection problems as they cannot capture the 3D spatial information that is critical to the detection of the target object. More recently, [64] proposed a 3D U-Net [51] like architecture to target the vertebrae localization problem in an image-to-image fashion. However, the proposed architecture cannot fully address the long-term contextual information in spinal images. To compensate this limitation, they further introduce a message passing and sparsity regularization algorithm for refinement.

4.2.2 Methodology

The overall architecture of the proposed method is illustrated in Fig. 4.2. We use a three-stage approach to solve the problem. In the first stage, a deep multitask 3D CNN is trained using randomly cropped 3D vertebrae samples. The idea of using 3D convolutional layers for medical images as well as cropping 3D samples for training is inspired by Dou et al. [16]. Compared with other deep learning approaches [59, 10] where only 2D convolutional layers were used, using 3D CNN retains the 3D spatial information of the input and encodes better feature representations. To learn a better model, the identification and localization tasks are trained simultaneously through MTL. In the second stage, we transform the trained multitask 3D CNN into a multitask 3D FCN by converting the fully connected layers to 3D convolutional layers. 3D FCN can be efficiently applied to 3D images of any size and produce a prediction map for the effective 3D samples. This idea is adapted from [57,43], and we use it to extract the features of all the positive samples of the input 3D image. Finally, in the third stage, the extracted sample features will be ordered and form a set

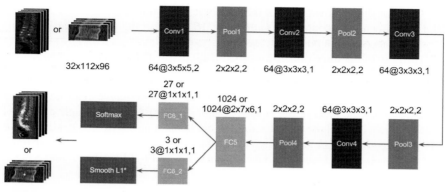

FIGURE 4.3

The architecture of the deep multitask 3D CNN/FCN. Note for CNN the input is a cropped image sample of size $32 \times 112 \times 196$ and the last two layers FC5 and FC6(_1 or _2) are fully connected layers. For FCN the input is a CT image of any size and the last two layers are convolutional layers.

of feature sequences. Those spatially ordered sample features will be used to train a bidirectional RNN (Bi-RNN) [55] that predicts the vertebrae locations and identities in the testing phase. The final results will then be generated via aggregation.

Stage I: deep multitask 3D CNN.   In this stage, we aim to train a network that takes a relatively small and fixed-size ($32 \times 112 \times 96$ in this work) 3D sample as the input and predicts the most likely vertebrae type and the corresponding centroid location. Note a sample may contain more than one vertebra and the network only predicts the one that is closest to the sample center. When applied to a CT image (see Section 4.2.2), this network can be used to effectively exploit the short-range contextual information.

As shown in Fig. 4.3, the proposed CNN has four convolutional layers, four pooling layers and three fully-connected layers. For convolutional layers, we pad the inputs such that the outputs from the layers have the same size as the inputs. For pooling layers, no padding is performed as we want to downsize the inputs for dense feature representation. The numbers associated with each convolutional layer denote the feature size, kernel size and stride size, respectively. The numbers above each fully-connected layer denote the output sizes. The feature and kernel sizes are chosen empirically with reference from [30,16,24]. The "FC5" layer serves as the feature layer that encodes the final features for each input image sample. "FC6_1" and "FC6_2" layers serve as the prediction layer for vertebrae identification and localization, respectively. The output size of "FC6_1" is 27 as we have 26 different vertebrae types plus the background and the output size of "FC6_2" is 3 because the location has 3 dimensions. The input sample size is $32 \times 112 \times 96$. We choose this size based on several considerations:

(1) This size should cover most of the vertebrae in the training set;

(2) Each dimension should be a multiple of 16 such that the feature map sizes are still integers after 4 pooling layers;

(3) The ratio of the three dimensions should approximate the shape of vertebrae.

The proposed CNN is trained using randomly cropped vertebrae samples. In particular, we call the samples that contain at least one vertebrae centroid *positive samples* and use the label of the closest vertebrae centroid (to the sample center) as the sample label. For those samples that do not contain any vertebrae centroids, we call them *negative samples* and assign the background label to those samples. In total, there are 26 vertebrae types with labels from C1–C7, T1–T12, L1–L5, and S1–S2. For convenience, we assign each of the label an integer with C1 $= 0, \ldots,$ S1 $= 25$, and background $= 26$.

To jointly learn vertebrae identification and localization, two losses are used for each of the tasks, respectively. The total loss is given by

$$L = L_{\text{id}} + \lambda L_{\text{loc}}, \tag{4.12}$$

where L_{id} denotes the identification loss, L_{loc} denotes the localization loss, and λ denotes the importance coefficient that controls the relative learning rate of the two tasks. We use a cross entropy softmax loss, which is commonly used for classification problems, for the identification task. Let $\{\mathbf{x}_0, \mathbf{x}_1, \ldots, \mathbf{x}_{N-1}\}$ be a set of N image samples and $\{\mathbf{y}_0, \mathbf{y}_1, \ldots, \mathbf{y}_{N-1}\}$ be a set of N ground-truth labels where each label is a one-hot vector denoted as $\mathbf{y_i} = [y_{i0}, y_{i1}, \ldots, y_{iP-1}]^T$, $y_{ij} \in \{0, 1\}$, $i \in \{0, 1, \ldots, N-1\}$, $j \in \{0, 1, \ldots, P-1\}$. The identification loss L_{id} can be written as

$$L_{\text{id}} = -\frac{1}{N} \sum_{i=0}^{N-1} \sum_{j=0}^{P-1} y_{ij} \log(f_{\text{id}}^j(\mathbf{x}_i; \mathbf{W})) + (1 - y_{ij}) \log(1 - f_{\text{id}}^j(\mathbf{x}_i; \mathbf{W})), \tag{4.13}$$

where f_{id}^j denotes jth output of the "FC6_1" layer and $\mathbf{W}$ denotes all the network parameters. For the localization task, it is a regression problem. Therefore, we use a smooth L_1 loss [17] for this task. Given a set of N ground-truth locations $\{\mathbf{p}_0, \mathbf{p}_1, \ldots, \mathbf{p}_{N-1}\}$ where $\mathbf{p}_i = [p_{i0}, p_{i1}, \ldots, p_{iD-1}]^T$, $i \in \{0, 1, \ldots, N-1\}$, the localization loss L_{loc} can be written as

$$L_{\text{loc}} = \frac{1}{m} \sum_{i=0}^{N-1} [y_{iP-1} = 0] \sum_{j=0}^{D-1} \text{smooth}_{L_1}(p_{ij} - f_{\text{loc}}^j(\mathbf{x}_i; \mathbf{W})), \tag{4.14}$$

where $m = \sum_{i=0}^{N-1} [y_{iP-1} = 0]$, f_{loc}^j is the jth output of the "FC6_2" layer, and $\text{smooth}_{L_1}(x)$ is the smooth L_1 loss that is given by

$$\text{smooth}_{L_1}(x) = \begin{cases} 0.5x^2, & \text{if } |x| < 1, \\ |x| - 0.5, & \text{otherwise.} \end{cases} \tag{4.15}$$

Note that only the locations for positive samples are meaningful. Thus, the localization loss will only be computed for positive samples and for negative samples the localization loss is zero. Here, we use the Iverson bracket indicator function $[y_{iP-1} = 0]$ to ignore negative samples, $P - 1$ indicates the background label, and $y_{iP-1} = 0$ means that the one-hot vector corresponds to a nonbackground label.

Stage II: deep multitask 3D FCN. We use the trained deep multitask 3D CNN to encode the short-range contextual information in a CT scan image. A straightforward approach is scanning the image in a sliding window manner by repeatedly cropping and processing overlapped image samples. When the input image is large, this approach can be very expensive and inefficient. As a solution, we propose to transform the CNN into an FCN. FCNs only contain convolutional and pooling layers. As pooling and convolution operation are computed using sliding windows, FCNs essentially process the input images in a sliding window manner but through the more efficient pooling and convolution operation.

When converting a CNN to an FCN, we must make sure the output of an FCN is identical to the output of a CNN if the input image size of FCN is the same as the input size required by CNN. This requires the convolutional layers of FCN should share the same weights and kernel layout as the corresponding fully connected layers in CNN. As denoted in Fig. 4.3, for the "FC5" layer, we convert it to a convolutional layer with parameters configured as "$1024@2 \times 7 \times 6, 1$". We use a kernel size of $2 \times 7 \times 6$ because the output feature map size from "Pool4" is $2 \times 7 \times 6$ when the input image size is the same as the sample size, i.e., $32 \times 112 \times 96$. Similarly, "FC6_1" and "FC6_2" are converted to convolutional layers with configurations of "$27@1 \times 1 \times 1, 1$" and "$3@1 \times 1 \times 1, 1$", respectively. After this conversion, the constructed FCN will have the same number of parameters and kernel layouts as the trained CNN. Thus, we use the trained parameters from CNN to initialize the FCN which, as a result, gives the same outputs as those from CNN.

As shown in Fig. 4.4, the FCN outputs two 3D score maps, one for identification and the other for localization. Each score is a vector indicating either the vertebrae label or the vertebrae location. The scores at the same location of the two maps can be mapped to the same image sample in the CT image space. As there are 4 pooling layers in the proposed FCN with each has a stride of 2, the effective sliding window stride is $2^4 = 16$. Therefore, for a score at $p_{score} = (x, y, z)$ of the output 3D score map, the corresponding image sample location at the input image is given by $p_{sample} = (16x, 16y, 16z)$. The identification score decides the vertebrae type of the image sample and the localization score gives the vertebrae centroid location in the sample. Assuming the predicted centroid location is $c_{score} = (a, b, c)$, the corresponding location at the image space is given by $c_{sample}(r, s, t) = (16x + a, 16y + b, 16z + c)$. For each of the predicted centroid location, we assign it with the vertebrae label from the corresponding identification score. The final results are a set of densely predicted centroid points, as demonstrated in Fig. 4.4, with each color indicating a different vertebrae type.

The proposed FCN can be used to extract feature sequence from the CT image, which will be further used to feed the RNN in the next stage (see Section 4.2.2).

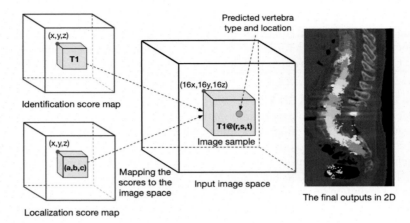

FIGURE 4.4

3D score maps and their mapping to the image space.

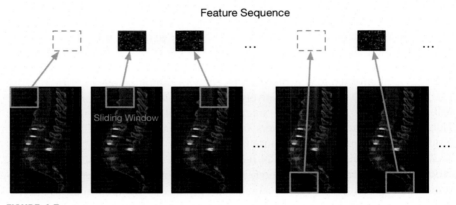

FIGURE 4.5

Feature sequence generation using the proposed FCN. Here, we resize the feature vectors to 2D for visualization purpose.

Fig. 4.5 illustrates the process of generating the feature sequence. Given an input image, the FCN implicitly processes it in a sliding window fashion. In addition to the 3D score maps, we can also obtain the feature maps from the intermediate layers and in this work we extract the high-level features from the "FC_5" layer. Since for each sample image we can obtain a feature map, the final output is a sequence of feature maps. Note we ignore the feature maps of background sample images as they contain no vertebrae and have little contribution to the vertebrae identification and localization.

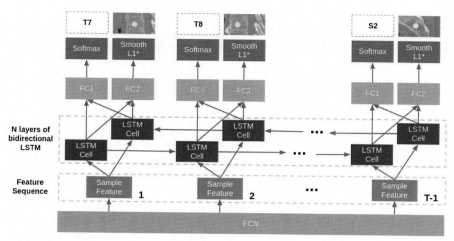

FIGURE 4.6

The architecture of the multitask Bi-RNN (unrolled in time).

Stage III: multitask bidirectional RNN. FCN can be used directly for vertebrae identification and localization by aggregating the predication results of all the positive samples. However, the limitation is that FCN can only encode short-range contextual information inside each sample image. But for vertebrae identification, long-range contextual information of neighboring vertebrae is also very helpful. For example, the algorithm may have difficulty distinguishing a vertebra between T2 and T3. However, if it knows that the vertebra above current vertebra is very likely to be T1 then it would be more confident to classify the current vertebra as T2 than T3. To this end, we propose to use RNN to encode the long-range contextual information between vertebrae. The idea is first converting a CT scan image into a sequence of spatially ordered vertebrae sample features using FCN and then feeding the sequence into an RNN that has already learned to encode the long-range contextual information among samples.

The architecture of the proposed RNN is illustrated in Fig. 4.6. Here, we use a Bi-RNN structure instead of a conventional one. Such a choice is based on the observation that the contextual information of current vertebra may come from two directions: the vertebrae above and below. The RNN cell used in the network is long-short term memory (LSTM) [25] cell which can handle long sequences. Each LSTM cell has 256 hidden states. As denoted in Fig. 4.6, a bidirectional LSTM layer consists of two LSTM cells of opposite directions. The outputs of the two LSTM cells are concatenated together to form the final output of the bidirectional LSTM layer. We stack N layers of such bidirectional LSTM to encode the input feature sequence. In our experiments $N = 3$, and we find minor performance difference with more bidirectional LSTM layers. Two fully-connected layers "FC1" and "FC2" are put at the top of the bidirectional LSTM layers for computing the classification and regression scores, respectively. The input at each timestep is a sample feature vector extracted from FCN as illustrated in Fig. 4.5. The RNN is also trained in a multitask learning manner. At the end of each timestep, there are two loss functions, one for the identification loss and the other for the localization loss. We use the same loss functions as the ones used in Stage I, but the total loss is accumulated over time

$$L = \sum_{t=0}^{T-1} L_{id}^t + \lambda L_{loc}^t. \tag{4.16}$$

To train the Bi-RNN, we need to generate a set of sample feature sequences from the training set. To increase the data variation, we first augment the training set by randomly cropping subimages (not the fixed-size samples) from the training CT scans. For each of the cropped subimages, we feed it through the FCN that samples the input image in a sliding window manner. Next, the features of the samples that are labeled as positive are kept and ordered based on the samples' relative spatial locations. Each of the spatially ordered sample feature sequences will be used as the training data for the Bi-RNN. Note the associated vertebrae labels and centroid points for each of the sample features can be easily calculated from the ground truth annotations that come with the CT scan images.

During the testing phase, each of the new CT scan image will first be processed by the FCN to generate the ordered sample feature sequence. Next, the sample feature sequence will be passed to the Bi-RNN which outputs the identification and localization results for each of the samples at each timestep. Note they are dense identification and localization results as the samples are overlapped. Finally, we aggregate the dense results using the median of the localization results that have the same identification label.

4.2.3 Experiments

The dataset used in all the experiments is a public dataset from CSI2014 [66]. It is considered challenging due to the variety of pathological cases, arbitrary of field-of-view and the existence of artificial implants. For all the experiments, we use the official split for training and testing as did by other state-of-the-art methods [19,10,64]. In total, there are 302 CT scans in this dataset; 242 CT scans from 125 patients are used for training and the rest 60 CT scans are held out for testing. During preprocessing, CT images are resampled such that the resolutions along the longitudinal, frontal and sagittal axes are 1.25, 1.0, and 1.0 mm, respectively. Vertebrae locations are first normalized according to the new resolution and then converted to the corresponding voxel locations of images or image samples. Each vertebra centroid location in the CT sans is annotated along with the corresponding vertebrae type. All the experiments are conducted using the TensorFlow [1] platform on two NVIDIA GTX Geforce 1070 GPUs.

Performance of deep multitask 3D CNN. To train and evaluate the performance of the proposed deep multitask 3D CNN, we randomly crop samples with size

Table 4.1 Ablation study of the proposed multitask 3D CNN.

	Cls. Accuracy	Loc. Error (mm)
2D CNN MTL	43.19%	8.74
3D CNN ID	48.52%	N/A
3D CNN LOC	N/A	7.05
3D CNN MTL	**52.39%**	**7.03**

$32 \times 112 \times 96$ from CT scans. During the sample generation, we make sure that all the vertebrae are evenly sampled and, on the average, there are about 40 samples for each vertebra. The network are trained for about 15 epochs with batch_size $= 24$, learning_rate $= 0.001$, weight_decay $= 0.0001$, momentum $= 0.9$, and $\lambda = 0.12$. The learning rate is reduced every 20,000 iteration by a factor of 0.4. All the hyperparameters and λ are chosen empirically with validation. For this study we are not interested in finding the best parameter settings for the model. In general, we find $\lambda = 0.12$ works better in a multitask scenario, and values close to 0.12 give minor performance difference. We refer readers to [65] for better multitask parameter choices. Two evaluation metrics are used, namely *sample classification accuracy* and *sample localization error*. Sample classification accuracy is the number of samples that are successfully classified among all the testing samples. Average sample localization error is defined as the average distances (in mm) between the predicted locations and vertebrae centroids

$$e = \frac{\sum_{i=1}^{N} ||l_{pred}^{i} - l_{gt}^{i}||}{N}, \tag{4.17}$$

where l_{pred}^{i} and l_{gt}^{i} denote the predicted location and the ground truth centroid for the ith positive sample, respectively.

To demonstrate the effectiveness of the proposed multitask 3D CNN, we compare our approach with 3 other baseline methods: 2D CNN MTL, 3D CNN ID, and 3D CNN LOC. For 2D CNN MTL, we convert all the 3D convolutional/pooling layers of the proposed network to their 2D versions. For 3D CNN ID and 3D CNN LOC, we remove the identification loss and the localization loss, respectively. We train theses three methods using the similar hyperparameters as the 3D CNN MTL. The evaluation results are shown in Table 4.1.

We can see that 2D CNN MTL only achieves 43.19% classification accuracy and 8.74 mm localization error, which is much worse than for its 3D counterpart. Since 2D convolution cannot encode the important spatial information of 3D images, the degradation in performance is expected. The classification accuracy of 3D CNN ID is 48.52% which is significantly better than 2D CNN MTL due to the use of 3D convolution. However, its performance is still worse than 3D CNN MTL, which achieves a 52.39% classification accuracy. This demonstrates that training identification and localization jointly is very helpful in improving the network's ability to distinguish different vertebrae. The localization errors of 3D CNN LOC and 3D CNN

Table 4.2 Comparison of the proposed method with the state-of-the-art methods.

Region	[19]			[10]			[64]		
	Id. Rate	Mean	Std	Id. Rate	Mean	Std	Id. Rate	Mean	Std
All	74.0%	13.20	17.83	84.2%	8.82	13.04	85%	8.6	**7.8**
Cervical	88.8%	6.81	10.02	91.8%	5.12	8.22	92%	5.6	**4.0**
Thoracic	61.8%	17.35	22.3	76.4%	11.39	16.48	81%	9.2	**7.9**
Lumbar	79.9%	13.05	12.45	88.1%	8.42	8.62	83%	11.0	10.8

Region	Ours CNN			Ours CNN+RNN			Ours CNN+Bi-RNN		
	Id. Rate	Mean	Std	Id. Rate	Mean	Std	Id. Rate	Mean	Std
All	83.8%	9.07	10.16	87.4%	6.59	8.71	**88.3%**	**6.47**	8.56
Cervical	91.2%	8.63	11.17	93.8%	4.99	5.53	**95.1%**	**4.48**	4.56
Thoracic	79.1%	9.56	10.08	81.7%	8.03	10.26	**84.0%**	**7.78**	10.17
Lumbar	85.1%	8.57	8.87	89.4%	6.15	8.29	**92.2%**	**5.61**	**7.68**

MTL are 7.05 and 7.03 mm, respectively. Such a close performance in localization error demonstrates that finding the vertebra centroids does not necessarily require recognizing vertebrae type which is consistent with common sense. However, the classification accuracy overall is not so good. This is because each cropped sample has a very narrow field-of-view that contains limited contextual information. Since different vertebrae are very similar in appearance, distinguishing between vertebrae, especially those neighboring ones, is very challenging without more contextual information.

To train the multitask Bi-RNN, we first randomly crop subimages of various sizes from the CT scans used for training. The number of cropped subimages is proportional to the number of vertebrae inside a CT scan. On average, 30 subimages are generated for each vertebra and in total, we obtain about 70,000 subimages. Due to memory limitation, the maximum subimage size is $96 \times 256 \times 256$, which covers a maximum of 8 vertebrae and gives long enough contextual information. For each of the subimage, we generate a sequence of sample features in the way described in Section 4.2.2. The average sequence length T is 266. We train the Bi-RNN for about 12 epochs with batch_size $= 256$, learning_rate $= 10^{-6}$, weight_decay $= 0.0001$, momentum $= 0.9$, and $\lambda = 0.10$. Again the hyperparameters are chosen empirically with validation. The trained Bi-RNN in combination with the trained FCN is used to evaluate the testing CT scans. We use *identification rate* and *localization error* as the evaluation metrics following the definition from [20].

Overall performance.   The overall performance results of the proposed method are given in Table 4.2. Here, we compare our method with three state-of-the-art methods on the same dataset. To demonstrate the effectiveness of the Bi-RNN, we also compare our method (denoted as CNN + Bi-RNN) with two baseline methods: 1) using CNN (denoted as CNN) only and 2) using CNN together with conventional RNN (denoted as CNN + RNN). For the CNN only baseline method, we use the trained FCN to generate dense predictions in a sliding window manner and the dense predictions for each vertebra will then be aggregated and refined to give the final identification and localization results. Table 4.2 shows the performance for all vertebrae types as well as the performance for each of the vertebrae categories (cervical, thoracic, and lumbar). Both the mean and standard deviation of the localization errors are measured. We can see from Table 4.2 that the proposed method outperforms both the state-of-the-art methods and the baseline methods in most of the measurements. For the standard deviation of the localization errors, the method from Dong et al. [64] gives similar performances with our method. This is because they used a message passing and sparsity regularization algorithm during the refinement step to suppress the outliers. This scheme can be also added to our method for further performance improvement. We then analyze the vertebra-wise performance of the proposed approach and compare it with the baseline methods. As shown in Fig. 4.7, we can find that the proposed approach performs better than the baseline methods on most vertebrae. This demonstrates that using RNN in combination with CNN can give better long-range contextual understanding and yield better performance. We also find that using Bi-RNN against conventional RNN can further boost the performance. This is consistent with the observation that contextual information comes from two directions (below and above) and should be addressed accordingly.

Success and failure cases.   Fig. 4.8 shows two successful identification and localization results. In the second and third columns, each colored point denotes the predicted vertebrae location for a sample. For images in Fig. 4.8(a)2 and Fig. 4.8(b)2, the colored points are from the CNN only baseline method that samples the image using FCN in a sliding window manner. For images of Fig. 4.8(a)3 and Fig. 4.8(b)3, the colored points are from the proposed method that makes predictions for each of the positive feature samples of the input sequence. As we can see here, the dense predictions from the proposed method are more concentrated around the vertebrae centroids which indicates more accurate prediction results. The fourth and fifth columns are the aggregated predictions from the dense predictions for the CNN only baseline method and the proposed method, respectively. Compared with the ground truths in the first column, we can see that both the proposed and CNN only baseline method perform well and the proposed method is slightly better than the CNN only baseline method.

Besides the success cases, we also investigate when the proposed method does not work. Fig. 4.9 shows two challenging examples that the CNN only baseline method or proposed method fail. For both examples, we show the results of the sagittal and frontal view, respectively. Fig. 4.9(a) shows a pathological example with quite blurred vertebra boundaries. We can see that most of the predictions by the CNN only baseline method are incorrect. On the other hand, the predictions from the proposed method follow the spine structure and in general are acceptable. Fig. 4.9(b) is even more challenging (arguably also to less experienced medical personnel) and both the baseline and proposed method fail.

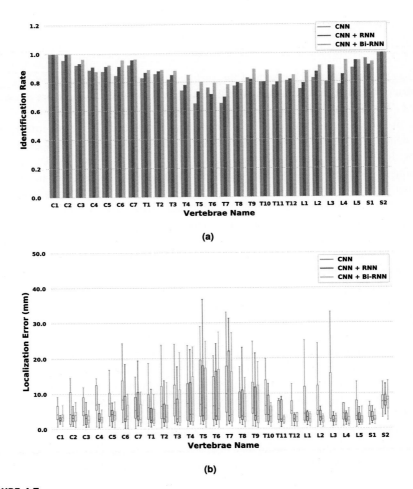

FIGURE 4.7

Vertebra-wise identification and localization results: (a) the identification accuracy of each vertebra; (b) the localization error statistics of each vertebra.

4.2.4 Discussion

We present a novel approach to vertebrae identification and localization from CT scans. Due to the similarity of vertebrae appearance and the variability of spinal images, such as arbitrary field-of-view, vertebrae curvatures, we develop a data-driven learning-based method to robustly capture both the short- and long-range contextual information that are critical for vertebrae identification and localization. For the short-range contextual information, we train an MTL 3D CNN that effectively extracts the features of vertebral samples by leveraging the domain information contained in both

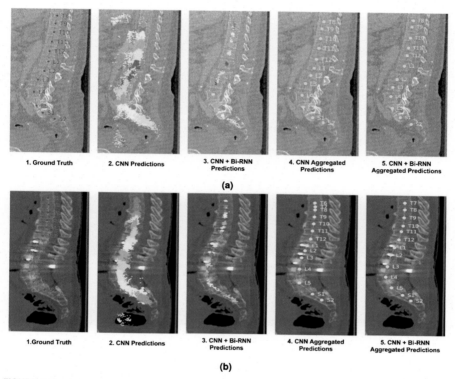

FIGURE 4.8

Two example successful cases of using the proposed method and the CNN only baseline method.

the vertebrae identification and localization tasks. The use of 3D convolutions enables it to encode 3D spatial information of CT volumes to yield a more robust model than the 2D counterparts. For the long-range contextual information, we develop a bidirectional MTL RNN that inherently learns the anatomic structure in a data-driven manner and exploits the contextual information among vertebral samples during testing phase. Experimental results demonstrate that the proposed MTL 3D CNN/FCN extracts better feature representations than its 2D or single-task counterparts, outperforming the state-of-the-art on a challenging dataset by a significant margin.

4.3 **Summary**

We have introduced deep neural network designs for medical object/landmark detection. In Section 4.1, we discussed the choices of detection models and detection tasks.

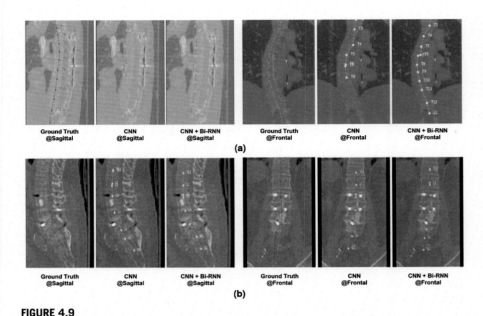

FIGURE 4.9

Two example failure cases of using the proposed method and the CNN only baseline method.

We presented specific examples of these choices and provided suggestions on the applications of the detection models and tasks. In Section 4.2, we included a case study on vertebrae localization and identification from spinal CT images and demonstrated how the design principles are applied in practice.

For the choices of detection models, we introduced three families of models in Section 4.1.1, namely the sliding-window based models, two/single-stage object detectors, and image-to-image models. In Section 4.2, we proposed a sliding-window based model based on multitask 3D FCN. We showed that using centroid regression as an extra task we could avoid the dense sliding-window and meanwhile improve the detection accuracy.

For the choices of detection tasks, we introduced anatomical object detection and anatomical landmark detection in Section 4.1.2. We highlighted the differences of these two tasks and gave examples on which task may be chosen to address the specific problem. We also provided several choices of the objective functions for each task and discussed the benefits of applying the different objective functions. In Section 4.2, we showed how anatomical landmark detection can be employed to label the vertebrae from CT images. For the objective functions, we used the point regression objective function and discussed its effectiveness on localizing and identifying the vertebrae.

References

[1] Martín Abadi, Ashish Agarwal, Paul Barham, Eugene Brevdo, Zhifeng Chen, Craig Citro, Greg S. Corrado, Andy Davis, Jeffrey Dean, Matthieu Devin, Sanjay Ghemawat, Ian Goodfellow, Andrew Harp, Geoffrey Irving, Michael Isard, Yangqing Jia, Rafal Jozefowicz, Lukasz Kaiser, Manjunath Kudlur, Josh Levenberg, Dandelion Mané, Rajat Monga, Sherry Moore, Derek Murray, Chris Olah, Mike Schuster, Jonathon Shlens, Benoit Steiner, Ilya Sutskever, Kunal Talwar, Paul Tucker, Vincent Vanhoucke, Vijay Vasudevan, Fernanda Viégas, Oriol Vinyals, Pete Warden, Martin Wattenberg, Martin Wicke, Yuan Yu, Xiaoqiang Zheng, TensorFlow: large-scale machine learning on heterogeneous systems, Software available from tensorflow.org, https://www.tensorflow.org/, 2015.

[2] Samah Al-Helo, Raja S. Alomari, Subarna Ghosh, Vipin Chaudhary, Gurmeet Dhillon, Al-Zoubi Moh'd B, Hazem Hiary, Thair M. Hamtini, Compression fracture diagnosis in lumbar: a clinical CAD system, International Journal of Computer Assisted Radiology and Surgery 8 (3) (2013) 461–469.

[3] Raja S. Alomari, Subarna Ghosh, Jaehan Koh, Vipin Chaudhary, Vertebral column localization, labeling, and segmentation, in: Spinal Imaging and Image Analysis, Springer, Berlin–Heidelberg, 2015, pp. 193–229.

[4] Ismail Ben Ayed, Kumaradevan Punithakumar, Rashid Minhas, Rohit Joshi, Gregory J. Garvin, Vertebral body segmentation in MRI via convex relaxation and distribution matching, in: International Conference on Medical Image Computing and Computer-Assisted Intervention, Springer, Berlin–Heidelberg, 2012, pp. 520–527.

[5] Wei Bian, Christopher P. Hess, Susan M. Chang, Sarah J. Nelson, Janine M. Lupo, Computer-aided detection of radiation-induced cerebral microbleeds on susceptibility-weighted MR images, NeuroImage: Clinical 2 (2013) 282–290.

[6] Joseph E. Burns, Imaging of the Spine: A Medical and Physical Perspective, Springer, Cham, 2015, pp. 3–29.

[7] Jinzheng Cai, Le Lu, Yuanpu Xie, Fuyong Xing, Lin Yang, Improving deep pancreas segmentation in CT and MRI images via recurrent neural contextual learning and direct loss function, in: Maxime Descoteaux, Lena Maier-Hein, Alfred Franz, Pierre Jannin, D. Louis Collins, Simon Duchesne (Eds.), Medical Image Computing and Computer-Assisted Intervention (MICCAI) 2017, Springer, Cham, 2017, pp. 674–682.

[8] Jinzheng Cai, Le Lu, Zizhao Zhang, Fuyong Xing, Lin Yang, Qian Yin, Pancreas segmentation in MRI using graph-based decision fusion on convolutional neural networks, in: International Conference on Medical Image Computing and Computer-Assisted Intervention, Springer, 2016, pp. 442–450.

[9] Nicolas Carion, Francisco Massa, Gabriel Synnaeve, Nicolas Usunier, Alexander Kirillov, Sergey Zagoruyko, End-to-end object detection with transformers, in: European Conference on Computer Vision, Springer, 2020, pp. 213–229.

[10] Hao Chen, Chiyao Shen, Jing Qin, Dong Ni, Lin Shi, Jack CY Cheng, Pheng-Ann Heng, Automatic localization and identification of vertebrae in spine CT via a joint learning model with deep neural networks, in: International Conference on Medical Image Computing and Computer-Assisted Intervention, Springer, 2015, pp. 515–522.

[11] Hao Chen, Lequan Yu, Qi Dou, Lin Shi, Vincent C.T. Mok, Pheng Ann Heng, Automatic detection of cerebral microbleeds via deep learning based 3D feature representation, in: 2015 IEEE 12th International Symposium on Biomedical Imaging (ISBI), IEEE, 2015, pp. 764–767.

[12] Hao Chen, Qi Dou, Dong Ni, Jie-Zhi Cheng, Jing Qin, Shengli Li, Pheng-Ann Heng, Automatic fetal ultrasound standard plane detection using knowledge transferred recurrent neural networks, in: International Conference on Medical Image Computing and Computer-Assisted Intervention, Springer, 2015, pp. 507–514.

[13] Jianxu Chen, Lin Yang, Yizhe Zhang, Mark Alber, Danny Z. Chen, Combining fully convolutional and recurrent neural networks for 3D biomedical image segmentation, in: Advances in Neural Information Processing Systems, 2016, pp. 3036–3044.

[14] Jifeng Dai, Yi Li, Kaiming He, Jian Sun, R-FCN: object detection via region-based fully convolutional networks, in: Advances in Neural Information Processing Systems, 2016, pp. 379–387.

[15] Bob D. De Vos, Jelmer M. Wolterink, Pim A. De Jong, Max A. Viergever, Ivana Išgum, 2D image classification for 3D anatomy localization: employing deep convolutional neural networks, in: Medical Imaging 2016: Image Processing, vol. 9784, International Society for Optics and Photonics, 2016, p. 97841Y.

[16] Qi Dou, Hao Chen, Lequan Yu, Lei Zhao, Jing Qin, Defeng Wang, Vincent C.T. Mok, Lin Shi, Pheng-Ann Heng, Automatic detection of cerebral microbleeds from MR images via 3D convolutional neural networks, IEEE Transactions on Medical Imaging 35 (5) (2016) 1182–1195.

[17] Ross Girshick, Fast R-CNN, arXiv preprint, arXiv:1504.08083, 2015.

[18] Ross Girshick, Jeff Donahue, Trevor Darrell, Jitendra Malik, Rich feature hierarchies for accurate object detection and semantic segmentation, in: Proceedings of the IEEE Conference on Computer Vision and Pattern Recognition, 2014, pp. 580–587.

[19] Ben Glocker, Darko Zikic, Ender Konukoglu, David R. Haynor, Antonio Criminisi, Vertebrae localization in pathological spine CT via dense classification from sparse annotations, in: International Conference on Medical Image Computing and Computer-Assisted Intervention, Springer, 2013, pp. 262–270.

[20] Ben Glocker, Johannes Feulner, Antonio Criminisi, David R. Haynor, Ender Konukoglu, Automatic localization and identification of vertebrae in arbitrary field-of-view CT scans, in: International Conference on Medical Image Computing and Computer-Assisted Intervention, Springer, Berlin–Heidelberg, 2012, pp. 590–598.

[21] Adam P. Harrison, Ziyue Xu, Kevin George, Le Lu, Ronald M. Summers, Daniel J. Mollura, Progressive and multi-path holistically nested neural networks for pathological lung segmentation from CT images, in: Maxime Descoteaux, Lena Maier-Hein, Alfred Franz, Pierre Jannin, D. Louis Collins, Simon Duchesne (Eds.), Medical Image Computing and Computer-Assisted Intervention – MICCAI 2017, Springer, Cham, 2017, pp. 621–629.

[22] Kaiming He, Georgia Gkioxari, Piotr Dollár, Ross Girshick, Mask R-CNN, in: Proceedings of the IEEE International Conference on Computer Vision, 2017, pp. 2961–2969.

[23] Kaiming He, Xiangyu Zhang, Shaoqing Ren, Jian Sun, Delving deep into rectifiers: surpassing human-level performance on ImageNet classification, in: Proceedings of the IEEE International Conference on Computer Vision, 2015, pp. 1026–1034.

[24] Kaiming He, Xiangyu Zhang, Shaoqing Ren, Jian Sun, Deep residual learning for image recognition, in: Proceedings of the IEEE Conference on Computer Vision and Pattern Recognition, 2016, pp. 770–778.

[25] Sepp Hochreiter, Jürgen Schmidhuber, Long short-term memory, Neural Computation 9 (8) (1997) 1735–1780.

[26] Paul F. Jaeger, Simon A.A. Kohl, Sebastian Bickelhaupt, Fabian Isensee, Tristan Anselm Kuder, Heinz-Peter Schlemmer, Klaus H. Maier-Hein, Retina U-Net: embarrassingly simple exploitation of segmentation supervision for medical object detection, in: Machine Learning for Health Workshop, PMLR, 2020, pp. 171–183.

[27] B. Michael Kelm, S. Kevin Zhou, Michael Suehling, Yefeng Zheng, Michael Wels, Dorin Comaniciu, Detection of 3D spinal geometry using iterated marginal space learning, in: International MICCAI Workshop on Medical Computer Vision, Springer, 2010, pp. 96–105.

[28] Dejan Knez, Janez Mohar, Robert J. Cirman, Boštjan Likar, Franjo Pernuš, Tomaž Vrtovec, Manual and computer-assisted pedicle screw placement plans: a quantitative comparison, in: International Workshop on Computational Methods and Clinical Applications for Spine Imaging, Springer, 2016, pp. 105–115.

[29] Bin Kong, Yiqiang Zhan, Min Shin, Thomas Denny, Shaoting Zhang, Recognizing end-diastole and end-systole frames via deep temporal regression network, in: International Conference on Medical Image Computing and Computer-Assisted Intervention, Springer, 2016, pp. 264–272.

[30] Alex Krizhevsky, Ilya Sutskever, Geoffrey E. Hinton, ImageNet classification with deep convolutional neural networks, in: F. Pereira, C.J.C. Burges, L. Bottou, K.Q. Weinberger (Eds.), Advances in Neural Information Processing Systems 25, Curran Associates, Inc., 2012, pp. 1097–1105.

[31] Hugo J. Kuijf, Jeroen de Bresser, Mirjam I. Geerlings, Mandy M.A. Conijn, Max A. Viergever, Geert Jan Biessels, Koen L. Vincken, Efficient detection of cerebral microbleeds on 7.0 T MR images using the radial symmetry transform, NeuroImage 59 (3) (2012) 2266–2273.

[32] Rajesh Kumar, Robotic assistance and intervention in spine surgery, in: Spinal Imaging and Image Analysis, Springer, Berlin–Heidelberg, 2015, pp. 495–506.

[33] Fabian Lecron, Jonathan Boisvert, Saïd Mahmoudi, Hubert Labelle, Mohammed Benjelloun, Fast 3D spine reconstruction of postoperative patients using a multilevel statistical model, in: International Conference on Medical Image Computing and Computer-Assisted Intervention, Springer, Berlin–Heidelberg, 2012, pp. 446–453.

[34] Fangzhou Liao, Ming Liang, Zhe Li, Xiaolin Hu, Sen Song, Evaluate the malignancy of pulmonary nodules using the 3-D deep leaky noisy-or network, IEEE Transactions on Neural Networks and Learning Systems 30 (11) (2019) 3484–3495.

[35] Haofu Liao, Addisu Mesfin, Jiebo Luo, Joint vertebrae identification and localization in spinal CT images by combining short- and long-range contextual information, IEEE Transactions on Medical Imaging 37 (5) (2018) 1266–1275.

[36] Tsung-Yi Lin, Piotr Dollár, Ross Girshick, Kaiming He, Bharath Hariharan, Serge Belongie, Feature pyramid networks for object detection, in: Proceedings of the IEEE Conference on Computer Vision and Pattern Recognition, 2017, pp. 2117–2125.

[37] Tsung-Yi Lin, Priya Goyal, Ross Girshick, Kaiming He, Piotr Dollár, Focal loss for dense object detection, in: Proceedings of the IEEE International Conference on Computer Vision, 2017, pp. 2980–2988.

[38] Cristian A. Linte, Kurt E. Augustine, Jon J. Camp, Richard A. Robb, David R. Holmes III, Toward virtual modeling and templating for enhanced spine surgery planning, in: Spinal Imaging and Image Analysis, Springer, Berlin–Heidelberg, 2015, pp. 441–467.

[39] David Liu, S. Kevin Zhou, Dominik Bernhardt, Dorin Comaniciu, Vascular landmark detection in 3D CT data, in: Medical Imaging 2011: Biomedical Applications in Molecular, Structural, and Functional Imaging, vol. 7965, International Society for Optics and Photonics, 2011, p. 796522.

[40] Jiamin Liu, Nathan Lay, Zhuoshi Wei, Le Lu, Lauren Kim, Evrim Turkbey, Ronald M. Summers, Colitis detection on abdominal CT scans by rich feature hierarchies, in: Medical Imaging 2016: Computer-Aided Diagnosis, vol. 9785, International Society for Optics and Photonics, 2016, p. 97851N.

[41] Li Liu, Wanli Ouyang, Xiaogang Wang, Paul Fieguth, Jie Chen, Xinwang Liu, Matti Pietikäinen, Deep learning for generic object detection: a survey, International Journal of Computer Vision 128 (2) (2020) 261–318.

[42] Wei Liu, Dragomir Anguelov, Dumitru Erhan, Christian Szegedy, Scott Reed, Cheng-Yang Fu, Alexander C. Berg, SSD: single shot multibox detector, in: European Conference on Computer Vision, Springer, 2016, pp. 21–37.

[43] Jonathan Long, Evan Shelhamer, Trevor Darrell, Fully convolutional networks for semantic segmentation, in: Proceedings of the IEEE Conference on Computer Vision and Pattern Recognition, 2015, pp. 3431–3440.

[44] Ma Jun, Le Lu, Yiqiang Zhan, Xiang Zhou, Marcos Salganicoff, Arun Krishnan, Hierarchical segmentation and identification of thoracic vertebra using learning-based edge detection and coarse-to-fine deformable model, in: International Conference on Medical Image Computing and Computer-Assisted Intervention, Springer, Berlin–Heidelberg, 2010, pp. 19–27.

[45] Y. Otake, S. Schafer, J.W. Stayman, W. Zbijewski, G. Kleinszig, R. Graumann, A.J. Khanna, J.H. Siewerdsen, Automatic localization of vertebral levels in X-ray fluoroscopy using 3D-2D registration: a tool to reduce wrong-site surgery, Physics in Medicine and Biology 57 (17) (2012) 5485.

[46] Christian Payer, Darko Štern, Horst Bischof, Martin Urschler, Regressing heatmaps for multiple landmark localization using CNNs, in: International Conference on Medical Image Computing and Computer-Assisted Intervention, Springer, 2016, pp. 230–238.

[47] Tomas Pfister, James Charles, Andrew Zisserman, Flowing ConvNets for human pose estimation in videos, in: Proceedings of the IEEE International Conference on Computer Vision, 2015, pp. 1913–1921.

[48] Adhish Prasoon, Kersten Petersen, Christian Igel, François Lauze, Erik Dam, Mads Nielsen, Deep feature learning for knee cartilage segmentation using a triplanar convolutional neural network, in: International Conference on Medical Image Computing and Computer-Assisted Intervention, Springer, 2013, pp. 246–253.

[49] Joseph Redmon, Santosh Divvala, Ross Girshick, Ali Farhadi, You only look once: unified, real-time object detection, in: Proceedings of the IEEE Conference on Computer Vision and Pattern Recognition, 2016, pp. 779–788.

[50] Shaoqing Ren, Kaiming He, Ross B. Girshick, Jian Sun, Faster R-CNN: towards real-time object detection with region proposal networks, in: Advances in Neural Information Processing Systems 28: Annual Conference on Neural Information Processing Systems 2015, December 7–12, 2015, Montreal, Quebec, Canada, 2015.

[51] Olaf Ronneberger, Philipp Fischer, Thomas Brox, U-Net: convolutional networks for biomedical image segmentation, in: International Conference on Medical Image Computing and Computer-Assisted Intervention, 2015.

[52] Holger R. Roth, Le Lu, Ari Seff, Kevin M. Cherry, Joanne Hoffman, Shijun Wang, Jiamin Liu, Evrim Turkbey, Ronald M. Summers, A new 2.5D representation for lymph node detection using random sets of deep convolutional neural network observations, in: International Conference on Medical Image Computing and Computer-Assisted Intervention, Springer, 2014, pp. 520–527.

[53] Oscar E. Ruiz, Julián Flórez, Robust CT to US 3D–3D registration by using principal component analysis and Kalman filtering, in: Computational Methods and Clinical Applications for Spine Imaging: Third International Workshop and Challenge, CSI 2015, Held in Conjunction with MICCAI 2015, Munich, Germany, October 5, 2015, Proceedings, vol. 9402, Springer, Berlin–Heidelberg, 2016, p. 52.

[54] Stefan Schmidt, Jörg Kappes, Martin Bergtholdt, Vladimir Pekar, Sebastian Dries, Daniel Bystrov, Christoph Schnörr, Spine detection and labeling using a parts-based graphical model, in: Information Processing in Medical Imaging, Springer, Berlin–Heidelberg, 2007, pp. 122–133.

[55] Mike Schuster, Kuldip K. Paliwal, Bidirectional recurrent neural networks, IEEE Transactions on Signal Processing 45 (11) (1997) 2673–2681.

[56] Alexander G. Schwing, Yefeng Zheng, Reliable extraction of the mid-sagittal plane in 3D brain MRI via hierarchical landmark detection, in: 2014 IEEE 11th International Symposium on Biomedical Imaging (ISBI), IEEE, 2014, pp. 213–216.

[57] Pierre Sermanet, David Eigen, Xiang Zhang, Michaël Mathieu, Rob Fergus, Yann LeCun, Overfeat: integrated recognition, localization and detection using convolutional networks, arXiv preprint, arXiv:1312.6229, 2013.

[58] Craig J. Simons, Loren Cobb, Bradley S. Davidson, A fast, accurate, and reliable reconstruction method of the lumbar spine vertebrae using positional MRI, Annals of Biomedical Engineering 42 (4) (2014) 833–842.

[59] Amin Suzani, Alexander Seitel, Yuan Liu, Sidney Fels, Robert N. Rohling, Purang Abolmaesumi, Fast automatic vertebrae detection and localization in pathological CT scans-a deep learning approach, in: International Conference on Medical Image Computing and Computer-Assisted Intervention, Springer, 2015, pp. 678–686.

[60] Jonathan J. Tompson, Arjun Jain, Yann LeCun, Christoph Bregler, Joint training of a convolutional network and a graphical model for human pose estimation, Advances in Neural Information Processing Systems 27 (2014) 1799–1807.

[61] Yinong Wang, Jianhua Yao, Joseph E. Burns, Jiamin Liu, Ronald M. Summers, Detection of degenerative osteophytes of the spine on PET/CT using region-based convolutional neural networks, in: International Workshop on Computational Methods and Clinical Applications for Spine Imaging, Springer, 2016, pp. 116–124.

[62] Ke Yan, Mohammadhadi Bagheri, Ronald M. Summers, 3D context enhanced region-based convolutional neural network for end-to-end lesion detection, in: International Conference on Medical Image Computing and Computer-Assisted Intervention, Springer, 2018, pp. 511–519.

[63] Dong Yang, Shaoting Zhang, Zhennan Yan, Chaowei Tan, Kang Li, Dimitris Metaxas, Automated anatomical landmark detection ondistal femur surface using convolutional neural network, in: 2015 IEEE 12th International Symposium on Biomedical Imaging (ISBI), IEEE, 2015, pp. 17–21.

[64] Dong Yang, Tao Xiong, Daguang Xu, Qiangui Huang, David Liu, S. Kevin Zhou, Zhoubing Xu, JinHyeong Park, Mingqing Chen, Trac D. Tran, Sang Peter Chin, Dimitris Metaxas, Dorin Comaniciu, Automatic vertebra labeling in large-scale 3D CT using deep image-to-image network with message passing and sparsity regularization, in: Marc Niethammer, Martin Styner, Stephen Aylward, Hongtu Zhu, Ipek Oguz, Pew-Thian Yap, Dinggang Shen (Eds.), Information Processing in Medical Imaging, Springer, Cham, 2017, pp. 633–644.

[65] Yongxin Yang, Timothy Hospedales, Deep multi-task representation learning: a tensor factorisation approach, arXiv preprint, arXiv:1605.06391, 2016.

[66] Jianhua Yao, Ben Glocker, Tobias Klinder, Shuo Li, Vertebrae localization and identification challenge, in: International Workshop and Challenge on Computational Methods and Clinical Applications for Spine Imaging, Springer, 2014.

[67] Jianhua Yao, Joseph E. Burns, Hector Munoz, Ronald M. Summers, Detection of vertebral body fractures based on cortical shell unwrapping, in: International Conference

on Medical Image Computing and Computer-Assisted Intervention, Springer, Berlin–Heidelberg, 2012, pp. 509–516.

[68] Yiqiang Zhan, Dewan Maneesh, Martin Harder, Xiang Sean Zhou, Robust MR spine detection using hierarchical learning and local articulated model, in: International Conference on Medical Image Computing and Computer-Assisted Intervention, Springer, Berlin–Heidelberg, 2012, pp. 141–148.

[69] Yiqiang Zhan, Maneesh Dewan, Martin Harder, Arun Krishnan, Xiang Sean Zhou, Robust automatic knee MR slice positioning through redundant and hierarchical anatomy detection, IEEE Transactions on Medical Imaging 30 (12) (2011) 2087–2100.

[70] Yipeng Zhang, Haofu Liao, Jin Xiao, Nisreen Al Jallad, Oriana Ly-Mapes, Jiebo Luo, A smartphone-based system for real-time early childhood caries diagnosis, in: Yipeng Hu, Roxane Licandro, J. Alison Noble, Jana Hutter, Stephen R. Aylward, Andrew Melbourne, Esra Abaci Turk, Jordina Torrents-Barrena (Eds.), Medical Ultrasound, and Preterm, Perinatal and Paediatric Image Analysis – First International Workshop, ASMUS 2020, and 5th International Workshop, PIPPI 2020, Held in Conjunction with MICCAI 2020, Lima, Peru, October 4–8, 2020, Proceedings, in: Lecture Notes in Computer Science, vol. 12437, Springer, 2020, pp. 233–242.

[71] Martin Zlocha, Qi Dou, Ben Glocker, Improving RetinaNet for CT lesion detection with dense masks from weak RECIST labels, in: International Conference on Medical Image Computing and Computer-Assisted Intervention, Springer, 2019, pp. 402–410.

Segmentation: intracardiac echocardiography contouring

5

CONTENTS

Image *segmentation* is a pixel-level classification of images. In general, there are two types of segmentations, namely semantic and instance segmentation. The former aims to obtain the semantic category of each pixel and the later aims to decide which object or instance that pixel belongs to. For medical image analysis, both segmentations are applied to delineate the boundaries of target objects or regions, such as 1) organ/substructure/cell segmentation and 2) lesion/nodule segmentation. Semantic segmentation is usually considered to address large and sparse objects, e.g., liver segmentation, while instance segmentation is required when the target objects are small and dense, e.g., cell or nuclei segmentation. The image segmentation results are usually leveraged for quantitative analysis of clinical parameters. For example, organ segmentation may be used for structural related analysis such as the volume of left ventricle. Lesion segmentation may be used for treatment planning and disease progression monitoring.

To obtain the segmented images, healthcare professionals such as radiologists or specialized clinicians first need to identify the region of interest (ROI) and then draw the precise boundaries of the ROI [15]. When it comes to 3D image segmentation such as the CT and MR images, this segmentation process is usually required to be done repetitively for each slice that contains the ROI. Such a manual segmentation of medical images is time consuming and prone to the intra- and inter-observer variability [45]. Therefore, computerized image segmentation solutions are often considered to automate and facilitate the segmentation process.

One of the challenges for automated medical image segmentation is the large variation of the input images. This could be either due to the variation of anatomy across different patients or variation of different imaging settings or devices. Early approaches to image segmentation such as clustering [13], watershed [30], and active contours [20], etc., either make assumptions about the geometry of the objects or require prior knowledge about the object's shape, and hence are prone to the variations of the input, which limits their wide-applicability in medical image segmentation.

In the past few years, the development of deep learning techniques has resulted in a new generation of image segmentation models which show significant performance improvement over the previous approaches [32]. The success of deep learning models is largely due to its ability to learn feature extraction in a data-driven manner (i.e., without relying on feature engineering or prior knowledge) and the feasibility to train at a relatively large scale (i.e., with large scale datasets and high-performance GPUs). As a result, deep learning models are less prone to the variations of medical images. Moreover, deep learning based solutions to medical image segmentation are often equipped with components, such as contracting path [38] or feature pyramid [26], to more effectively extract the hierarchical visual features at pixel-level.

This chapter introduces how to design deep learning models for medical image segmentation. In Section 5.1, we first present several typical families of deep segmentation models and discuss the pros and cons of using these models. Next, we introduce two major segmentation tasks and their corresponding training objectives. We differentiate these two segmentation tasks and discuss which medical problems can be better addressed by these tasks. Finally, we connect the medical image segmentation task with the medical image restoration tasks and present three cases that image restoration may facilitate the image segmentation. In Section 5.2, we provide a case study for medical image segmentation. In particular, we address the segmentation of cardiac structure from intracardiac echocardiography (ICE) images. We follow the design principle introduced in Section 5.1.3 and present a joint 3D image inpainting and segmentation model to better address the ICE image segmentation problem [24].

5.1 Design principles

5.1.1 Choice of deep neural networks

Fully convolutional networks.   A fully convolutional neural network (FCN) is a special type of CNN that only contains convolutional layers As a result of using only convolutional layers, FCNs can work with input images of any size, while standard CNNs only accept fixed-size images. Any standard CNN can be easily converted to an FCN by replacing the fully connected layers with convolutional layers. The fully connected layers whose inputs are from convolutional layers can be replaced by a convolutional layer with the kernel size equal to the output feature map size of the previous convolutional layer. The fully connected layers whose inputs are from other fully connected layers can be just replaced by a convolutional layer with a kernel size of 1×1.

The first work that utilizes FCN for image segmentation was proposed by Long et al. [27] in 2014. Since image segmentation can be viewed as a classification problem where each pixel in the image needs to be categorized, an intuitive approach to image segmentation through CNNs would be using the feature map from last convolutional layer as the score map for pixel classification. However, due to pooling and "valid" convolution, directly applying FCNs would only produce coarse prediction maps. To handle this problem, Long et al. [27] used deconvolutional layers at the end of FCN to obtain a dense prediction map. Deconvolution is essentially an upsampling operation and it has several advantages over other upsampling methods: 1) deconvolution is nonlinear, 2) upsampling using deconvolution can be trained end-to-end in FCNs, and 3) deconvolution can be efficiently implemented using convolution.

FCN is among the early efforts showing that deep neural networks can be trained to address the image segmentation problem effectively. Following its success, FCN has been soon adapted for medical image segmentation to solve problems such as tumor segmentation [47] and skin lesion segmentation [51]. However, despite its popularity and success, conventional FCN model has several limitations: 1) it does not address well the contextual information; 2) it does not combine well the local and global features; and 3) it is not easily transferable to 3D images [32]. Therefore, FCN is rarely used in recent medical image segmentation solutions. And as we will show next, many other works have been proposed to address the limitation of FCNs.

CNN with graphical models. As we have mentioned previously, FCN ignores the context of the scenes to be segmented and hence results in noisy segmentation. To incorporate the context information, one idea is to introduce graphical models such as Markov Random Fields (MRFs) and their variant Conditional Random Fields (CRFs). CRFs can potentially model the contextual relationships between object classes. Particularly, fully connected CRFs, when implemented with an efficient inference algorithm [22], have demonstrated the ability to model the long-range relationships between pixels and produce sharp boundaries and fine-grained segmentation.

Therefore, many approaches have been proposed to combine CNNs with CRFs. One of the seminal works in this direction is DeepLab [9] which includes fully connected CRFs in a postprocessing step to refine the outputs from the CNN segmentation model. The main idea is to regard the CNN outputs as the unary potentials of fully connected CRFs and then apply grid search to find the parameters for the pairwise potentials. DeepLab shows that fully connected CRFs can localize segment boundaries with a higher accuracy and yield fine-grained segmentations. However, in this approach, the training of CNN is disconnected with CRFs which arguably may not fully leverage the strength of CRFs, since it is not able to guide the parameter updates during CNN training. To address this issue, Zheng et al. [55] proposed an approach called CRF-RNN that models CRF with a recurrent neural network.

Since CRF-RNN could be jointly trained with CNN, the entire approach was end-to-end trainable and the resulting model significantly outperformed the disconnected CNN+CRF counterpart.

Introducing CRFs after CNN is very helpful to refine the weak and coarse segmentation predictions. However, it should be pointed out that later deep learning based approaches [54,11,52] to image segmentation gradually abandoned CRFs or other graphical models. The main reason is that the latter approaches have strong CNNs consisting of encoder–decoder components. When combined with other designs such as dilated convolution [10] or feature pyramid [26], the CNNs can already output sharp and fine-grained segmentation boundaries, which makes the graphical models unnecessary.

Encoder–decoder networks. The encoder–decoder networks are one of the most popular choices for medical image segmentation. An encoder–decoder network usually has a symmetric architecture with equal number of encoding and decoding convolutional layers. The encoder extracts and downsamples visual feature representations from the input. The decoder then upsamples the visual features and decodes pixel-level predictions. Early encoder–decoder approaches [34,2] simply stack the encoder and decoder in a sequential manner without the capability to leverage the high-resolution features from the early encoder layers. As a result, they cannot output sharp and precise segmentations.

U-Net [38] is a seminal encoder–decoder network for medical image segmentation. It introduces an important idea of contracting path that shuttles the encoder features to decoder layers. In this way, the decoder can make better use of the high-resolution semantic information from early encoding stage. Therefore, it localizes better the objects and outputs more precise segmentation boundaries. U-Net heavily influenced the subsequent encoder–decoder network designs [31,58]. Nowadays, when we talk about encoder–decoder networks, we usually mean those with contracting paths.

Following U-Net, Milletari et al. [31] proposed V-Net to address the segmentation of volumetric medical images. They introduced 3D convolutional layers into an encoder–decoder architecture similar to U-Net. With 3D convolution layers, the network is able to directly consume 3D images for better extraction of 3D semantics. Zhou et al. [58] introduced U-Net++ with nested U-Net architectures for medical image segmentation. They improved the original U-Net architecture with redesigned contracting paths. In addition to the skip connections between the encoder and decoder, they also introduced extra upsample/decoding units to decode the higher-resolution features at earlier stages and each encoding–decoding submodule formed a UNet-like structure itself. Through this design, it could bring the feature semantics between the encoder and decoder closer and exploited better the multiscale features.

5.1.2 Choice of segmentation tasks and objectives

Medical image segmentation can be divided into two categories, semantic and instance segmentation.

Semantic segmentation.   Semantic segmentation is the most common type of medical image segmentation. The goal of semantic segmentation is to classify each pixel in the image and identify regions with similar semantic meaning. In medical image computing, semantic segmentation is usually applied to identify the boundary of organs or lesions, e.g., the delineation of retinal vessels [44,53] and the segmentation of brain tumors [37,33]. There are two popular choices of objective functions for semantic segmentation, the pixel-wise cross entropy loss and the Dice loss [31]. Let x_i be the ith pixel of a medical image **X**. Semantic segmentation aims to obtain the class label y_i of each pixel x_i, $i \in \{1, \dots, N\}$, where N is the total number of pixels in **X**. Let p_i be the model's prediction of pixel x_i. We can define the cross entropy loss as

$$\mathcal{L}_{\text{CE}} = -\frac{1}{N} \sum_{i=1}^{N} w(\mathbf{X}) y_i \log p_i + (1 - y_i) \log (1 - p_i). \qquad (5.1)$$

For simplicity, here we assume a binary classification where $y_i \in \{0, 1\}$; $w(\mathbf{X})$ is a weight to balance the frequency of foreground ($y_i = 1$) and background ($y_i = 0$) pixels. When $w(\mathbf{X}) = 1$, $\mathcal{L}_{\text{CE}}$ is the standard cross entropy loss. Cross entropy loss is the most widely used loss objective due to its effectiveness under different evaluation metrics [4,18]. However, when the evaluation metric is the Dice coefficient, another popular choice of loss objective is the Dice loss [31,46],

$$\mathcal{L}_{\text{Dice}} = -\frac{\sum_{i=1}^{N} y_i p_i}{\sum_{i=1}^{N} (y_i + p_i) + \epsilon} - \frac{\sum_{i=1}^{N} (1 - y_i)(1 - p_i)}{\sum_{i=1}^{N} (1 - y_i) + (1 - p_i) + \epsilon}, \qquad (5.2)$$

where ϵ is a small number to improve numeric stability when the predictions and ground truths are empty or full.

Instance segmentation.   In many biomedical applications, healthcare professionals are usually interested in identifying the boundaries of each individual object of interest, e.g., the identification of each cell in microscopy images [12,39] or the recognition of each individual glandular structure in histology images [7,50]. Semantic segmentation may not well serve this purpose since it only groups image regions by semantic categories and does not provide information at the instance or object level. Instance segmentation addresses this problem by providing segmentation result for each individual instance. Let x_i be the ith pixel of a medical image **X**. Instance segmentation aims to obtain both the class label y_i and the instance label z_i of each pixel x_i, $i \in \{1, \dots, N\}$, where N is the total number of pixels in **X**. For example, in gland instance segmentation, y_i denotes whether the gland is benign or malignant and z_i denotes the id of the gland that pixel x_i belongs to.

Early approaches to instance segmentation are multitask learning based approaches [7,50], where in addition to the semantic segmentation loss $\mathcal{L}_{\text{mask}}$ these methods also include auxiliary loss $\mathcal{L}_{\text{aux}}$ that provides information about each individual instance,

$$\mathcal{L} = \mathcal{L}_{\text{mask}} + \mathcal{L}_{\text{aux}}. \qquad (5.3)$$

For example, $\mathcal{L}_{aux}$ could be a contour loss [7] that encourages the network to predict the contours of each instance; $\mathcal{L}_{aux}$ could also be an object detection loss [50], and the network learns to predict the class label and bounding box of each instance. With auxiliary information, the segmentation of each individual instance could then be obtained via a postprocessing step. However, the semantic segmentation plus auxiliary task(s) based approaches usually have lesser accuracy [14] mostly due to the unreliableness of the auxiliary task [12] or the errors introduced in fusing the auxiliary information and semantic segmentation.

Another approach is to regard the instance segmentation as a combination of object detection and semantic segmentation, and address the problem by first predicting the bounding box of each instance then performing semantic segmentation within the predicted bounding boxes. The most well-known approach in this category is Mask R-CNN [16] which extends the popular object detection method Faster R-CNN [36] with an object mask prediction branch so that the instance-level semantic masks can be efficiently and accurately obtained. For such detection followed by segmentation strategy, the objective function can be written as

$$\mathcal{L} = \mathcal{L}_{box} + \mathcal{L}_{class} + \mathcal{L}_{mask}. \qquad (5.4)$$

Here, $\mathcal{L}_{box}$ is the bounding box loss, $\mathcal{L}_{class}$ is the object classification loss, and $\mathcal{L}_{class}$ is the object semantic mask loss. Note that unlike the other approaches which perform multitask learning at the image-level, this approach only trains multiple tasks at the instance-level. With this strategy, the instance segmentation can be trained end-to-end without requiring the fusing of multiple tasks in the postprocessing. Due to its efficiency and effectiveness, Mask R-CNN has quickly been adapted to solve medical problems such as microscopic algae detection [39] and nuclei segmentation [19,48].

5.1.3 Image restoration for segmentation

Image restoration is the task of recovering a corrupted or noisy image into its original or clean state. In medical imaging, it often refers to the denoising, deblurring, or artifact removal from the medical images, which often happens during the acquisition of the medical images but can also be applied in the postprocessing steps to improve the image quality. Moreover, it may also refer to the removal of the lesions or simply the inpainting of a cropped region. Image restoration techniques are usually leveraged to facilitate the analysis of medical images, and one way is to help with the medical image segmentation.

Image restoration as preprocessing for image segmentation.   The most straightforward way is to apply image restoration in the preprocessing of an image segmentation solution. For example, a low-dose CT image is usually noisy and hence the anatomy boundary may not be well presented. In this case, a CT image denoising method [8] may be applied to improve the structural and contrast details of the CT image. The denoised image can then be consumed by the segmentation methods for more robust segmentation results [21]. Similarly, in MR image segmentation, the existence of lesions may compromise the performance of the segmentation software.

Thus, a lesion inpainting method [29] can be used to remove the lesions from the MR images. However, it should be noted that the deep learning based segmentation methods are more robust to the various quality of the input images, particularly when there are enough training samples. Therefore, image restoration methods as preprocessing are less applicable to the deep learning based segmentation approaches.

Joint image restoration and segmentation.   Instead of treating image restoration and segmentation as two independent tasks and only applying image restoration via preprocessing, another way is to jointly learn from image restoration and segmentation. There are two motivations for such a joint learning. First, both tasks are not independent, but share some similarities. The ability to restore the image can be partially leveraged to recognize objects from the image, and usually the best segmentation is achieved when the quality of input images is high [5]. Second, compared to image segmentation, training image restoration tasks usually require no labels (or only weak labels). Therefore, via a joint learning with image restoration, the image segmentation can implicitly benefit from the unsupervised learning of image restoration. This is particularly useful when it is infeasible to collect a significant number of segmentation labels.

This joint learning of image restoration and segmentation has been recently shown effective on different deep learning based medical image segmentation approaches. Buchholz et al. [5] proposed a DenoiSeg model to jointly learn the denoising and segmentation of microscopy images. This model is based on the U-Net [38] architecture for segmentation and employs the Noise2Void [23] approach for unsupervised denoising. It shows that joint learning with a denoising task can consistently improve the performance of the U-Net segmentation model when only a few labeled microscopy images are available. Lyu et al. [28] proposed an $A^3DSegNet$ model where, in addition to the joint metal artifact reduction and vertebrae segmentation, it can also transform imaging modality under the same network architecture. This approach includes multiple combinations of unpaired image transformations. Hence, it can also obviate the need for the dense segmentation annotations in one imaging modality while achieving reasonable segmentation performance due to the joint training. In Section 5.2, we introduce how the joint learning of 3D image inpainting and segmentation can improve the performance of cardiac structure segmentation in intracardiac echocardiography images.

Image restoration for unsupervised image segmentation.   The image restoration tasks such as image inpainting, while usually trained in an unsupervised manner, can provide information about the foreground and background and hence may be leveraged for unsupervised image segmentation. For example, in image inpainting, if an object is partially occluded, it is possible to recover the object based on the existing context information. However, if an object is entirely occluded, then the inpainting model will be unable to recover the object. Based on this property, Savarese et al. [42] proposed to achieve the unsupervised foreground–background segmentation by maximizing the inpainting error. They argued that when the foreground and background are well segmented then no context information can be inferred for the

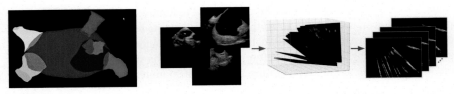

FIGURE 5.1

Left: graphical illustration of LA and its surrounding structures: blue, LA; green, left atrial appendage (LAA); red, left inferior pulmonary vein (LIPV); purple, left superior pulmonary vein (LSPV); white, right inferior pulmonary vein (RIPV); yellow, right superior pulmonary vein (RSPV). Right: 3D sparse ICE volume generation using the location information associated with each ICE image.

foreground/background inpainting, which results in the maximum inpainting errors. Following a similar idea, Wolf et al. [49] proposed an unsupervised instance segmentation method to separate cells in microscopy images. They showed that, when combined with simple foreground detection, their method can achieve comparable instance segmentation performance to fully supervised methods.

5.2 Case study: intracardiac echocardiography contouring

Atrial fibrillation (AF) refers to rapid and irregular beating of the atria, which affected about 2% to 3% of the population in Europe and North America as of 2014 [59]. One of its treatments is to perform catheter ablation to destroy the atypical tissues that trigger the abnormal heart rhythm. During catheter ablation, intracardiac echocardiography (ICE) is often used to guide the intervention. Compared with other imaging modalities such as transesophageal echocardiography, ICE provides better patient tolerance, requiring no general anaesthesia [3]. Moreover, modern ICE devices are equipped with an embedded position sensor that measures the precise 3D location of the ICE transducer. Such spatial geometry information associated with the ICE image is key to this study.

Some gross morphological and architectural features of the left atrium (LA) and its surrounding structures (left atrial appendage (LAA), left inferior pulmonary vein (LIPV), left superior pulmonary vein (LSPV), right inferior pulmonary vein (RIPV), and right superior pulmonary vein (RSPV)) are important to AF interventions, and recognizing these features relies on a clear view of LA's surrounding structures (see Fig. 5.1(a)) and their junctions with the LA [40]. However, due to the limitations of 2D ICE and the difficulty in manual manipulation of the ICE transducer, these 3D anatomical structures may not be sufficiently observed in certain views. This introduces difficulties to electrophysiologists as well as echocardiography image analysis algorithms that attempt automatic multicomponent contouring or segmentation (we use contouring and segmentation interchangeably in this work).

Existing approaches to 2D echocardiogram segmentation only focus on single cardiac chamber such as left ventricle (LV) [25,41,57] or LA [1]. They are designed to distinguish between the blood tissues and the endocardial structures which is relatively easy due to the significant difference in appearance. When it comes to multiple cardiac components (chambers and their surrounding structures), where the boundaries cannot be clearly recognized, these methods may fail. To the best of our knowledge, this work is the first to handle the multicomponent echocardiogram segmentation from 2D ICE images. To the best of our knowledge, this work is the first to handle the multicomponent echocardiogram segmentation from 2D ICE images.

Recently, deep convolutional neural networks (CNNs) have achieved unprecedented success in medical image analysis, including segmentation [56]. A direct approach to our problem would be applying an existing CNN model for 2D ICE segmentation. However, our baseline method of training a CNN to directly generate segmentation masks from 2D ICE images does not demonstrate satisfactory performance, especially for the less-observed pulmonary veins. Such a baseline solely relies on the brute force of big data to cover all possible variations, which is difficult to achieve. To go beyond brute force, we further integrate knowledge to boost contouring performance. Such knowledge stems from two sources: (i) *3D geometry information* provided by a position sensor embedded inside an ICE catheter and (ii) *3D image appearance information* exemplified by cross-modality computed tomography (CT) volumes that contain the same anatomical structures.

5.2.1 Methodology

The proposed method consists of three parts. Using the 3D geometry knowledge, we first form a 3D sparse volume based on the 2D ICE images. Then, to tap into the 3D image appearance knowledge, we design a multitask 3D network with an adversarial formulation. The network performs cross-modality volume completion and sparse volume segmentation simultaneously for collaborative structural understanding and consistency. Finally, taking as inputs both the original 2D ICE image and the 2D mask projected from the generated 3D mask, we design a network to refine the 2D segmentation results.

3D sparse volume formation.   We take as inputs a set of 2D ICE images, each including part of the heart in its field of view and with its 3D position from a magnetic localization system. We use the location information to map all 2D ICE images (Fig. 5.1(b)-left) to 3D space (Fig. 5.1(b)-middle), thus forming a sparse ICE volume (Fig. 5.1(b)-right). The generated 3D sparse ICE volume keeps the spatial relationships among individual ICE views. A segmentation method based on the sparse volume can take this advantage for better anatomical understanding and structural consistency.

3D sparse volume segmentation and completion.   The architecture of the proposed 3D segmentation and completion network (3D-SCNet) is illustrated in Fig. 5.2(a). The network consists of a generator G_{3d} and two discriminators D_{3d}^c and

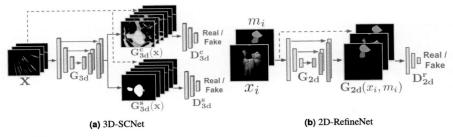

(a) 3D-SCNet   **(b)** 2D-RefineNet

FIGURE 5.2

The network architectures of the proposed method.

D_{3d}^s. Taking the sparse ICE volume $\mathbf{x}$ as input, the generator G_{3d} performs 3D segmentation and completion simultaneously and outputs a segmentation map $G_{3d}^s(\mathbf{x})$, as well as a dense volume $G_{3d}^c(\mathbf{x})$. During training, the ground truth of $G_{3d}^c(\mathbf{x})$ is a CT volume instead of a dense ICE volume as we lack the training data of the latter. The ICE images and the CT volumes are from *completely different* patients. This inherently indicates a challenging *cross-modality volume completion* problem with unpaired data. We target this problem through adversarial learning and mesh pairing (see Section 5.2.2). The two discriminators judge the realness of the outputs from the generator. When trained adversarially together with a generator, they make sure the generator's outputs are more perceptually realistic. Following conditional GAN [17], we also allow the discriminators to take $\mathbf{x}$ as the input to further improve adversarial training.

The segmentation task s and completion task c are trained jointly in a multitask learning (MTL) fashion [6]. The adversarial loss for a task $t \in \{s, c\}$ can be written as

$$\mathcal{L}_{adv}^t = \mathbb{E}_{\mathbf{x}, y_t \sim p(\mathbf{x}, y_t)}[\log D_{3d}^t(\mathbf{x}, y_t)] + \mathbb{E}_{\mathbf{x} \sim p(\mathbf{x})}[1 - \log D_{3d}^t(\mathbf{x}, G_{3d}^t(\mathbf{x}))], \quad (5.5)$$

where p denote the data distributions. For a real data y_t, i.e., the ground-truth segmentation map or CT volume, D_{3d}^t is trained to predict a "real" label. For the generated data $G_{3d}^t(\mathbf{x})$, D_{3d}^t learns to give a "fake" label. On the other hand, the generator G_{3d} is trained to deceive D_{3d}^t by making $G_{3d}^t(\mathbf{x})$ as "real" as possible.

Adversarial loss alone, however, does not give a strong structural regularization to the training [35]. Hence, we use reconstruction loss to measure the pixel-level error between the generator outputs and the ground truths. For the segmentation task, we first convert the score map to a multichannel map with each channel denoting the binary segmentation map of a target anatomy and then apply an L_2 loss $\mathcal{L}_{rec}^s$ between $G_{3d}^s(\mathbf{x})$ and y_s. For the completion task, the L_1 loss $\mathcal{L}_{rec}^c$ between $G_{3d}^s(\mathbf{x})$ and y_c is measured. We use L_1 loss against L_2 loss for this task due to the observation that outputs from L_2 loss are usually overly smoothed. The total loss of the sparse volume segmentation and completion network is given by

$$\mathcal{L}_{3d} = \sum_{t \in \{c,s\}} \lambda_{\text{rec}}^t \mathcal{L}_{\text{rec}}^t + \lambda_{\text{adv}}^t \mathcal{L}_{\text{adv}}^t, \tag{5.6}$$

where λ_{rec}^t and λ_{adv}^t are corresponding weighting coefficients.

We use a 3D UNet-like network [38] as the generator. There are 8 consecutive downsampling blocks, followed by 8 consecutive upsampling blocks in the network. We use skip connections to shuttle feature maps between two symmetric blocks. Each downsampling block contains a 3D convolutional layer, a batch normalization layer and a leaky ReLU layer. Similarly, each upsampling layer contains a 3D deconvolutional layer, a batch normalization layer and a ReLU layer. The convolutional and deconvolutional layers have the same parameter settings: $4 \times 4 \times 4$ kernel size, $2 \times 2 \times 2$ stride size, and $1 \times 1 \times 1$ padding size. Finally, a tanh function is attached at the end of the generator to bound the network outputs. The two discriminators D_{3d}^s and D_{3d}^c have identical network architecture with each of them having 3 downsampling blocks, followed by a 3D convolutional layer and a sigmoid layer. The downsampling blocks for the discriminators are the same as those used in the generator. The final 3D convolutional layer ($3 \times 3 \times 3$ kernel size, $1 \times 1 \times 1$ stride size, and $1 \times 1 \times 1$ padding size) and sigmoid layer are used for realness classification.

2D contour refinement. As shown in Fig. 5.2(b), the 2D refinement network (2D-RefineNet) has a similar structure to the 3D-SCNet. Actually, G_{2d} and D_{2d}^r have almost the same structure as their 3D counterparts, except that the convolutional and deconvolutional layers are now in 2D. The inputs to the 2D-RefineNet is a 2D ICE image x_i together with its corresponding 2D segmentation map m_i where m_i is obtained by projecting $G_{3d}^s(\mathbf{x})$ onto x_i. The training of the 2D-RefineNet is also performed in an adversarial fashion and conditional GAN is used to allow D_{2d}^r observing the generator inputs. We compute the adversarial loss L_{adv}^r the same way as Eq. (5.5) and use the L_2 distance between the refinement network output $G_{2d}(x_i, m_i)$ and the ground-truth 2D segmentation map y_r as the reconstruction loss L_{rec}^r. The total loss is

$$\mathcal{L}_{2d} = \lambda_{\text{rec}}^r \mathcal{L}_{\text{rec}}^r + \lambda_{\text{adv}}^r \mathcal{L}_{\text{adv}}^r, \tag{5.7}$$

where λ_{rec}^r and λ_{adv}^r are the corresponding weighting coefficients.

5.2.2 Experiments

Dataset and preprocessing. The left atrial ICE images used in this study are collected using a clinical system with each image associated with a homogeneous matrix that projects the ICE image to a common coordinate system. We perform both 2D and 3D annotations on the ICE images for the cardiac components of interest, i.e., LA, LAA, LIPV, LSPV, RIPV, and RSPV. For the 2D annotations, contours of all the plausible components in the current view are annotated. For the 3D annotations, ICE images from the same patient and at the same cardiac phase are first projected to 3D

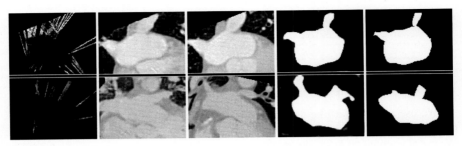

FIGURE 5.3

Sparse volume segmentation and completion results for 2 cases. Columns from left to right: (a) sparse ICE volume; (b) completed CT volume; (c) the paired "ground-truth" CT volume; (d) predicted and (e) ground-truth 3D segmentation map.

and 3D mesh models of the target components are then manually annotated. Note that in clinical practice multiple 2D ICE clips are acquired to dynamically image a patient's LA anatomy. In this study, we focus only on gated 2D ICE images and leave dynamic modeling for future study. 3D segmentation masks are generated using these mesh models. In total, the whole database has 150 patients. For each patient, there are 20–80 gated frames for use. We have 3D annotations for all 150 patients. For 2D annotations, we annotated 100 patients, resulting in a total of 11,782 annotated ICE images. By anatomical components, we have in 2D 4669 LA, 1104 LAA, 1799 LIPV, 1603 LSPV, 1309 RIPV, and 1298 RSPV annotations. So, the LA is mostly observed and the LAA and PVs are less observed. For a subset of 1568 2D ICE images, we have 2–3 expert annotations per image to compute interrater reliability (IRR).

As we do not have dense ICE volumes available for training, we use CT volumes instead as the ground truth for the completion task. Each CT volume we use is associated with an LA mesh model. To pair with a sparse ICE volume, we pick the CT volume whose LA mesh model is closest to that of the targeting sparse ICE volume (after Procrustes analysis [43]). In total, 414 CT volumes are available, which gives enough anatomical variability for the mesh pairing. All the data used for 3D training are augmented with random perturbations in scale, rotation, and translation to increase the generalizability of the model.

Training and evaluation. We train the 3D-SCNet and 2D-RefineNet using Adam optimization with $lr = 0.005$, $\beta_1 = 0.5$, $\beta_2 = 0.999$. The 3D-SCNet is trained for about 25 epochs with $\lambda_{adv}^s = 0.2$, $\lambda_{adv}^c = 1$, $\lambda_{rec}^s = 1000$, $\lambda_{rec}^c = 100$. The 2D-RefineNet is trained for about 25 epochs with $\lambda_{adv}^r = 1$, $\lambda_{rec}^r = 1000$. All λs are chosen empirically and we train the models using 5-fold cross-validation. The segmentation results are evaluated using the Dice metric and average symmetric surface distance (ASSD).

Results. The outputs from the 3D network model are shown in Fig. 5.3. We can observe that the model not only gives satisfying segmentation outputs, Fig. 5.3(d), but also gives a good estimation about the CT volume, Fig. 5.3(b). Especially, we

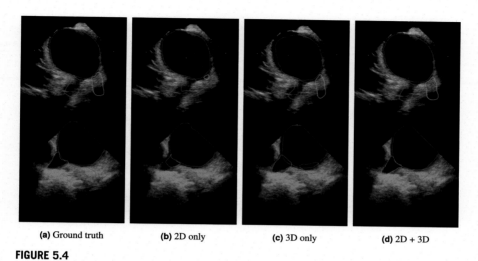

    (a) Ground truth   **(b)** 2D only   **(c)** 3D only   **(d)** 2D + 3D

FIGURE 5.4

Samples of 2D ICE contouring results from different models.

note that the estimated completion outputs do not give structurally exact results as the "ground truth" but instead try to match the content from the sparse volume. Since the "ground truth" CT volume is paired based on mesh models, this difference is expected. It demonstrates that the completion outputs are based on the sparse volume and the system only tries to complete the missing region such that it looks like a "real" CT volume. We also quantitatively evaluate the performance of the 3D sparse volume segmentation and obtain the following Dice scores: LA (89.5%), LAA (50.0%), LIPV (52.9%), LSPV (43.4%), RIPV (62.43%), RSPV (57.6%), and overall (86.1%). This shows that using the limited information from sparse volumes our model can still achieve satisfactory 3D segmentation performance. As we will show in later experiments, the segmentation accuracy, actually, is even higher in the region where 2D ICE images are presented. We also notice that *it is vital to use the 3D appearance information* – the training fails to converge in our experiment of learning the 3D network without using the 3D appearance information from CT.

    Fig. 5.4 shows the 2D ICE contouring results using different models: the "2D only" model that is trained directly with the 2D ICE images, the "3D only" model by projecting the predicted 3D segmentation results onto the corresponding ICE image, and the "2D + 3D" model by refining the outputs from 3D-SCNet using 2D-RefineNet. We observe from the first row that the "3D only" outputs give better estimation about the PVs (red and orange) than the "2D only" outputs. This is because the PVs in the current 2D ICE view are not clearly presented which is more challenging to the "2D only" model. While for the "3D only" model, it makes use of the information from other views and hence predicts better the PV locations. Finally, we see that the outputs from the "2D + 3D" model combines the knowledge from both the 2D and 3D models and generally gives superior outputs than these two mod-

Table 5.1 2D segmentation accuracy of different models. The results are evaluated in terms of Dice metric (%) and ASSD (mm).

	2D only		3D only		2D+3D		IRR	
	Dice	**ASSD**	**Dice**	**ASSD**	**Dice**	**ASSD**	**Dice**	**ASSD**
LA	94.3	0.623	93.5	0.693	**95.4**	**0.537**	89.6	1.340
LAA	68.2	1.172	66.5	1.206	**71.2**	**1.106**	68.8	1.786
LIPV	70.1	0.918	71.7	0.904	**72.4**	**0.856**	69.9	1.459
LSPV	65.9	1.275	67.8	**0.916**	**71.1**	1.197	62.9	1.582
RIPV	69.6	0.927	71.7	0.889	**73.8**	**0.786**	71.4	1.378
RSPV	63.3	0.872	70.4	**0.824**	**70.5**	0.862	57.8	1.633
Total	91.0	0.839	89.8	0.834	**92.1**	**0.791**	88.6	1.432

els. Similar results can also be found in the second row where we see the "2D + 3D" model not only predicts the location of the PVs (purple and brown) better by making use of the 3D information but also refines the output according to the 2D view.

The quantitative results of these models are given in Table 5.1. The "3D only" model in general has better performance in PVs and worse performance in LA and LAA than the "2D only" model. This is because LA and LAA usually have a clear view in 2D ICE images, unlike the PVs. The "2D + 3D" model combines the advantages of the "2D only" and "3D only" model and in general yields the best performance. The IRR scores from human experts are relatively lower, especially for the LSPV and RSPV. This is expected as these two structures are difficult to view with ICE. The IRR scores are generally lower than those from our models, which demonstrates the benefit of using an automatic segmentation model – better consistency.

5.2.3 Discussion

We presented a knowledge fusion plus deep learning approach to ICE contouring of multiple LA components. First, it uses 3D geometry and cross-modality appearance knowledge for better anatomical understanding and structural consistency. Then, it refines the contours in 2D by exploiting the detailed 2D appearance information. We showed that the proposed model indeed benefits from the integrated knowledge and gives superior performance over the models trained individually. In the future, we will investigate the use of temporal information for better modeling and the clinical utility of the generated dense 3D cross-modality views.

5.3 Summary

We have introduced how to design deep neural networks for medical image segmentation. In Section 5.1, we presented several design principles, namely how to choose backbone neural networks for image segmentation, how to choose segmentation tasks and learning objectives, and how to combine the image restoration tasks to facilitate the image segmentation. Then in Section 5.2, we provided a case study to show how these design principles are implemented in practice.

For the choice of segmentation models, we introduced three families of deep neural networks for segmentation in Section 5.1.1, i.e., FCNs, CNN with graphical models, and encoder–decoder models. In Section 5.2, we proceeded with the encoder–decoder model design and provided examples of designing 2D and 3D UNet-like [38] encoder–decoder models for ICE image segmentation.

We covered two commonly encountered medical image segmentation tasks in Section 5.1.2, i.e., semantic and instance segmentation. We provided scenarios for which segmentation tasks may be considered in clinical applications. We also introduced different learning objectives for each segmentation task and provided guidance on the choices of learning objectives. In Section 5.2, we gave details on how the semantic segmentation is applied to delineate the cardiac structures from ICE images.

Finally, we noted the connection between image restoration and image segmentation in Section 5.1.3 and presented three ways of leveraging image restoration to facilitate image segmentation. In Section 5.2, we introduced how 3D ICE image inpainting (one of the image restoration tasks) can be jointly trained with 3D ICE image segmentation. We showed that the joint learning provides better 3D understanding of the cardiac structure and, as a result, gives better segmentation performance than a 2D only segmentation model.

References

[1] Gregory Allan, Saman Nouranian, Teresa Tsang, Alexander Seitel, Maryam Mirian, John Jue, Dale Hawley, Sarah Fleming, Ken Gin, Jody Swift, et al., Simultaneous analysis of 2D echo views for left atrial segmentation and disease detection, IEEE Transactions on Medical Imaging 36 (1) (2017) 40–50.

[2] Vijay Badrinarayanan, Alex Kendall, Roberto Cipolla, Segnet: a deep convolutional encoder–decoder architecture for image segmentation, IEEE Transactions on Pattern Analysis and Machine Intelligence 39 (12) (2017) 2481–2495.

[3] Thomas Bartel, Silvana Müller, Angelo Biviano, Rebecca T. Hahn, Why is intracardiac echocardiography helpful? Benefits, costs, and how to learn, European Heart Journal 35 (2) (2013) 69–76.

[4] Jeroen Bertels, Tom Eelbode, Maxim Berman, Dirk Vandermeulen, Frederik Maes, Raf Bisschops, Matthew B. Blaschko, Optimizing the Dice score and Jaccard index for medical image segmentation: theory and practice, in: International Conference on Medical Image Computing and Computer-Assisted Intervention, Springer, 2019, pp. 92–100.

[5] Tim-Oliver Buchholz, Mangal Prakash, Deborah Schmidt, Alexander Krull, Florian Jug, DenoiSeg: joint denoising and segmentation, in: European Conference on Computer Vision, Springer, 2020, pp. 324–337.

[6] Rich Caruana, Multitask learning, in: Learning to Learn, Springer, 1998, pp. 95–133.

[7] Hao Chen, Xiaojuan Qi, Lequan Yu, Pheng-Ann Heng, DCAN: deep contour-aware networks for accurate gland segmentation, in: Proceedings of the IEEE Conference on Computer Vision and Pattern Recognition, 2016, pp. 2487–2496.

[8] Hu Chen, Yi Zhang, Mannudeep K. Kalra, Feng Lin, Yang Chen, Peixi Liao, Jiliu Zhou, Ge Wang, Low-dose CT with a residual encoder–decoder convolutional neural network, IEEE Transactions on Medical Imaging 36 (12) (2017) 2524–2535.

[9] Liang-Chieh Chen, George Papandreou, Iasonas Kokkinos, Kevin Murphy, Alan L. Yuille, Semantic image segmentation with deep convolutional nets and fully connected CRFs, arXiv preprint, arXiv:1412.7062, 2014.

[10] Liang-Chieh Chen, George Papandreou, Iasonas Kokkinos, Kevin Murphy, Alan L. Yuille, Deeplab: semantic image segmentation with deep convolutional nets, atrous convolution, and fully connected CRFs, IEEE Transactions on Pattern Analysis and Machine Intelligence 40 (4) (2017) 834–848.

[11] Liang-Chieh Chen, Yukun Zhu, George Papandreou, Florian Schroff, Hartwig Adam, Encoder–decoder with atrous separable convolution for semantic image segmentation, in: Proceedings of the European Conference on Computer Vision (ECCV), 2018, pp. 801–818.

[12] Long Chen, Martin Strauch, Dorit Merhof, Instance segmentation of biomedical images with an object-aware embedding learned with local constraints, in: International Conference on Medical Image Computing and Computer-Assisted Intervention, Springer, 2019, pp. 451–459.

[13] Nameirakpam Dhanachandra, Khumanthem Manglem, Yambem Jina Chanu, Image segmentation using K-means clustering algorithm and subtractive clustering algorithm, Procedia Computer Science 54 (2015) 764–771.

[14] Abdul Mueed Hafiz, Ghulam Mohiuddin Bhat, A survey on instance segmentation: state of the art, International Journal of Multimedia Information Retrieval (2020) 1–19.

[15] Intisar Rizwan I. Haque, Jeremiah Neubert, Deep learning approaches to biomedical image segmentation, Informatics in Medicine Unlocked 18 (2020) 100297.

[16] Kaiming He, Georgia Gkioxari, Piotr Dollár, Ross Girshick, Mask R-CNN, in: Proceedings of the IEEE International Conference on Computer Vision, 2017, pp. 2961–2969.

[17] Phillip Isola, Jun-Yan Zhu, Tinghui Zhou, Alexei A. Efros, Image-to-image translation with conditional adversarial networks, in: Proceedings of the IEEE Conference on Computer Vision and Pattern Recognition, 2017, pp. 1125–1134.

[18] Shruti Jadon, A survey of loss functions for semantic segmentation, in: 2020 IEEE Conference on Computational Intelligence in Bioinformatics and Computational Biology (CIBCB), IEEE, 2020, pp. 1–7.

[19] Hwejin Jung, Bilal Lodhi, Jaewoo Kang, An automatic nuclei segmentation method based on deep convolutional neural networks for histopathology images, BMC Biomedical Engineering 1 (1) (2019) 1–12.

[20] Michael Kass, Andrew Witkin, Demetri Terzopoulos, Snakes: active contour models, International Journal of Computer Vision 1 (4) (1988) 321–331.

[21] Prabhpreet Kaur, Gurvinder Singh, Parminder Kaur, A review of denoising medical images using machine learning approaches, Current Medical Imaging 14 (5) (2018) 675–685.

[22] Philipp Krähenbühl, Vladlen Koltun, Efficient inference in fully connected CRFs with Gaussian edge potentials, Advances in Neural Information Processing Systems 24 (2011) 109–117.

[23] Alexander Krull, Tim-Oliver Buchholz, Florian Jug, Noise2void-learning denoising from single noisy images, in: Proceedings of the IEEE/CVF Conference on Computer Vision and Pattern Recognition, 2019, pp. 2129–2137.

[24] Haofu Liao, Yucheng Tang, Gareth Funka-Lea, Jiebo Luo, Shaohua Kevin Zhou, More knowledge is better: cross-modality volume completion and 3D+2D segmentation for intracardiac echocardiography contouring, in: Alejandro F. Frangi, Julia A. Schnabel, Christos Davatzikos, Carlos Alberola-López, Gabor Fichtinger (Eds.), Medical Image Computing and Computer Assisted Intervention – MICCAI 2018 – 21st International Conference, Granada, Spain, September 16–20, 2018, Proceedings, Part II, in: Lecture Notes in Computer Science, vol. 11071, Springer, 2018, pp. 535–543.

[25] Ning Lin, Weichuan Yu, James S. Duncan, Combinative multi-scale level set framework for echo image segmentation, Medical Image Analysis 7 (4) (2003) 529–537.

[26] Tsung-Yi Lin, Piotr Dollár, Ross Girshick, Kaiming He, Bharath Hariharan, Serge Belongie, Feature pyramid networks for object detection, in: Proceedings of the IEEE Conference on Computer Vision and Pattern Recognition, 2017, pp. 2117–2125.

[27] Jonathan Long, Evan Shelhamer, Trevor Darrell, Fully convolutional networks for semantic segmentation, in: Proceedings of the IEEE Conference on Computer Vision and Pattern Recognition, 2015, pp. 3431–3440.

[28] Yuanyuan Lyu, Haofu Liao, Heqin Zhu, S. Kevin Zhou, A^3DSegNet: anatomy-aware artifact disentanglement and segmentation network for unpaired segmentation, artifact reduction, and modality translation, in: International Conference on Information Processing in Medical Imaging, Springer, 2021, pp. 360–372.

[29] José V. Manjón, José E. Romero, Roberto Vivo-Hernando, Gregorio Rubio, Fernando Aparici, Maria de la Iglesia-Vaya, Thomas Tourdias, Pierrick Coupé, Blind MRI brain lesion inpainting using deep learning, in: International Workshop on Simulation and Synthesis in Medical Imaging, Springer, 2020, pp. 41–49.

[30] Fernand Meyer, Topographic distance and watershed lines, Signal Processing 38 (1) (1994) 113–125.

[31] Fausto Milletari, Nassir Navab, Seyed-Ahmad Ahmadi, V-Net: fully convolutional neural networks for volumetric medical image segmentation, in: 2016 Fourth International Conference on 3D Vision (3DV), IEEE, 2016, pp. 565–571.

[32] Shervin Minaee, Yuri Y. Boykov, Fatih Porikli, Antonio J. Plaza, Nasser Kehtarnavaz, Demetri Terzopoulos, Image segmentation using deep learning: a survey, IEEE Transactions on Pattern Analysis and Machine Intelligence (2021).

[33] Andriy Myronenko, 3D MRI brain tumor segmentation using autoencoder regularization, in: International MICCAI Brainlesion Workshop, Springer, 2018, pp. 311–320.

[34] Hyeonwoo Noh, Seunghoon Hong, Bohyung Han, Learning deconvolution network for semantic segmentation, in: Proceedings of the IEEE International Conference on Computer Vision, 2015, pp. 1520–1528.

[35] Deepak Pathak, Philipp Krahenbuhl, Jeff Donahue, Trevor Darrell, Alexei A. Efros, Context encoders: feature learning by inpainting, arXiv preprint, arXiv:1604.07379, 2016.

[36] Shaoqing Ren, Kaiming He, Ross B. Girshick, Jian Sun, Faster R-CNN: towards real-time object detection with region proposal networks, in: Advances in Neural Information Processing Systems 28: Annual Conference on Neural Information Processing Systems 2015, December 7–12, 2015, Montreal, Quebec, Canada, 2015, pp. 91–99.

[37] Mina Rezaei, Konstantin Harmuth, Willi Gierke, Thomas Kellermeier, Martin Fischer, Haojin Yang, Christoph Meinel, A conditional adversarial network for semantic segmentation of brain tumor, in: International MICCAI Brainlesion Workshop, Springer, 2017, pp. 241–252.

[38] Olaf Ronneberger, Philipp Fischer, Thomas Brox, U-Net: convolutional networks for biomedical image segmentation, in: International Conference on Medical Image Computing and Computer-Assisted Intervention, 2015.

[39] Jesus Ruiz-Santaquiteria, Gloria Bueno, Oscar Deniz, Noelia Vallez, Gabriel Cristobal, Semantic versus instance segmentation in microscopic algae detection, Engineering Applications of Artificial Intelligence 87 (2020) 103271.

[40] Damián Sánchez-Quintana, José Ramón López-Mínguez, Yolanda Macías, José Angel Cabrera, Farhood Saremi, Left atrial anatomy relevant to catheter ablation, Cardiology Research and Practice (2014).

[41] Alessandro Sarti, Cristiana Corsi, Elena Mazzini, Claudio Lamberti, Maximum likelihood segmentation of ultrasound images with Rayleigh distribution, IEEE Transactions on Ultrasonics, Ferroelectrics, and Frequency Control 52 (6) (2005) 947–960.

[42] Pedro Savarese, Sunnie S.Y. Kim, Michael Maire, Greg Shakhnarovich, David McAllester, Information-theoretic segmentation by inpainting error maximization, in: Proceedings of the IEEE/CVF Conference on Computer Vision and Pattern Recognition, 2021, pp. 4029–4039.

[43] Peter H. Schönemann, A generalized solution of the orthogonal Procrustes problem, Psychometrika 31 (1) (1966) 1–10.

[44] Jaemin Son, Sang Jun Park, Kyu-Hwan Jung, Retinal vessel segmentation in fundoscopic images with generative adversarial networks, arXiv preprint, arXiv:1706.09318, 2017.

[45] Martijn P.A. Starmans, Sebastian R. van der Voort, Jose M. Castillo Tovar, Jifke F. Veenland, Stefan Klein, Wiro J. Niessen, Radiomics: data mining using quantitative medical image features, in: Handbook of Medical Image Computing and Computer Assisted Intervention, Elsevier, 2020, pp. 429–456.

[46] Carole H. Sudre, Wenqi Li, Tom Vercauteren, Sebastien Ourselin, M. Jorge Cardoso, Generalised Dice overlap as a deep learning loss function for highly unbalanced segmentations, in: Deep Learning in Medical Image Analysis and Multimodal Learning for Clinical Decision Support, Springer, 2017, pp. 240–248.

[47] Guotai Wang, Wenqi Li, Sébastien Ourselin, Tom Vercauteren, Automatic brain tumor segmentation using cascaded anisotropic convolutional neural networks, in: International MICCAI Brainlesion Workshop, Springer, 2017, pp. 178–190.

[48] Shidan Wang, Ruichen Rong, Donghan M. Yang, Junya Fujimoto, Shirley Yan, Ling Cai, Lin Yang, Danni Luo, Carmen Behrens, Edwin R. Parra, et al., Computational staining of pathology images to study the tumor microenvironment in lung cancer, Cancer Research 80 (10) (2020) 2056–2066.

[49] Steffen Wolf, Fred A. Hamprecht, Jan Funke, H.H.M.I. Janelia, V.A. Ashburn, Inpainting networks learn to separate cells in microscopy images, in: BMVC, 2020.

[50] Yan Xu, Yang Li, Yipei Wang, Mingyuan Liu, Yubo Fan, Maode Lai, I. Eric, Chao Chang, Gland instance segmentation using deep multichannel neural networks, IEEE Transactions on Biomedical Engineering 64 (12) (2017) 2901–2912.

[51] Yading Yuan, Ming Chao, Yeh-Chi Lo, Automatic skin lesion segmentation using deep fully convolutional networks with Jaccard distance, IEEE Transactions on Medical Imaging 36 (9) (2017) 1876–1886.

[52] Yuhui Yuan, Xilin Chen, Jingdong Wang, Object-contextual representations for semantic segmentation, in: Computer Vision–ECCV 2020: 16th European Conference, Glasgow, UK, August 23–28, 2020, Proceedings, Part VI 16, Springer, 2020, pp. 173–190.

[53] Yishuo Zhang, Albert C.S. Chung, Deep supervision with additional labels for retinal vessel segmentation task, in: International Conference on Medical Image Computing and Computer-Assisted Intervention, Springer, 2018, pp. 83–91.

[54] Hengshuang Zhao, Jianping Shi, Xiaojuan Qi, Xiaogang Wang, Jiaya Jia, Pyramid scene parsing network, in: Proceedings of the IEEE Conference on Computer Vision and Pattern Recognition, 2017, pp. 2881–2890.

[55] Shuai Zheng, Sadeep Jayasumana, Bernardino Romera-Paredes, Vibhav Vineet, Zhizhong Su, Dalong Du, Chang Huang, Philip H.S. Torr, Conditional random fields as recurrent neural networks, in: Proceedings of the IEEE International Conference on Computer Vision, 2015, pp. 1529–1537.

[56] K. Zhou, H. Greenspan, D. Shen, Deep Learning for Medical Image Analysis, The MICCAI Society Book Series, Elsevier Science, 2017, https://books.google.com/books?id=WVqfDAAAQBAJ.

[57] Shaohua Kevin Zhou, Shape regression machine and efficient segmentation of left ventricle endocardium from 2D B-mode echocardiogram, Medical Image Analysis 14 (4) (2010) 563–581.

[58] Zongwei Zhou, Md. Mahfuzur Rahman Siddiquee, Nima Tajbakhsh, Jianming Liang, UNet++: a nested U-Net architecture for medical image segmentation, in: Deep Learning in Medical Image Analysis and Multimodal Learning for Clinical Decision Support, Springer, 2018, pp. 3–11.

[59] M. Zoni-Berisso, F. Lercari, T. Carazza, S. Domenicucci, Epidemiology of atrial fibrillation: European perspective, Clinical Epidemiology 6 (2014) 213–220.

Registration: 2D/3D rigid registration

CONTENTS

Image registration is the task of transforming two or more images so that the content of the images is aligned in the same coordinate system. In medical image registration, we usually have medical images of the same subject but captured under different clinical scenarios. The goal for medical image registration is to align the anatomical structures of the medical images to facilitate the later healthcare delivery. Medical image registration establishes the correspondence between clinical regions of interest and thus the information extracted from one image could readily be applied to another. For example, we may have two images, one captured before the surgery and the other captured during the surgery. If the coordinate correspondences between the images are available, then the clinical findings and annotations (e.g., the location of lesions) obtained before the surgery can be directly leveraged to guide the surgery without the reannotation of the intraoperative image.

Medical image registration is a broad topic due to the variety of medical data and the different physical properties of anatomical structures. First, the medical images may have many different modalities (e.g., MR, CT, or X-ray) and dimensionalities (2D or 3D). Combinations of the different imaging data result in different medical image registration settings (e.g., unimodal registration, multimodal registration, 2D/3D registration, 3D/3D registration, etc.). Second, depending on the different anatomical structures under investigation, the registration could either be rigid or deformable. For example, in bone registration where the relative location of bones does not change over time, rigid registration may be considered. In the registration of neuroimaging data where local changes of the brain may happen, deformable registration is desired.

Given these variations in registration settings, manual registration can be quite challenging and time consuming, especially with multimodal and deformable registration scenarios. It not only requires specialized tools, but also clinicians with high expertise. Therefore, automatic registration systems have been developed. An image registration system usually takes a pair of images, the moving image and the fixed image, as input. It outputs the transformation parameters from which we can warp the moving image so that its content is aligned with the fixed image. Most of the traditional registration methods are similarity-based approaches with handcrafted similarity metrics that measure the similarity between the fixed and moving images. The optimal transformation parameters are usually iteratively searched until the image similarity is maximized. However, it remains challenging to find an appropriate similarity metric when the fixed and moving images are different in appearance. Meanwhile, computing the similarity may have nonnegligible computational cost and when the transformation searching space is high-dimensional, it will introduce significant computational burden and prohibit real-time registration.

Deep learning based methods are initially introduced to address the limitations of the traditional registration approaches. The data-driven nature and the ability to extract hierarchical features have made it possible to learn similarity metrics directly from medical images. This is particularly useful for multimodal or interpatient registration cases where handcrafted similarity metrics are less robust. Meanwhile, deep learning frameworks all have GPU acceleration support, and thereby deep learning based registration models are more capable of handling computationally expensive transformation parameter search. Moreover, recent development has shown that it is even possible to have deep neural networks directly estimate the transformation parameters to avoid transformation parameter search and speed up the registration. In particular, such a direct transformation estimation can be achieved in an unsupervised manner which lowers the data requirement for training and encourages practical use.

In this chapter, we first review the design principles that are applicable to medical image registrations in general, regardless of specific registration settings. Specifically, in Section 6.1, we introduce four categories of deep learning based registration approaches and cover the seminal works published in the recent years. For each category, we also provide an overview of the design and the choices for learning the deep image registration. Next, in Section 6.2, we focus on the 2D/3D rigid registration setting and provide a case study [20]. Unlike the conventional registration approaches, we reformulate the registration as a point tracking problem. In this way, we establish the correspondence between the moving and fixed images. The transformation parameters can then be obtained by aligning the corresponding points in the moving and fixed images.

6.1 **Design principles**
6.1.1 **Deep similarity based registration**

Similarity based approach is a commonly used strategy for medical image registration. In similarity based registration, we first define a similarity metric between the moving image and the fixed image. Then, the transformation parameters can be derived by identifying the transformation that maximizes the similarity. Traditionally, the similarity metrics are handcrafted such as sum of squared differences (SSD), cross-correlation (CC), mutual information (MI), etc. However, these metrics are sensitive to the initial location of the moving image and are usually infeasible when the moving image and the fixed image have different modalities. Therefore, deep learning methods are proposed in the recent years for more robust similarity measurement.

6.1.1.1 *Problem definition and choice of objective functions*

Let $\mathbf{X}_m$ and $\mathbf{X}_f$ be the moving and fixed images for registration, respectively. In deep similarity metric learning, the goal is to train a deep neural network $g(\mathbf{X}_m, \mathbf{X}_f; \mathbf{W})$ that estimates the similarity between $\mathbf{X}_m$ and $\mathbf{X}_f$. Here, $\mathbf{W}$ denotes the weights of g. Once g is obtained, we could apply it to the iterative-based registration methods [18,35] where the target transformation $\mathcal{T}$ between $\mathbf{X}_m$ and $\mathbf{X}_f$ is iteratively searched via an optimization method that maximizes the image similarity.

To learn the similarity metric, a straightforward approach is to regard the problem as a binary classification problem. When $\mathbf{X}_m$ and $\mathbf{X}_f$ are similar, i.e., they are registered, we ask the model to classify them as a positive sample. Otherwise, we ask the model to classify them as a negative sample. The most commonly used loss function for this task is the binary cross entropy loss

$$\mathcal{L}_{\mathrm{CE}} = -\frac{1}{N}\sum_{i=1}^{N} y_i \log p_i + (1-y_i)\log(1-p_i), \qquad (6.1)$$

where y_i denotes the ground-truth label and p_i denotes the deep learning model's output. Alternatively, we may also consider using the Hinge loss

$$\mathcal{L}_{\mathrm{Hinge}} = \frac{1}{N}\sum_{i=1}^{N}\max(0, 1-y_i p_i), \qquad (6.2)$$

which demonstrates better performance in similarity metric learning [35].

If the landmarks are annotated on the fixed and moving images, we may also measure the target registration error (TRE). Let $\mathbf{p}_m = \{\mathbf{p}_m^i\}_1^M$ and $\mathbf{p}_f = \{\mathbf{p}_f^i\}_1^M$ be the locations of landmarks on the moving and fixed images, respectively. The TRE is the average distances between the transformed $\mathbf{p}_m$ and $\mathbf{p}_f$,

$$e_i = \frac{1}{M}\sum_{j=1}^{M}\|\mathcal{T}_i(\mathbf{p}_m^j) - \mathbf{p}_f^j\|_2, \qquad (6.3)$$

and the TRE loss is then given as

$$\mathcal{L}_{\text{TRE}} = \frac{1}{N} \sum_{i=1}^{N} \|e_i - \hat{e}_i\|_2, \tag{6.4}$$

where $\hat{e}_i$ denotes the model's prediction of the TRE. The TRE loss accounts for the extent of the similarity. Compared with the binary classification, which treats all negative samples equally regard less of the similarity differences, this is a more desirable property as it facilitates the later optimization for the transformation parameter search.

6.1.1.2 Deep learning models for similarity metric learning

One of the earliest deep learning based medical image registration approaches was proposed by Wu et al. [44,43] where they applied unsupervised feature learning approaches, such as independent subspace analysis or autoencoding, to extract representative visual features from the moving and fixed images. This unsupervised approach was feasible since they aimed at unimodal medical image registration where both the moving and fixed images were brain MR images of the same type. Therefore, the learned visual features could be directly used for similarity measurement. However, when it comes to multimodal medical image registration where the visual similarity should be more semantically defined, the unsupervised feature learning is infeasible. To address the multimodal medical image registration, Cheng et al. [4] proposed a supervised deep similarity metric learning approach. In this supervised approach, the deep neural network took both the moving and fixed images as the input and directly output a similarity score. To achieve this metric learning for registration, they formulated the problem as a binary classification problem and a positive prediction indicated that the input pair was registered.

While supervised similarity metric learning is feasible for multimodal medical image registration, formulating the problem as binary classification ignores the degree of misalignment. Therefore, Eppenhof et al. [12] proposed to directly regress the TRE which is a common metric that measures the displacement between the moving and fixed images. However, in this way, the learned TRE metric can be nonsmooth and nonconvex. To address this issue, Haskins et al. [14] proposed a multipass solution where the moving image was perturbed N times and the average of the associated TRE estimates was used as the metric output. This approach smoothed the metric and hence improved the optimization.

6.1.2 Reinforcement learning based registration

The similarity based approaches typically require sampling a significant set of moving images during the optimization process which results in high computational cost. Meanwhile, when the initial position of the moving image is not properly placed, the deep neural network will not correctly measure the image similarity which leads to unsuccessful transformation parameter search. To address this issue, we may consider applying reinforcement learning (RL) based approaches for more efficient transformation parameter search. Instead of applying similarity measure and searching the transformation parameters via sampling, the RL-based methods first train an agent that predicts the most possible transformation parameter search direction and then the registration is iteratively repeated until a fixed number of steps is reached.

6.1.2.1 Problem definition and choice of objective functions

In RL-based registration, the goal is to train an agent (in terms of deep neural networks) $g(\mathbf{X}_m, \mathbf{X}_f, s; \mathbf{W}) \rightarrow \mathbb{R}^{|A|}$ that takes the moving image $\mathbf{X}_m$ and fixed image $\mathbf{X}_f$ as the input and estimates rewards for each of the $|A|$ actions at state s. Here, the state s is determined by the current transformation parameters and the registration is completed if the optimal state is reached, i.e., the target transformation parameter is found; $A = \{a_i\}$ is a set of actions that the agent may take. Each action a_i defines a transformation parameter search direction which can be regard as an analogy to the gradient in optimization. At each iteration, we take the action that gives the maximum reward where a reward is usually decided by the current distance to the target transformation parameters. To train the agent, we compute the L_2 loss between the ground-truth and predicted reward

$$\mathcal{L}_{\text{RL}} = \frac{1}{N} \sum_{n=1}^{N} \sum_{i=1}^{|A|} \| g_i(\mathbf{X}_m, \mathbf{X}_f, s; \mathbf{W}) - r_i \|_2, \qquad (6.5)$$

where r_i denotes the ground-truth reward and g_i denotes the predicted reward by the agent for action a_i.

6.1.2.2 Deep learning models for reinforcement learning based registration

Liao et al. [21] were the first to formulate the registration as a Markov decision process (MDP) and address the problem under a reinforcement learning framework. However, this method required the agent to be trained on a large number of samples such that the registration can follow the expected trajectory. To mitigate this issue, Miao et al. [24] introduced a multiagent design to the RL-based registration for more robust parameter search. While their proposed approach achieved improved performance, the problem with the RL-based approaches were that they still could not guarantee convergence which hence limited their registration accuracy. Therefore, they are usually used to find a good initial pose for the registration, and a combination with an optimization-based method is applied for better performance.

6.1.3 Supervised transformation estimation

The development of deep neural networks has made it possible to directly estimate the transformation parameters in one step. That is, taking a pair of moving and fixed images as input, the deep neural network directly outputs the expected transformation parameters for registration. This is a step further than the RL-based approaches in the effort of speeding up the registration. Since no iterative sampling of the moving images is required, it significantly reduces the computational cost. Such a speedup is particularly helpful for deformable registration where the solution space is high dimensional. But it may also benefit the rigid registration in the case of identifying the initial registration pose.

6.1.3.1 Problem definition and choice of objective functions

Let $\mathcal{T}_\theta$ be a target transformation so that the warped moving image $\mathcal{T}_\theta \circ \mathbf{X}_m$ aligns with the fixed image $\mathbf{X}_f$. Here, $\mathcal{T}_\theta$ is parameterized by θ from which a displacement vector field can be derived. For example, in rigid registration, θ usually comprises the 6D parameters of the homography matrix. In deformable registration, θ could be the control points for B-spline interpolation. The goal of transformation estimation is to train a network $g(\mathbf{X}_m, \mathbf{X}_f; \mathbf{W})$ that predicts the transformation parameter $\hat{\theta}$. In a supervised setting, the ground-truth parameters θ are available, and we apply L_2 loss to directly regress the transformation parameters,

$$\mathcal{L}_{\text{STE}} = \frac{1}{N} \sum_{i=1}^{N} \|\theta_i - \hat{\theta}_i\|_2. \tag{6.6}$$

6.1.3.2 Deep learning models for supervised transformation estimation

The supervised transformation estimation has been initially proposed to address the rigid image registration problem. Miao et al. [25] proposed the first deep learning based approach for rigid 2D/3D registration where they trained the convolutional neural networks (CNNs) to directly regress the 3D pose given a pair of DRR and X-ray images. However, this approach was generally too ambitious and hence relied on the existence of opaque objects, such as medical implants, that provided strong features for robustness. Moreover, to train the regression model, synthetic data were used in their approach to obtain the ground-truth transformation parameters and the corresponding X-ray images. However, the synthetic X-ray images used for training were visually different from the clinical X-ray images and hence the model may result in poor generalizability in clinical application. To address this limitation, Zheng et al. [47] proposed a pairwise domain adaptation (PDA) module for supervised rigid 2D/3D registration. With the PDA module, the knowledge learned from synthetic images could be better adapted to the clinical images and hence mitigated the discrepancy between the training and clinical application.

Supervised transformation estimation is more desirable for deformable registration. On the one hand, the deformable registration has higher dimension in transformation parameter space which makes the iterative search in solution space more challenging and costly. On the other hand, there is a strong spatial correlation between the deformable transformation field and the fixed and moving image pairs. This spatial correlation can be more effectively formulated via CNNs, especially with the encoder–decoder architectures like U-Net [31]. One of the earliest supervised transformation estimation approaches for deformable registration was proposed by Yang et al. [45,46]. They used an encoder–decoder CNN to predict the deformable map.

However, instead of directly estimating the displacement of the pixels/voxels, they proposed to predicting the initial momentum of the large deformation diffeomorphic metric mapping (LDDMM) registration model from which the displacement can be derived. The LDDMM model retained the smoothness of the displacement which yielded better registration than the direct displacement estimation by CNN.

One of the limitations for supervised parameter estimation is the lack of training data. To address this limitation, Uzunova et al. [37] proposed a data augmentation model to synthesize the training samples. In their approach, the data augmentation was data-driven where a statistical appearance model was applied to learn the generation of deformed samples from the training data. Compared with the manually specified data augmentation schemes, such as affine transformations, noise and global changes in brightness, the proposed data-driven augmentation could synthesize more realistic ground-truth samples from only a few images. With the synthesized training datasets, they then adapted the FlowNet [11] architecture for the CNN-based displacement deformation field estimation. Other than synthesizing deformed samples, Rohe et al. [30] proposed to obtain ground-truth deformation field from the segmentation maps of two MRI images. In particular, given two segmentation maps, they applied an iterative log-approximation scheme to generate the reference stationary velocity field (SVF), which is a diffeomorphic deformation parametrization. After obtaining the reference SVFs, they trained an SVF-Net that predicts SVF from a pair of moving and fixed MRI inputs. For the architecture of the SVF-Net, they applied a U-Net-like [31] structure so that the SVF estimation was achieved in an image-to-image manner.

6.1.4 Unsupervised transformation estimation

Similar to supervised transformation estimation, unsupervised transformation estimation also aims to directly predict the transformation parameters in one step. But unlike the supervised transformation estimation, it does not require the availability of ground-truth transformation parameters for training and hence obviates the need to synthesize training samples. In unsupervised transformation estimation, the goal is to have the deep neural networks to predict transformation parameters so that the similarity between the deformed/transformed moving image and the fixed image is maximized. Since the moving and fixed images are readily available, the training can be achieved in a self-supervised manner without labeled ground-truth transformation parameters. The key enabler for such an approach is the spatial transformer network (STN) [15] which introduces a spatial transformer module that provides efficient and differentiable deformation of the input features. Therefore, this module can be easily incorporated into deep neural networks so that any operations with the deformed features can be backpropagated through the model.

6.1.4.1 Problem definition and choice of objective functions

In unsupervised transformation estimation, we aim to train a deep neural network $g(\mathbf{X}_m, \mathbf{X}_f; \mathbf{W})$ that minimizes the dissimilarity between the warped image $\mathcal{T}_{\hat{\theta}_i} \circ \mathbf{X}_m$

and the fixed image $\mathbf{X}_f$,

$$\mathcal{L}_{\text{UTE}} = \frac{1}{N} \sum_{i=1}^{N} -S(\mathcal{T}_{\hat{\theta}_i} \circ \mathbf{X}_m^i, \mathbf{X}_f^i) + R(\mathcal{T}_{\hat{\theta}_i}). \tag{6.7}$$

Here, S is a similarity metric that measures the similarity of two images; $\hat{\theta}_i = g(\mathbf{X}_m^i, \mathbf{X}_f^i; \mathbf{W})$ is the network's prediction of the transformation parameter; R is a regularization term, such as total variation [41], that encourages the predicted transformation field $\mathcal{T}_{\hat{\theta}_i}$ to be smooth. The loss function is usually implemented with variations of STN so that the generation of the transformation field and the warping of the moving image are differentiable and the self-supervised training is achieved. For the choices of the similarity metric S, we may consider the mean square error, mutual information [40], and cross correlation [1].

6.1.4.2 Deep learning models for unsupervised transformation estimation

de Vos et al. [9,8] introduced one of the first solutions that applied STN for unsupervised transformation estimation. The proposed DLIR framework supported both rigid image registration, where the network predicted the affine transformation parameters for the spatial transformer, and deformable image registration, where the network predicted the B-spline control points for the spatial transformer. As such, the DLIR framework was capable of a two-stage coarse-to-fine registration by applying the rigid registration in the first stage and then applying deformable registration thereafter. For the image similarity metric, they employed the normalized cross correlation (NCC) similarity, and the training was to minimize the NCC dissimilarity between the transformed moving image and the fixed image.

While such a coarse-to-fine registration approach achieved promising deformable registration performance, it did not operate the registration at full resolution. At its finest level, the transformation was determined by the B-spline control points, which may not capture small deformations between images. To address this limitation, Li et al. [19] and Balakrishnan et al. [2] proposed to predict the dense deformation field which controlled the deformation at pixel/voxel-level and could be directly applied to warp the moving image. Both approaches leveraged image-to-image architectures, such as FCN [22] and U-Net [31], to achieve the dense deformation field prediction at full resolution. However, the problem with dense deformation field estimation was that the predicted deformation field may not be smooth. Therefore, Dalca et al. [6] introduced scaling and squaring layers after the image-to-image networks to estimate the stationary velocity field which was not only smooth but also diffeomorphic. Meanwhile, they also formulated the problem under a probabilistic generative model and hence their approach could also produce uncertainty estimation alongside with the deformation field estimation.

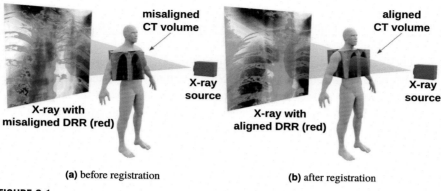

(a) before registration   **(b)** after registration

FIGURE 6.1

Overlay of the DRRs and X-rays before and after the 2D/3D registration. For visualization purpose, only the bone region of the DRRs are projected and recolored with red to distinguish from the X-rays.

6.2 Case study: 2D/3D medical image registration

In 2D/3D rigid registration for intervention, the goal is to find a rigid pose of a preintervention 3D data, e.g., computed tomography (CT), such that it aligns with a 2D intraintervention image of a patient, e.g., fluoroscopy. In practice, CT is usually a preferred 3D preintervention data as digitally reconstructed radiographs (DRRs) can be produced from CT using ray casting [34]. The generation of DRRs simulates how an X-ray is captured, which makes them visually similar to the X-rays. Therefore, they are leveraged to facilitate the 2D/3D registration as we can observe the misalignment between the CT and patient by directly comparing the intraintervention X-ray and the generated DRR (see Fig. 6.1 and Section 6.2.1 for details).

One of the most commonly used 2D/3D registration strategies [23] is through an optimization-based approach, where a similarity metric is first designed to measure the closeness between the DRRs and the 2D data, and then the 3D pose is iteratively searched and optimized for the best similarity score. However, the iterative pose searching scheme usually suffers from two problems. First, the generation of DRRs incurs high computation, and the iterative pose searching requires a significant number of DRRs for the similarity measure, making it computationally slow. Second, iterative pose searching relies on a good initialization. When the initial position is not close enough to the correct one, the method may converge to local extrema, and the registration fails. Although many studies have been proposed to address these two problems [7,26,27,17,10,16,32], trade-offs still have to be made between sampling good starting points and less costly registration.

In recent years, the development of deep neural networks (DNNs) has enabled a learning-based strategy for medical image registration [24,36,21,25] that aims to estimate the pose of the 3D data without searching and sampling the pose space at a large scale. Despite the efficiency, there are still two limitations of the existing learning-based methods. First, the learning-based methods usually require generating a huge number of DRRs for training. The corresponding poses for the DRRs have to be dense in the entire searching space to avoid overfitting. Considering that the number of required DRRs is exponential with respect to the dimension of the pose space (which is usually six), this is computationally prohibitive, thus making the learning-based methods less reliable during testing. Second, the current state-of-the-art learning-based methods [24,36,21] require an iterative refinement of the estimated pose and use DNNs to predict the most plausible update direction for faster convergence. However, the iterative approach still introduces a nonnegligible computational cost, and the DNNs may direct the searching to an unseen state, which fails the registration quickly.

In this chapter, we introduce a novel learning-based approach, which is referred to as a Point-Of-Interest Network for Tracking and Triangulation (POINT^2). POINT^2 directly aligns the 3D data with the patient by using DNNs to establish a point-to-point correspondence between multiple views (i.e., captured at different projection angles) of DRRs and X-ray images. The 3D pose is then estimated by aligning the matched points. Specifically, these are achieved by tracking a set of points of interest (POIs). For 2D correspondence, we use the POI tracking network to map the 2D POIs from the DRRs to the X-ray images. For 3D correspondence, we develop a triangulation layer that projects the tracked POIs in the X-ray images of multiple views back into 3D. We highlight that since the point-to-point correspondence is established in a shift-invariant manner, the requirement of dense sampling in the entire pose space is avoided.

The contributions of this work are as follows:

- A novel learning-based multiview 2D/3D rigid registration method that directly measures the 3D misalignment by exploiting the point-to-point correspondence between the X-rays and DRRs, which avoids the costly and unreliable iterative pose searching, and thus delivers faster and more robust registration.
- A novel POI tracking network constructed using a Siamese U-Net with POI convolution to enable a fine-grained feature extraction and effective POI similarity measure, and more importantly, to offer a shift-invariant 2D misalignment measure that is robust to in-plane offsets (i.e., the translation and rotation offset are within the DRR or X-ray imaging plane).
- A unified framework of the POI tracker and the triangulation layer, which enables (i) end-to-end learning of informative 2D features and (ii) 3D pose estimation.
- An extensive evaluation on a large-scale and challenging clinical cone-beam CT (CBCT) dataset, which shows that the proposed method performs significantly better than the state-of-the-art learning-based approaches, and, when used as an initial pose estimator, it also greatly improves the robustness and speed of the state-of-the-art optimization-based approaches.

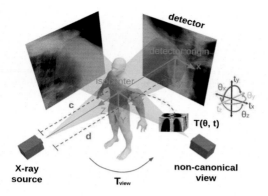

FIGURE 6.2

The X-ray imaging model of the canonical-view (bottom-left to upper-right) and a non-canonical view (bottom-right to upper-left).

6.2.1 Problem formulation

Following the convention in the literature [23], we assume a 2D/3D rigid registration problem and also assume that the 3D data is a CT or CBCT volume, which is the most accessible and allows the generation of DRR. For the 2D data, we use X-rays. As single-view 2D/3D registration is an ill-posed problem (due to the ambiguity introduced by the out-plane offset), X-rays from multiple views are usually captured during the intervention. Therefore, we also follow the literature [23] and tackle a multiview 2D/3D registration problem. Without loss of generality, most of the studies in this work are conducted under two views, and it is easy to extend our work to the cases with more views.

2D/3D rigid registration with DRRs. In 2D/3D rigid registration, the misalignment between the patient and the CT volume $\mathbf{V}$ is formulated through a transformation matrix $\mathbf{T}$ that brings $\mathbf{V}$ from its initial location to the patient's location under the same coordinate. As illustrated in Fig. 6.2, $\mathbf{T}$ is usually parameterized by three translations $\mathbf{t} = (t_x, t_y, t_z)^T$ and three rotations $\boldsymbol{\theta} = (\theta_x, \theta_y, \theta_z)^T$ about the axes, and can be written as a 4×4 matrix under the homogeneous coordinates,

$$\mathbf{T} = \begin{bmatrix} \mathbf{R}(\boldsymbol{\theta}) & \mathbf{t} \\ 0 & 1 \end{bmatrix}, \tag{6.8}$$

where $\mathbf{R}$ is the rotation matrix that controls the rotation of $\mathbf{V}$ around the origin.

As demonstrated in Fig. 6.1, casting simulated X-rays through the CT volume creates a DRR on the detector. Similarly, passing a real X-ray beam through the patient's body gives an X-ray image. Hence, the misalignment between the CT volume and the patient can be observed from the detector by comparing the DRR and the X-ray image. Given a transformation matrix $\mathbf{T}$ and a CT volume $\mathbf{V}$, the DRR $\mathbf{I}^D$ can be computed by

$$\mathbf{I}^{D}(\mathbf{x}) = \int_{\mathbf{p}\in l(\mathbf{x})} \mathbf{V}(\mathbf{T}^{-1}\mathbf{p})d\mathbf{p}, \tag{6.9}$$

where $l(\mathbf{x})$, whose parameters are determined by the imaging model, is a line segment connecting the X-ray source and a point $\mathbf{x}$ on the detector. Therefore, let $\mathbf{I}^{X}$ denote the X-ray image, the 2D/3D registration can be seen as finding the optimal $\mathbf{T}^{*}$ such that $\mathbf{I}^{X}$ and $\mathbf{I}^{D}$ are aligned.

X-ray imaging model.   An X-ray imaging system is usually modeled as a pinhole camera [5,13], as illustrated in Fig. 6.2, where the X-ray source serves as the camera center and the X-ray detector serves as the image plane. Following the convention in X-ray imaging [5], we assume an isocenter coordinate system whose origin lies at the isocenter. Without loss of generality, we also assume the imaging model is calibrated, and there is no X-ray source offset and detector offset. Thus, the X-ray source, the isocenter, and the detector's origin are collinear, and the line from the X-ray source to the isocenter (referred to as the principal axis) is perpendicular to the detector. Let d denote the distance between the X-ray source and the detector origin, and c denote the distance between the X-ray source and the isocenter, then for a point $\mathbf{X} = (X, Y, Z)^{T}$ in the isocenter coordinates, its projection $\mathbf{x}$ on the detector is given by

$$\mathbf{x}' = \mathbf{K}\begin{bmatrix}\mathbf{I} & \mathbf{h}\end{bmatrix}\begin{pmatrix}\mathbf{X}\\1\end{pmatrix}, \tag{6.10}$$

where

$$\mathbf{K} = \begin{bmatrix} -d & 0 & 0 \\ 0 & -d & 0 \\ 0 & 0 & 1 \end{bmatrix}, \quad \mathbf{h} = \begin{pmatrix} 0 \\ 0 \\ -c \end{pmatrix}.$$

Here $\mathbf{x}' = (x', y', z')$ is defined under the homogeneous coordinates and its counterpart under the detector coordinates can be written as $\mathbf{x} = (x, y) = (x'/z', y'/z')$.

In general, an X-ray is usually not captured at the canonical view as discussed above. Let $\mathbf{T}_{\text{view}}$ be a transformation matrix that converts a canonical view to a noncanonical view (Fig. 6.2), then the projection of $\mathbf{X}$ for the noncanonical view can be written as

$$\mathbf{x}' = \mathbf{K}\begin{bmatrix}\mathbf{R}_{\text{view}} & \mathbf{t}_{\text{view}} + \mathbf{h}\end{bmatrix}\begin{pmatrix}\mathbf{X}\\1\end{pmatrix}, \tag{6.11}$$

where $\mathbf{R}_{\text{view}}$ and $\mathbf{t}_{\text{view}}$ perform the rotation and translation, respectively, as in Eq. (6.8). Similarly, we can rewrite Eq. (6.9) at a noncanonical view as

$$\mathbf{I}_{\text{view}}^{D}(\mathbf{x}) = \int_{\mathbf{p}\in l(\mathbf{x})} \mathbf{V}(\mathbf{T}^{-1}\mathbf{T}_{\text{view}}^{-1}\mathbf{p})d\mathbf{p}. \tag{6.12}$$

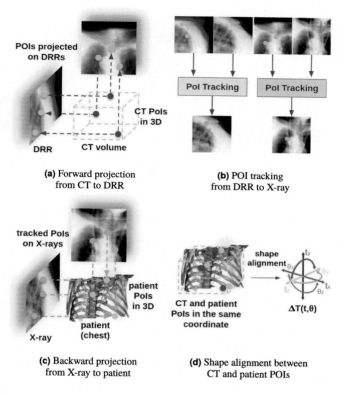

(a) Forward projection
from CT to DRR

(b) POI tracking
from DRR to X-ray

(c) Backward projection
from X-ray to patient

(d) Shape alignment between
CT and patient POIs

FIGURE 6.3

Overview of the proposed POINT^2 method. For better visualization, we apply different colormaps to DRR and X-ray images and adjust their contrast.

6.2.2 Methodology

An overview of the proposed method with two views is shown in Fig. 6.3. Given a set of DRR and X-ray pairs of different views, our approach first selects a set of POIs in 3D from the CT volume and projects them to each DRR using Eq. (6.11) as shown in Fig. 6.3(a). Then, the approach measures the misalignment between each pair of DRR and X-ray by tracking the projected DRR POIs from the X-ray (Fig. 6.3(b)). Using the tracked POIs on the X-rays, we can estimate their corresponding 3D POIs on the patient through triangulation (Fig. 6.3(c)). Finally, by aligning CT POIs with patient POIs, the pose misalignment $\mathbf{T}^*$ between the CT and the patient can be calculated (Fig. 6.3(d)).

POINT.   One of the key components of the proposed method is a Point-Of-Interest Network for Tracking (POINT) that finds the point-to-point correspondence between two images, that is, we use this network to track the POIs from DRR to X-ray. Specifically, the network takes a DRR and X-ray pair ($\mathbf{I}^D$, $\mathbf{I}^X$) and a set of projected DRR

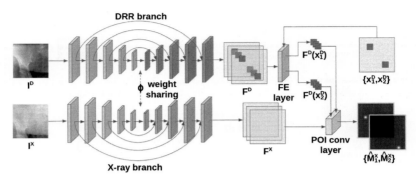

FIGURE 6.4

The architecture of the POINT network.

POIs $\{\mathbf{x}_1^D, \mathbf{x}_2^D, \ldots, \mathbf{x}_m^D\}$ as the input and outputs the tracked X-ray POIs in the form of heatmaps $\{\hat{\mathbf{M}}_1^X, \hat{\mathbf{M}}_2^X, \ldots, \hat{\mathbf{M}}_m^X\}$.

The structure of the network is illustrated in Fig. 6.4. We construct this network under a Siamese architecture [3,38] with each branch ϕ having an U-Net-like structure [31]. The weights of the two branches are shared. Each branch takes an image as the input and performs fine-grained feature extraction at pixel-level. Thus, the output is a feature map with the same resolution as the input image, and for an image with size $M \times N$, the size of the feature map is $M \times N \times C$ where C is the number of channels. We denote the extracted feature maps of DRR and X-ray as $\mathbf{F}^D = \phi(\mathbf{I}^D)$ and $\mathbf{F}^X = \phi(\mathbf{I}^X)$, respectively.

With feature map $\mathbf{F}^D$, the feature vector of a DRR POI $\mathbf{x}_i^D$ can be extracted by interpolating $\mathbf{F}^D$ at $\mathbf{x}_i^D$. The feature extraction layer (FE layer) in Fig. 6.4 performs this operation and we denote its output as a feature kernel $\mathbf{F}^D(\mathbf{x}_i^D)$. For a richer feature representation, the neighbor feature vectors around $\mathbf{x}_i^D$ may also be used. A neighbor of size K gives in total $(2K + 1) \times (2K + 1)$ feature vectors and the feature kernel $\mathbf{F}^D(\mathbf{x}_i^D)$ in this case has a size $(2K + 1) \times (2K + 1) \times C$.

Similarly, a feature kernel at $\mathbf{x}$ of the X-ray feature map can be extracted and denoted as $\mathbf{F}^X(\mathbf{x})$. Then, we may apply a similarity operation to $\mathbf{F}^D(\mathbf{x}_i^D)$ and $\mathbf{F}^X(\mathbf{x})$ to give a similarity score of the two locations $\mathbf{x}_i^D$ and $\mathbf{x}$. When the similarity check is operated exhaustively over all locations on the X-ray, the location $\mathbf{x}^*$ with the highest similarity score is regarded as the corresponding POI of $\mathbf{x}_i^D$ on the X-ray. Such an exhaustive search on $\mathbf{F}^X$ can be performed effectively with convolution and is denoted as a POI convolution layer in Fig. 6.4. The output of the layer is a heatmap $\hat{\mathbf{M}}_i^X$ and is computed by

$$\hat{\mathbf{M}}_i^X = \mathbf{F}^X * (\mathbf{W} \odot \mathbf{F}^D(\mathbf{x}_i^D)), \tag{6.13}$$

where $\mathbf{W}$ is a learned weight that selects the features for better similarity. Each element $\hat{\mathbf{M}}_i^X(\mathbf{x})$ denotes a similarity score of the corresponding location $\mathbf{x}$ on the X-ray.

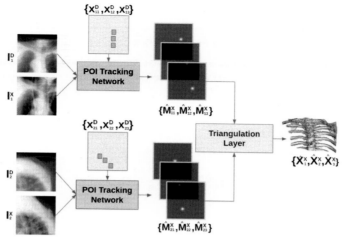

FIGURE 6.5

The overall framework of POINT^2.

POINT^2. With the tracked POIs from different views of X-rays, we can obtain their 3D locations on the patient using triangulation as shown in Fig. 6.3(c). However, this work seeks a uniform solution that formulates the POINT network and the triangulation under the same framework so that the two tasks can be trained jointly in an end-to-end fashion which could potentially benefit the learning of the tracking network. An illustration of this end-to-end design for two views is shown in Fig. 6.5. For an n-view 2D/3D registration problem, the proposed design will include n POINT networks as discussed above. Each of the networks will track POIs for the designated view and, therefore, the weights are not shared among the networks. Given a set of DRR and X-ray pairs $\{(\mathbf{I}_1^D, \mathbf{I}_1^X), (\mathbf{I}_2^D, \mathbf{I}_2^X), \ldots, (\mathbf{I}_n^D, \mathbf{I}_n^X)\}$ of the n views, these networks output the tracked X-ray POIs of each view in the form of heatmaps.

After obtaining the heatmaps, we introduce a triangulation layer that localizes a 3D point by forming triangles to it from the 2D tracked POIs from the heatmaps. Formally, we denote $\mathcal{M}_j = \{\hat{\mathbf{M}}_{1j}^X, \hat{\mathbf{M}}_{2j}^X, \ldots, \hat{\mathbf{M}}_{nj}^X\}$ the set of heatmaps from different views but all corresponding to the same 3D POI $\hat{\mathbf{X}}_j^X$. Here, $\hat{\mathbf{M}}_{ij}^X$ is the heatmap of the jth X-ray POI from the ith view, and we obtain the 2D X-ray POI by

$$\hat{\mathbf{x}}_{ij}^X = \frac{1}{\sum_{\mathbf{x}} \hat{\mathbf{M}}_{ij}^X(\mathbf{x})} \sum_{\mathbf{x}} \hat{\mathbf{M}}_{ij}^X(\mathbf{x})\mathbf{x}. \tag{6.14}$$

Next, we rewrite Eq. (6.11) as

$$\mathbf{D}(\mathbf{x})\mathbf{R}_{\text{view}}\mathbf{X} = c\mathbf{x} - \mathbf{D}(\mathbf{x})\mathbf{t}_{\text{view}}, \tag{6.15}$$

where

$$\mathbf{D}(\mathbf{x}) = \begin{bmatrix} d & 0 & \\ 0 & d & \mathbf{x} \end{bmatrix}.$$

Thus, by applying Eq. (6.15) for each view, we can get

$$\begin{cases} \mathbf{D}(\hat{\mathbf{x}}_{1j}^X)\mathbf{R}_1\hat{\mathbf{X}}_j^X = c\hat{\mathbf{x}}_{1j}^X - \mathbf{D}(\hat{\mathbf{x}}_{1j}^X)\mathbf{t}_1, \\ \mathbf{D}(\hat{\mathbf{x}}_{2j}^X)\mathbf{R}_2\hat{\mathbf{X}}_j^X = c\hat{\mathbf{x}}_{2j}^X - \mathbf{D}(\hat{\mathbf{x}}_{2j}^X)\mathbf{t}_2, \\ \quad\quad\quad \vdots \\ \mathbf{D}(\hat{\mathbf{x}}_{nj}^X)\mathbf{R}_n\hat{\mathbf{X}}_j^X = c\hat{\mathbf{x}}_{nj}^X - \mathbf{D}(\hat{\mathbf{x}}_{nj}^X)\mathbf{t}_n. \end{cases} \tag{6.16}$$

Let

$$\mathbf{A} = \begin{bmatrix} \mathbf{D}(\hat{\mathbf{x}}_{1j}^X)\mathbf{R}_1 \\ \mathbf{D}(\hat{\mathbf{x}}_{2j}^X)\mathbf{R}_2 \\ \vdots \\ \mathbf{D}(\hat{\mathbf{x}}_{nj}^X)\mathbf{R}_n \end{bmatrix}, \quad \mathbf{b} = \begin{bmatrix} c\hat{\mathbf{x}}_{1j}^X - \mathbf{D}(\hat{\mathbf{x}}_{1j}^X)\mathbf{t}_1 \\ c\hat{\mathbf{x}}_{2j}^X - \mathbf{D}(\hat{\mathbf{x}}_{2j}^X)\mathbf{t}_2 \\ \vdots \\ c\hat{\mathbf{x}}_{nj}^X - \mathbf{D}(\hat{\mathbf{x}}_{nj}^X)\mathbf{t}_n \end{bmatrix}, \tag{6.17}$$

then $\hat{\mathbf{X}}_j^X$ is given by

$$\hat{\mathbf{X}}_j^X = \mathbf{A}^+\mathbf{b}. \tag{6.18}$$

The triangulation can be plugged into a loss function that regulates the training of POINT networks of different views,

$$\mathcal{L} = \frac{1}{mn} \sum_i \sum_j \text{BCE}(\sigma(\hat{\mathbf{M}}_{ij}^X), \sigma(\mathbf{M}_{ij}^X)) + \frac{w}{n} \sum_j ||\hat{\mathbf{X}}_j^X - \mathbf{X}_j^X||_2, \tag{6.19}$$

where $\mathbf{M}_{ij}^X$ is the ground-truth heatmap, $\mathbf{X}_j^X$ is the ground-truth 3D POI, BCE is the pixel-wise binary cross entropy function, σ is the sigmoid function, and w is a weight balancing the losses between tracking and triangulation errors.

Shape alignment. Let $\mathbf{P}^D = [\mathbf{X}_1^D \ \mathbf{X}_2^D \ \dots \ \mathbf{X}_m^D]$ be the selected CT POIs, and $\mathbf{P}^X = [\hat{\mathbf{X}}_1^X \ \hat{\mathbf{X}}_2^X \ \dots \ \hat{\mathbf{X}}_m^X]$ be the estimated 3D POIs under the homogeneous coordinates. The shape alignment finds a transformation matrix $\mathbf{T}^*$ such that the transformed $\mathbf{P}^D$ aligns closely with $\mathbf{P}^X$, i.e.,

$$\mathbf{T}^* = \arg\min_{\mathbf{T}} ||\mathbf{T}\mathbf{P}^D - \mathbf{P}^X||_F \text{ such that } \mathbf{R}\mathbf{R}^T = \mathbf{I}. \tag{6.20}$$

This problem is solved analytically through Procrustes analysis [33].

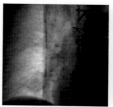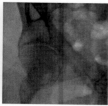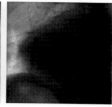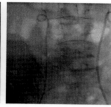

FIGURE 6.6

Sample raw X-ray images of our dataset.

6.2.3 Experiments

Dataset. The dataset we use in the experiments is a cone-beam CT (CBCT) dataset captured for radiation therapy. The dataset contains 340 raw CBCT scans with each has 780 X-ray images. Each X-ray image comes with a geometry file that provides the registration ground truth, as well as the information to reconstruct the CBCT volume. Each CBCT volume is reconstructed from the 780 X-ray images, and in total we have 340 CBCT volumes (one for each CBCT scan). We use 300 scans for training and validation, and 40 scans for testing. The size of the CBCT volumes is $448 \times 448 \times 768$ with 0.5 mm voxel spacing, and the size of the X-ray images is 512×512 with 0.388 mm pixel spacing. During the experiments, the CBCT volumes are treated as the 3D preintervention data, and the corresponding X-ray images are treated as the 2D intraintervention data. Sample X-ray images from our dataset are shown in Fig. 6.6. Note that unlike many existing approaches [27,29,42] that evaluate their methods on small datasets (typically about 10 scans) which are captured under relatively ideal scenarios, we use a significantly larger dataset with complex clinical settings, e.g., diverse field-of-views, surgical instruments/implants, various image contrast and quality, etc.

We consider two common views during the experiment: the anterior–posterior view and the lateral view. Hence, only X-rays that are close to ($\pm5°$) these views are used for training and testing. Note that this selection does not tightly constrain the diversity of the X-rays as the patient may be subject to movements with regard to the operating bed. To train the proposed method, X-ray and DRR pairs are selected and generated with a maximum of $10°$ rotation offset and 20 mm translation offset. We first invert all the raw X-ray images and then apply histogram equalization to both the inverted X-ray images and DRRs to facilitate the similarity measurement. For each of the scan, we also annotate their landmarks on the reconstructed CBCT volume for further evaluation.

Implementation and training details. We implement the proposed approach under the Pytorch [28] framework with GPU acceleration. For the POINT network, each of the Siamese branch ϕ has five encoding blocks (BatchNorm, Conv, and LeakyReLU) followed by five decoding blocks (BatchNorm, Deconv, and ReLU), thus forming a symmetric structure, and we use skip-connections to shuttle the lower-

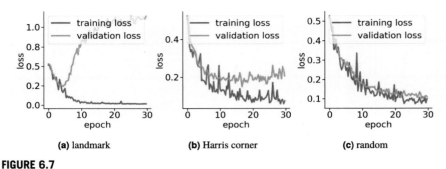

(a) landmark **(b)** Harris corner **(c)** random

FIGURE 6.7

Training and validation losses of different POI selection methods.

level features from an encoding block to its symmetric decoding counterpart. The triangulation layer is implemented according to Eq. (6.18) with the backpropagation automatically supported by Pytorch. We train the proposed approach in a two-stage fashion. In the first stage, we train the POINT network of each view independently for 30 epochs. Then, we fine-tune POINT^2 for 20 epochs. We find this mechanism converges faster than training POINT^2 from scratch. For the optimization, we use the minibatch stochastic gradient descent with 0.01 learning rate for the first stage and 0.001 for the second. We set the loss weight as $w = 0.01$, which we empirically find it works well during training. For the X-ray imaging model, we use $d = 1500$ mm and $c = 1000$ mm.

Ablation study. This section discusses an ablation study of the proposed POINT network. As the network tracks POIs in 2D, we use mean projected distance (mPD) [39] to evaluate different models with specific design choices. The evaluation results are given in Table 6.1.

The first step of the proposed approach requires selecting a set of POIs to set up a point-to-point correspondence. In this experiment, we investigate different POI selection strategies. First, we investigate directly using landmarks as the POIs since they usually have strong semantic meaning and can be annotated before the intervention. Second, we also investigate an automatic solution that uses the Harris corners as the POIs to avoid the labor work of annotation. Finally, we try random POI selection.

As shown in Fig. 6.7(a), we find our approach is prone to overfitting when trained with landmark POIs. This is actually reasonable as each CBCT volume only contains about a dozen of landmarks, which in total is about 3000 POIs. Considering the variety of the field of views of our dataset, this is far from enough and leads to the overfitting. For the Harris corners, a few hundred of POIs are selected from each CBCT volume, and we can see an improvement in performance, but the overfitting still exists (Fig. 6.7(b)). We find the use of random POIs gives the best performance and generalizes well to unseen data (Fig. 6.7(c)). This seemly surprising observation is, in fact, reasonable as it forces the model to learn a more general way to extract

Table 6.1 Ablation study of the proposed POINT network.

#	Kernel size			POI type			Weight		mPD (mm)
	1	3	5	land.	Harris	rand.	w/	w/o	
1	✓					✓	✓		8.46
2		✓				✓	✓		**8.12**
3			✓			✓	✓		9.49
4		✓			✓		✓		9.87
5		✓		✓			✓		12.72
6		✓				✓		✓	11.26

features at a fine-grained level, instead of memorizing some feature points that may look different when projected from a different view.

We also explore two design options for the POI convolution layer. First, it is worth knowing that how much neighborhood information around the POI is necessary to extract a distinctive feature while the learning can still be easily generalized. To this end, we try different sizes of the feature kernel for POI convolution as given in Eq. (6.13). Rows 1–3 in Table 6.1 show the performance of the POINT network with different feature kernel sizes. We observe that a 1×1 kernel does not give features distinctive enough for better similarity measure and a 5×5 kernel seems to include too much neighborhood information (and use more computation) that is harder for the model to figure out a general representation. In general, a 3×3 kernel serves better for the feature similarity measure. It should also be noted that a 1×1 kernel does not mean only the information at the current pixel location is used since each element of $\mathbf{F}^D$ or $\mathbf{F}^X$ is supported by the receptive field of the U-Net that readily provides rich neighborhood information. Second, we compare the performance of the POINT network with or without having the weight W in Eq. (6.13). Rows 2 and 6 show that it is critical to have a weighted feature kernel convolution so that discriminate features can be highlighted in the similarity measure.

The POINT network benefits from the shift invariant property of the convolution operation, which makes it less sensitive to the in-plane offset of the DRRs. Fig. 6.8 shows some tracking results from the POINT network. Here the odd rows show the (a) X-ray and (b)–(d) DRR images. The heatmap below each DRR shows the tracking result between this DRR and the leftmost X-ray image. The red and the blue marks on the X-ray and DRR images denote the POIs. The red and blue marks on the heatmaps are the ground-truth and tracked POIs, respectively. The green blobs are the heatmap responses and they are used to generate the tracked POIs (blue) according to Eq. (6.14). The numbers under each DRR denote the mPD scores before and after the tracking. As we can observe that the tracking results are consistently good, no matter how much initial offset there is between the DRR and the X-ray image. This shows that our POINT network indeed benefits from the POI convolution layer and provide more consistent outputs regardless of the in-plane offsets.

2D/3D registration.   We compare our method with one learning-based (MDP [24]) and three optimization-based methods (Opt-GC [7], Opt-GO [7], and Opt-NGI [26]).

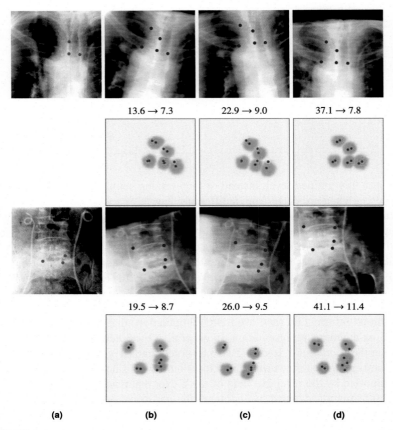

FIGURE 6.8

POI tracking results: (a) X-ray image; (b)–(d) DRR images with different in-plane offsets. The heatmaps of the tracking results are all aligned with the X-ray images and appear similar, showing the shift-invariant property.

To further evaluate the performances of the proposed method as an initial pose estimator, we also compare two approaches that use MDP or our method to initialize the optimization. We denote these two approaches as MDP+opt and POINT^2+opt, respectively. Finally, we investigate the registration performance of our method that only uses the POINT network without the triangulation layer, and denote the corresponding models as POINT and POINT+opt. For MDP+opt, POINT+opt and POINT^2+opt, we use the Opt-GC method during the optimization as we find it converges faster when the initial pose is close to the global optima.

Following the standard in 2D/3D registration [39], the performances of the proposed method and the baseline methods are evaluated with mean target registration error (mTRE), i.e., the mean distance (in mm) between the patient landmarks and the

Table 6.2 2D/3D registration performance comparing with the state-of-the-art results.

	mTRE (mm)			GFR	Reg. time
	50th	**75th**	**95th**		
Initial	20.4	24.4	29.7	92.9%	N/A
Opt-NGI [26]	**0.62**	25.2	57.8	40.0%	23.5 s
Opt-GO [7]	6.53	23.8	44.7	45.1%	22.8 s
Opt-GC [7]	7.40	25.7	56.5	47.7%	22.1 s
MDP [24]	5.40	8.62	27.6	<u>16.4%</u>	1.74 s
POINT	5.63	<u>7.72</u>	<u>12.8</u>	18.6%	**0.75 s**
POINT^2	<u>4.22</u>	**5.70**	**9.84**	**4.9%**	<u>0.78 s</u>
MDP [24] + Opt	<u>1.06</u>	<u>2.25</u>	24.6	15.6%	3.21 s
POINT + Opt	1.19	4.67	<u>21.8</u>	<u>14.8%</u>	**2.16 s**
POINT^2 + Opt	**0.55**	**0.96**	**5.67**	**2.7%**	<u>2.25 s</u>

aligned CT landmarks in 3D. The mTRE results are reported in forms of the 50th, 75th, and 95th percentiles to demonstrate the robustness of the compared methods. In addition, we also report the gross failure rate (GFR) and average registration time, where GFR is defined as the percentage of the tested cases with a TRE greater than 10 mm [24].

The evaluation results are given in Table 6.2. We find that the optimization-based methods generally require a good initialization for accurate registration. Otherwise, they fail quickly. Opt-NGI overall is less sensitive to the initial location than Opt-GO and Opt-GC, with more than half of the registration results have less than 1 mm mTRE. Despite the high accuracy, it still suffers from the high failure rate and long registration time and so do the Opt-GO and Opt-GC methods. On the other hand, MDP achieves a better GFR and registration time by learning a function that guides the iterative pose searching. This also demonstrates the benefit of using a learning-based approach to guide the registration. However, due to the problem we have mentioned in Section 6.1.2.2, it still has a relatively high GFR and a noticeable registration time. In contrast, our base model POINT already achieves comparable performance to MDP; however, it runs over twice faster. Further, by including the triangulation layer, POINT^2 performs significantly better than both POINT and MDP in terms of mTRE and GFR. It means that the triangulation layer that brings the 3D information to the training of the POINT network is indeed useful.

In addition, we notice that when our method is combined with an optimization based method (POINT^2 + Opt) the GFR is greatly reduced, which demonstrates that our method provides initial poses that are close to the global optima such that the optimization is unlikely to fall into local optima. The speed is also significantly improved due to faster convergence and less sampling over the pose space.

6.2.4 Limitations

First, similar to other learning-based approaches, our method requires a considerably large dataset from the targeting medical domain to learn reliable feature representations. When the data is insufficient, the proposed method may fail. Second, although our method alone is quite robust and its accuracy is state-of-the-art through a combination with the optimization-based approach, it is still desirable to come up with a more elegant solution to solve the problem directly. Finally, due to the use of triangulation, our method requires X-rays from at least two views to be available. Therefore, for the applications where only a single view is acceptable, our method will render an estimate of registration parameter with inherent ambiguity.

6.2.5 Discussion

We proposed a fast and robust method for 2D/3D registration. The proposed method avoids the often costly and unreliable iterative pose searching by directly aligning the CT with the patient through a novel POINT^2 framework, which first establishes the point-to-point correspondence between the pre- and intra-intervention data in both 2D and 3D, and then performs a shape alignment between the matched points to estimate the pose of the CT. We evaluated the proposed POINT^2 framework on a challenging and large-scale CBCT dataset and showed that 1) a robust POINT network should be trained with random POIs, 2) a good POI convolution layer should be convolved with weighted 3×3 feature kernel, and 3) the POINT network is not sensitive to in-plane offsets. We also demonstrated that the proposed POINT^2 framework is significantly more robust and faster than the state-of-the-art learning-based approach. When used as an initial pose estimator, we also showed that the POINT^2 framework can greatly improve the speed and robustness of the current optimization-based approach while attaining a higher registration accuracy. Finally, we discussed several limitations of the POINT^2 framework which we will address in our future work.

6.3 Summary

We have presented how to leverage deep learning models to solve problems in medical image registration. As medical image registration is a broad topic, in Section 6.1, we focus on the two popular directions in addressing medical image registration with deep learning, namely deep iterative registration and transformation estimation based registration.

For deep iterative registration, there are two possible ways that deep learning can be applied to facilitate the iterative transformation parameter search, i.e., how to better measure the image similarity and how to better find the searching direction. In Section 6.1.1, we showed how to design deep learning models to learn the similarity between the fixed and moving images. We provided several choices of learning the similarity metrics and then introduce seminal works that address the similarity learning under different registration settings. In Section 6.1.2, we showed how the reinforcement learning can be leveraged to predict the transformation parameter search direction, and then presented two pioneer works that apply the RL-based solutions for 2D/3D rigid registration.

For transformation estimation-based registration, there are two possible settings that a deep transformation estimation model can be trained, i.e., the supervised transformation estimation and the unsupervised transformation estimation. In Section 6.1.3, we first introduced the idea of transformation estimation with deep neural networks and then demonstrated how to train a transformation estimation model when ground-truth transformation parameters are available. Next, in Section 6.1.4, we discussed the benefit and feasibility of training transformation estimation models without groundtruth labels. We introduced an objective function based on the similarity measure and denoted its connection with the spatial transformer module to enable the end-to-end training of the network. We summarized the approaches by the seminal works and noted the advantages and disadvantages of applying the related models for transformation estimation.

In Section 6.2, we limited the problem to the 2D/3D rigid registration and investigate how the problem can be addressed in practice. We gave a formal introduction to the 2D/3D rigid registration problem setting and proposed a Point-Of-INterest Tracking (POINT) based registration approach. Specifically, we provided details on how to design a U-Net based Siamese network for tracking and how to establish 3D point correspondences from the 2D tracking maps. We showed that the proposed approach achieves better registration performance while being more computationally efficient than the RL-base and optimization-based approaches.

References

[1] Brian B. Avants, Charles L. Epstein, Murray Grossman, James C. Gee, Symmetric diffeomorphic image registration with cross-correlation: evaluating automated labeling of elderly and neurodegenerative brain, Medical Image Analysis 12 (1) (2008) 26–41.

[2] Guha Balakrishnan, Amy Zhao, Mert R. Sabuncu, John Guttag, Adrian V. Dalca, An unsupervised learning model for deformable medical image registration, in: Proceedings of the IEEE Conference on Computer Vision and Pattern Recognition, 2018, pp. 9252–9260.

[3] Luca Bertinetto, Jack Valmadre, Joao F. Henriques, Andrea Vedaldi, Philip H.S. Torr, Fully-convolutional Siamese networks for object tracking, in: European Conference on Computer Vision, Springer, 2016, pp. 850–865.

[4] Xi Cheng, Li Zhang, Yefeng Zheng, Deep similarity learning for multimodal medical images, Computer Methods in Biomechanics and Biomedical Engineering: Imaging & Visualization 6 (3) (2018) 248–252.

[5] International Electrotechnical Commission, et al., Radiotherapy Equipment: Coordinates, Movements and Scales, IEC, 2008.

[6] Adrian V. Dalca, Guha Balakrishnan, John Guttag, Mert R. Sabuncu, Unsupervised learning for fast probabilistic diffeomorphic registration, in: International Conference on Medical Image Computing and Computer-Assisted Intervention, Springer, 2018, pp. 729–738.

[7] T. De Silva, A. Uneri, M.D. Ketcha, S. Reaungamornrat, G. Kleinszig, S. Vogt, N. Aygun, S.F. Lo, J.P. Wolinsky, J.H. Siewerdsen, 3D–2D image registration for target localization in spine surgery: investigation of similarity metrics providing robustness to content mismatch, Physics in Medicine and Biology 61 (8) (2016) 3009.

[8] Bob D. de Vos, Floris F. Berendsen, Max A. Viergever, Hessam Sokooti, Marius Staring, Ivana Išgum, A deep learning framework for unsupervised affine and deformable image registration, Medical Image Analysis 52 (2019) 128–143.

[9] Bob D. de Vos, Floris F. Berendsen, Max A. Viergever, Marius Staring, Ivana Išgum, End-to-end unsupervised deformable image registration with a convolutional neural network, in: Deep Learning in Medical Image Analysis and Multimodal Learning for Clinical Decision Support, Springer, 2017, pp. 204–212.

[10] Joyoni Dey, Sandy Napel, Targeted 2D/3D registration using ray normalization and a hybrid optimizer, Medical Physics 33 (12) (2006) 4730–4738.

[11] Alexey Dosovitskiy, Philipp Fischer, Eddy Ilg, Philip Hausser, Caner Hazirbas, Vladimir Golkov, Patrick Van Der Smagt, Daniel Cremers, Thomas Brox, Flownet: learning optical flow with convolutional networks, in: Proceedings of the IEEE International Conference on Computer Vision, 2015, pp. 2758–2766.

[12] Koen A.J. Eppenhof, Josien P.W. Pluim, Error estimation of deformable image registration of pulmonary CT scans using convolutional neural networks, Journal of Medical Imaging 5 (2) (2018) 024003.

[13] Richard Hartley, Andrew Zisserman, Multiple View Geometry in Computer Vision, Cambridge University Press, 2003.

[14] Grant Haskins, Jochen Kruecker, Uwe Kruger, Sheng Xu, Peter A. Pinto, Brad J. Wood, Pingkun Yan, Learning deep similarity metric for 3D MR–TRUS image registration, International Journal of Computer Assisted Radiology and Surgery 14 (3) (2019) 417–425.

[15] Max Jaderberg, Karen Simonyan, Andrew Zisserman, et al., Spatial transformer networks, Advances in Neural Information Processing Systems 28 (2015) 2017–2025.

[16] H-S. Jans, A.M. Syme, S. Rathee, B.G. Fallone, 3D interfractional patient position verification using 2D-3D registration of orthogonal images, Medical Physics 33 (5) (2006) 1420–1439.

[17] Ali Khamene, Peter Bloch, Wolfgang Wein, Michelle Svatos, Frank Sauer, Automatic registration of portal images and volumetric CT for patient positioning in radiation therapy, Medical Image Analysis 10 (1) (2006) 96–112.

[18] Stefan Klein, Marius Staring, Keelin Murphy, Max A. Viergever, Josien PW Pluim, Elastix: a toolbox for intensity-based medical image registration, IEEE Transactions on Medical Imaging 29 (1) (2009) 196–205.

[19] Hongming Li, Yong Fan, Non-rigid image registration using fully convolutional networks with deep self-supervision, arXiv preprint, arXiv:1709.00799, 2017.

[20] Haofu Liao, Wei-An Lin, Jiarui Zhang, Jingdan Zhang, Jiebo Luo, Shaohua Kevin Zhou, Multiview 2D/3D rigid registration via a point-of-interest network for tracking and triangulation, in: IEEE Conference on Computer Vision and Pattern Recognition, CVPR 2019, Long Beach, CA, USA, June 16–20, 2019, Computer Vision Foundation / IEEE, 2019, pp. 12638–12647.

[21] Rui Liao, Shun Miao, Pierre de Tournemire, Sasa Grbic, Ali Kamen, Tommaso Mansi, Dorin Comaniciu, An artificial agent for robust image registration, in: Proceedings of the Thirty-First AAAI Conference on Artificial Intelligence, February 4–9, 2017, San Francisco, California, USA, 2017, pp. 4168–4175.

[22] Jonathan Long, Evan Shelhamer, Trevor Darrell, Fully convolutional networks for semantic segmentation, in: Proceedings of the IEEE Conference on Computer Vision and Pattern Recognition, 2015, pp. 3431–3440.

[23] Primoz Markelj, Dejan Tomaževič, Bostjan Likar, Franjo Pernuš, A review of 3D/2D registration methods for image-guided interventions, Medical Image Analysis 16 (3) (2012) 642–661.

[24] Shun Miao, Sebastien Piat, Peter Walter Fischer, Ahmet Tuysuzoglu, Philip Walter Mewes, Tommaso Mansi, Rui Liao, Dilated FCN for multi-agent 2D/3D medical image registration, in: Proceedings of the Thirty-Second AAAI Conference on Artificial Intelligence, (AAAI-18), the 30th Innovative Applications of Artificial Intelligence (IAAI-18), and the 8th AAAI Symposium on Educational Advances in Artificial Intelligence (EAAI-18), New Orleans, Louisiana, USA, February 2–7, 2018, 2018, pp. 4694–4701.

[25] Shun Miao, Z. Jane Wang, Rui Liao, A CNN regression approach for real-time 2D/3D registration, IEEE Transactions on Medical Imaging 35 (5) (2016) 1352–1363.

[26] Yoshito Otake, Adam S. Wang, J. Webster Stayman, Ali Uneri, Gerhard Kleinsig, Sebastian Vogt, A. Jay Khanna, Ziya L. Gokaslan, Jeffrey H. Siewerdsen, Robust 3D–2D image registration: application to spine interventions and vertebral labeling in the presence of anatomical deformation, Physics in Medicine and Biology 58 (23) (2013) 8535.

[27] Yoshito Otake, Mehran Armand, Robert S. Armiger, Michael D. Kutzer, Ehsan Basafa, Peter Kazanzides, Russell H. Taylor, Intraoperative image-based multiview 2D/3D registration for image-guided orthopaedic surgery: incorporation of fiducial-based C-arm tracking and GPU-acceleration, IEEE Transactions on Medical Imaging 31 (4) (2012) 948–962.

[28] Adam Paszke, Sam Gross, Francisco Massa, Adam Lerer, James Bradbury, Gregory Chanan, Trevor Killeen, Zeming Lin, Natalia Gimelshein, Luca Antiga, Alban Desmaison, Andreas Kopf, Edward Yang, Zachary DeVito, Martin Raison, Alykhan Tejani, Sasank Chilamkurthy, Benoit Steiner, Lu Fang, Junjie Bai, Soumith Chintala, PyTorch: an imperative style, high-performance deep learning library, in: H. Wallach, H. Larochelle, A. Beygelzimer, F. d'Alché-Buc, E. Fox, R. Garnett (Eds.), Advances in Neural Information Processing Systems 32, Curran Associates, Inc., 2019, pp. 8024–8035.

[29] Franjo Pernus, et al., 3D-2D registration of cerebral angiograms: a method and evaluation on clinical images, IEEE Transactions on Medical Imaging 32 (8) (2013) 1550–1563.

[30] Marc-Michel Rohé, Manasi Datar, Tobias Heimann, Maxime Sermesant, Xavier Pennec, SVF-Net: learning deformable image registration using shape matching, in: International Conference on Medical Image Computing and Computer-Assisted Intervention, Springer, 2017, pp. 266–274.

[31] Olaf Ronneberger, Philipp Fischer, Thomas Brox, U-Net: convolutional networks for biomedical image segmentation, in: International Conference on Medical Image Computing and Computer-Assisted Intervention, 2015.

[32] Daniel B. Russakoff, Torsten Rohlfing, Kensaku Mori, Daniel Rueckert, Anthony Ho, John R. Adler, Calvin R. Maurer, Fast generation of digitally reconstructed radiographs using attenuation fields with application to 2D–3D image registration, IEEE Transactions on Medical Imaging 24 (11) (2005) 1441–1454.

[33] George A.F. Seber, Multivariate Observations, vol. 252, John Wiley & Sons, 2009.

[34] George W. Sherouse, Kevin Novins, Edward L. Chaney, Computation of digitally reconstructed radiographs for use in radiotherapy treatment design, International Journal of Radiation Oncology, Biology, Physics 18 (3) (1990) 651–658.

[35] Martin Simonovsky, Benjamín Gutiérrez-Becker, Diana Mateus, Nassir Navab, Nikos Komodakis, A deep metric for multimodal registration, in: International Conference

on Medical Image Computing and Computer-Assisted Intervention, Springer, 2016, pp. 10–18.

[36] Daniel Toth, Shun Miao, Tanja Kurzendorfer, Christopher A. Rinaldi, Rui Liao, Tommaso Mansi, Kawal Rhode, Peter Mountney, 3D/2D model-to-image registration by imitation learning for cardiac procedures, International Journal of Computer Assisted Radiology and Surgery (2018) 1–9.

[37] Hristina Uzunova, Matthias Wilms, Heinz Handels, Jan Ehrhardt, Training CNNs for image registration from few samples with model-based data augmentation, in: International Conference on Medical Image Computing and Computer-Assisted Intervention, Springer, 2017, pp. 223–231.

[38] Jack Valmadre, Luca Bertinetto, João Henriques, Andrea Vedaldi, Philip H.S. Torr, End-to-end representation learning for correlation filter based tracking, in: Computer Vision and Pattern Recognition (CVPR), 2017 IEEE Conference on, IEEE, 2017, pp. 5000–5008.

[39] Everine B. Van de Kraats, Graeme P. Penney, Dejan Tomazevic, Theo Van Walsum, Wiro J. Niessen, Standardized evaluation methodology for 2D–3D registration, IEEE Transactions on Medical Imaging 24 (9) (2005) 1177–1189.

[40] Paul Viola, William M. Wells III, Alignment by maximization of mutual information, International Journal of Computer Vision 24 (2) (1997) 137–154.

[41] Valery Vishnevskiy, Tobias Gass, Gabor Szekely, Christine Tanner, Orcun Goksel, Isotropic total variation regularization of displacements in parametric image registration, IEEE Transactions on Medical Imaging 36 (2) (2016) 385–395.

[42] Jian Wang, Roman Schaffert, Anja Borsdorf, Benno Heigl, Xiaolin Huang, Joachim Hornegger, Andreas Maier, Dynamic 2D/3D rigid registration framework using point-to-plane correspondence model, IEEE Transactions on Medical Imaging 36 (9) (2017) 1939–1954.

[43] Guorong Wu, Minjeong Kim, Qian Wang, Brent C. Munsell, Dinggang Shen, Scalable high-performance image registration framework by unsupervised deep feature representations learning, IEEE Transactions on Biomedical Engineering 63 (7) (2015) 1505–1516.

[44] Guorong Wu, Minjeong Kim, Qian Wang, Yaozong Gao, Shu Liao, Dinggang Shen, Unsupervised deep feature learning for deformable registration of MR brain images, in: International Conference on Medical Image Computing and Computer-Assisted Intervention, Springer, 2013, pp. 649–656.

[45] Xiao Yang, Roland Kwitt, Marc Niethammer, Fast predictive image registration, in: Deep Learning and Data Labeling for Medical Applications, Springer, 2016, pp. 48–57.

[46] Xiao Yang, Roland Kwitt, Martin Styner, Marc Niethammer, Quicksilver: fast predictive image registration–a deep learning approach, NeuroImage 158 (2017) 378–396.

[47] Jiannan Zheng, Shun Miao, Z. Jane Wang, Rui Liao, Pairwise domain adaptation module for CNN-based 2D/3D registration, Journal of Medical Imaging 5 (2) (2018) 021204.

Deep network design for medical image reconstruction, synthesis, and selected applications

Reconstruction: supervised artifact reduction

CONTENTS

Medical image *reconstruction* refers to the process of generating interpretable visual representations of a human body from the raw data captured by an imaging system. Tomographic reconstruction is the most studied medical image reconstruction and the representative imaging types, including CT, MR, PET, ultrasound imaging, etc. In this chapter, we focus on CT and MR images which are the two most common imaging modalities, but at a high-level the deep learning methods introduced for CT and MR apply to other imaging modalities as well.

While there could be many steps involved in tomographic reconstruction [46], at a high level, it includes two major steps, the acquisition of the sensor data and the transformation of the sensor data to image data. Therefore, when it comes to improving the reconstruction via computing methods, it usually means improving 1) the quality of the sensor data, 2) the domain transformation from sensor data domain to image data domain, and 3) the quality of the image data after transformation.

Traditionally, these three possible ways of improvements are addressed with mathematical and numerical solutions which are human-designed and by definition suboptimal. Deep learning based reconstruction aims to address the problem with deep neural networks in a data-driven way, i.e., learning the reconstruction directly by fitting the training data. The recent progress has shown that deep learning models can address many computer vision problems well in such a way.

In this chapter, we particularly focus on the supervised learning of reconstruction via deep neural networks. We assume the paired low- and high-quality imaging data are given. The deep neural network takes the low-quality imaging data as input and learns to output the high-quality imaging data. In Section 7.1, we introduce design principles for supervised models that improve reconstruction in image domain (Section 7.1.1), sensor domain (Section 7.1.2), and dual-domain (Section 7.1.3). Next, we provide two case studies to illustrate the application of deep learning models to solve practical medical image reconstruction problems. Specifically, in Section 7.2, we present an image domain approach to address the sparse-view artifact reduction problem [29]. In Section 7.3, we present a dual-domain approach to address the metal artifact reduction problem [31].

7.1 Design principles

7.1.1 Image domain approaches

The most straightforward way of introducing deep learning is to directly apply to the reconstructed image. That is, we first apply a conventional reconstruction method to convert the raw sensor data to a medical image. Due to the limitation of the conventional reconstruction method, the reconstructed image may be low-quality, e.g., low-resolution, noisy or containing artifacts. Hence, we then apply a deep learning model that takes the low-quality medical image as the input and outputs an improved image, e.g., higher resolution, less noisy or artifact reduced. We call such an approach the image domain approach. Since the image domain approach only works with the reconstructed image and does not involve the sensor data or the conventional reconstruction pipeline, we could directly apply the existing image-to-image deep neural networks, such as U-Net [42], to solve the problem.

7.1.1.1 Problem definition and choice of objective functions

Let $\mathbf{X}$ be a reconstructed image using the conventional method. The image domain approach aims to train a deep neural network $g(\mathbf{X}; \mathbf{W_g})$ whose output $\hat{\mathbf{X}}$ improves the quality of $\mathbf{X}$; g is usually designed under the deep image-to-image neural network setting and a common choice of the loss function is

$$\mathcal{L}_{\text{recon}} = \mathbb{E}_{\mathbf{X}, \mathbf{X}_{\text{gt}}}[\|\hat{\mathbf{X}} - \mathbf{X}_{\text{gt}}\|_2 + \lambda R(\hat{\mathbf{X}})], \qquad (7.1)$$

where $\mathbf{X}_{gt}$ is the ground-truth high-quality image of $\mathbf{X}$; R is a regularization function so that $\hat{\mathbf{X}}$ satisfies certain constraints, e.g., total variation [14]. However, applying this loss usually results in overly smoothed image. To address this problem, one could apply the adversarial loss which applies a discriminator so that the generated image

$\hat{\mathbf{X}}$ visually looks similar to the images from the domain of $\mathbf{X}_{gt}$,

$$\mathcal{L}_{adv} = \mathbb{E}_{\mathbf{X}}[\log d(\mathbf{X}_{gt}; W_d)] + \mathbb{E}_{\hat{\mathbf{X}}}[1 - \log d(\hat{\mathbf{X}}; W_d)]. \tag{7.2}$$

Here d is a discriminator. It takes a generated image $\hat{\mathbf{X}}$ or a real image $\mathbf{X}_{gt}$ as input and decides if the input images are generated or real. The adversarial training aims to play a minimax game. On the one hand, it aims to train the discriminator d so that it outputs 0 when the input is a generated image and 1 when the input is a real image. On the other hand, it aims to train the generator g so that the generated image looks like a real image and the discriminator outputs 1 on the generated image. Applying the adversarial loss usually gives results visually closer to the high-quality medical images. But it should be pointed out that its correctness in terms of clinical use is not guaranteed.

7.1.1.2 Deep learning models for image domain reconstruction

There are many works leveraging deep neural networks (DNNs) for image domain reconstruction. One of the earliest DNN enabled works in this area used a 3-layer convolutional neural network (CNN) to reduce noise from LDCT images [6] and achieved superior performance than traditional approaches. Following the same idea, Chen et al. [5] advanced [6] with a deeper network under the encoder–decoder architecture. They used a residual encoder–decoder architecture to reduce the noise from LDCT images and achieved superior performance than the traditional approaches. Peng et al. [41] proposed a Spatially Aware Interpolation NeTwork (SAINT) to better learn CT image enhancement with 3D spatial awareness and, at the same time, maintain a relatively low computational cost. However, the outputs from these methods were often overly smoothed due to mean square error (MSE) loss. To address this problem, Yang et al. [55] proposed to use the perceptual loss [21] to regularize the training for sharper outputs. More recently, Wolterink et al. [50] introduced generative adversarial networks (GANs) [12] into their architecture to obtain more realistic outputs and this work was further improved by Yang et al. [56] where a combination of perceptual loss [21] and adversarial loss was used. Furthermore, Gjesteby et al. [11], Xu et al. [53], and Wang et al. [47] proposed to reduce metal artifact directly in the CT image domain. The metal artifacts considered in these works were mild and thus could be effectively reduced by a CNN. We will show in our experiments that image domain enhancement is not sufficient for mitigating intense metal shadows.

7.1.2 Sensor domain approaches

Another way of improving medical image reconstruction is to apply deep learning models to correct the sensor domain data. The sensor domain data is the raw data that acquired by the imaging devices. For example, in CT imaging this means correcting the sinogram images and in MR imaging this means correcting the k-space data. In a sensor domain approach, we first apply deep neural networks to correct the imperfections of the sensor domain data, and then we apply the reconstruction algorithms to convert the corrected sensor domain data to the image domain data. The image domain data obtained in this way will have higher quality since the imaging artifacts usually come from the imperfections of the sensor domain data which have been corrected in the earlier step by the deep learning model. Similar to the image domain approaches, the sensor domain approaches also leverage deep image-to-image networks for the correction.

7.1.2.1 Problem definition and choice of objective functions

Let $\mathbf{Y}$ be the raw sensor domain data. The sensor domain approach aims to train a deep neural network $g(\mathbf{Y}; \mathbf{W}_g)$ that outputs the corrected sensor domain data $\hat{\mathbf{Y}}$. To train g, we can simply apply the mean squared error (MSE) loss,

$$\mathcal{L}_{\text{recon}} = \mathbb{E}_{\mathbf{Y}, \mathbf{Y}_{\text{gt}}} \|\hat{\mathbf{Y}} - \mathbf{Y}_{\text{gt}}\|_2, \tag{7.3}$$

where $\mathbf{Y}_{\text{gt}}$ is the ground-truth sensor domain data from which we can reconstruct the high-quality image domain data. Note that in some cases, the sensor domain data is locally compromised. Therefore, we can have the neural network to only focus on the compromised region via masking operation, i.e.,

$$\mathcal{L}_{\text{image\_recon}} = \mathbb{E}_{\mathbf{Y}, \mathbf{Y}_{\text{gt}}} \|\hat{\mathbf{Y}} \odot \mathbf{M} - \mathbf{Y}_{\text{gt}} \odot \mathbf{M}\|_2, \tag{7.4}$$

where $\odot$ denotes a masking operator that selects the compromised region in the sensor domain data according to the mask $\mathbf{M}$. For example, in CT imaging the sinogram image may be compromised by the metal objects and hence introduces metal artifacts in the CT image. Thus, $\mathbf{M}$ indicates the metal trace region that is covered by the metal object. In MR imaging, $\mathbf{M}$ may indicate the missing k-space lines in undersampled MR image reconstruction. Meanwhile, it is easy to incorporate the inverse Fourier transformation as part of the deep learning pipeline. Therefore, for MR imaging, instead of matching the ground-truth k-space data, we can choose to directly match the ground-truth MR image,

$$\mathcal{L}_{\text{image\_recon}} = \mathbb{E}_{\mathbf{Y}, \mathbf{Y}_{\text{gt}}} \|\text{IFT}(\hat{\mathbf{Y}}) - \text{IFT}(\mathbf{Y}_{\text{gt}})\|_2, \tag{7.5}$$

where $\text{IFT}(\cdot)$ is a differentiable inverse Fourier transformation layer that converts the k-space data to MR image. Finally, similar to the image domain approaches, we can also apply the adversarial loss to the corrected sensor domain data so that it visually looks similar to the ground-truth sensor domain data. The loss function is the same as in Eq. (7.1).

7.1.2.2 Deep learning models for sensor domain reconstruction

For CT image reconstruction, motivated by the success of DNNs in solving inverse problems, Gjesteby et al. [10] and Park et al. [38] proposed to refine sinograms using a CNN for improved consistency. Zhang et al. [60] proposed a CNNMAR model to first estimate a prior image by a CNN and then correct sinogram similar to NMAR.

However, even with the strong expressive power of CNNs, these approaches still suffer from secondary artifacts due to inconsistent sinograms.

For MR image reconstruction, Akccakaya et al. [2] proposed to apply DNNs for k-space data interpolation and hence achieve fast MR imaging. They showed that, compared with the linear interpolation approaches, the nonlinear k-space data interpolation via DNNs produces better MR images both visually and quantitatively. Han et al. [15] also proposed to directly interpolate the missing k-space data using DNNs. Their idea is based on the ALOHA algorithm [19]. But instead of doing the low-rank Hankel matrix completion, they applied DNNs to learn the k-space interpolation in a data-driven way. Following a similar idea, Lee et al. [26] proposed an ALOHA-based deep learning approach for reference-free EPI ghost correction in MR images.

7.1.3 Dual-domain approaches

Learning from single domain has its limitations. For image domain approaches, the artifacts after reconstruction are nonlocal and the images may be structurally corrupted, which makes it challenging to recover the underlying information in the artifact affected regions. This is not the case for sensor domain approaches where the data is usually locally compromised. Hence, the deep neural networks only need to focus on the compromised part of the data and keep the integrity of the uncompromised part. The problem with the sensor domain approaches is that the imperfections from the sensor domain correction will be translated to nonlocal artifacts in the image domain. Even an insignificant error in the sensor domain data will be amplified after the reconstruction, and hence result in secondary artifact in the image domain.

Dual-domain approaches aim to address this problem via deep neural networks that consider both the image domain and sensor domain. The approaches involve components that correct errors in both domains and jointly learn corrections in an end-to-end manner. The main enabler is the inclusion of the domain transformation function as part of the neural network which bridges the sensor domain learning and the image domain learning.

7.1.3.1 Problem definition and choice of objective functions

Let $\mathbf{Y}$ be a raw sensor domain data that is compromised during the acquisition, and t be a domain transformation function that converts the sensor domain data to image domain, i.e., $\mathbf{X} = t(\mathbf{Y})$. The dual-domain approach aims train a deep neural network $g(\mathbf{Y}; \mathbf{W})$ that directly outputs an image domain data $\hat{\mathbf{X}}$ that improves the quality of $\mathbf{X}$. The dual-domain approach has a cascade form and comprises a sensor domain part followed by an image domain part, i.e., $g(\mathbf{Y}; \mathbf{W}) = g_i(t(g_s(\mathbf{Y}; \mathbf{W}_s)); \mathbf{W}_i)$. Here g_s denotes the sensor domain network that improves the quality of the sensor domain data and g_i denotes the image domain network that improves the quality of the image domain data; t is differentiable, and therefore g_s and g_i can be trained jointly in an end-to-end manner. To train the dual-domain network, we can simply combine the loss functions for each domain,

$$\mathcal{L}_{\text{dual}}(\hat{\mathbf{Y}}, \hat{\mathbf{X}}, \mathbf{Y}_{\text{gt}}, \mathbf{X}_{\text{gt}}) = \lambda_s \mathcal{L}_{\text{sensor}}(\hat{\mathbf{Y}}, \mathbf{Y}_{\text{gt}}) + \lambda_i \mathcal{L}_{\text{image}}(\hat{\mathbf{X}}, \mathbf{X}_{\text{gt}}), \qquad (7.6)$$

where $\hat{\mathbf{Y}}$ is the output of the sensor domain network g_s, $\hat{\mathbf{X}}$ is the output of the image domain network g_i, $\mathbf{Y}_{gt}$ is the ground-truth sensor domain data, and $\mathbf{X}_{gt}$ is the ground-truth image domain data; λ_s and λ_i are hyperparameters that balance between the sensor domain loss $\mathcal{L}_{sensor}$ and the image domain loss $\mathcal{L}_{image}$.

For the choices of $\mathcal{L}_{sensor}$ and g_s, we may follow Sections 7.1.2.1 and 7.1.2.2. Similarly, for the choices of $\mathcal{L}_{image}$ and g_i, we may follow Sections 7.1.1.1 and 7.1.1.2. For the choices of t, if it is CT imaging, t could be the Radon transformation, and, if it is MR imaging, t could be the inverse Fourier transformation. It is worth noting that if $\lambda_s = 0$ and g_s is an identity function, the approach is the same as an image domain approach. If $\lambda_i = 0$ and g_i is an identity function, the approach is the same as a sensor domain approach. Moreover, if the inverse function of t exists, the output of g could be transformed back to the sensor domain, which forms a cycle. Therefore, multiple dual-domain networks could be stacked together for iterative reconstruction.

7.1.3.2 Deep learning models for dual-domain reconstruction

For MR imaging, one of the earliest dual-domain approaches was proposed by Eo et al. [9] for undersampled MR imaging. They proposed a model called KIKI-net that consists of a K-net for k-space completion and an I-net for image restoration. Several K-nets and I-nets were connected in an interleaved fashion for iterative MR reconstruction. They showed that this interleaved K-net and I-net placement outperformed the single domain counterparts and hence demonstrated the effectiveness of the dual-domain learning. Following a similar idea, Zhou et al. [66] proposed a DuDoR net that learns from both the k-space domain and the image domain iteratively with recurrent blocks. In their approach, both the image domain network and the k-space domain network were implemented with dilated residual dense networks (DRD-Net). Meanwhile, the T1 data was introduced to provide prior knowledge for improved reconstruction.

For CT imaging, Lin et al. [31] (Section 7.3) proposed to address the metal artifact reduction problem with dual-domain learning. In particular, they proposed a sinogram domain network for sinogram domain metal trace completion and an image domain network for image domain metal artifact reduction. To enable the joint learning from both the sinogram and image domains, they introduced a differentiable Radon inversion layer that could computational effectively reconstruct CT images from sinogram data and meanwhile attain gradients for backpropagation. Following this idea, Hu et al. [17] and Zhou et al. [67] proposed to apply the dual-domain learning for the sparse-view and limited angle CT reconstruction, respectively.

7.2 Case study: sparse-view artifact reduction

Cone-beam computed tomography (CBCT) is a variant of computed tomography (CT). Compared with conventional CT, which is usually imaged with fan-shaped X-ray beams requiring multiple rotations of the gantry, CBCT provides rapid volume acquisition by using cone-shaped source of radiation such that only a single rotation of the gantry is necessary. Therefore, CBCT usually has shorter examination time, resulting in fewer patient motion artifacts and better X-ray tube efficiency. One way to further shorten the acquisition time and enhance the healthcare experience is to take fewer X-ray measurements during each CBCT scan. However, due to the "cone-beam" projection geometry, CBCT images usually contain more pronounced streak artifacts than CT images and this is even worse when fewer X-ray projections are used during the CBCT reconstruction [4]. In this work, we aim to develop a postprocessing method that alleviates the side-effect of sparse-view CBCT reconstruction by effectively reducing the cone-beam artifacts.

This work proposes to perform sparse-view CBCT artifact reduction with DNNs. Specifically, we train an image-to-image generative model with the perceptual loss to obtain outputs that are perceptually close to the densely reconstructed CBCT images. In order to address the artifacts at various levels, we further contribute to the literature with a novel discriminator architecture based on feature pyramid networks (FPN) [30] and a differential modulated focus map such that the adversarial training is biased to the artifacts at multiple scales. The proposed approach is evaluated on clinical CBCT images. Experimental results demonstrate that our method outperforms strong baseline methods both qualitatively and quantitatively.

7.2.1 Background

A number of approaches have been proposed to address the artifacts [61,48,28,16,36, 44] that are commonly encountered in CBCT images. One of the predominant artifacts in CBCT imaging is the metal artifact. It is caused by the metallic objects that implanted into patients. Metal artifacts reduction (MAR) methods usually [61,48] correct this type of artifact by reconstructing the CBCT images with modified projection data where metallic implants are segmented and replaced with the boundary pixels. Another predominant artifact is the beam hardening artifact which is often observed when X-ray beams pass through high density materials such as bone or metal. Existing works in cone-beam artifacts reduction address this artifact by either generating spectrally independent projection data [28] or estimating the projection error introduced by high-density objects [16]. Some other works propose to correct the scatter artifact through a beam stop array for scatter projection estimation [36] or correct the respiratory motion artifact with a respiratory correlation algorithm that assign projects to corresponding breathing phases [44]. However, to our best knowledge, no scheme has been proposed to correct the cone-beam artifacts introduced by sparse-view CBCT reconstruction in a postprocessing step. The current methods, due to the nature of the targeting artifacts, cannot be directly adapted to handle this task. On the other hand, instead of reducing artifacts from CBCT images directly, many other systems [52,64] propose to introduce better sparse-view reconstruction methods that yield less artifacts. Although encouraging improvements have been made, the image quality from the current solutions is still not satisfactory when only a small number of views are used. This work attempts to fill this gap by refining the sparsely reconstructed CBCT images through a novel cone-beam artifact reduction method.

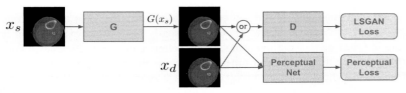

FIGURE 7.1

Overall architecture of the proposed method.

7.2.2 Methodology

Let x_s be a sparse-view CBCT image, which is reconstructed from a sparse set or low number of projections (or views) and x_d be its dense-view counterpart, which is reconstructed from a dense set or high number of projections (or views). The proposed method is formulated under an image-to-image generative model as illustrated in Fig. 7.1 where we train a generator that transforms x_s to an ideally artifact-free image that looks like x_d. The discriminator is used for the adversarial training, and the perceptual network is included for additional perceptual and structural regularization. We use LSGAN [33] against a regular GAN to achieve more stable adversarial learning. The adversarial objective functions for the proposed model can be written as

$$\min_{D} \mathcal{L}_A(D; G, \Lambda) = \mathbb{E}_{\mathbf{X}_d}[\|\Lambda \odot (D(x_d) - \mathbf{1})\|^2] + \mathbb{E}_{\mathbf{X}_s}[\|\Lambda \odot D(G(x_s))\|^2], \quad (7.7)$$

$$\min_{G} \mathcal{L}_A(G; D, \Lambda) = \mathbb{E}_{\mathbf{X}_s}[\|\Lambda \odot (D(G(x_s)) - \mathbf{1})\|^2], \quad (7.8)$$

where Λ is a focus map detailed in Section 7.2.2.2. Note that here we apply a PatchGAN-like [18] design to the discriminator such that the realness is patch based and the output is a score map. The generator G and discriminator D are trained in an adversarial fashion. The discriminator is trained to distinguish between x_d and the generated CBCT image $G(x_s)$ (Eq. (7.7)). While the generator is trained to generate CBCT image samples as "real" as possible such that the discriminator cannot tell if it is from the data distribution of x_d or generated by G (Eq. (7.8)).

Training with the adversarial loss alone usually introduces additional artifacts. Therefore, we adapt the choice of [56] by using a perceptual loss to induce the learning and give more realistic outputs. Letting $\phi^{(i)}(\cdot)$ denote the feature maps extracted by the ith layer of the perceptual network ϕ and N_i denote the number of elements in $\phi^{(i)}(\cdot)$, the perceptual loss can be computed by

$$\mathcal{L}_P = \frac{1}{N_i}\|\phi^{(i)}(x_d) - \phi^{(i)}(G(x_s))\|_1. \quad (7.9)$$

In this work, the perceptual network ϕ is a pretrained VGG16-net [43], and we empirically find that $i = 8$ works well.

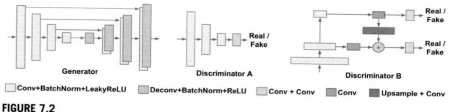

FIGURE 7.2

Detailed network structure of the generator and discriminator.

7.2.2.1 Network structure

The generator is based on an encoder–decoder architecture [40] with skip connections between the encoding and decoding blocks to form a U-Net-like [42] structure. As shown in Fig. 7.2, the generator has four encoding blocks and four decoding blocks. Each encoding block contains a convolutional layer followed by a batch normalization layer and a leaky ReLU layer. Similarly, each decoding block contains a deconvolutional layer followed by a batch normalization layer and an ReLU layer. Both the convolutional and deconvolutional layers have a 4 × 4 kernel with a stride of 2 such that they can downsample and upsample the outputs, respectively. Outputs from the encoding blocks are shuttled to the corresponding decoding blocks using skip connections without passing through the middle "bottleneck" layers. This design allows the low-level context information from the encoding blocks to be used directly together with the decoded high-level information during generation. We find the adversarial training with this design converges faster than a typical DCGAN.

A typical discriminator (Fig. 7.2 Discriminator A) usually contains a set of encoding blocks followed by a classification block to determine the input's realness. In this case, the discrimination is performed at a fixed-granularity which is fine when the task is a generative task such as style transfer or image translation, or there is a systematic error to be fixed such as JPEG decompression or superresolution. For sparse-view CBCT images, the artifacts appear randomly with different scales. To capture such a variation of artifacts, we propose a discriminator that handles the adversarial training at different granularities.

The core idea is to create a feature pyramid and perform discrimination at multiple scales. As illustrated in Fig. 7.2 Discriminator B, the network uses two classification blocks to make decision based on different levels of semantic feature maps. Here, we adapt the design from FPN [30] so that the feature pyramid has strong semantics at all scales. Specifically, we first use three encoding blocks to extract features at different levels. Next, we use an upsample block to incorporate stronger semantic features from the top layer into the outputs of the middle layer. The upsample block consists of a bilinear unsampling layer and a 3 × 3 convolutional layer (to smooth the outputs). Because the feature maps from encoding blocks have different channel sizes, we place a lateral block (essentially a 1 × 1 convolutional layer) after each encoding block to match this channel difference. In the end, there are two classification blocks to make joint decisions on the semantics at different scales.

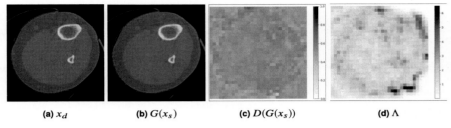

(a) x_d **(b)** $G(x_s)$ **(c)** $D(G(x_s))$ **(d)** Λ

FIGURE 7.3

Saturated (c) score map $D(G(x_s))$ and (d) focus map Λ computed between (a) dense-view CBCT image x_d and (b) generated CBCT image $G(x_s)$.

Each classification block contains a 3×3 convolutional layer followed by a 1×1 convolutional layer. Let $D_1(x)$ and $D_2(x)$ denote the outputs from the two classification blocks, then adversarial loss with FPN as the discriminator can be given by $\min_D \mathcal{L}_A(D; G, \Lambda_1, \Lambda_2) = \sum_{i=1}^{2} \mathcal{L}_A(D_i; G, \Lambda_i)$ and $\min_G \mathcal{L}_A(G; D, \Lambda_1, \Lambda_2) = \sum_{i=1}^{2} \mathcal{L}_A(G; D_i, \Lambda_i)$. We have also experimented with deeper discriminators with more classification blocks for richer feature semantics, but found that they contribute only minor improvements over the current setting.

7.2.2.2 Focus map

When an image from the generator looks mostly "real" (Fig. 7.3(b)), the score map (Fig. 7.3(c)) output by the discriminator will be overwhelmed by borderline scores (those values close to 0.5). This saturates the adversarial training as borderline scores make little contribution to the weight update of the discriminator. To address this problem, we propose to introduce a modulation factor to the adversarial loss such that the borderline scores are down-weighted during training. Observing that when a generated region is visually close to the corresponding region of a dense-view image (Fig. 7.3(a)), it is more likely to be "real" and causes the discriminator to give a borderline score, we therefore use a feature difference map (Fig. 7.3(d)) to perform this modulation.

Let $\phi_{m,n}^{(j)}(\cdot)$ denote the (m, n)th feature vector of $\phi^{(j)}(\cdot)$, then the (m, n)th element of the feature difference map Λ between x_d and $G(x_s)$ is defined as

$$\lambda_{m,n} = \frac{1}{Z_j} \|\phi_{m,n}^{(j)}(x_d) - \phi_{m,n}^{(j)}(G(x_s))\|, \tag{7.10}$$

where Z_j is a normalization term given by

$$Z_j = \frac{1}{N_j} \sum_{m,n} \|\phi_{m,n}^{(j)}(x_d) - \phi_{m,n}^{(j)}(G(x_s))\|. \tag{7.11}$$

We use the same perceptual network ϕ as that used for computing the perceptual loss and j is chosen to match the resolution of $D_1(x)$ and $D_2(x)$. For the VGG16-net, we use $j = 16$ for Λ_1 and $j = 9$ for Λ_2.

7.2.3 Experiments

7.2.3.1 Dataset and models

Datasets. The CBCT images used in this study is obtained by a multisource CBCT scanner dedicated for lower extremities. In total, knee images from 27 subjects are under investigation. Each subject is associated with a sparse-view image and a dense-view image that are reconstructed using 67 and 200 projection views, respectively. Each image is processed slice by slice along the sagittal direction where the streak artifacts are most pronounced. During the training, patches of 256×256 are randomly cropped from the slices and used as the inputs to the models.

Models. Three variants of the proposed methods as well as two other baseline methods are compared:

(i) Baseline-MSE: a similar approach to [50] by combining MSE loss with GAN. 3D UNet (which is identical to the 2D UNet used in this work with all the 2D convolutional and deconvolutional layers replaced by their 3D counterparts) and LSGAN are used for fair comparison;

(ii) Baseline-Perceptual: a similar approach to [56] by combining perceptual loss with GAN. It is also based on our UNet and LSGAN infrastructure for fair comparison;

(iii) Ours-FPN: our method using FPN as the discriminator and setting $\Lambda_1 = \Lambda_2 = 1$;

(iv) Ours-Focus: our method using focus map and conventional discriminator (Fig. 7.2 Discriminator A);

(v) Ours-Focus+FPN: our method using focus map as well as the FPN discriminator.

We train all the models using Adam optimization with the learning rate $lr = 10^{-4}$ and $\beta_1 = 0.5$. We use $\lambda_a = 1.0$, $\lambda_m = 100$, and $\lambda_p = 10$ to control the weights between the adversarial loss, the MSE loss and perceptual loss. The values are chosen empirically and are the same for all models (if applicable). All the models are trained for 50 epochs with 5-fold cross-validation.

7.2.3.2 Results

Fig. 7.4 shows the qualitative results of the models. Though the baseline methods overall have some improvements over the sparse-view image, they still cannot handle the streak artifacts very well. "Baseline-Perceptual" produces less pronounced artifacts than "Baseline-MSE," which demonstrates that using perceptual loss and processing the images slice by slice in 2D give better results than MSE loss with 3D generator. Our models (Fig. 7.4(e)–(f)) in general produce less artifacts than the

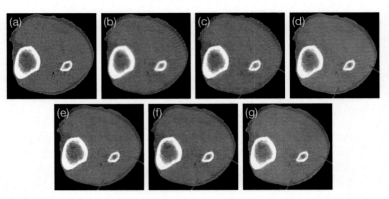

FIGURE 7.4

Qualitative sparse-view CBCT artifact reduction results by different models. The same brightness and contrast enhancement are applied to the images for better but uniform visualization: (a) x_d, (b) x_s, (c) Baseline-MSE, (d) Baseline-Perceptual, (e) Ours-Focus, (f) Ours-FPN, (g) Ours-Focus+FPN.

baseline models. We can barely see the streak artifacts from their outputs. Visually, they produce similar outputs and the result from "Ours-Focus+FPN" is slightly better than "Ours-FPN" and "Ours-Focus." This means that using FPN as the discriminator or applying a modulation factor to the adversarial loss can indeed induce the training to artifacts reduction.

We further investigate the image characteristics of each model in a region of interest (ROI). A good model should have similar image characteristics to the dense-view images in ROIs. When looking at the pixel-wise difference between the dense-view ROI and the model ROI, no structure information should be observed resulting a random noise map. Fig. 7.5(a) shows the ROI differences of the models. We can see a clear bone structure from the ROI difference map between x_s and x_d (Fig. 7.5(a) third row) which demonstrates a significant difference in image characteristics between these two images. For "Baseline-MSE," the bone structure is less recognizable, showing more similar image characteristics. For "Baseline-Perceptual" and our models, we can hardly see the structural information and mostly observe random noises. This indicates that these models have very similar image characteristics to a dense-view image. We also measure the mean and standard deviation of the pixel values within the ROI. We can see that our models have very close statistics with x_d. Especially, the pixel value statistics of "Ours-Focus" and "Ours-Focus+FPN" are almost identical to x_d, demonstrating better image characteristics.

We then evaluate the models quantitatively by comparing their outputs with the corresponding dense-view CBCT image. Three evaluation metrics are used: structural similarity (SSIM), peak signal-to-noise ratio (PSNR), and root mean square error (RMSE). Higher values for SSIM and PSNR and lower values for RMSE indicate better performance. We can see from Table 7.1 that the baseline methods give bet-

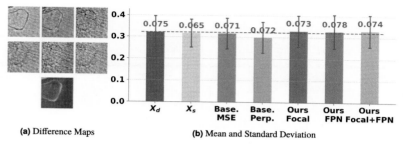

(a) Difference Maps   (b) Mean and Standard Deviation

FIGURE 7.5

ROI characteristics. (a) Patches are obtained by subtracting the corresponding ROI from x_d (third row). First row from left to right: x_s, Baseline-MSE, Baseline-Perceptual. Second row from left to right: Ours-Focus, Ours-FPN, Ours-Focus+FPN. (b) Each bar indicates the mean value of the ROI. The numbers on the top of each bar indicate the standard deviations. The vertical lines indicates the changes of the mean value when ± standard deviations is applied. Pixel values are normalized to [0, 1].

Table 7.1 Quantitative sparse-view CBCT artifact reduction results of different models.

	x_s	Baseline		Ours		
		MSE	Perc.	Focus	FPN	FPN+Focus
SSIM	0.839	0.849	0.858	0.879	0.871	0.884
PSNR(dB)	34.07	34.24	35.39	36.26	36.38	36.14
RMSE(10^{-2})	1.98	1.96	1.70	1.54	1.52	1.56

ter scores than x_s. Similar to the case in qualitative evaluation, "Baseline-Perceptual" performs better than "Baseline-MSE." Our methods consistently outperform the baseline methods by a significant margin. "Ours-FPN" gives best performance in PSNR and RMSE. However, PSNR and RMSE only measure the pixel level difference between two images. To measure the performance in perceived similarity, SSIM is usually a better choice, and we find "Ours-FPN+Focus" has a slightly better performance on this metric. This confirms our observation in qualitative evaluation.

7.2.4 Discussion

We have presented a novel approach to reducing the artifacts from sparsely reconstructed CBCT images. To the best of our knowledge, this is the first work that addresses the artifacts introduced by sparse-view CBCT reconstruction in a postprocessing step. We target this problem using an image-to-image generative model with a perceptual loss as regulation. The model generates perceptually realistic outputs while making the artifacts less pronounced. To further suppress the streak artifacts, we have also proposed a novel FPN based discriminator and a focus map to induce the adversarial training. Experimental results show that the proposed mechanism ad-

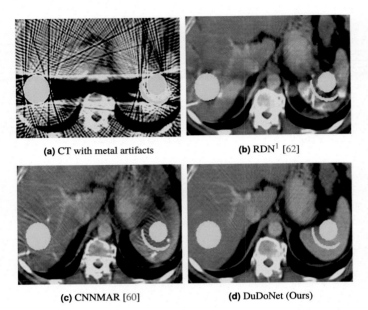

(a) CT with metal artifacts   (b) RDN[1] [62]

(c) CNNMAR [60]   (d) DuDoNet (Ours)

FIGURE 7.6

(a) Sample MAR results for a CT image with intense metal artifact. Metal implants are colored in yellow. (b) Artifacts are not fully reduced and a "white band" is present between the two implants. (c) Organ boundaries on the right are smeared out. (d) DuDoNet effectively reduces metal shadows and recovers fine details.

dresses the streak artifacts much better and the proposed models outperform strong baseline methods both qualitatively and quantitatively.

7.3 Case study: metal artifact reduction

Computed tomography (CT) images reconstructed from X-ray projections allow effective medical diagnosis and treatment. However, due to increasingly common metallic implants, CT images are often adversely affected by metal artifacts which not only exhibit undesirable visual effects but also increase the possibility of false diagnosis. This creates the problem of metal artifact reduction (MAR), for which existing solutions are inadequate.

Unlike typical image restoration tasks such as superresolution [25,62,49,65], compression artifact removal [59,13], and denoising [7,32,27], metal artifacts are often *structured and nonlocal* (e.g., streaking and shadowing artifacts as in Fig. 7.6(a)). Modeling such artifacts in the image domain is extremely difficult. Therefore, before the emergence of deep learning, most existing works [23,8,35,34] proposed to reduce metal artifact in the X-ray projection (sinogram) domain. The metal-corrupted

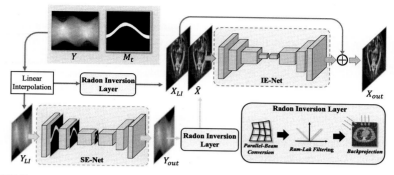

FIGURE 7.7

The proposed Dual Domain Network (DuDoNet) for MAR. Given a degraded sinogram Y and a metal trace mask $\mathcal{M}_t$, DuDoNet reduces metal artifacts by simultaneously refining in the sinogram and image domains.

regions are viewed as missing, and replaced by interpolated values. However, as the projections are taken from a single object under certain geometry, physical constraints should be satisfied by the enhanced sinogram. Otherwise, severe *secondary artifacts* can be introduced in the reconstructed CT images.

Recently, motivated by the success of deep learning in solving ill-posed inverse problems [62,49,27,37,58,45], several works have been proposed to overcome the difficulties in MAR. Wang et al. [47] applied the pix2pix model [18] to reduce metal artifact in the CT image domain. Zhang et al. [60] proposed to first estimate a prior image by a convolutional neural network (CNN). Based on the prior image, metal-corrupted regions in the sinogram are filled with surrogate data through several post-processing steps for reduced secondary artifact. Park et al. [38] applied U-Net [42] to directly restore metal-corrupted sinograms. Although metal artifacts can be reduced by these deep learning approaches, we will show that, despite the strong expressive power of deep neural networks, either image domain enhancement or sinogram domain enhancement is limited in being able to restore metal shadows and secondary artifact.

We hereby propose Dual Domain Network (DuDoNet) to address these problems by *learning two CNNs on dual domains to restore sinograms and CT images simultaneously*. Our intuition is that image domain enhancement can be improved by fusing information from the sinogram domain, and inconsistent sinograms can be corrected by the learning signal backpropagated from the image domain to reduce secondary artifacts. Specifically, we propose a novel network (Fig. 7.7) consisting of three parts: *a sinogram enhancement network (SE-Net), a Radon inversion layer (RIL), and an image enhancement network (IE-Net)*. To address the issue that in the sinogram domain, information about small metal implants tends to vanish in higher layers of the network due to downsampling, we propose a mask pyramid U-Net architecture for SE-Net, which retains metal mask information across multiple scales. The key to our dual-domain learning is RIL that reconstructs CT images using the filtered back-projection (FBP) algorithm and efficiently backpropagates gradients from the image domain to the sinogram domain. Based on RIL, we introduce a Radon consistency loss to penalize secondary artifacts in the image domain. Finally, IE-Net refines CT images via residual learning. Extensive experiments on CT images from hundreds of patients demonstrate that dual-domain enhancement generates superior artifact-reduced CT images.

In summary, we make the following contributions:

- We propose an end-to-end trainable dual-domain refinement network for MAR. The network is able to recover details corrupted by metal artifacts.
- We propose a mask pyramid (MP) U-Net to improve sinogram refinement. The MP architecture improves performance especially when small metallic implants are dominated by the nonmetal regions.
- We propose a Radon inversion layer (RIL) to enable efficient end-to-end dual-domain learning. RIL can benefit the community through its ubiquitous use in various reconstruction algorithms [51,20,1,63].
- We propose a Radon consistency (RC) loss to penalize secondary artifacts in the image domain. Gradients of the loss in the image domain are back-propagated through RIL to the sinogram domain for improved consistency.

7.3.1 Background

Tissues inside the human body such as bones and muscles have different X-ray attenuation coefficients μ. If we consider a 2D slice of human body, the distribution of the attenuation coefficients $X = \mu(x, y)$ represents the underlying anatomical structure. The principle of CT imaging is based on the fundamental Fourier Slice Theorem, which guarantees that the 2D function X can be reconstructed solely from its dense 1D projections. In CT imaging, projections of the anatomical structure X are inferred by the emitted and received X-ray intensities through the Lambert–Beer Law [3]. We consider the following CT model under a polychromatic X-ray source with energy distribution $\eta(E)$:

$$Y = -\log \int \eta(E) \exp\{-\mathcal{P}X(E)\}\, dE, \qquad (7.12)$$

where $\mathcal{P}$ is the projection generation process, and Y represents the projection data (sinogram). The 2D $X(E)$ is the anatomical structure (CT image) we want to recover from the measured projection data Y.

For normal body tissues, $X(E)$ is almost constant with respect to the X-ray energy E. If we let $X = X(E)$, then

$$Y = \mathcal{P}X. \qquad (7.13)$$

Therefore, given measured projection data Y, the CT image $\hat{X}$ can be inferred by using a reconstruction algorithm $\hat{X} = \mathcal{P}^{\dagger}Y$ [22] where $\mathcal{P}^{\dagger}$ denotes the linear operation for reconstruction.

However, when metallic implants $I_M(E)$ are present, $X(E) = X + I_M(E)$, where $X(E)$ has large variations with respect to E due to I_M. Eq. (7.12) becomes

$$Y = \mathcal{P}X - \log \int \eta(E) \exp\{-\mathcal{P}I_M(E)\} dE, \qquad (7.14)$$

where the region of $\mathcal{P}I_M$ in Y will be referred to as *metal trace* in the rest of the paper. When the reconstruction algorithm $\mathcal{P}^\dagger$ is applied,

$$\mathcal{P}^\dagger Y = \hat{X} - \mathcal{P}^\dagger \log \int \eta(E) \exp\{-\mathcal{P}I_M(E)\} dE. \qquad (7.15)$$

The term after $\hat{X}$ in (7.15) is the metal artifact. It is clear that perfect MAR can be achieved only if the last term in Eq. (7.15) is suppressed while the term $\hat{X}$ is unaffected. However, it is generally an ill-posed problem since both terms contribute to the region of metal trace.

7.3.1.1 Inpainting-based methods

One commonly adopted strategy in MAR is to formulate sinogram completion as an image inpainting task. Data within the metal trace are viewed as missing and filled through interpolation. Linear interpolation (LI) [23] is a widely used method in MAR due to its simplicity. Meyer et al. [35] proposed the NMAR algorithm, where sinograms are normalized by tissue priors before performing LI. NMAR requires proper tissue segmentation in the image domain, which is unreliable when severe metal artifacts are present. Mehranian et al. [34] restored sinograms by enforcing sparsity constraints in the wavelet domain. In general, inpainting-based approaches fail to replace the data of $\mathcal{P}X$ in (7.14) within metal trace by consistent values. *It is this introduced inconsistency in sinogram data that leads to noticeable secondary artifacts after reconstruction.*

7.3.1.2 MAR by iterative reconstruction

In iterative reconstruction, MAR can be formulated as the following optimization problem:

$$\hat{X} = \min_X \|(1 - \mathcal{M}_t) \odot (\mathcal{P}X - Y)\|^2 + \lambda R(X), \qquad (7.16)$$

where $\mathcal{M}_t$ is the metal trace mask; $\mathcal{M}_t = 1$ on the metal trace and $\mathcal{M}_t = 0$ otherwise; R is some regularization function, e.g., total variation (TV) [14] and sparsity constraints in the wavelet domain [57]. Eq. (7.16) is often solved through iterative approaches such as the split Bregman algorithm. Iterative reconstruction usually suffers from long processing time as they require multiplying and inverting huge matrices in each iteration. More importantly, hand-crafted regularization $R(X)$ does not capture the structure of metal artifacts and would result in an over-smoothed reconstruction. Recently, Zhang et al. [57] proposed a reweighted JSR method which combines NMAR into (7.16) and jointly solves for X and interpolated sinogram. Similar to NMAR, the weighting strategy in reweighted JSR requires tissue segmentation. In a phantom study, better performance against NMAR is achieved by reweighted JSR. However, the improvements remain limited for nonphantom CT images.

7.3.2 Methodology

As shown in Fig. 7.7, our proposed model consists of three parts: (a) a sinogram enhancement network (SE-Net), (b) a Radon inversion layer (RIL), and (c) an image enhancement network (IE-Net). Inputs to the model include a degraded sinogram $Y \in \mathbb{R}^{H_s \times W_s}$ and the corresponding metal trace mask $\mathcal{M}_t \in \{0, 1\}^{H_s \times W_s}$. Notice that we use H_s to represent the detector size and W_s to represent the number of projection views. The region where $\mathcal{M}_t = 1$ is the metal trace. Given the inputs, we first apply LI [23] to generate an initial estimate for the sinogram data within metal trace. The resulting interpolated sinogram is denoted by Y_{LI}. SE-Net then restores Y_{LI} within the metal trace through a mask pyramid U-Net architecture. To maintain sinogram consistency, we introduce a Radon consistency (RC) loss. A sinogram will be penalized by the RC loss if it leads to secondary artifacts in the image domain after passing through RIL. Finally, the reconstructed CT image $\hat{X} \in \mathbb{R}^{H_c \times W_c}$ is refined by IE-Net via residual learning.

7.3.2.1 Sinogram enhancement network

Sinogram enhancement is extremely challenging since geometric consistency should be retained to prevent secondary artifact in the reconstructed CT image, so prior works only replace data within the metal trace. Similarly, given a metal-corrupted sinogram Y and metal trace mask $\mathcal{M}_t$, SE-Net $\mathcal{G}_s$ learns to restore the region of Y_{LI} in $\mathcal{M}_t = 1$. In sinogram domain enhancement, when the metal size is small, or equivalently, the metal trace is small, information about metal trace is dominated by nonmetal regions in higher layers of network due to downsampling. To retain the mask information, we propose to fuse $\mathcal{M}_t$ through a mask pyramid U-Net architecture. The output of SE-Net is written as

$$Y_{out} = \mathcal{M}_t \odot \mathcal{G}_s(Y_{LI}, \mathcal{M}_t) + (1 - \mathcal{M}_t) \odot Y_{LI}. \qquad (7.17)$$

We use an L_1 loss to train SE-Net,

$$\mathcal{L}_{\mathcal{G}_s} = \|Y_{out} - Y_{gt}\|_1, \qquad (7.18)$$

where Y_{gt} is the ground-truth sinogram without metal artifact.

7.3.2.2 Radon inversion layer

Although sinogram inconsistency is reduced by SE-Net, there is no existing mechanism to penalize secondary artifacts in the image domain. The missing key element is an efficient and *differentiable* reconstruction layer. Therefore, we propose a novel RIL f_R to reconstruct CT images from sinograms and at the same time allow backpropagation of gradients. We highlight that trivially inverting $\mathcal{P}$ in existing deep learning frameworks would require a time and space complexity of $\mathcal{O}(H_s W_s H_c W_c)$, which is prohibitive due to limited GPU memory.

In this work, we consider the projection process $\mathcal{P}$ as the Radon transform under fan-beam geometry with arc detectors [22]. The distance between an X-ray source and its rotation center is D. The resulting fan-beam sinograms Y_{fan} are represented in coordinates (γ, β). To reconstruct CT images from $Y_{fan}(\gamma, \beta)$, we adopt the fan-beam filtered backprojection (FBP) algorithm as the forward operation of RIL.

Our RIL consists of three modules: (a) a parallel-beam conversion module, (b) a filtering module, and (c) a backprojection module. The parallel-beam conversion module transforms $Y_{fan}(\gamma, \beta)$ to its parallel-beam counterpart $Y_{para}(t, \theta)$ through a change of variables. The FBP algorithm in coordinates (t, θ) becomes more effective and memory-efficient than in (γ, β). Parallel-beam FBP is then realized by the subsequent filtering and backprojection modules.

Parallel-beam conversion module. We utilize the property that a fan beam sinogram $Y_{fan}(\gamma, \beta)$ can be converted to its parallel beam counterpart $Y_{para}(t, \theta)$ through the following change of variables [22]:

$$\begin{cases} t = D \sin\gamma, \\ \theta = \beta + \gamma. \end{cases} \tag{7.19}$$

The change of variable in (7.19) is implemented by grid sampling in (t, θ), which allows backpropagation of gradients. With Y_{para}, CT images can be reconstructed through the following Ram-Lak filtering and backprojection modules.

Ram-Lak filtering module. We apply the Ram-Lak filtering to Y_{para} in the Fourier domain,

$$Q(t, \theta) = \mathcal{F}_t^{-1} \left\{ |\omega| \cdot \mathcal{F}_t \left\{ Y_{para}(t, \theta) \right\} \right\}, \tag{7.20}$$

where $\mathcal{F}_t$ and $\mathcal{F}_t^{-1}$ are the Discrete Fourier Transform (DFT) and inverse Discrete Fourier Transform (iDFT) with respect to the detector dimension.

Backprojection module. The filtered parallel-beam sinogram Q is backprojected to the image domain for every projection angle θ by the following formula:

$$X(u, v) = \int_0^\pi Q(u \cos\theta + v \sin\theta, \theta) d\theta. \tag{7.21}$$

It is clear from (7.21) that the computation is highly parallel. We make a remark here regarding the property of RIL f_R. Due to the backprojection nature of f_R, the derivative with respect to the input Y_{out} is actually the projection operation $\mathcal{P}$. That is, any loss in the image domain will be aggregated and projected to the sinogram domain. This desirable property enables joint learning in sinogram and image domains.

Radon consistency loss. With the differentiable RIL, we introduce the following Radon consistency (RC) loss to penalize secondary artifacts in $\hat{X} = f_R(Y_{out})$ after reconstruction:

$$\mathcal{L}_{RC} = \| f_R(Y_{out}) - X_{gt} \|_1, \tag{7.22}$$

where X_{gt} is the ground truth CT image without metal artifact.

Difference from DL-based reconstruction.   Our RIL is designed to combine the image formation process (CT reconstruction) with deep neural networks and achieve improved MAR by dual-domain consistency learning. Methods in [51,20,1,63] target *image formation via deep learning*, which is not the main focus of this work.

7.3.2.3 Image enhancement network

Since our ultimate goal is to reduce visually undesirable artifacts in image domain, we further apply a U-Net $\mathcal{G}_i$ to enhance $\hat{X}$ by residual learning,

$$X_{out} = X_{LI} + \mathcal{G}_i(\hat{X}, X_{LI}), \tag{7.23}$$

where $X_{LI} = f_R(Y_{LI})$ is reconstructed from Y_{LI}, the linearly interpolated sinogram; $\mathcal{G}_i$ is also optimized by L_1 loss,

$$\mathcal{L}_{\mathcal{G}_i} = \|X_{out} - X_{gt}\|_1. \tag{7.24}$$

The full objective function of our model is

$$\mathcal{L} = \mathcal{L}_{\mathcal{G}_s} + \mathcal{L}_{RC} + \mathcal{L}_{\mathcal{G}_i}. \tag{7.25}$$

One could tune and balance each term in (7.25) for better performance. However, we found that the default setting works sufficiently well.

7.3.3 Experiments

Following the de facto practice in the literature [60], our evaluations consider simulated metal artifacts on real patient CTs. Various effects are considered including polychromatic X-ray, partial volume effect, and Poisson noise. The simulated artifacts exhibit complicated structures and cannot be easily modeled by a very deep CNN. All the compared approaches are evaluated on the same dataset, and superior performance is achieved by our method.

Metal artifact dataset.   Recently, Yan et al. [54] released a large-scale CT dataset DeepLesion for lesion detection. Due to its high diversity and quality, we use a subset of images from DeepLesion to synthesize metal artifact; 4000 images from 320 patients are used in the training set and 200 images from 12 patients are used in the test set. All images are resized to 416×416. We collect a total of 100 metal shapes; 90 metal shapes are paired with the 4000 images, yielding 360,000 combinations in the training set; 10 metal shapes are paired with the 200 images, yielding 2000 combinations in the test set. In the training set, the sizes of the metal implants range from 16 to 4967 pixels. In the test set, the sizes of the metal implants range from 32 to 2054 pixels.

We adopt similar procedures as in [60] to synthesize metal-corrupted sinograms and CT images. We assume a polychromatic X-ray source with spectrum $\eta(E)$ in Fig. 7.8. To simulate Poisson noise in the sinogram, we assume the incident X-ray has 2×10^7 photons. Metal partial volume effect is also considered. The distance from

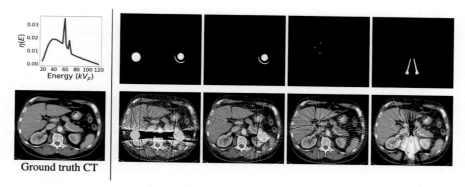

FIGURE 7.8

Sample simulated metal artifact on patient CT. The X-ray spectrum is shown in the upper-left corner. Metallic implants are colored in yellow for better visualization.

the X-ray source to the rotation center is set to 39.7 cm, and 320 projection views are uniformly spaced between 0 and 360 degrees. The resulting sinograms have size 321×320. Fig. 7.8 shows some sample images with simulated metal artifacts.

Evaluation metrics.   We choose peak signal-to-noise ratio (PSNR) and structured similarity index (SSIM) for quantitative evaluations. In DeepLesion, each CT image is provided with a dynamic range, within which the tissues are clearly discernible. We use the dynamic range as the peak signal strength when calculating PSNR.

Implementation details.   We implement our model using the PyTorch [39] framework. All the sinograms have size 321×320, and all the CT images have size 416×416. To train the model, we use the Adam [24] optimizer with $(\beta_1, \beta_2) = (0.5, 0.999)$, and a batch size of 8. The learning rate starts from 2×10^{-4}, and is halved for every 30 epochs. The model is trained on two Nvidia 1080Ti for 380 epochs.

7.3.3.1 Ablation study

In this section, we evaluate the effectiveness of different components in the proposed approach. Performance is evaluated on the artifact-reduced CT images. When evaluating SE-Nets without image domain refinement, we use the reconstructed CT images $\hat{X}$. We experiment on the following configurations:

A) SE-Net$_0$: The sinogram enhancement network without mask pyramid network.
B) SE-Net: The full sinogram enhancement module.
C) IE-Net: Image enhancement module. IE-Net is applied to enhance X_{LI} without $\hat{X}$.
D) SE-Net$_0$+IE-Net: Dual domain learning with SE-Net$_0$ and IE-Net.
E) SE-Net+IE-Net: Dual domain learning with SE-Net and IE-Net.

Table 7.2 Quantitative evaluations for different components in DuDoNet.

PSNR(dB)/SSIM	Large Metal ——————————————→ Small Metal					Average
A) SE-Net$_0$	22.88/0.7850	24.52/0.8159	27.38/0.8438	28.61/0.8549	28.93/0.8581	26.46/0.8315
B) SE-Net	23.06/0.7868	24.71/0.8178	27.66/0.8463	28.91/0.8575	29.19/0.8604	26.71/0.8337
C) IE-Net	27.54/0.8840	29.49/0.9153	31.96/0.9368	34.38/0.9498	33.90/0.9489	31.45/0.9269
D) SE-Net$_0$+IE-Net	28.46/0.8938	30.67/0.9232	33.71/0.9458	36.17/0.9576	35.74/0.9571	32.95/0.9355
E) SE-Net+IE-Net	28.28/0.8921	30.49/0.9221	33.76/0.9456	36.26/0.9576	36.01/0.9574	32.96/0.9350
F) SE-Net$_0$+IE-Net+RCL	28.97/0.8970	31.14/0.9254	34.21/0.9476	36.58/0.9590	36.15/0.9586	33.41/0.9375
G) SE-Net+IE-Net+RCL	29.02/0.8972	31.12/0.9256	34.32/0.9481	36.72/0.9595	36.36/0.9592	33.51/0.9379

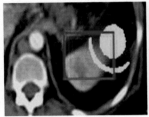 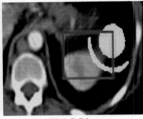 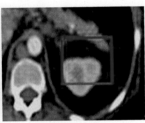

Without RC loss   With RC loss   Ground Truth

FIGURE 7.9

Visual comparisons between models without RC loss (E in Table 7.2) and our full model (G in Table 7.2).

F) SE-Net$_0$+IE-Net+RCL: Dual domain learning with Radon consistency loss.
G) SE-Net+IE-Net+RCL: Our full network.

Notice that the configurations including SE-Net$_0$, SE-Net, and IE-Net are single domain enhancement approaches.

Table 7.2 summarizes the performance of different models. Since there are totally 10 metal implants in the test set, for conciseness, we group the results according to the size of metal implants. The sizes of the 10 metal implants are: [2054, 879, 878, 448, 242, 115, 115, 111, 53, 32] in pixels. We simply put every two masks into one group.

From E and G, it is clear that the use of the RC loss improves the performance over all metal sizes for at least 0.3 dB. In Fig. 7.9, the model trained with RC loss better recovers the shape of the organ.

From F and G, we observe an interesting trend that the proposed mask pyramid architecture results in ~0.2 dB gain when the metal size is small, and the performance is nearly identical when the metal is large. The reason is that the mask pyramid retains metal information across multiple scales. Fig. 7.10 demonstrates that in the proximity of small metal implants, the model with mask pyramid recovers the fine details.

Effect of dual domain learning.   In the proposed framework, IE-Net enhances X_{LI} by fusing information from SE-Net. We study the effect of dual-domain learning by visually comparing our full pipeline (G in Table 7.2) with single domain enhance-

Without MP   With MP   Ground Truth

FIGURE 7.10

Visual comparisons between models without MP (F in Table 7.2) and our full model (G in Table 7.2).

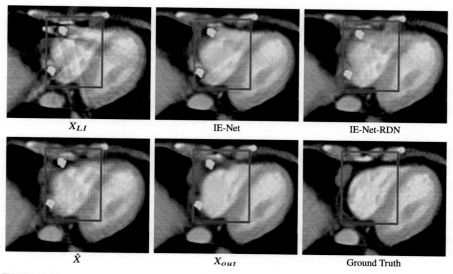

X_{LI} IE-Net   IE-Net-RDN

$\hat{X}$ X_{out} Ground Truth

FIGURE 7.11

Visual comparisons between models without SE-Net (top row IE-Net and IE-Net-RDN) and our full model (bottom row $\hat{X}$ and X_{out}).

ment IE-Net (C in Table 7.2). In addition to the U-Net architecture, we also consider IE-Net with RDN architecture, which is denoted as IE-Net-RDN. Visual comparisons are shown in Fig. 7.11. We observe that single domain models IE-Net and IE-Net-RDN fail to recover corrupted organ boundaries in X_{LI}. In our dual-domain refinement network, SE-Net first recovers inconsistent sinograms and reduces secondary artifacts as in $\hat{X}$. IE-Net then refines $\hat{X}$ to recover the fine details.

Effect of LI sinogram.   The inputs to our network are the linear interpolated sinogram Y_{LI} and its reconstructed CT X_{LI}. One possible alternative is to directly input

Table 7.3 Quantitative evaluation of MAR approaches in terms of PSNR and SSIM.

PSNR(dB)/SSIM	Large Metal ────────────────────→ Small Metal					Average
LI	20.20/0.8236	22.35/0.8686	26.76/0.9098	28.50/0.9252	29.53/0.9312	25.47/0.8917
NMAR	21.95/0.8333	24.43/0.8813	28.63/0.9174	30.84/0.9281	31.69/0.9402	27.51/0.9001
cGAN-CT	26.71/0.8265	24.71/0.8507	29.80/0.8911	31.47/0.9104	27.65/0.8876	28.07/0.8733
RDN-CT	28.61/0.8668	28.78/0.9027	32.40/0.9264	34.95/0.9446	34.00/0.9376	31.74/0.9156
CNNMAR	23.82/0.8690	26.78/0.9097	30.92/0.9394	32.97/0.9513	33.11/0.9520	29.52/0.9243
DuDoNet (Ours)	**29.02/0.8972**	**31.12/0.9256**	**34.32/0.9481**	**36.72/0.9595**	**36.36/0.9592**	**33.51/0.9379**

the metal corrupted sinogram and CT, and let the network learn to restore the intense artifacts. However, we experimentally found out this alternative approach does not perform well. Metal shadows and streaking artifacts are not fully suppressed.

7.3.3.2 Comparison with state-of-the-art methods

In this section, we compare our model with the following methods: LI [23], NMAR [35], cGAN-CT [47], RDN-CT [62], and CNNMAR [60]. We use cGAN-CT to refer the approach by Wang et al. [47] which applies cGAN for image domain MAR. RDN [62] was originally proposed for image superresolution (SR). The fundamental building unit of RDN is the residual dense block (RDB). Recently, it has been shown that by stacking multiple RDBs or its variant, the residual in residual dense blocks (RRDBs) [49], local details in natural images can be effectively recovered. We build a very deep architecture with 10 RDBs (~80 conv layers) for direct image domain enhancement, which is denoted by RDN-CT. Specifically, we select $D = 10$, $C = 8$, $G = 64$, following the notations in [62]. Inputs to RDN-CT are 128×128 patches.

Quantitative comparisons. Table 7.3 shows quantitative comparisons. We observe that the state-of-the-art sinogram inpainting approach CNNMAR achieves higher SSIM than image enhancement approaches (e.g., RDN and cGAN-CT) especially when the size of metal is small. The reason is that sinogram inpainting only modifies data within the metal trace and recovers the statistics reasonably well. In most of the cases, CNNMAR also outperforms cGAN-CT in terms of PSNR. However, when CNN is sufficiently deep (e.g., RDN-CT), image enhancement approaches generally achieve higher PSNR. Our dual-domain learning approach jointly restores sinograms and CT images, which attains the best performance in terms of both PSNR and SSIM *consistently in all categories*.

Visual comparisons. Fig. 7.12 shows visual comparisons. Fig. 7.12(a) considers metal artifacts resulted from two small metallic implants. From the zoomed figure (with metal artifact), we can perceive severe streaking artifacts and intense metal shadows between the two implants. We observe that sinogram inpainting approaches such as LI, NMAR, and CNNMAR effectively reduce metal shadows. However, fine details are either corrupted by secondary artifacts as in LI or blurred as in NMAR and CNNMAR. Image domain approaches such as cGAN-CT and RDN-CT produce

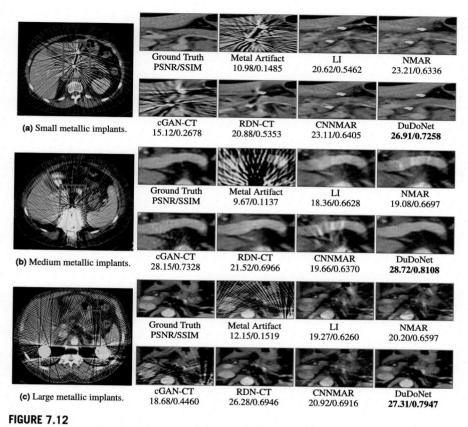

FIGURE 7.12

Visual comparisons on MAR for different types of metallic implants.

sharper CT images but fail to suppress metal shadows. Our method effectively reduces metal shadows and at the same time retains fine details. Fig. 7.12(b) shows a degraded CT image with long metal implants. We observe similar trend that sinogram inpainting approaches do not perform well in regions with intense streaking artifact. In this example, image domain methods reduce most of the artifacts. It is possibly due to that fact that the pattern of the artifact in Fig. 7.12(b) is monotonous compared to Figs. 7.12(a) and 7.12(c). However, noticeable speckle noise is present in the result by cGAN-CT, and RDN-CT does not fully recover details in the middle. Fig. 7.12(c) considers metal artifacts result from two large metallic implants. Likewise, sinogram inpainting methods and direct image domain enhancement have limited capability of suppressing metal artifacts.

Table 7.4 Comparison of running time measured in seconds.

LI [23]	NMAR [35]	cGAN-CT [47]	RDN-CT [62]	CNNMAR [60]	DuDoNet (Ours)
0.0832	0.4180	0.0365	0.5150	0.6043	0.1335

7.3.3.3 Running time comparisons

On an Nvidia 1080Ti GPU, it takes 0.24 ms for RIL to reconstruct a sinogram of size 321×320 to a CT image of size 416×416, and 11.40 ms for backpropagation of gradients. RIL requires 16 MB of memory for forward pass and 25 MB for backpropagation. In Table 7.4 we compare the running time of different MAR approaches. With the running time of LI included, DuDoNet runs almost $4\times$ faster than the very deep architecture RDN while achieving superior performance.

7.3.4 Discussion

We presented the dual-domain network for metal artifact reduction. In particular, we proposed to jointly improve sinogram consistency and refined CT images through a novel Radon inversion layer and a Radon consistency loss, along with a mask pyramid U-Net. Experimental evaluations demonstrate that while state-of-the-art MAR methods suffer from secondary artifacts and very-deep neural networks have limited capability of directly reducing metal artifacts in image domain, our dual-domain model can effectively suppress metal shadows and recover details for CT images. At the same time, our network is computationally more efficient. Future work includes investigating the potential of the dual-domain learning framework for other signal recovery tasks, such as superresolution, noise reduction, and CT reconstruction from sparse X-ray projections.

7.4 Summary

We have introduced how to design supervised deep learning models to address medical image reconstruction problems. We note that medical image reconstruction is the process of transforming the sensor domain data (measured by imaging devices) to the image domain data (that is interpretable by healthcare professionals). Therefore, we show how to develop sensor domain approaches, image domain approaches, and dual-domain approaches to improve the medical image reconstruction performance.

Section 7.1 elaborated the design principles for the three categories of approaches. Specifically, in Section 7.1.1, we showed that deep neural networks can be directly applied to the image domain data in a postprocessing step to reduce the artifacts after reconstruction. Then, in Section 7.2, we provided a case study to demonstrate how to implement an image domain approach for sparse-view artifact reduction.

In Section 7.1.2, we showed how to leverage deep neural networks to correct the sensor domain data so that the compromised imaging information is addressed in an earlier stage. Although many ideas for image domain approaches could be directly applied to the sensor domain, we note that problems present differently in the sensor domain and highlight the designs that are specific to sensor domain approaches.

Finally, in Section 7.1.3, we showed that it is feasible to design deep learning models to address the problems from both the image and sensor domains. More importantly, such a dual-domain approach can be implemented under a unified framework so that the learning from both domains can be achieved in an end-to-end manner. To elaborate this dual-domain learning, we also provided a case study in Section 7.3 where we introduced a novel network called DuDoNet for joint sinogram domain and image domain metal artifact reduction.

References

[1] J. Adler, O. Öktem, Learned primal–dual reconstruction, IEEE Transactions on Medical Imaging 37 (6) (2018) 1322–1332.

[2] Mehmet Akçakaya, Steen Moeller, Sebastian Weingärtner, Kâmil Uğurbil, Scan-specific robust artificial-neural-networks for k-space interpolation (RAKI) reconstruction: database-free deep learning for fast imaging, Magnetic Resonance in Medicine 81 (1) (2019) 439–453.

[3] Beer, Bestimmung der Absorption des rothen Lichts in farbigen Flüssigkeiten, Annalen der Physik und Chemie 162 (5) (1852) 78–88.

[4] Junguo Bian, Jeffrey H. Siewerdsen, Xiao Han, Emil Y. Sidky, Jerry L. Prince, Charles A. Pelizzari, Xiaochuan Pan, Evaluation of sparse-view reconstruction from flat-panel-detector cone-beam CT, Physics in Medicine and Biology 55 (22) (2010) 6575.

[5] Hu Chen, Yi Zhang, Mannudeep K. Kalra, Feng Lin, Yang Chen, Peixi Liao, Jiliu Zhou, Ge Wang, Low-dose CT with a residual encoder-decoder convolutional neural network, IEEE Transactions on Medical Imaging 36 (12) (2017) 2524–2535.

[6] Hu Chen, Yi Zhang, Weihua Zhang, Peixi Liao, Ke Li, Jiliu Zhou, Ge Wang, Low-dose CT denoising with convolutional neural network, in: Biomedical Imaging (ISBI 2017), 2017 IEEE 14th International Symposium on, IEEE, 2017, pp. 143–146.

[7] Kostadin Dabov, Alessandro Foi, Vladimir Katkovnik, Karen Egiazarian, Image denoising by sparse 3-D transform-domain collaborative filtering, IEEE Transactions on Image Processing 16 (8) (2007) 2080–2095.

[8] Xinhui Duan, Li Zhang, Yongshun Xiao, Jianping Cheng, Zhiqiang Chen, Yuxiang Xing, Metal artifact reduction in CT images by sinogram TV inpainting, in: Nuclear Science Symposium Conference Record, 2008. NSS'08. IEEE, IEEE, 2008, pp. 4175–4177.

[9] Taejoon Eo, Yohan Jun, Taeseong Kim, Jinseong Jang, Ho-Joon Lee, Dosik Hwang, KIKI-net: cross-domain convolutional neural networks for reconstructing undersampled magnetic resonance images, Magnetic Resonance in Medicine 80 (5) (2018) 2188–2201.

[10] L. Gjesteby, Q. Yang, Y. Xi, Y. Zhou, J. Zhang, G. Wang, Deep learning methods to guide CT image reconstruction and reduce metal artifacts, in: SPIE Medical Imaging, 2017.

[11] Lars Gjesteby, Qingsong Yang, Yan Xi, Bernhard Claus, Yannan Jin, Bruno De Man, Ge Wang, Reducing metal streak artifacts in CT images via deep learning: pilot results, in: The 14th International Meeting on Fully Three-Dimensional Image Reconstruction in Radiology and Nuclear Medicine, 2017, pp. 611–614.

[12] Ian Goodfellow, Jean Pouget-Abadie, Mehdi Mirza, Bing Xu, David Warde-Farley, Sherjil Ozair, Aaron Courville, Yoshua Bengio, Generative adversarial nets, in: Advances in Neural Information Processing Systems, 2014.

[13] Jun Guo, Hongyang Chao, Building dual-domain representations for compression artifacts reduction, in: European Conference on Computer Vision, Springer, 2016, pp. 628–644.

[14] H. Gupta, K.H. Jin, H.Q. Nguyen, M.T. McCann, M. Unser, Iterative metal artifact reduction for X-ray computed tomography using unmatched projector/backprojector pairs, IEEE Transactions on Medical Imaging 43 (6) (2016) 3019–3033.

[15] Yoseo Han, Leonard Sunwoo, Jong Chul Ye, k-Space deep learning for accelerated MRI, IEEE Transactions on Medical Imaging 39 (2) (2019) 377–386.

[16] Jiang Hsieh, Robert C. Molthen, Christopher A. Dawson, Roger H. Johnson, An iterative approach to the beam hardening correction in cone beam CT, Medical Physics 27 (1) (2000) 23–29.

[17] Dianlin Hu, Jin Liu, Tianling Lv, Qianlong Zhao, Yikun Zhang, Guotao Quan, Juan Feng, Yang Chen, Limin Luo, Hybrid-domain neural network processing for sparse-view CT reconstruction, IEEE Transactions on Radiation and Plasma Medical Sciences 5 (1) (2020) 88–98.

[18] Phillip Isola, Jun-Yan Zhu, Tinghui Zhou, Alexei A. Efros, Image-to-image translation with conditional adversarial networks, in: Proceedings of the IEEE Conference on Computer Vision and Pattern Recognition, 2017, pp. 1125–1134.

[19] Kyong Hwan Jin, Dongwook Lee, Jong Chul Ye, A general framework for compressed sensing and parallel MRI using annihilating filter based low-rank Hankel matrix, IEEE Transactions on Computational Imaging 2 (4) (2016) 480–495.

[20] Kyong Hwan Jin, Michael T. McCann, Emmanuel Froustey, Michael Unser, Deep convolutional neural network for inverse problems in imaging, IEEE Transactions on Image Processing 26 (9) (2017) 4509–4522.

[21] Justin Johnson, Alexandre Alahi, Li Fei-Fei, Perceptual losses for real-time style transfer and super-resolution, in: European Conference on Computer Vision, Springer, 2016, pp. 694–711.

[22] Avinash C. Kak, Malcolm Slaney, Principles of Computerized Tomographic Imaging, Society for Industrial and Applied Mathematics, 2001.

[23] Willi A. Kalender, Robert Hebel, Johannes Ebersberger, Reduction of CT artifacts caused by metallic implants, Radiology 164 (2) (1987) 576–577.

[24] Diederik Kingma, Jimmy Ba, Adam: a method for stochastic optimization, arXiv preprint, arXiv:1412.6980, 2014.

[25] Christian Ledig, Lucas Theis, Ferenc Huszár, Jose Caballero, Andrew Cunningham, Alejandro Acosta, Andrew P. Aitken, Alykhan Tejani, Johannes Totz, Zehan Wang, et al., Photo-realistic single image super-resolution using a generative adversarial network, in: The IEEE Conference on Computer Vision and Pattern Recognition (CVPR), vol. 2, 2017, p. 4.

[26] Juyoung Lee, Yoseob Han, Jae-Kyun Ryu, Jang-Yeon Park, Jong Chul Ye, k-Space deep learning for reference-free EPI ghost correction, Magnetic Resonance in Medicine 82 (6) (2019) 2299–2313.

[27] Jaakko Lehtinen, Jacob Munkberg, Jon Hasselgren, Samuli Laine, Tero Karras, Miika Aittala, Timo Aila, Noise2Noise: learning image restoration without clean data, in: International Conference on Machine Learning (ICML), vol. 80, 2018, pp. 2965–2974.

[28] Yinsheng Li, John Garrett, Guang-Hong Chen, Reduction of beam hardening artifacts in cone-beam CT imaging via SMART-RECON algorithm, in: Medical Imaging 2016: Physics of Medical Imaging, vol. 9783, International Society for Optics and Photonics, 2016, p. 97830W.

[29] Haofu Liao, Zhimin Huo, William J. Sehnert, Shaohua Kevin Zhou, Jiebo Luo, Adversarial sparse-view CBCT artifact reduction, in: Alejandro F. Frangi, Julia A. Schnabel, Christos Davatzikos, Carlos Alberola-López, Gabor Fichtinger (Eds.), Medical Image Computing and Computer Assisted Intervention – MICCAI 2018 – 21st International Conference, Granada, Spain, September 16–20, 2018, Proceedings, Part I, in: Lecture Notes in Computer Science, vol. 11070, Springer, 2018, pp. 154–162.

[30] Tsung-Yi Lin, Piotr Dollár, Ross Girshick, Kaiming He, Bharath Hariharan, Serge Belongie, Feature pyramid networks for object detection, in: Proceedings of the IEEE Conference on Computer Vision and Pattern Recognition, 2017, pp. 2117–2125.

[31] Wei-An Lin, Haofu Liao, Cheng Peng, Xiaohang Sun, Jingdan Zhang, Jiebo Luo, Rama Chellappa, Shaohua Kevin Zhou, DuDoNet: dual domain network for CT metal artifact reduction, in: IEEE Conference on Computer Vision and Pattern Recognition, CVPR 2019, Long Beach, CA, USA, June 16–20, 2019, Computer Vision Foundation / IEEE, 2019, pp. 10512–10521.

[32] Markku Makitalo, Alessandro Foi, Optimal inversion of the Anscombe transformation in low-count Poisson image denoising, IEEE Transactions on Image Processing 20 (1) (2011) 99–109.

[33] Xudong Mao, Qing Li, Haoran Xie, Raymond Y.K. Lau, Zhen Wang, Stephen Paul Smolley, Least squares generative adversarial networks, in: Proceedings of the IEEE International Conference on Computer Vision, 2017, pp. 2794–2802.

[34] Abolfazl Mehranian, Mohammad Reza Ay, Arman Rahmim, Habib Zaidi, X-ray CT metal artifact reduction using wavelet domain L0 sparse regularization, IEEE Transactions on Medical Imaging 32 (2013) 1707–1722.

[35] Esther Meyer, Rainer Raupach, Michael Lell, Bernhard Schmidt, Marc Kachelrieß, Normalized metal artifact reduction (NMAR) in computed tomography, Medical Physics (2010).

[36] Ruola Ning, Xiangyang Tang, David Conover, X-ray scatter correction algorithm for cone beam CT imaging, Medical Physics 31 (5) (2004) 1195–1202.

[37] J. Pan, W. Ren, Z. Hu, M. Yang, Learning to deblur images with exemplars, IEEE Transactions on Pattern Analysis and Machine Intelligence (2018).

[38] Hyung Suk Park, Yong Eun Chung, Sung Min Lee, Hwa Pyung Kim, Jin Keun Seo, Sinogram-consistency learning in CT for metal artifact reduction, arXiv preprint, arXiv:1708.00607, 2017.

[39] Adam Paszke, Sam Gross, Soumith Chintala, Gregory Chanan, Edward Yang, Zachary DeVito, Zeming Lin, Alban Desmaison, Luca Antiga, Adam Lerer, Automatic differentiation in PyTorch, in: NIPS-W, 2017.

[40] Deepak Pathak, Philipp Krahenbuhl, Jeff Donahue, Trevor Darrell, Alexei A. Efros, Context encoders: feature learning by inpainting, arXiv preprint, arXiv:1604.07379, 2016.

[41] Cheng Peng, Wei-An Lin, Haofu Liao, Rama Chellappa, S. Kevin Zhou, SAINT: spatially aware interpolation NeTwork for medical slice synthesis, in: 2020 IEEE/CVF Conference on Computer Vision and Pattern Recognition, CVPR 2020, Seattle, WA, USA, June 13–19, 2020, Computer Vision Foundation / IEEE, 2020, pp. 7747–7756.

[42] Olaf Ronneberger, Philipp Fischer, Thomas Brox, U-Net: convolutional networks for biomedical image segmentation, in: International Conference on Medical Image Computing and Computer-Assisted Intervention, 2015.

[43] Karen Simonyan, Andrew Zisserman, Very deep convolutional networks for large-scale image recognition, CoRR, arXiv:1409.1556 [abs], 2014.

[44] Jan-Jakob Sonke, Lambert Zijp, Peter Remeijer, Marcel van Herk, Respiratory correlated cone beam CT, Medical Physics 32 (4) (2005) 1176–1186.

[45] Dmitry Ulyanov, Andrea Vedaldi, Victor Lempitsky, Deep image prior, in: The IEEE Conference on Computer Vision and Pattern Recognition (CVPR), 2018.

[46] Ge Wang, Jong Chul Ye, Bruno De Man, Deep learning for tomographic image reconstruction, Nature Machine Intelligence 2 (12) (2020) 737–748.

[47] Jianing Wang, Yiyuan Zhao, Jack H. Noble, Benoit M. Dawant, Conditional generative adversarial networks for metal artifact reduction in CT images of the ear, in: Medical Image Computing and Computer Assisted Intervention (MICCAI), 2018.

[48] Qingli Wang, Liang Li, Li Zhang, Zhiqiang Chen, Kejun Kang, A novel metal artifact reducing method for cone-beam CT based on three approximately orthogonal projections, Physics in Medicine and Biology 58 (1) (2012) 1.

[49] Xintao Wang, Ke Yu, Shixiang Wu, Jinjin Gu, Yihao Liu, Chao Dong, Yu Qiao, Chen Change Loy, ESRGAN: enhanced super-resolution generative adversarial networks, in: The European Conference on Computer Vision Workshops (ECCVW), 2018.

[50] Jelmer M. Wolterink, Tim Leiner, Max A. Viergever, Ivana Išgum, Generative adversarial networks for noise reduction in low-dose CT, IEEE Transactions on Medical Imaging 36 (12) (2017) 2536–2545.

[51] Tobias Würfl, Florin C. Ghesu, Vincent Christlein, Andreas Maier, Deep learning computed tomography, in: Medical Image Computing and Computer Assisted Intervention (MICCAI), Springer International Publishing, 2016, pp. 432–440.

[52] Dan Xia, David A. Langan, Stephen B. Solomon, Zheng Zhang, Buxin Chen, Hao Lai, Emil Y. Sidky, Xiaochuan Pan, Optimization-based image reconstruction with artifact reduction in C-arm CBCT, Physics in Medicine and Biology 61 (20) (2016) 7300.

[53] Shiyu Xu, Hao Dang, Deep residual learning enabled metal artifact reduction in CT, in: Medical Imaging 2018: Physics of Medical Imaging, vol. 10573, International Society for Optics and Photonics, 2018, p. 105733O.

[54] Ke Yan, Xiaosong Wang, Le Lu, Ling Zhang, Adam P. Harrison, Mohammadhadi Bagheri, Ronald M. Summers, Deep lesion graphs in the wild: relationship learning and organization of significant radiology image findings in a diverse large-scale lesion database, in: The IEEE Conference on Computer Vision and Pattern Recognition (CVPR), 2018.

[55] Qingsong Yang, Pingkun Yan, Mannudeep K. Kalra, Ge Wang, CT image denoising with perceptive deep neural networks, arXiv preprint, arXiv:1702.07019, 2017.

[56] Qingsong Yang, Pingkun Yan, Yanbo Zhang, Hengyong Yu, Yongyi Shi, Xuanqin Mou, Mannudeep K. Kalra, Ge Wang, Low dose CT image denoising using a generative adversarial network with Wasserstein distance and perceptual loss, arXiv preprint, arXiv:1708.00961, 2017.

[57] Haimiao Zhang, Bin Dong, Baodong Liu, A reweighted joint spatial-Radon domain CT image reconstruction model for metal artifact reduction, SIAM Journal on Imaging Sciences 11 (2018) 707–733.

[58] He Zhang, Vishal M. Patel, Densely connected pyramid dehazing network, in: The IEEE Conference on Computer Vision and Pattern Recognition (CVPR), 2018.

[59] Xiaoshuai Zhang, Wenhan Yang, Yueyu Hu, Jiaying Liu, DMCNN: dual-domain multiscale convolutional neural network for compression artifacts removal, in: 2018 25th IEEE International Conference on Image Processing (ICIP), IEEE, 2018, pp. 390–394.

[60] Yanbo Zhang, Hengyong Yu, Convolutional neural network based metal artifact reduction in X-ray computed tomography, IEEE Transactions on Medical Imaging 37 (6) (2018) 1370–1381.

[61] Yongbin Zhang, Lifei Zhang, X. Ronald Zhu, Andrew K. Lee, Mark Chambers, Lei Dong, Reducing metal artifacts in cone-beam CT images by preprocessing projection data, International Journal of Radiation Oncology, Biology, Physics 67 (3) (2007) 924–932.

[62] Yulun Zhang, Yapeng Tian, Yu Kong, Bineng Zhong, Yun Fu, Residual dense network for image super-resolution, in: The IEEE Conference on Computer Vision and Pattern Recognition (CVPR), 2018.

[63] Z. Zhang, X. Liang, X. Dong, Y. Xie, G. Cao, A sparse-view CT reconstruction method based on combination of DenseNet and deconvolution, IEEE Transactions on Medical Imaging 37 (6) (2018) 1407–1417.

[64] Zheng Zhang, Xiao Han, Erik Pearson, Charles Pelizzari, Emil Y. Sidky, Xiaochuan Pan, Artifact reduction in short-scan CBCT by use of optimization-based reconstruction, Physics in Medicine and Biology 61 (9) (2016) 3387.

[65] Zhisheng Zhong, Tiancheng Shen, Yibo Yang, Zhouchen Lin, Chao Zhang, Joint sub-bands learning with clique structures for wavelet domain super-resolution, arXiv preprint, arXiv:1809.04508, 2018.

[66] Bo Zhou, S. Kevin Zhou, DuDoRNet: learning a dual-domain recurrent network for fast MRI reconstruction with deep T1 prior, in: Proceedings of the IEEE/CVF Conference on Computer Vision and Pattern Recognition, 2020, pp. 4273–4282.

[67] Bo Zhou, S. Kevin Zhou, James S. Duncan, Chi Liu, Limited view tomographic reconstruction using a cascaded residual dense spatial-channel attention network with projection data fidelity layer, IEEE Transactions on Medical Imaging 40 (7) (2021) 1792–1804.

Reconstruction: unsupervised artifact reduction

8

CONTENTS

We have covered supervised learning approaches for medical image reconstruction in the previous chapter. However, for many clinical applications, it is impractical to develop supervised models due to the absence of paired training data. For example, in metal artifact reduction, the artifacts originate from the metal implants. It is impractical to capture a pair of spatially aligned images, one with metal implants and the other without metal implants. In fluorescence microscopy, the images are inherently noisy due to the extremely low number of photons captured by the microscopic detector. Hence, there are no ground-truth clean images available at all.

To address these scenarios, we introduce unsupervised learning approaches in this chapter. That is, given the low-quality medical data, either from the sensor or image domain, we present models that can learn medical image reconstruction without ground-truth high-quality data. Learning in such a way is considerably challenging. However, due to the advances in deep learning, substantial progress has been made in this direction. One key enabler is the introduction of generative adversarial networks (GANs) [9]. GANs can generate data that is statistically close to the training samples, and in the context of medical image reconstruction, it means the generation of high-quality medical images without supervision. This is an appealing property; when combined with other GAN-based techniques, such as conditional GAN [28], CycleGAN [46], or UNIT [23], it opens up opportunities for learning medical image reconstruction from unpaired training samples. Another key enabler is the feasibility of self-supervised learning with deep neural networks. In particular, it has been shown that deep neural networks perform surprisingly well on many inverse problems by simply reconstructing the corrupted input or its corrupted variant [20,17,1,36,32].

This chapter is organized as follows. In Section 8.1, we introduce the design principles for two types of unsupervised learning approaches, unpaired and self-supervised learning approaches. For each approach, we introduce the problem setting, choices of objective functions or learning strategies, and seminal works. Next, in Section 8.2, we provide a case study that addresses metal artifact reduction via unpaired learning [21]. Specifically, we present an artifact disentanglement network that learns to disentangle the metal artifacts from the input images and outputs the artifact-free images. We provide details in the design of network architecture and loss functions to demonstrate how unpaired learning can be applied in practice.

8.1 Design principles
8.1.1 Unpaired learning approaches

In unpaired learning of medical image reconstruction, we assume that both low- and high-quality medical images are available for training. But there is no pairwise correspondence between low- and high-quality images. That is, given a low-quality image from the training set, we do not know the ground-truth high-quality image. The goal is to train a deep neural network that transforms the low-quality image to a high-quality one, under this unpaired setting and without direct supervision. Architecture-wise, the problem can still be addressed with deep image-to-image networks. The major difference is the learning part, and in the next section, we give detailed learning strategies and objective functions for unpaired learning of medical image reconstruction.

8.1.1.1 Problem definition and choice of objective functions

Conditional GAN [28]. Let $\mathcal{I}^a$ be a domain of low-quality images and $\mathcal{I}$ be a domain of high-quality images. The unpaired learning aims to learn a mapping $g^* : \mathcal{I}^a \to \mathcal{I}$ without paired dataset $\mathcal{P} \subset \{(\mathbf{X}^a, \mathbf{X}) | \mathbf{X}^a \in \mathcal{I}^a, \mathbf{X} \in \mathcal{I}, g^*(\mathbf{X}^a) = \mathbf{X}\}$. One way to address this unpaired learning problem is to apply conditional generative adversarial networks (cGANs) [28,14]. An image-to-image cGAN aims to train a generator g that takes the low-quality image $\mathbf{X}^a$ as input (and thus conditioned on $\mathbf{X}^a$), and its output $\hat{\mathbf{X}}$ improves the quality of $\mathbf{X}^a$, i.e., $\hat{\mathbf{X}} = g(\mathbf{X}^a)$. Meanwhile, cGAN also trains a discriminator d that distinguishes between images from the high-quality domain $\mathcal{I}$ and images from the generator $\hat{\mathcal{I}} = \{\hat{\mathbf{X}} | \hat{\mathbf{X}} = g(\mathbf{X}^a), \mathbf{X}^a \in \mathcal{I}^a\}$. The objective function of cGAN can be expressed as

$$\mathcal{L}_{\text{cGAN}}(g, d) = \mathbb{E}_{\mathcal{I}}[\log d(\mathbf{X})] + \mathbb{E}_{\mathcal{I}^a}[\log 1 - d(g(\mathbf{X}^a))]. \tag{8.1}$$

Here d and g play a minimax game. On the one hand, when training d, we aim to maximize $\mathcal{L}_{\text{cGAN}}$ so that d outputs 1 on $\mathbf{X}$ and 0 on $g(\mathbf{X}^a)$. On the other hand, when training g, we aim to minimize $\mathcal{L}_{\text{cGAN}}$ so that d outputs 1 on $g(\mathbf{X}^a)$, i.e.,

$$g^* = \arg\min_g \max_d \mathcal{L}_{\text{cGAN}}(g, d). \tag{8.2}$$

Since during training $\mathbf{X}$ and $\mathbf{X}^a$ are not necessarily paired, we obviate the need for paired datasets and achieve unpaired learning with cGAN. However, because the discriminator simply categorizes the inputs, cGAN only encourages the generated images $\hat{\mathbf{X}}$ to be semantically similar to high-quality domain images, and thus there is no guarantee that $\hat{\mathbf{X}}$ and $\mathbf{X}^a$ are spatially aligned. To address this limitation, we may consider applying CycleGAN.

CycleGAN [46]. In CycleGAN, we introduce another generator $f : \mathcal{I} \rightarrow \mathcal{I}^a$ that learns to map images from the high-quality domain to the low-quality domain. Accordingly, we also train a discriminator d_f that learns to distinguish between images from the low-quality domain $\mathcal{I}^a$ and images from $\hat{\mathcal{I}}^a = \{\hat{\mathbf{X}}^a | \hat{\mathbf{X}}^a = f(\mathbf{X}), \mathbf{X} \in \mathcal{I}\}$. CycleGAN applies cGAN loss to train the generator f,

$$f^* = \arg\min_f \max_{d_f} \mathcal{L}_{\text{cGAN}}(f, d_f). \tag{8.3}$$

More importantly, CycleGAN also applies a cycle-consistency loss to encourage the generation consistency between g and f so that the inputs and outputs of these two generators are spatially aligned,

$$\mathcal{L}_{\text{cc}}(g, f) = \mathbb{E}_{\mathcal{I}}[\|g(f(\mathbf{X})) - \mathbf{X}\|_1] + \mathbb{E}_{\mathcal{I}^a}[\|f(g(\mathbf{X}^a)) - \mathbf{X}^a\|_1], \tag{8.4}$$

and the full CycleGAN loss is

$$\mathcal{L}_{\text{CycleGAN}}(g, f, d, d_f) = \mathcal{L}_{\text{cGAN}}(g, d_g) + \mathcal{L}_{\text{cGAN}}(f, d_f) + \lambda\mathcal{L}_{\text{cc}}(g, f), \tag{8.5}$$

where d_g is the discriminator for g and λ is a loss weight.

8.1.1.2 Deep learning models for unpaired learning of medical image reconstruction

Following the idea by the pix2pix framework [14], many works introduced image-to-image cGAN to address medical image reconstruction problems, such as low-dose CT denoising [38], fast MRI dealiasing [42], and Fourier ptychography reconstruction [35]. However, most of these approaches used a content loss to minimize the differences between the model's prediction and the ground truth, and thus they did not satisfy the requirement for unpaired learning. Wolterink et al. [38] proposed to apply cGAN loss alone without content loss. In this way, they obviated the need for paired data and showed that the model could still improve the quality of the reconstructed CT image. However, they did not achieve noticeable improvement over the traditional iterative reconstruction method.

To better address unpaired learning, other works proposed to introduce CycleGAN with dedicated designs for medical image reconstruction. Kang et al. [16]

introduced CycleGAN for multiphase CT denoising. In addition to cGAN loss and cycle-consistency loss, they also applied an identity loss that enforced the model to reconstruct its inputs when they were from the target domain. This design was based on the observation that multiphase CT may include samples from the high-dose CT domain, due to the phase–dose misalignment. Lee et al. [19] proposed to apply SpCycleGAN [4] for fluorescence microscopy reconstruction. Specifically, they introduced a 3-Way SpCycleGAN that applied SpCycleGAN along the x, y, and z directions of fluorescence volumes. In this way, they extended SpCycleGAN with better 3D context understanding.

8.1.2 Self-supervised learning approaches

While unpaired learning can address medical image reconstruction problems without paired training data, it still requires the availability of high-quality images. However, for some problems, it is only the low-quality images that are captured, and the high-quality images are never observed. To handle such a problem setting, we may consider self-supervised learning. Specifically, we aim to train a deep image-to-image network for medical image reconstruction with only samples from the low-quality image domain. In self-supervised learning, we achieve this goal by establishing correspondence between the network's prediction and input (or variants of the input). In the next section, we present choices of objective functions that address medical image denoising under different self-supervised learning settings.

8.1.2.1 Problem definition and choice of objective functions

Noise2Noise [20].   Let $\mathbf{X}_i^a \in \mathcal{I}^a$ be a noisy image that can be decomposed into $\mathbf{X}_i^a = \mathbf{X}_i + \mathbf{A}_i$, where $\mathbf{X}_i \in \mathcal{I}$ is a clean image and $\mathbf{A}_i \in \mathcal{A}$ is an additive noise component, which has zero mean and unknown distribution. In Noise2Noise, we assume there exists a set of paired noisy images $\mathcal{P} = \{(\mathbf{X}_i^a, \mathbf{X}_i^{a'}) | \mathbf{X}_i^a = \mathbf{X}_i + \mathbf{A}_i, \mathbf{X}_i^{a'} = \mathbf{X}_i + \mathbf{A}_i'\}_i$, where $\mathbf{A}_i$ and $\mathbf{A}_i'$ are two independently sampled noises from $\mathcal{A}$. This is a mild assumption for certain medical image reconstruction problems, such as cryo-TEM, where it is possible to independently acquire images of the same subject [3]. Given this paired noisy image set, we aim to train a deep image-to-image network $\hat{\mathbf{X}} = g(\mathbf{X}^a)$ that reduces the noise from $\mathbf{X}^a$. The loss function for training g is a simple

$$\mathcal{L}_{\text{Noise2Noise}} = \frac{1}{N} \sum_{i=1}^{N} \| g(\mathbf{X}_i^a) - \mathbf{X}_i^{a'} \|^2. \tag{8.6}$$

This loss function is simple due the fact that $\mathcal{A}$ has zero mean, and $\mathbf{A}_i$ and $\mathbf{A}_i'$ are independent. This means $\mathbb{E}_{\mathcal{A}}[\mathbf{X}_i^{a'} | \mathbf{X}_i^a] = \mathbf{X}_i$, and for an infinite dataset, minimizing Eq. (8.6) with a noisy target is the same as minimizing it with ground truth $\mathbf{X}_i$.

Noise2Void [17].   While Noise2Noise works well in practice, it bears the problem of requiring paired noisy images for training, which is not always satisfied for medical image reconstruction. In Noise2Void, we make two more assumptions (which generally hold) about the medical images. First, the value of a clean image $\mathbf{X}$ at a pixel location $\mathbf{p}$ is not statistically independent of the values from its neighborhood $\mathcal{N}(\mathbf{p})$ within a certain radius, i.e., $p(\mathbf{X}(\mathbf{p})|\mathbf{X}(\mathbf{p}')) \neq p(\mathbf{X}(\mathbf{p}))$, $\mathbf{p}' \in \mathcal{N}(\mathbf{p})$. Second, the noises at different pixel locations are conditionally independent given $\mathbf{X}$, i.e., $p(\mathbf{A}|\mathbf{X}) = \prod_i p(\mathbf{A}(\mathbf{p}_i)|\mathbf{X})$. With these two assumptions, we can then go a step further by only requiring a dataset $\mathcal{I}^a = \{\mathbf{X}_i^a\}_i$ with unpaired noisy images. The goal is then training a denoising network g using images from $\mathcal{I}^a$. To this end, we consider simply requiring g to reconstruct the noisy input image itself,

$$\mathcal{L}_{\text{Noise2Void}} = \frac{1}{N} \sum_{i=1}^{N} \|g(\mathbf{X}_i^a) - \mathbf{X}_i^a\|^2. \tag{8.7}$$

This idea looks daunting as g would likely degenerate to an identity function that maps any input to itself. To avoid this degeneration, Noise2Void introduces a *blind-spot* design for g, where the receptive field of g will have a blind spot in its center. That is, when predicting the value of $\hat{\mathbf{X}}(\mathbf{p})$ for a pixel at location $\mathbf{p}$, g cannot use the value of $\mathbf{X}^a(\mathbf{p})$ but only the values of its neighbors within the receptive field $\mathcal{N}_{\text{RF}}$. Thus, we prohibit g to learn an identity function in the trivial way. Meanwhile, given the two assumptions we made for Noise2Void, we know that $\mathbb{E}_{\mathcal{A}}[\mathbf{X}_i^a(\mathbf{p})|\mathbf{X}_i^a(\mathcal{N}_{\text{RF}} - \{\mathbf{p}\})] = \mathbf{X}_i(\mathbf{p})$. Therefore, minimizing Eq. (8.7) with itself as target is equivalent to minimizing with ground truth.

Deep image prior [36].   So far, we have introduced self-supervised approaches that can learn from a set of noisy images without direct supervision. In deep image prior, we aim to address an even more challenging setting where the noisy image prior is not given, i.e., no observations of any noisy images for training. Instead, we formulate the denoising process as an optimization problem and tune parameters of the deep neural network separately for each image that we want to reduce the noise. Specifically, let $g(\mathbf{z}; \theta)$ be a deep neural network where $\mathbf{z}$ is a fixed random tensor, and θ is the network's parameters. We optimize θ so that the network's output matches the observed noisy input $\mathbf{X}^a$,

$$\theta^* = \arg\min_{\theta} \|g(\mathbf{z}; \theta) - \mathbf{X}^a\|^2, \tag{8.8}$$

and the denoised image can be obtained by

$$\mathbf{X}^* = g(\mathbf{z}; \theta^*). \tag{8.9}$$

This seemly naive approach works surprisingly well on several inverse problems, including image denoising. Its success suggests that deep neural network by design has already captured a strong prior that favors nature-looking images over noisy ones. Meanwhile, this setting without noisy image prior is common for conventional medical image reconstruction where an image is reconstructed from only the measured sensor data without any prior images involved. Inspired by this, Eq. (8.8) can also be modified so that the network's output is consistent with the sensor domain measurement,

$$\theta^* = \arg\min_{\theta} \| f(g(\mathbf{z}; \theta)) - \mathbf{Y} \|^2. \tag{8.10}$$

Here, f is a forward imaging model that maps the image domain data to sensor domain, and $\mathbf{Y}$ is the measured sensor domain data from which a noisy image may be reconstructed.

8.1.2.2 Deep learning models for self-supervised learning of medical image reconstruction

The Noise2Noise method [20] has shown to be very effective (can be as effective as the supervised methods as shown in the original paper) in image denoising. Therefore, it has soon been adapted to denoise medical images. The original Noise2Noise paper has already demonstrated the application of Noise2Noise for undersampled MRI image denoising. However, the original paper required the existence of fully-sampled MRI for the synthesis of paired noisy samples. To address this limitation, Yaman et al. [40] proposed to generate the noisy pairs directly from subsampled MRI images. They randomly split the k-space data of the subsampled MRI into two complementary parts. For each part, a subsampled MRI was reconstructed and hence formed a noisy pair. Wu et al. [39] applied Noise2Noise for CT perfusion (CTP) image denoising. In their approach, they used the adjacent CTP frames as the paired noisy samples. Bepler et al. [2] proposed a method called Topaz-Denoise based on Noise2Noise. They applied the method for cryoEM and cryoET denoising where the paired noisy observations were generated from movie frames collected in the normal cryoEM process.

To address the cases where paired noisy images were not available, Krull et al. [17] proposed the Noise2Void method, and they demonstrated its effectiveness on fluorescence microscopy noising. Batson et al. [1] proposed a method called Noise2Self to address self-supervised learning of denoising without paired noisy images. Similar to Noise2Void, Noise2Self also avoided the learning of identity functions. But instead of the *blind-spot* design, Noise2Self introduced $\mathcal{J}$-invariant neural networks which had a theoretical guarantee against fitting the noise.

Deep image prior (DIP) [36] has the most relaxed requirement for unsupervised learning of medical image denoising since it does not even require any noisy image for training. However, the problem with DIP is that it cannot address the noises as effective as Noise2Noise or Noise2Void. Therefore, it is usually applied together with regular reconstruction regimes. Since both are training data-free, it makes them a good fit to work together. Gong et al. [8] introduced the DIP idea for PET image reconstruction. They proposed a conditional DIP so that the reconstruction could also leverage information from MRI priors of the same patient. More importantly, they included DIP as part of the reconstruction pipeline so that imaging physics could also be considered in DIP optimization. Yoo et al. [44] proposed to leverage DIP for dynamic MRI reconstruction. They improved the original DIP formulation so that it could joint optimize for spoke-shared measurements, resulting in time-dependent

DIP. Moreover, they applied Eq. (8.10) for the optimization to enforce the reconstruction consistency with the measurements.

8.2 Case study: metal artifact reduction

Metal artifact is one of the commonly encountered problems in computed tomography (CT). It arises when a patient carries metallic implants, e.g., dental fillings and hip prostheses. Compared to body tissues, metallic materials attenuate X-rays significantly and nonuniformly over the spectrum, leading to inconsistent X-ray projections. The mismatched projections will introduce severe streaking and shading artifacts in the reconstructed CT images, which significantly degrade the image quality and compromise the medical image analysis as well as the subsequent healthcare delivery.

To reduce the metal artifacts, many efforts have been made over the past decades [5]. Conventional approaches [15,26] address the metal artifacts by projection completion, where the metal traces in the X-ray projections are replaced by estimated values. After the projection completion, the estimated values need to be consistent with the imaging content and the underlying projection geometry. When the metallic implant is large, it is challenging to satisfy these requirements and thus secondary artifacts are often introduced due to an imperfect completion. Moreover, the X-ray projection data, as well as the associated reconstruction algorithms, are often held out by the manufactures, which limits the applicability of the projection based approaches.

A workaround to the limitations of the projection-based approaches is to address the metal artifacts directly in the CT images. However, since the formation of metal artifacts involves complicated mechanisms such as beam hardening, scatter, noise, and the nonlinear partial volume effect [5], it is very challenging to model and reduce metal artifacts in the CT images with traditional approaches. Therefore, recent approaches [45,37,12,6] to metal artifact reduction (MAR) propose to use deep neural networks (DNNs) to inherently address the modeling of metal artifacts, and their experimental results show promising MAR performances. All the existing DNN-based approaches are supervised methods that require pairs of anatomically identical CT images, one with and the other without metal artifacts, for training. As it is clinically impractical to acquire such pairs of images, most of the supervised methods resort to synthesizing metal artifacts in CT images to simulate the pairs. However, due to the complexity of metal artifacts and the variations of CT devices, the synthesized artifacts may not accurately reproduce the real clinical scenarios, and the performances of these supervised methods tend to degrade in clinical applications.

In this work, we aim to address the challenging yet more practical unsupervised setting where *no paired CT images are available and required for training.* To this end, we reformulate the artifact reduction problem as an artifact disentanglement problem. As illustrated in Fig. 8.1, we assume that any artifact-affected image consists of an artifact component (i.e., metal artifacts, noises, etc.) and a content component (i.e., the anatomical structure). Our goal is to disentangle these two components

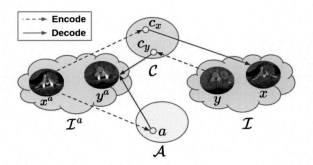

FIGURE 8.1

Artifact disentanglement. The content and artifact components of an image x^a from the artifact-affected domain $\mathcal{I}^a$ is mapped separately to the content space $\mathcal{C}$ and the artifact space $\mathcal{A}$, i.e., artifact disentanglement. An image y from the artifact-free domain $\mathcal{I}$ contains no artifact and thus is mapped only to the content space. Decoding without artifact code removes the artifact from an artifact-affected image (blue arrows $x^a \rightarrow x$) while decoding with the artifact code adds artifacts to an artifact-free image (red arrows $y \rightarrow y^a$).

in the latent space, and artifact reduction can be readily achieved by reconstructing CT images without the artifact component. Fundamentally, this artifact disentanglement without paired images is made possible by grouping the CT images into two groups, one with metal artifacts and the other without metal artifacts. In this way, we introduce an *inductive bias* [24] that a model may inherently learn artifact disentanglement by comparing between these two groups. More importantly, the artifact disentanglement assumption guides manipulations in the latent space. This can be leveraged to include additional inductive biases that apply self-supervisions between the outputs of the model (see Section 8.2.2.2) and thus obviate the need for paired images.

Specifically, we propose an artifact disentanglement network (ADN) with specialized encoders and decoders that handle the encoding and decoding of the artifact and content components separately for the unpaired inputs. Different combinations of the encoders and decoders support different forms of image translations (see Section 8.2.2.1), e.g., artifact reduction, artifact synthesis, self-reconstruction, and so on. ADN exploits the relationships between the image translations for unsupervised learning. Extensive experiments show that our method achieves comparable performance to the existing supervised methods on a synthesized dataset. When applied to clinical datasets, all the supervised methods do not generalize well due to a significant domain shift, whereas ADN delivers consistent MAR performance and significantly outperforms the compared supervised methods.

8.2.1 Background

Conventional metal artifact reduction.   Most conventional approaches address metal artifacts in X-ray projections. A straightforward way is to directly correct the X-ray measurement of the metallic implants by modeling the underlying physical effects such as beam hardening [30,11], scatter [25], and so on. However, the metal traces in projections are often corrupted. Thus, instead of projection correction, a more common approach is to replace the corrupted region with estimated values. Early approaches [7,15] fill the corrupted regions by linear interpolation which often introduces new artifacts due to the inaccuracy of the interpolated values. To address this issue, a state-of-the-art approach [26] introduces a prior image to normalize the X-ray projections before the interpolation.

Deep metal artifact reduction.   A number of studies have recently been proposed to address MAR with DNNs. RL-ARCNN [12] introduces residual learning into a deep convolutional neural network (CNN) and achieves better MAR performance than standard CNN. DestreakNet [6] proposes a two-streams approach that can take a pair of NMAR [26] and detail images as the input to jointly reduce metal artifacts. CNNMAR [45] uses CNN to generate prior images in the CT image domain to help the correction in the projection domain. Both DestreakNet and CNNMAR show significant improvements over the existing non-DNN based methods on synthesized datasets. cGANMAR [37] leverages generative adversarial networks (GANs) [9] to further improve the DNN-based MAR performance.

Unsupervised image-to-image translation.   Image artifact reduction can be regarded as a form of image-to-image translation. One of the earliest unsupervised methods in this category is CycleGAN [46] where a cycle-consistency design is proposed for unsupervised learning. MUNIT [13] and DRIT [18] improve CycleGAN for diverse and multimodal image generation. However, these unsupervised methods aim at image synthesis and do not have suitable components for artifact reduction. Another recent work that is specialized for artifact reduction is deep image prior (DIP) [36], which, however, only works for less structured artifacts such as additive noise or compression artifacts.

8.2.2 Methodology

Let $\mathcal{I}^a$ be the domain of all artifact-affected CT images and $\mathcal{I}$ be the domain of all artifact-free CT images. We denote $\mathcal{P} = \{(x^a, x) \mid x^a \in \mathcal{I}^a, x \in \mathcal{I}, f(x^a) = x\}$ as a set of paired images, where $f : \mathcal{I}^a \to \mathcal{I}$ is an MAR model that removes the metal artifacts from x. In this work, we assume no such paired dataset is available and we propose to learn f with unpaired images.

As illustrated in Fig. 8.1, the proposed method disentangles the artifact and content components of an artifact-affected image x^a by encoding them separately into a content space $\mathcal{C}$ and an artifact space $\mathcal{A}$. If the disentanglement is well addressed, the encoded content component $c_x \in \mathcal{C}$ should contain no information about the artifact while preserving all the content information. Thus, decoding from c_x should

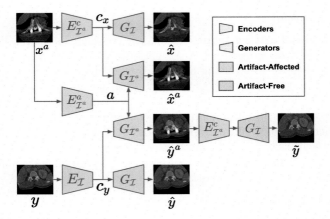

FIGURE 8.2

Overview of the proposed artifact disentanglement network (ADN). Taking any two unpaired images, one from $\mathcal{I}^a$ and the other from $\mathcal{I}$, as the inputs, ADN supports four different forms of image translations: $\mathcal{I}^a \to \mathcal{I}$, $\mathcal{I} \to \mathcal{I}^a$, $\mathcal{I} \to \mathcal{I}$, and $\mathcal{I}^a \to \mathcal{I}^a$.

give an artifact-free image x which is the artifact-removed counterpart of x^a. On the other hand, it is also possible to encode an artifact-free image y into the content space which gives a content code c_y. If c_y is decoded together with an artifact code $a \in \mathcal{A}$, we obtain an artifact-affected image y^a. In the following sections, we introduce an artifact disentanglement network (ADN) that learns these encodings and decodings without paired data.

8.2.2.1 Encoders and decoders

The architecture of ADN is shown in Fig. 8.2. It contains a pair of artifact-free image encoder $E_{\mathcal{I}} : \mathcal{I} \to \mathcal{C}$ and decoder $G_{\mathcal{I}} : \mathcal{C} \to \mathcal{I}$ and a pair of artifact-affected image encoder $E_{\mathcal{I}^a} = \{E^c_{\mathcal{I}^a} : \mathcal{I}^a \to \mathcal{C}, E^a_{\mathcal{I}^a} : \mathcal{I}^a \to \mathcal{A}\}$ and decoder $G_{\mathcal{I}^a} : \mathcal{C} \times \mathcal{A} \to \mathcal{I}^a$. The encoders map an image sample from the image domain to the latent space and the decoders map a latent code from the latent space back to the image domain. Note that unlike a conventional encoder, $E_{\mathcal{I}^a}$ consists of a content encoder $E^c_{\mathcal{I}^a}$ and an artifact encoder $E^a_{\mathcal{I}^a}$, which encode the content and artifacts separately to achieve artifact disentanglement.

Specifically, given two unpaired images $x^a \in \mathcal{I}^a$ and $y \in \mathcal{I}$, $E^c_{\mathcal{I}^a}$ and $E_{\mathcal{I}}$ map the content component of x^a and y to the content space $\mathcal{C}$, respectively; $E^a_{\mathcal{I}^a}$ maps the artifact component of x^a to the artifact space $\mathcal{A}$. We denote the corresponding latent codes as

$$c_x = E^c_{\mathcal{I}^a}(x^a), \quad a = E^a_{\mathcal{I}^a}(x^a), \quad c_y = E_{\mathcal{I}}(y). \tag{8.11}$$

Here $G_{\mathcal{I}^a}$ takes a content code and an artifact code as the input and outputs an artifact-affected image. Decoding from c_x and a should reconstruct x^a and decoding from c_y

and a should add artifacts to y,

$$\hat{x}^a = G_{\mathcal{I}^a}(c_x, a), \quad \hat{y}^a = G_{\mathcal{I}^a}(c_y, a). \qquad (8.12)$$

Here $G_{\mathcal{I}}$ takes a content code as the input and outputs an artifact-free image. Decoding from c_x should remove the artifacts from x^a and decoding from c_y should reconstruct y,

$$\hat{x} = G_{\mathcal{I}}(c_x), \quad \hat{y} = G_{\mathcal{I}}(c_y). \qquad (8.13)$$

Note that $\hat{y}^a$ can be regarded as a synthesized artifact-affected image whose artifacts come from x^a and content comes from y. Thus, by reapplying $E^c_{\mathcal{I}^a}$ and $G_{\mathcal{I}}$, it should remove the synthesized artifacts and recover y,

$$\tilde{y} = G_{\mathcal{I}}(E^c_{\mathcal{I}^a}(\hat{y}^a)). \qquad (8.14)$$

8.2.2.2 Learning

For ADN, learning an MAR model $f : \mathcal{I}^a \to \mathcal{I}$ means learning the two key components $E^c_{\mathcal{I}^a}$ and $G_{\mathcal{I}}$; $E^c_{\mathcal{I}^a}$ encodes only the content of an artifact-affected image and $G_{\mathcal{I}}$ generates an artifact-free image with the encoded content code. Thus, their composition readily results in an MAR model, $f = G_{\mathcal{I}} \circ E^c_{\mathcal{I}^a}$. However, without paired data, it is challenging to directly address the learning of these two components. Therefore, we learn $E^c_{\mathcal{I}^a}$ and $G_{\mathcal{I}}$ together with other encoders and decoders in ADN. In this way, different learning signals can be leveraged to regularize the training of $E^c_{\mathcal{I}^a}$ and $G_{\mathcal{I}}$, and removes the requirement of paired data.

The learning aims at encouraging the outputs of the encoders and decoders to achieve the artifact disentanglement. That is, we design loss functions so that ADN outputs the intended images as denoted in Eqs. (8.12)–(8.14). An overview of the relationships between the loss functions and ADN's outputs is shown in Fig. 8.3. We can observe that ADN enables five forms of losses, namely two adversarial losses $\mathcal{L}^{\mathcal{I}}_{\text{adv}}$ and $\mathcal{L}^{\mathcal{I}^a}_{\text{adv}}$, an artifact consistency loss $\mathcal{L}_{\text{art}}$, a reconstruction loss $\mathcal{L}_{\text{rec}}$, and a self-reduction loss $\mathcal{L}_{\text{self}}$. The overall objective function is formulated as the weighted sum of these losses,

$$\mathcal{L} = \lambda_{\text{adv}}(\mathcal{L}^{\mathcal{I}}_{\text{adv}} + \mathcal{L}^{\mathcal{I}^a}_{\text{adv}}) + \lambda_{\text{art}}\mathcal{L}_{\text{art}} + \lambda_{\text{rec}}\mathcal{L}_{\text{rec}} + \lambda_{\text{self}}\mathcal{L}_{\text{self}}, \qquad (8.15)$$

where the λ's are hyperparameters that control the importance of each term.

Adversarial loss. By manipulating the artifact component in the latent space, ADN outputs $\hat{x}$ (Eq. (8.13)) and $\hat{y}^a$ (Eq. (8.12)), where the former removes artifacts from x^a and the latter adds artifacts to y. Learning to generate these two outputs is crucial to the success of artifact disentanglement. However, since there are no paired images, it is impossible to simply apply regression losses, such as the L_1 or L_2 loss, to minimize the difference between ADN's outputs and the ground truths. To address this problem, we adopt the idea of adversarial learning [9] by introducing two discriminators $D_{\mathcal{I}^a}$ and $D_{\mathcal{I}}$ to regularize the plausibility of $\hat{x}$ and $\hat{y}^a$. On the one hand, $D_{\mathcal{I}^a}/D_{\mathcal{I}}$ learns to distinguish whether an image is generated by ADN or sampled from $\mathcal{I}^a/\mathcal{I}$. On

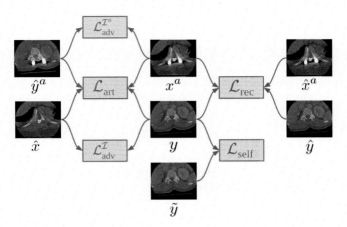

FIGURE 8.3

An illustration of the relationships between the loss functions and ADN's inputs and outputs.

the other hand, ADN learns to deceive $D_{\mathcal{I}^a}$ and $D_{\mathcal{I}}$ so that they cannot determine if the outputs from ADN are generated images or real images. In this way, $D_{\mathcal{I}^a}$, $D_{\mathcal{I}}$ and ADN can be trained without paired images. Formally, the adversarial loss can be written as

$$\mathcal{L}_{adv}^{\mathcal{I}} = \mathbb{E}_{\mathcal{I}}[\log D_{\mathcal{I}}(y)] + \mathbb{E}_{\mathcal{I}^a}[1 - \log D_{\mathcal{I}}(\hat{x})],$$
$$\mathcal{L}_{adv}^{\mathcal{I}^a} = \mathbb{E}_{\mathcal{I}^a}[\log D_{\mathcal{I}^a}(x^a)] + \mathbb{E}_{\mathcal{I},\mathcal{I}^a}[1 - \log D_{\mathcal{I}^a}(\hat{y}^a)], \qquad (8.16)$$
$$\mathcal{L}_{adv} = \mathcal{L}_{adv}^{\mathcal{I}} + \mathcal{L}_{adv}^{\mathcal{I}^a}.$$

Reconstruction loss. Despite the artifact disentanglement, there should be no information lost or model-introduced artifacts during the encoding and decoding. For artifact reduction, the content information should be fully encoded and decoded by $E_{\mathcal{I}^a}^c$ and $G_{\mathcal{I}}$. For artifact synthesis, the artifact and content components should be fully encoded and decoded by $E_{\mathcal{I}^a}^a$, $E_{\mathcal{I}}$, and $G_{\mathcal{I}^a}$. However, without paired data, the intactness of the encoding and decoding cannot be directly regularized. Therefore, we introduce two forms of reconstruction to inherently encourage the encoders and decoders to preserve the information. Specifically, ADN requires $\{E_{\mathcal{I}^a}, G_{\mathcal{I}^a}\}$ and $\{E_{\mathcal{I}}, G_{\mathcal{I}}\}$ serve as autoencoders when encoding and decoding from the same image,

$$\mathcal{L}_{rec} = \mathbb{E}_{\mathcal{I},\mathcal{I}^a}[||\hat{x}^a - x^a||_1 + ||\hat{y} - y||_1]. \qquad (8.17)$$

Here, the two outputs $\hat{x}^a$ (Eq. (8.12)) and $\hat{y}$ (Eq. (8.13)) of ADN reconstruct the two inputs x^a and y, respectively. As a common practice in image-to-image translation problem [14], we use L_1 loss instead of L_2 loss to encourage sharper outputs.

Artifact consistency loss. The adversarial loss reduces metal artifacts by encouraging $\hat{x}$ to resemble a sample from $\mathcal{I}$. But the $\hat{x}$ obtained in this way is only anatomically plausible not anatomically precise, i.e., $\hat{x}$ may not be anatomically correspondent to x^a. A naive solution to achieve the anatomical preciseness without paired data is to directly minimize the difference between $\hat{x}$ and x^a with an L_1 or L_2 loss. However, this will induce $\hat{x}$ to contain artifacts, and thus conflicts with the adversarial loss and compromises the overall learning. ADN addresses the anatomical preciseness by introducing an artifact consistency loss,

$$\mathcal{L}_{\text{art}} = \mathbb{E}_{\mathcal{I},\mathcal{I}^a}[||(x^a - \hat{x}) - (\hat{y}^a - y)||_1]. \tag{8.18}$$

This loss is based on the observation that the difference between x^a and $\hat{x}$ and the difference between $\hat{y}^a$ and y should be close due to the use of the same artifact. Unlike a direct minimization of the difference between x^a and $\hat{x}$, $\mathcal{L}_{\text{art}}$ only requires x^a and $\hat{x}$ to be anatomically close but not exactly close and vice versa, for $\hat{y}^a$ and y.

Self-reduction loss. ADN also introduces a self-reduction mechanism. It first adds artifacts to y which creates $\hat{y}^a$ and then removes the artifacts from $\hat{y}^a$ which results $\tilde{y}$. Thus, we can pair $\hat{y}^a$ with y to regularize the artifact reduction in Eq. (8.14) with regression,

$$\mathcal{L}_{\text{self}} = \mathbb{E}_{\mathcal{I},\mathcal{I}^a}[||\tilde{y} - y||_1]. \tag{8.19}$$

8.2.2.3 Network architectures

We formulate the building components, i.e., the encoders, decoders, and discriminators, as convolutional neural networks (CNN). Table 8.1 lists their detailed architectures. As we can see, the building components consist of a stack of building blocks, where some of the structures are inspired by the state-of-the-art approaches for image translation [46,13].

As shown in Fig. 8.4, there are five different types of blocks. The residual, downsampling and upsampling blocks are the core blocks of the encoders and decoders. The downsampling block (Fig. 8.4(b)) uses strided convolution to reduce the dimensionality of the feature maps for better computational efficiency. Compared with the max pooling layers, strided convolution adaptively selects the features for downsampling, which demonstrates better performance for generative models [33]. The residual block (Fig. 8.4(a)) includes residual connections to allow low-level features to be considered in the computation of high-level features. This design shows better performance for deep neural networks [10]. The upsampling block (Fig. 8.4(c)) converts feature maps back to their original dimension to generate the final outputs. We use an upsample layer (nearest neighbor interpolation) followed with a convolutional layer for the upsampling. We choose this design instead of the deconvolutional layer to avoid the "checkerboard" effect [29]. The padding of all the convolutional layers in the blocks of the encoders and decoders are reflection padding. It provides better results along the edges of the generated images.

It is worth noting that we propose a special way to merge the artifact code and the content code during the decoding of an artifact-affected image. We refer to this

Table 8.1 Architecture of the building components. "Channel (Ch.)," "Kernel," "Stride," and "Padding (Pad.)" denote the configurations of the convolution layers in the blocks.

Network	Block/Layer	Count	Ch.	Kernel	Stride	Pad.
$E_{\mathcal{I}}$ / $E_{\mathcal{I}^a}$	down.	1	64	7	1	3
	down.	1	128	4	2	1
	down.	1	256	4	2	1
	residual	4	256	3	1	1
E_a	down.	1	64	7	1	3
	down.	1	128	4	2	1
	down.	1	256	4	2	1
$G_{\mathcal{I}}$	residual	4	256	3	1	1
	up.	1	128	5	1	2
	up.	1	64	5	1	2
	final	1	1	7	1	3
$G_{\mathcal{I}^a}$	residual	4	256	3	1	1
	merge	1	256	1	1	0
	up.	1	128	5	1	2
	merge	1	128	1	1	0
	up.	1	64	5	1	2
	merge	1	64	1	1	0
	final	1	1	7	1	3
$D_{\mathcal{I}}$ / $D_{\mathcal{I}^a}$	conv	1	64	4	2	1
	relu	1	–	–	–	–
	down.	1	128	4	2	1
	down.	1	256	4	1	1
	conv	1	1	4	1	1

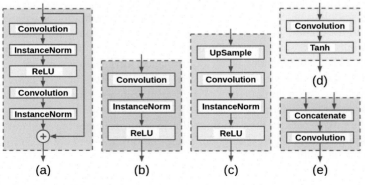

(a)   (b)   (c)   (d)

FIGURE 8.4

Basic building blocks of the encoders and decoders: (a) residual block, (b) downsampling block, (c) upsampling block, (d) final block, and (e) merging block.

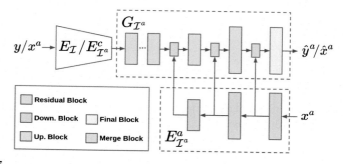

FIGURE 8.5

Detailed architecture of the proposed artifact pyramid decoding (APD). The artifact-affected decoder $G_{\mathcal{I}^a}$ uses APD to effectively merge the artifact code from $E_{\mathcal{I}^a}$.

design as *artifact pyramid decoding* (APD) in respect to the feature pyramid network (FPN) [22]. For artifact encoding and decoding, we aim to effectively recover the details of the artifacts. A feature pyramid design, which includes high-definition features with relatively cheaper costs, serves well for this purpose. Fig. 8.5 demonstrates the detailed architecture of APD. Here $E_{\mathcal{I}^a}$ consists of several downsampling blocks and outputs feature maps at different scales, i.e., a feature pyramid; $G_{\mathcal{I}^a}$ consists of a stack of residual, merge, upsample, and final blocks. It generates the artifact-affected images by merging the artifact code at different scales during the decoding. The merging blocks (Fig. 8.4(e)) in $G_{\mathcal{I}^a}$ first concatenate the content feature maps and artifact feature maps along the channel dimension, and then use a 1×1 convolution to locally merge the features.

8.2.3 Experiments

8.2.3.1 Baselines

We compare the proposed method with nine methods that are closely related to our problem. Two of the compared methods are conventional methods, LI [15] and NMAR [26]. These two methods are widely used approaches to MAR. Three of the compared methods are supervised methods: CNNMAR [45], UNet [34], and cGAN-MAR [37]. CNNMAR and cGANMAR are two recent approaches that are dedicated to MAR. U-Net is a general CNN framework that shows effectiveness in many image-to-image problems. The other four compared methods are unsupervised methods: CycleGAN [46], DIP [36], MUNIT [13], and DRIT [18]. These methods are currently state-of-the-art approaches to unsupervised image-to-image translation problems.

As for the implementations of the compared methods, we use their officially released code whenever possible. For LI and NMAR, there is no official code, and we adopt the implementations that are used in CNNMAR. For U-Net, we use a publicly available implementation [27] in PyTorch. For cGANMAR, we train the model with the official code of Pix2Pix [14] as cGANMAR is identical to Pix2Pix at the backend.

8.2.3.2 Datasets

We evaluate the proposed method on one synthesized dataset and two clinical datasets. We refer to them as SYN, CL1, and CL2, respectively. For SYN, we randomly select 4118 artifact-free CT images from DeepLesion [41] and follow the method from CNNMAR [45] to synthesize metal artifacts. CNNMAR is one of the state-of-the-art supervised approaches to MAR. To generate the paired data for training, it simulates the beam hardening effect and Poisson noise during the synthesis of metal-affected polychromatic projection data from artifact-free CT images. As beam hardening effect and Poisson noise are two major causes of metal artifacts, and for a fair comparison, we apply the metal artifact synthesis method from CNNMAR in our experiments. We use 3918 of the synthesized pairs for training and validation and the remaining 200 pairs for testing.

For CL1, we choose the vertebrae localization and identification dataset from CSI2014 [43]. This is a challenging CT dataset for localization problems with a significant portion of its images containing metallic implants. We split the CT images from this dataset into two groups, one with artifacts and the other without artifacts. First, we identify regions with HU values greater than 2500 as the metal regions. Then, CT images whose largest-connected metal regions have more than 400 pixels are selected as artifact-affected images. CT images with the largest HU values less than 2000 are selected as artifact-free images. After this selection, the artifact-affected group contains 6270 images and the artifact-free group contains 21,190 images. We withhold 200 images from the artifact-affected group for testing.

For CL2, we investigate the performance of the proposed method under a more challenging *cross-modality* setting. Specifically, the artifact-affected images of CL2 are from a cone-beam CT (CBCT) dataset collected during spinal interventions. Images from this dataset are very noisy. The majority of them contain metal artifacts while the metal implants are mostly not within the imaging field of view. There are in total 2560 CBCT images from this dataset, among which 200 images are withheld for testing. For the artifact-free images, we reuse the CT images collected from CL1.

Note that LI, NMAR, and CNNMAR require the availability of raw X-ray projections which, however, are not provided by SYN, CL1, and CL2. Therefore, we follow the literature [45] by synthesizing the X-ray projections via forward projection. For SYN, we first forward project the artifact-free CT images and then mask out the metal traces. For CL1 and CL2, there are no ground-truth artifact-free CT images available. Therefore, the X-ray projections are obtained by forward projecting the artifact-affected CT images. The metal traces are also segmented and masked out for projection interpolation.

8.2.3.3 Training and testing

We implement our method under the PyTorch deep learning framework [31] and use the Adam optimizer with 1×10^{-4} learning rate to minimize the objective function. For the hyperparameters, we use $\lambda_{adv}^{\mathcal{I}} = \lambda_{adv}^{\mathcal{I}^a} = 1.0$, $\lambda_{rec} = \lambda_{self} = \lambda_{art} = 20.0$ for SYN and CL1, and use $\lambda_{adv}^{\mathcal{I}} = \lambda_{adv}^{\mathcal{I}^a} = 1.0$, $\lambda_{rec} = \lambda_{self} = \lambda_{art} = 5.0$ for CL2.

Table 8.2 Quantitative comparison with baseline methods on the SYN dataset.

	Method	Metrics	
		PSNR	**SSIM**
Conventional	LI [15]	32.0	91.0
	NMAR [26]	32.1	91.2
Supervised	CNNMAR [45]	32.5	91.4
	UNet [34]	**34.8**	93.1
	cGANMAR [37]	34.1	**93.4**
Unsupervised	CycleGAN [46]	30.8	72.9
	DIP [36]	26.4	75.9
	MUNIT [13]	14.9	7.5
	DRIT [18]	25.6	79.7
	Ours	<u>33.6</u>	<u>92.4</u>

Due to the artifact synthesis, SYN contains paired images for supervised learning. To simulate the unsupervised setting for SYN, we evenly divide the 3918 training pairs into two groups. For one group, only artifact-affected images are used and their corresponding artifact-free images are withheld. For the other group, only artifact-free images are used and their corresponding artifact-affected images are withheld. During the training of the unsupervised methods, we randomly select one image from each of the two groups as the input.

To train the supervised methods with CL1, we first synthesize metal artifacts using the images from the artifact-free group of CL1. Then, we train the supervised methods with the synthesized pairs. During testing, the trained models are applied to the testing set containing only clinical metal artifact images. To train the unsupervised methods, we randomly select one image from the artifact-affected group and the other from the artifact-free group as the input. In this way, the artifact-affected images and artifact-free images are sampled evenly during training which helps with the data imbalance between the artifact-affected and artifact-free groups.

For CL2, synthesizing metal artifacts is not possible due to the unavailability of artifact-free CBCT images. Therefore, for the supervised methods, we directly use the models trained for CL1. In other words, the supervised methods are trained on synthesized CT images (from CL1) and tested on clinical CBCT images (from CL2). For the unsupervised models, each time we randomly select one artifact-affected CBCT image and one artifact-free CT image as the input for training.

8.2.3.4 Performance on synthesized data

SYN contains paired data, allowing for both quantitative and qualitative evaluations. Following the convention in the literature, we use peak signal-to-noise ratio (PSNR) and structural similarity index (SSIM) as the metrics for the quantitative evaluation. For both metrics, higher values are better. Table 8.2 and Fig. 8.6 show the quantitative and qualitative evaluation results, respectively.

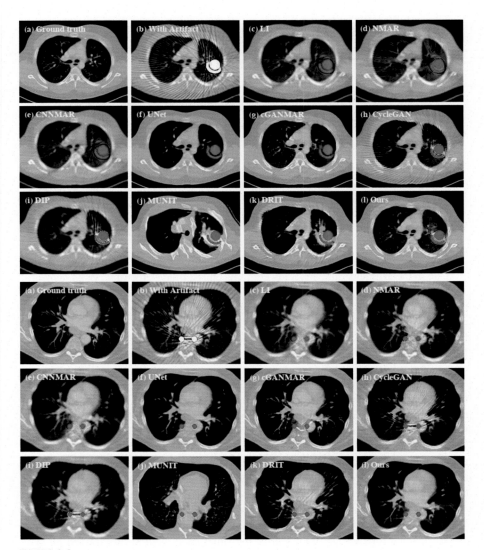

FIGURE 8.6

Qualitative comparison with baseline methods on the SYN dataset. For better visualization, we segment out the metal regions through thresholding and color them in red.

We observe that our proposed method performs significantly better than the other unsupervised methods. MUNIT focuses more on diverse and realistic outputs (Fig. 8.6(j)) with less constraint on structural similarity. CycleGAN and DRIT perform better as both the two models also require the artifact-corrected outputs to be able to transform back to the original artifact-affected images. Although this helps preserve content information, it also encourages the models to keep the artifacts. Therefore, as shown in Figs. 8.6(h) and 8.6(k), the artifacts cannot be effectively reduced. DIP does not reduce many metal artifacts in the input image (Fig. 8.6(i)) as it is not designed to handle the more structured metal artifacts.

We also find that the performance of our method is on par with the conventional and supervised methods. The performance of U-Net is close to that of cGANMAR which at its backend uses an U-Net-like architecture. However, due to the use of GAN, cGANMAR produces sharper outputs (Fig. 8.6(g)) than U-Net (Fig. 8.6(f)). As for PSNR and SSIM, both methods only slightly outperform our method. LI, NMAR, and CNNMAR are all projection interpolation based methods. NMAR is better than LI as it uses prior images to guide the projection interpolation. CNNMAR uses CNN to learn the generation of the prior images and thus shows better performance than NMAR. As we can see, ADN performs better than these projection interpolation based approaches both quantitatively and qualitatively.

8.2.3.5 Performance on clinical data

Next, we investigate the performance of the proposed method on clinical data. Since there are no ground truths available for the clinical images, only qualitative comparisons are performed. The qualitative evaluation results of CL1 are shown in Fig. 8.7. Here, all the supervised methods are trained with paired images that are synthesized from the artifact-free group of CL1. We can see that UNet and cGANMAR do not generalize well when applied to clinical images (Figs. 8.7(f) and 8.7(g)). LI, NMAR, and CNNMAR are more robust as they correct the artifacts in the projection domain. However, the projection domain corrections also introduce secondary artifacts (Figs. 8.7(c), 8.7(d), and 8.7(e)). For the more challenging CL2 dataset (Fig. 8.8), all the supervised methods fail. This is not totally unexpected as the supervised methods are trained using only CT images because of the lack of artifact-free CBCT images. As the metallic implants of CL2 are not within the imaging field of view, there are no metal traces available and the projection interpolation based methods do not work (Figs. 8.8(c), 8.8(d), and 8.8(e)). Similar to the cases with SYN, the other unsupervised methods also show inferior performances when evaluated on both the CL1 and CL2 datasets. In contrast, our method removes the dark shadings and streaks significantly without introducing secondary artifacts.

8.2.3.6 Ablation study

We perform an ablation study to understand the effectiveness of several designs of ADN. All the experiments are conducted with the SYN dataset so that both the quantitative and qualitative performances can be analyzed. Table 8.3 and Fig. 8.9 show the experimental results, where the performances of ADN (M4) and its three variants (M1–M3) are compared. M1 refers to the model trained with only the adversarial loss $\mathcal{L}_{adv}$. M2 refers to the model trained with both the adversarial loss $\mathcal{L}_{adv}$ and the reconstruction loss $\mathcal{L}_{rec}$. M3 refers to the model trained with the adversarial loss $\mathcal{L}_{adv}$, the reconstruction loss $\mathcal{L}_{rec}$, and the artifact consistency loss $\mathcal{L}_{art}$. M4 refers to the

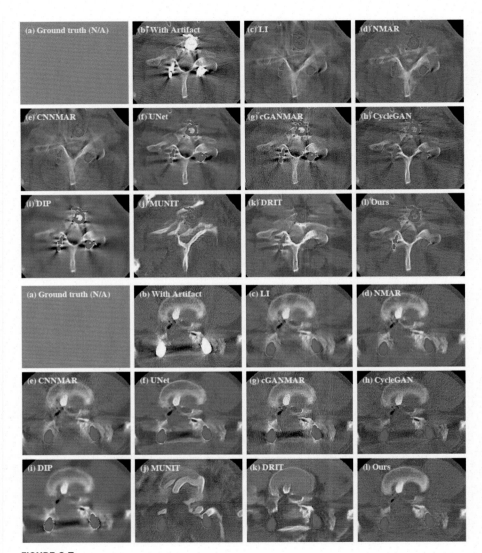

FIGURE 8.7

Qualitative comparison with baseline methods on the CL1 dataset. For better visualization, we obtain the metal regions through thresholding and color them with red.

model trained with all the losses, i.e., ADN. We use M4 and ADN interchangeably in the experiments.

From Fig. 8.9, we can observe that M1 generates artifact-free images that are structurally similar to the inputs. However, with only adversarial loss, there is no support that the content of the generated images should exactly match the inputs. Thus,

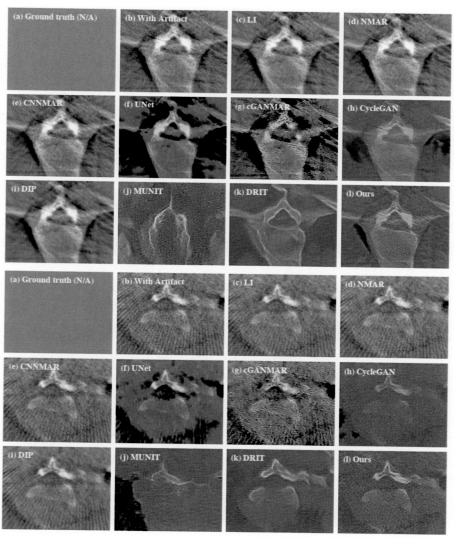

FIGURE 8.8

Qualitative comparison with baseline methods on the CL2 dataset.

we can see that many details of the inputs are lost and some anatomical structures are mismatched. In contrast, the results from M2 maintain most of the anatomical details of the inputs. This demonstrates that learning to reconstruct the inputs is helpful to guide the model to preserve the details of the inputs. However, as the reconstruction loss is applied in a self-reconstruction manner, there is no direct penalty for the

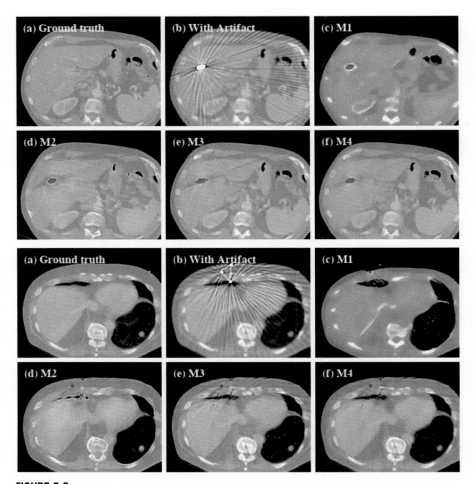

FIGURE 8.9

Qualitative comparison of different variants of ADN. The compared models (M1–M4) are trained with different combinations of the loss functions discussed in Section 8.2.2.2.

anatomical reconstruction error during the artifact reduction. Thus, we can still observe some minor anatomical imperfections from the outputs of M2.

M3 improves M2 by including the artifact consistency loss. This loss directly measures the pixel-wise anatomical differences between the inputs and the generated outputs. As shown in Fig. 8.9, the results of M3 precisely preserve the content of inputs and suppress most of the metal artifacts. For M4, we can find that the outputs are further improved. This shows that the self-reduction mechanism, which allows the model to reduce synthesized artifacts, is indeed helpful. The quantitative results

Table 8.3 Quantitative comparison of different variants of ADN. The compared models (M1–M4) are trained with different combinations of the loss functions discussed in Section 8.2.2.2.

Method	Metrics	
	PSNR	**SSIM**
M1 ($\mathcal{L}_{adv}$ only)	21.7	61.5
M2 (M1 with $\mathcal{L}_{rec}$)	26.3	82.1
M3 (M2 with $\mathcal{L}_{art}$)	32.8	91.6
M4 (M3 with $\mathcal{L}_{self}$)	**33.6**	**92.4**

are provided in Table 8.3. We can see that they are consistent with our qualitative observations in Fig. 8.9.

8.2.3.7 Artifact synthesis

In addition to artifact reduction, ADN also supports unsupervised artifact synthesis. This functionality arises from two designs. First, the adversarial loss $\mathcal{L}_{adv}^{\mathcal{I}^a}$ encourages the output $\hat{y}^a$ to be a sample from $\mathcal{I}^a$, i.e., the metal artifact should look real. Second, the artifact consistency loss $\mathcal{L}_{art}$ induces $\hat{y}^a$ to contain the metal artifacts from x^a and suppresses the synthesis of the content component from x. This section investigates the effectiveness of these two designs. The experiments are performed with the CL1 dataset as learning to synthesize clinical artifacts is more practical and challenging than learning to synthesize the artifacts from SYN, whose artifacts are already synthesized. Fig. 8.10 shows the experimental results, where each row is an example of artifact synthesis. Images on the left are the clinical images with metal artifacts. Images in the middle are the clinical images without artifacts. Images on the right are the artifact synthesis results by transferring the artifacts from the left image to the middle image. As we can see, except the positioning of the metal implants, the synthesized artifacts look realistic. The metal artifacts merge naturally into the artifact-free images making it really challenging to notice that the artifacts are actually synthesized. More importantly, it is only the artifacts that are transferred and almost no content is transferred to the artifact-free images. Note that our model is data-driven. If there is an anatomical structure or lesion that looks like metal artifacts, it might also be transferred.

8.2.4 Discussion

Applications to artifact reduction. Given the flexibility of ADN, we expect many applications to artifact reduction in medicine, where obtaining paired data is usually impractical. First, as we have already demonstrated, ADN can be applied to address metal artifacts. It reduces metal artifacts directly with CT images, which is critical to the scenarios when researchers or healthcare practitioners have no access to the raw

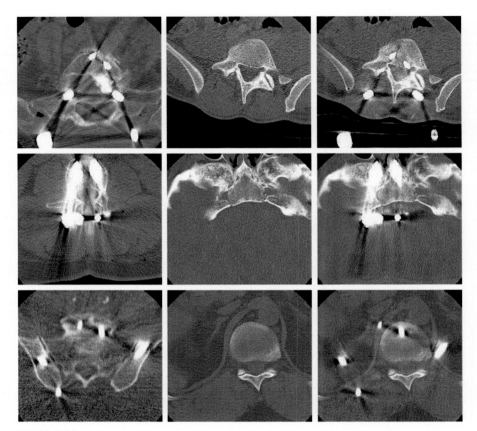

FIGURE 8.10

Metal artifact transfer: (left) clinical images with metal artifacts x^a; (middle) clinical images without metal artifacts y; (right) metal artifacts on the left column transferred to the artifact-free images in the middle $\hat{y}^a$.

projection data as well as the associated reconstruction algorithms. For the manufacturers, ADN can be applied in a post-processing step to further improve the in-house MAR algorithm that addresses metal artifacts in the projection data during the CT reconstruction.

Second, even though our problem under investigation is MAR, ADN should work with other artifact reduction problems as well. In the problem formulation, ADN does not make any assumption about the nature of the artifacts. Therefore, if we change to other artifact reduction problems such as deblurring, destreaking, denoising, etc., ADN should also work. Actually, in the experiments, the input images from CL1 (Fig. 8.7(b)) are slightly noisy while the outputs of ADN are more smooth. Similarly, input images from CL2 (Fig. 8.8(b)) contain different types of artifacts, such as noise, streaking artifacts, and so on, and ADN handles them well.

Applications to artifact synthesis.   By combining $E^a_{\mathcal{I}^a}$, $E_{\mathcal{I}}$, and $G_{\mathcal{I}^a}$, ADN can be applied to synthesize artifacts in an artifact-free image. As we have shown in Fig. 8.10, the synthesized artifacts look natural and realistic, which may potentially have practical applications in medical image analysis. For example, a CT image segmentation model may not work well when metal artifacts are present as there are not enough metal-affected images in the dataset. By using ADN, we could significantly increase the number of metal-affected images in the dataset via the realistic metal artifact synthesis. In this way, ADN may potentially improve the performance of the CT segmentation model.

We present an unsupervised learning approach to MAR. Through the development of an artifact disentanglement network, we have shown how to leverage artifact disentanglement to achieve different forms of image translations as well as self-reconstructions that eliminate the requirement of paired images for training. To understand the effectiveness of this approach, we have performed extensive evaluations on one synthesized and two clinical datasets. The evaluation results demonstrate the feasibility of using unsupervised learning method to achieve comparable performance to the supervised methods with synthesized dataset. More importantly, the results also show that directly learning MAR from clinical CT images under an unsupervised setting is a more feasible and robust approach than simply applying the knowledge learned from synthesized data to clinical data. We believe our findings in this work will stimulate more applicable research for medical image artifact reduction under an unsupervised setting.

8.3 Summary

We have introduced unsupervised learning approaches to medical image reconstruction. In practice, it is not always possible to capture paired low- and high-quality medical images to train deep image-to-image networks. Therefore, we present unsupervised learning methods that learn deep image reconstruction without such paired data. Specifically, we introduce two categories of unsupervised learning approaches for medical image reconstruction, unpaired and self-supervised approaches. Unpaired learning approaches have access to both low- and high-quality image sets during training but the pairwise correspondences between images of these two sets are not given or available. Self-supervised learning approaches have access to only low-quality images, and hence they resort to supervisory signals from the input low-quality images themselves.

For unpaired learning approaches, we provide detailed design principles in Section 8.1.1. We show how to leverage two types of GAN models, cGAN [28,14] and CycleGAN [46], to train deep image-to-image networks from unpaired low-quality and high-quality images. For each type of model, we also introduce specific works in the literature to demonstrate its applications to different medical image reconstruction problems. Next, in Section 8.2, we provide a case study that applies unpaired learning to CT metal artifact reduction. We propose a model called artifact disentanglement network (ADN) that substantially extends cGAN to disentangle metal artifacts in latent space, which we show addressing better the unpaired learning. We use this model to further illustrate some practical network architecture designs and objective function choices.

For self-supervised learning approaches, we summarize three seminal models, namely Noise2Noise [20], Noise2Void [17], and DIP [36], that address self-supervised image reconstruction under different problem settings. Specifically, Noise2Noise works when paired noisy samples exist; Noise2Void requires only a set of noisy samples without noisy pairs; DIP can address the cases with just a single noisy image. In Section 8.1.2, we first show how each of the models works under these problem settings. Then, we associate these models with particular medical image reconstruction problems and demonstrate how they are applied in practice.

References

[1] Joshua Batson, Loic Royer, Noise2self: blind denoising by self-supervision, in: International Conference on Machine Learning, PMLR, 2019, pp. 524–533.

[2] Tristan Bepler, Kotaro Kelley, Alex J. Noble, Bonnie Berger, Topaz-Denoise: general deep denoising models for cryoEM and cryoET, Nature Communications 11 (1) (2020) 1–12.

[3] Tim-Oliver Buchholz, Mareike Jordan, Gaia Pigino, Florian Jug, Cryo-care: content-aware image restoration for cryo-transmission electron microscopy data, in: 2019 IEEE 16th International Symposium on Biomedical Imaging (ISBI 2019), IEEE, 2019, pp. 502–506.

[4] Chichen Fu, Soonam Lee, David Joon Ho, Shuo Han, Paul Salama, Kenneth W. Dunn, Edward J. Delp, Three dimensional fluorescence microscopy image synthesis and segmentation, in: Proceedings of the IEEE Conference on Computer Vision and Pattern Recognition Workshops, 2018, pp. 2221–2229.

[5] Lars Gjesteby, Bruno De Man, Yannan Jin, Harald Paganetti, Joost Verburg, Drosoula Giantsoudi, Ge Wang, Metal artifact reduction in CT: where are we after four decades?, IEEE Access 4 (2016) 5826–5849.

[6] Lars Gjesteby, Hongming Shan, Qingsong Yang, Yan Xi, Bernhard Claus, Yannan Jin, Bruno De Man, Ge Wang, Deep neural network for CT metal artifact reduction with a perceptual loss function, in: Proceedings of the Fifth International Conference on Image Formation in X-Ray Computed Tomography, 2018.

[7] Gary H. Glover, Norbert J. Pelc, An algorithm for the reduction of metal clip artifacts in CT reconstructions, Medical Physics 8 (6) (1981) 799–807.

[8] Kuang Gong, Ciprian Catana, Jinyi Qi, Quanzheng Li, PET image reconstruction using deep image prior, IEEE Transactions on Medical Imaging 38 (7) (2018) 1655–1665.

[9] Ian Goodfellow, Jean Pouget-Abadie, Mehdi Mirza, Bing Xu, David Warde-Farley, Sherjil Ozair, Aaron Courville, Yoshua Bengio, Generative adversarial nets, in: Advances in Neural Information Processing Systems, 2014.

[10] Kaiming He, Xiangyu Zhang, Shaoqing Ren, Jian Sun, Deep residual learning for image recognition, in: Proceedings of the IEEE Conference on Computer Vision and Pattern Recognition, 2016, pp. 770–778.

[11] Jiang Hsieh, Robert C. Molthen, Christopher A. Dawson, Roger H. Johnson, An iterative approach to the beam hardening correction in cone beam CT, Medical Physics 27 (1) (2000) 23–29.

[12] Xia Huang, Jian Wang, Fan Tang, Tao Zhong, Yu Zhang, Metal artifact reduction on cervical CT images by deep residual learning, Biomedical Engineering Online 17 (1) (2018) 175.

[13] Xun Huang, Ming-Yu Liu, Serge J. Belongie, Jan Kautz, Multimodal unsupervised image-to-image translation, in: Computer Vision – ECCV 2018, 2018.

[14] Phillip Isola, Jun-Yan Zhu, Tinghui Zhou, Alexei A. Efros, Image-to-image translation with conditional adversarial networks, in: Proceedings of the IEEE Conference on Computer Vision and Pattern Recognition, 2017, pp. 1125–1134.

[15] Willi A. Kalender, Robert Hebel, Johannes Ebersberger, Reduction of CT artifacts caused by metallic implants, Radiology 164 (2) (1987) 576–577.

[16] Eunhee Kang, Hyun Jung Koo, Dong Hyun Yang, Joon Bum Seo, Jong Chul Ye, Cycle-consistent adversarial denoising network for multiphase coronary CT angiography, Medical Physics 46 (2) (2019) 550–562.

[17] Alexander Krull, Tim-Oliver Buchholz, Florian Jug, Noise2void-learning denoising from single noisy images, in: Proceedings of the IEEE/CVF Conference on Computer Vision and Pattern Recognition, 2019, pp. 2129–2137.

[18] Hsin-Ying Lee, Hung-Yu Tseng, Jia-Bin Huang, Maneesh Singh, Ming-Hsuan Yang, Diverse image-to-image translation via disentangled representations, in: Computer Vision – ECCV 2018, 2018.

[19] Soonam Lee, Shuo Han, Paul Salama, Kenneth W. Dunn, Edward J. Delp, Three dimensional blind image deconvolution for fluorescence microscopy using generative adversarial networks, in: 2019 IEEE 16th International Symposium on Biomedical Imaging (ISBI 2019), IEEE, 2019, pp. 538–542.

[20] Jaakko Lehtinen, Jacob Munkberg, Jon Hasselgren, Samuli Laine, Tero Karras, Miika Aittala, Timo Aila, Noise2Noise: learning image restoration without clean data, in: International Conference on Machine Learning (ICML), vol. 80, 2018, pp. 2965–2974.

[21] Haofu Liao, Wei-An Lin, S. Kevin Zhou, Jiebo Luo, ADN: artifact disentanglement network for unsupervised metal artifact reduction, IEEE Transactions on Medical Imaging 39 (3) (2020) 634–643.

[22] Tsung-Yi Lin, Piotr Dollár, Ross Girshick, Kaiming He, Bharath Hariharan, Serge Belongie, Feature pyramid networks for object detection, in: Proceedings of the IEEE Conference on Computer Vision and Pattern Recognition, 2017, pp. 2117–2125.

[23] Ming-Yu Liu, Thomas Breuel, Jan Kautz, Unsupervised image-to-image translation networks, in: Advances in Neural Information Processing Systems, 2017, pp. 700–708.

[24] Francesco Locatello, Stefan Bauer, Mario Lucic, Sylvain Gelly, Bernhard Schölkopf, Olivier Bachem, Challenging common assumptions in the unsupervised learning of disentangled representations, arXiv preprint, arXiv:1811.12359, 2018.

[25] Esther Meyer, Clemens Maaß, Matthias Baer, Rainer Raupach, Bernhard Schmidt, Marc Kachelrieß, Empirical scatter correction (ESC): a new CT scatter correction method and its application to metal artifact reduction, in: IEEE Nuclear Science Symposium & Medical Imaging Conference, IEEE, 2010, pp. 2036–2041.

[26] Esther Meyer, Rainer Raupach, Michael Lell, Bernhard Schmidt, Marc Kachelrieß, Normalized metal artifact reduction (NMAR) in computed tomography, Medical Physics (2010).

[27] Alexandre Milesi, U-Net: semantic segmentation with PyTorch, https://github.com/milesial/Pytorch-UNet, 2017.

[28] Mehdi Mirza, Simon Osindero, Conditional generative adversarial nets, arXiv preprint, arXiv:1411.1784, 2014.

[29] Augustus Odena, Vincent Dumoulin, Chris Olah, Deconvolution and checkerboard artifacts, Distill 1 (10) (2016) e3.

[30] Hyoung Suk Park, Dosik Hwang, Jin Keun Seo, Metal artifact reduction for polychromatic X-ray CT based on a beam-hardening corrector, IEEE Transactions on Medical Imaging 35 (2) (2015) 480–487.

[31] Adam Paszke, Sam Gross, Francisco Massa, Adam Lerer, James Bradbury, Gregory Chanan, Trevor Killeen, Zeming Lin, Natalia Gimelshein, Luca Antiga, Alban Desmaison, Andreas Kopf, Edward Yang, Zachary DeVito, Martin Raison, Alykhan Tejani, Sasank Chilamkurthy, Benoit Steiner, Lu Fang, Junjie Bai, Soumith Chintala, PyTorch: an imperative style, high-performance deep learning library, in: H. Wallach, H. Larochelle, A. Beygelzimer, F. d'Alché-Buc, E. Fox, R. Garnett (Eds.), Advances in Neural Information Processing Systems 32, Curran Associates, Inc., 2019, pp. 8024–8035.

[32] Yuhui Quan, Mingqin Chen, Tongyao Pang, Hui Ji, Self2self with dropout: learning self-supervised denoising from single image, in: Proceedings of the IEEE/CVF Conference on Computer Vision and Pattern Recognition, 2020, pp. 1890–1898.

[33] Alec Radford, Luke Metz, Soumith Chintala, Unsupervised representation learning with deep convolutional generative adversarial networks, arXiv preprint, arXiv:1511.06434, 2015.

[34] Olaf Ronneberger, Philipp Fischer, Thomas Brox, U-Net: convolutional networks for biomedical image segmentation, in: International Conference on Medical Image Computing and Computer-Assisted Intervention, 2015.

[35] Nguyen Thanh, Yujia Xue, Yunzhe Li, Lei Tian, George Nehmetallah, Deep learning approach to Fourier ptychographic microscopy, Optics Express (2018).

[36] Dmitry Ulyanov, Andrea Vedaldi, Victor Lempitsky, Deep image prior, in: The IEEE Conference on Computer Vision and Pattern Recognition (CVPR), 2018.

[37] Jianing Wang, Yiyuan Zhao, Jack H. Noble, Benoit M. Dawant, Conditional generative adversarial networks for metal artifact reduction in CT images of the ear, in: Medical Image Computing and Computer Assisted Intervention (MICCAI), 2018.

[38] Jelmer M. Wolterink, Tim Leiner, Max A. Viergever, Ivana Išgum, Generative adversarial networks for noise reduction in low-dose CT, IEEE Transactions on Medical Imaging 36 (12) (2017) 2536–2545.

[39] Dufan Wu, Hui Ren, Quanzheng Li, Self-supervised dynamic CT perfusion image denoising with deep neural networks, IEEE Transactions on Radiation and Plasma Medical Sciences 5 (3) (2020) 350–361.

[40] Burhaneddin Yaman, Seyed Amir Hossein Hosseini, Steen Moeller, Jutta Ellermann, Kâmil Uğurbil, Mehmet Akçakaya, Self-supervised physics-based deep learning MRI reconstruction without fully-sampled data, in: 2020 IEEE 17th International Symposium on Biomedical Imaging (ISBI), IEEE, 2020, pp. 921–925.

[41] Ke Yan, Xiaosong Wang, Le Lu, Ronald M. Summers, DeepLesion: automated mining of large-scale lesion annotations and universal lesion detection with deep learning, Journal of Medical Imaging (2018).

[42] Guang Yang, Simiao Yu, Hao Dong, Greg Slabaugh, Pier Luigi Dragotti, Xujiong Ye, Fangde Liu, Simon Arridge, Jennifer Keegan, Yike Guo, et al., DAGAN: deep de-aliasing generative adversarial networks for fast compressed sensing MRI reconstruction, IEEE Transactions on Medical Imaging 37 (6) (2017) 1310–1321.

[43] Jianhua Yao, Ben Glocker, Tobias Klinder, Shuo Li, Vertebrae localization and identification challenge, in: International Workshop and Challenge on Computational Methods and Clinical Applications for Spine Imaging, Springer, 2014.

[44] Jaejun Yoo, Kyong Hwan Jin, Harshit Gupta, Jerome Yerly, Matthias Stuber, Michael Unser, Time-dependent deep image prior for dynamic MRI, IEEE Transactions on Medical Imaging (2021).

[45] Yanbo Zhang, Hengyong Yu, Convolutional neural network based metal artifact reduction in X-ray computed tomography, IEEE Transactions on Medical Imaging 37 (6) (2018) 1370–1381.

[46] Jun-Yan Zhu, Taesung Park, Phillip Isola, Alexei A. Efros, Unpaired image-to-image translation using cycle-consistent adversarial networks, in: International Conference on Computer Vision (ICCV), 2017.

Synthesis: novel radiography view synthesis

CONTENTS

Medical data synthesis refers to the process of generating unseen medical data as if it was clinically captured or produced. In general, medical data synthesis has two forms, unconditional and conditional. Unconditional synthesis randomly generates medical data that is statistically close to samples from real/clinical data distribution. Conditional synthesis, on the other hand, generates samples that match or align with some given inputs. Conventional approaches to medical data synthesis are usually conditional synthesis approaches. They require the availability of some image descriptions or observed data, such as physical parameter values, segmentation maps, or imaging atlas, which may not be easily accessible for certain clinical applications. Meanwhile, they implement simple or handcrafted functions to transform data from one modality to another, and thus cannot produce diverse and realistic results.

This chapter is focused on machine learning models for medical data synthesis. Unlike those conventional approaches which are typically physical-, or registration-based [60], machine learning-based approaches train parametrized models and learn synthesis in a data-driven way. They do not explicitly model or simulate the generation process of medical data, which results in fewer requirements for conditional inputs or can be even addressed unconditionally. Moreover, with the development of deep learning, especially the introduction of deep generative models [22,42,17,73], we have been equipped with tools to address medical data synthesis in more flexible ways and meanwhile obtain high-quality synthetic data.

Deep Network Design for Medical Image Computing. https://doi.org/10.1016/B978-0-12-824383-1.00018-6

Because of this feasibility, deep learning-based synthesis methods have enabled a broad range of clinical applications. For example, medical data synthesis can be applied to address medical image reconstruction problems. In particular, it can be applied to extreme cases where only a very limited number of sensor data are available. Besides, synthesizing unseen medical data can address privacy issues and avoid leaking patient-specific or sensitive information by sharing synthetic data. This property can also be leveraged for educational purposes where we may provide synthetic data to medical students to facilitate their medical study. Moreover, they can help to simplify clinical pipelines. In particular, for the cases where multiple modalities of imaging data are necessary, synthesizing medical images can reduce the required number of modalities for acquisition and/or provide complementary anatomy information.

The rest of this chapter is structured as follows. In Section 9.1, we introduce design principles for machine learning-based medical data synthesis. Specifically, we cover three categories, unconditional synthesis, homogeneous domain synthesis, and heterogeneous domain synthesis. In Section 9.2, we take a step further with heterogeneous domain synthesis by providing a case study about synthesizing novel radiography views [59]. We demonstrate how the introduction of heterogeneous domain synthesis between X-ray and CT image domains could be applied to better synthesize X-ray images at novel views.

9.1 Design principles

9.1.1 Unconditional synthesis

Unconditional synthesis is the generation of medical data without conditioning on extra inputs. When it comes to generative modeling, it means to model the full joint distribution of training data, and sampling from the modeled distribution results in data samples statistically close to training data. In terms of medical image synthesis, it means to train generative models that can produce (via random sampling) diverse and unseen medical images that are visually indistinguishable from the training samples. Unconditional synthesis is the most basic form of image synthesis and the original generative models [22,42,17,73] are proposed to address image synthesis in this setting. The most popular type of generative models for image synthesis are generative adversarial networks (GANs), and in this section we introduce GANs for unconditional medical image synthesis.

9.1.1.1 Problem definition and choice of objective functions

Let $\mathcal{I}$ be a target medical image domain. We train a GAN to address the unconditional synthesis of images from $\mathcal{I}$. A GAN consists of two subnets, a generator g and a discriminator d. The generator g takes a random noise $\mathbf{z} \sim p_{\mathbf{z}}(\mathbf{z})$ as input and generates an image $g(\mathbf{z})$. The discriminator d takes an image as input and decides if the input is a sample from $\mathcal{I}$ or generated by g. For a vanilla GAN [22], d is formulated as a binary classifier and outputs a scalar $d(\mathbf{x})$ that represents the probability of the input being a sample from $\mathcal{I}$. In adversarial modeling, g and d play a minimax game which can be described as follows:

$$\min_g \max_d \mathcal{L}_{\text{GAN}}(g, d) = \mathbb{E}_{\mathbf{x} \sim p_{\mathcal{I}}}[\log d(\mathbf{x})] + \mathbb{E}_{\mathbf{z} \sim p_{\mathbf{z}}}[\log(1 - d(g(\mathbf{z})))]. \quad (9.1)$$

Here, we simultaneously train g and d. When training d (and thus fixing g's parameters), we maximize Eq. (9.1) which encourages d to predict 1 for samples from $\mathcal{I}$ (the first term) and predict 0 for samples generated by g (the second term). When training g (and thus fixing d's parameters), we minimize Eq. (9.1). That is, we encourage g to generate samples statistically close to samples from $\mathcal{I}$ so that d cannot correctly classify $g(\mathbf{z})$ and output high probability value (the second term). In this way, the progression of one subnet is leveraged to improve the other. For g and d with sufficient capacity, when both subnets cannot be further improved, we reach a point where $p_{\mathcal{I}} = p_g$, i.e., sampling an image from g is essentially sampling an image from $\mathcal{I}$.

Improvements to unconditional GANs. While GANs have solid theoretical foundation, it is well known that the training process of vanilla GANs is brittle. Therefore, many efforts have been made to stabilize the training of GANs and generate diverse, high-resolution and realistic images. Specifically, for unconditional image synthesis, there are generally two ways to improve GANs: 1) improving the network architectures and the related training strategies; and 2) improving the objective functions. Next, we introduce several ideas that improve GANs along these two directions.

The vanilla GAN implements g and d with multilayer perceptrons which do not have enough capacity to handle the generation of high-resolution and high-quality images. To address this limitation, Radford et al. [61] proposed a DCGAN model that implements g and d with convolutional layers. They provided details in the architecture design and adversarial training to demonstrate the dedication to stabilizing GANs for image generalization. Zhang et al. [82] proposed a SAGAN that introduced a self-attention mechanism into convolutional GANs, which showed significant generation quality improvement. Based on SAGAN, Brock et al. [7] introduced BigGAN with tricks and techniques for large GAN training. They showed that, using large networks, BigGAN improved SAGAN by a large margin. The StyleGAN family [38,37,36] currently holds one of the best performing GANs in natural image synthesis. StyleGAN is originally developed from PGGAN [39] and includes style-based designs for better control of the generation.

In addition to improving the architectures and related training strategies, some other researchers seek to improve GAN's objective function, which largely contributes to the instability of GAN training. As pointed out by Arjovsky et al. [2], the original objective function of GANs has problems such as vanishing gradients, mode collapse, unbounded gradients, and undefined distribution distance measure. To address the vanishing gradients problem, vanilla GAN proposed an alternative logistic loss [22] that does not saturate when the discriminator rejects with high confidence. However, this solution will then likely introduce the mode collapse problem due to the inverted KL-divergence it aims to minimize [2]. Therefore, other researchers proposed GAN losses, such as least squares loss [52] or hinge loss [48], that do not saturate when the discriminator progresses. The most well-known one is the Wasserstein GAN [3], which not only avoids vanishing gradients but also induces weak topology and hence has better chance to converge. The problem with Wasserstein GAN is that it requires the discriminator to be K-Lipschitz which may not be always satisfied during the optimization. To address this problem Gulrajani et al. [25] introduced a gradient penalty term to encourage the discriminator to be 1-Lipschitz. Moreover, requiring the discriminator be K-Lipschitz also addresses the unbounded gradients problem since it means bounding the gradients with norm K almost everywhere. Following this idea, Miyato et al. [54] introduced spectrum normalization layers that impose the discriminator be 1-Lipschitz by construction. Finally, the f-divergence family of GANs [56] (which includes vanilla GANs) may have undefined f-divergence measure when the model or data are confined to low-dimensional manifolds. Therefore, Arjovsky et al. [2] proposed to introduce noises to both the real and generated data to smoothen the distribution and thus with enough bandwidth of the noise the f-divergence is well-defined. However, the noises are high-dimensional (in comparison to the support of the generator) and as a result requires considerable more number of samples for parameter estimation. Roth et al. [63,53] further showed that adding noises to inputs can be approximated by regularizing with gradient penalty which avoids sampling the high-dimensional noise data.

9.1.1.2 Deep learning models for unconditional medical image synthesis

Motivated by the rapid development of GANs for unconditional natural image synthesis, GANs had also been applied to synthesize medical images in the past few years. The initial attempts were merely trying GANs to understand their feasibility in medical image synthesis, and tests had been made to see if medical professionals could tell the synthesized images from the clinical ones. For example, Chuquicusma et al. [14] applied DCGAN [61] to synthesize lung lesions from CT images. The synthesized lesion patches mostly looked reasonable, but they were still far from realistic. Han et al. [26] tried both DCGAN [61] and WGAN [3] for brain MR image synthesis. They showed that WGAN generated MR images with much better quality than DCGAN and hence made it more challenging for medical professionals to identify the synthesized images. More recently, Fetty et al. [18] leveraged the more advanced StyleGAN [38] for both CT and MR image synthesis. Their results demonstrated that it was feasible to generate realistic medical images even at high-resolution. Meanwhile, they also investigated the manipulation of GAN latent space and showed the possibility of controlling the content of medical image synthesis.

Another application of unconditional medical image synthesis is for data augmentation. Salehinejad et al. [64] tried DCGAN for chest X-ray synthesis. The trained models were then applied to augment the X-ray dataset and balanced the number of images for each pathology category. The authors showed that, with GAN augmented datasets, they were able to train X-ray pathology classification models with much improved performance. Similarly, Frid-Adar et al. [19] applied DCGAN to synthesize liver lesions in CT images and achieved better liver lesion classification performance with augmented datasets. These two works only addressed data augmentation for classification problems which could be simply handled by training generative models separately for each category or applying Auxiliary Classifier GAN [57]. When it comes image segmentation, they are not applicable. Bowles et al. [6] proposed to address the more challenging image segmentation problems. Specifically, they trained PGGANs [39] to augment datasets for CT and MR image segmentation. Since training segmentation models required the availability of ground-truth segmentation masks, they proposed to model the joint probability of image and segmentation mask with GANs and had the PGGAN to generate outputs with two channels, one containing CT/MR images and the other containing the corresponding segmentation labels.

9.1.2 Homogeneous domain synthesis

Homogeneous domain synthesis aims to address the conditional synthesis between images of homogeneous domains. Here we use the term homogeneous domain to indicate that the source and target domain images may not necessarily have the same modality, but the captured content (e.g., anatomical structures) are spatially and semantically aligned. For example, we may be given a chest CT image of a patient and want to synthesize the corresponding MR image as if MR scan was given to the patient. Similarly, we may be also interested in the image translation between different variations of MR images (e.g., T1-to-T2) or between different decompositions of X-ray images [1].

Therefore, when dealing with a homogeneous domain synthesis problem, we usually formulate the problem as an image-to-image translation problem where we aim to develop models to transform images from source domain to target domain. We expect a transformed image spatially maintains the content of the input source domain image but has style or characteristics of target domain images. Explicitly modeling such a transformation is challenging, and sometimes the problem might be even ill-posed. Hence, we consider addressing the problem in a data-driven way and train deep image-to-image networks for homogeneous domain synthesis.

9.1.2.1 Problem definition and choice of objective functions

Let $\mathcal{X}$ be the source domain and $\mathcal{Y}$ be the target domain. For homogeneous domain synthesis, we aim to train a deep image-to-image network g that takes $\mathbf{X} \in \mathcal{X}$ as the input and outputs an image $\hat{\mathbf{Y}}$ that is close to images from domain $\mathcal{Y}$, i.e., $\hat{\mathbf{Y}} = g(\mathbf{X}; \mathbf{W})$ where $\mathbf{W}$ are the parameters of g that we aim to optimize. For the choices of network architecture, any deep image-to-image networks are applicable. The most widely used one is U-Net [62] but we may also consider some more recent architectures such as UNet++ [85], nnU-Net [33] and TransUNet [11].

Learning with paired images. For the objective functions, when we have paired images available, i.e., given an image $\mathbf{X}$ from source domain, we have access to its corresponding ground truth image $\mathbf{Y}$ from target domain, we can simply minimize the MSE loss to train g,

$$\mathcal{L}_{\mathrm{MSE}}(g) = \mathbb{E}_{\mathbf{XY}} \| g(\mathbf{X}; \mathbf{W}) - \mathbf{Y} \|_2. \tag{9.2}$$

Applying MSE loss may result in overly smoothed images. To address this problem, we may consider introducing the adversarial loss

$$\mathcal{L}_{adv}(g, d_g) = \mathbb{E}_{\mathbf{Y}}[\log d_g(\mathbf{Y})] + \mathbb{E}_{\mathbf{X}}[\log 1 - d_g(g(\mathbf{X}))]. \qquad (9.3)$$

Here, d_g is a discriminator, and it is trained together with g in an adversarial way as we have introduced in Section 9.1.1.1. Applying the adversarial loss only may cause spatial misalignment between the input and output images. Therefore, the MSE loss and adversarial loss are usually applied together to balance between the spatial alignment and realness. The loss can be written as

$$\mathcal{L}_{paired}(g, d_g) = \mathcal{L}_{adv}(g, d_g) + \lambda \mathcal{L}_{MSE}(g). \qquad (9.4)$$

Learning with unpaired images. While this loss generally works well, the limitation is that it requires the availability of paired images which may not always be satisfied in practice. Instead, we usually have to deal with the unpaired learning scenario, where we have access to images from both domain $\mathcal{X}$ and domain $\mathcal{Y}$, but for a given image $\mathbf{X} \in \mathcal{X}$ we do not know the paired ground truth $\mathbf{Y} \in \mathcal{Y}$. For example, when synthesizing CT from MR images, it is usually impractical to obtain a pair of anatomically aligned CT and MR images from the same patient as it requires scanning with CT and MR simultaneously. For the same patient, we can only capture CT and MR at different times which results in unaligned images. To align the CT and MR, we may resort to multimodal registration which, however, is another challenging task. In a more common setting, we are only provided with a CT from one patient and an MR from another, and hence even registration is impossible. Therefore, it necessitates learning homogeneous domain synthesis directly with unpaired images. The most widely adopted solution for this problem is CycleGAN [86] which introduces a cycle consistency loss,

$$\mathcal{L}_{cycle}(g, f) = \mathbb{E}_{\mathbf{Y}}[\|g(f(\mathbf{Y})) - \mathbf{Y}\|_1] + \mathbb{E}_{\mathbf{X}}[\|f(g(\mathbf{X})) - \mathbf{X}\|_1], \qquad (9.5)$$

where f is a generator that maps images from $\mathcal{Y}$ to $\mathcal{X}$; $\mathcal{L}_{cycle}$ can be thought of as a replacement for the MSE loss (i.e., $\mathcal{L}_{MSE}$) in paired learning. It only requires access to marginal distributions of $\mathcal{Y}$ and $\mathcal{X}$, and thus obviates the need for paired images. Taking the adversarial losses into consideration, the total loss for unpaired learning can be written as

$$\mathcal{L}_{unpaired}(g, f, d_g, d_f) = \mathcal{L}_{adv}(g, d_g) + \mathcal{L}_{adv}(f, d_f) + \lambda \mathcal{L}_{cycle}(g, f), \qquad (9.6)$$

where $\mathcal{L}_{adv}(f, d_f)$ is the adversarial loss for training f, and d_f is the corresponding discriminator of f.

9.1.2.2 Deep learning models for homogeneous domain synthesis
Homogeneous domain synthesis has been applied to address various problems in medical image computing. Liu et al. [49] applied homogeneous domain synthesis to

improve the quality of PET/MR imaging. They proposed to use a convolution autoencoder (CAE) network to estimate the different materials (e.g., air, bone, and soft tissue) from MR images and then synthesize pseudo-CT images from the CAE outputs. The pseudo-CT images can be used to correct photon attenuation maps which are crucial for accurate PET acquisition. Hwang et al. [32] proposed to improve the PET imaging without relying on MR images. They used a CAE network to synthesize CT attenuation maps from μ-maps derived from the MLAA algorithm. They showed that CAE networks gave more accurate estimation of CT attenuation than applying only MLAA, and hence resulted in better PET reconstruction quality.

Han et al. [27] proposed to synthesize CT images from MR images and leverage the synthesized CT to facilitate radiotherapy dose planning. In their approach, they trained a U-Net for MR–CT translation under the paired learning setting. The limitation of this approach was that the paired images were obtained via deformable registration which however could not perfectly align CT and MR images. To address this problem, Wolterink et al. [75] proposed to train a CycleGAN under the unpaired learning setting. Their method was able to generate CT images that aligned with the input MR better than CT–MR registration, and therefore had more potential than paired learning methods in addressing the radiotherapy dose planning

Chartsias et al. [9] leveraged fully convolution neural networks for multicontrast MR synthesis. They proposed to map MR images with different modalities to a shared modality-invariant latent space. In this way, they could take an arbitrary number of MR modalities (of the same patient) as the input and synthesize any other target MR modalities of interest. While being flexible to the input and output MR modalities, the limitation of this approach was that it was developed under the paired learning setting where the input MR modalities and the ground-truth MR modalities were expected to be aligned. Dar et al. [16] addressed the unpaired learning of multicontrast MR synthesis with CycleGAN. The problem with this approach was that it only supported the bidirectional synthesis of a pair of MR modalities. When more modalities were to consider, it would require training a significant number of CycleGAN models and hence make it computationally prohibitive. To address this problem, Lee et al. [45] proposed a model called CollaGAN that learned the joint manifold of multiple MR modalities. It extended CycleGAN to the multidomain image-to-image translation setting and could estimate any missing modality from a given set of available modalities.

9.1.3 Heterogeneous domain synthesis

Heterogeneous domain synthesis is the conditional synthesis between two heterogeneous domains. That is, given a sample from source domain, we aim to generate the corresponding sample from target domain. However, unlike homogeneous domain synthesis, the input and output samples from source and target domains are not spatially aligned. They may only contain contents that are aligned in terms of semantics and/or some physical laws. For example, in medical imaging, we may deal with both the sensor domain (e.g., X-ray images) and image domain (e.g., CT images) data.

Although both domains can capture the same information of a subject, the representations of information are different and there is no correspondence between the sensor domain data and image domain data at pixel or voxel level. We may also be interested in the generation between medical image and text, such as generating medical reports from imaging data or synthesizing medical images given medical reports. In such cases, we have to work with the more challenging scenario where the input and output are only semantically aligned.

Due to the significant differences between source and target domains, the focus for heterogeneous domain synthesis is to design models to close the domain gap, and introduce prior knowledge to facilitate cross-domain generation. First, it requires designing deep neural networks with specialized encoder and decoder for source and target domains, respectively, so that they account for the dimensionality and modality differences between domains. For example, in X-ray to CT synthesis, the input image is 2D, and the output is 3D. Thus, the network should have an encoder that works for 2D images and a decoder that outputs 3D images. More importantly, the encoder and decoder design should facilitate this transition in dimensionality. Similarly, in medical image to text synthesis, the network should have dedicated components for the encoding and decoding of image and text, respectively. Meanwhile, they should work coherently so that the generated text matches the input image.

Second, the network design may also include prior knowledge about the source and target domains. This is particularly useful for heterogeneous domain synthesis problems since they are often ill-posed, and thus data-driven only approaches with conventional deep neural networks may not be well suited to address these problems. Introducing prior knowledge into the network design could help narrow down the searching space and facilitate the learning. For example, in single view 3D reconstruction, it has been shown that the state-of-the-art methods with encoder–decoder architectures tend to rely on recognition rather than reconstruction when generating 3D shapes [71]. Therefore, it could be beneficial to introduce prior knowledge of reconstruction to network design. This would help the model understand better about reconstruction and avoid being biased to recognition.

As for objective functions, most of the existing heterogeneous domain synthesis problems are formulated under the supervised learning assumption. Some widely used loss functions, such as MSE loss and cross-entropy loss, are applicable to these problems. Therefore, in this section, we will not give details on the loss function choices but focus on the network designs with an emphasis on the two directions we have just introduced.

9.1.3.1 Deep learning models for heterogeneous domain synthesis

One common scenario of heterogeneous domain synthesis is single- or few-image tomography, where we are given one or a few X-ray images from which we aim to reconstruct a CT image. This is an ill-posed problem and does not have unique solution. Thus, it cannot be directly addressed by conventional CT reconstruction approaches. Instead, it can be regarded as a heterogeneous domain synthesis problem, and the goal is to synthesize the most plausible CT image from the given X-rays. One of the earliest deep learning based approaches to this problem was proposed by Henzler et al. [28]. They applied an encoder–decoder network with skip connections similar to U-Net [62]. To address the transition from 2D to 3D, they identified that the decoder's outputs were already 3D, and the third dimension originally represented 2D features. Thus, they proposed to regard the feature dimension as the third spatial dimension of 3D volume. In this way, they could directly use the U-Net structure for 2D-to-3D image generation without dedicated architecture change. However, this also meant that there would be no 3D feature extraction which limited the expressiveness of the model. Kasten et al. [40] proposed to generate 3D knee bones from biplanar X-ray images. Similar to Henzler et al., they also used a U-Net-like structure for this 2D-to-3D image generation. The difference was they used a 3D U-Net so as to address the generation directly in 3D. For the input, since 3D U-Net assumed 3D input, they proposed to repeat the X-ray images along the third spatial dimension to construct a pseudo-3D volume and the biplanar X-ray images were concatenated along the channel dimension. While in this way they handled better 3D generation, the limitation was the use of 3D U-Net which significantly increased the computational cost compared 2D U-Net. Ying et al. [79] proposed an X2CT-GAN to reconstruct CT from biplanar X-rays. In this approach, they introduced a hybrid U-Net with 2D encoder and 3D decoder for 2D-to-3D image reconstruction. Moreover, they also introduced specialized connection modules to 1) bridge 2D encoder and 3D decoder, 2) shuttle low-level 2D features from encoder to decoder, and 3) fuse features of biplanar X-rays. With these dedicated designs for 2D-to-3D generation, their method showed improved CT reconstruction performance.

Another example of heterogeneous domain synthesis is the generation between medical image and medical reports. Jing et al. [34] were the first to investigate the generation of medical reports for given X-ray images. They followed the idea from image captioning [76,35,80] by encoding X-ray images with convolutional neural network and generating report paragraphs with LSTM [30]. Inspired by Xu et al. [76], they also applied semantic attentions so that the generation could focus on diagnostic related content. Yuan et al. [81] proposed to encode multiple semantic information (i.e., visual features, radiography observations, and medical concepts.) for better understanding of radiography content. And more importantly, the decoder could leverage these encoded semantics for better generation of the medical reports. Yang et al. [78] proposed an XRayGAN to generate X-ray images from medical reports, which could then be applied to train radiology students. In particular, this model used LSTMs [30] to encode medical reports at both word- and sentence-level. Then, the text-embeddings were sent to a multiscale conditional GAN (MSCGAN) to synthesize X-ray images. The MSCGAN consisted of progressive generators for lateral and frontal X-ray views, respectively, and hence could generate high-resolution biplanar X-ray images at a time.

Besides adapting network architectures, many others considered also introducing prior knowledge to facilitate the heterogeneous domain synthesis. Unberath et al. [72] addressed the problem of synthesizing digitally reconstructed radiographs (DRRs). The conventional synthesis method cannot produce DRRs that are visually close to real X-ray images. The major reason is that conventional DDR generation process does not accurately model X-ray image formation. To address this limitation, Unberath et al. proposed a DeepDRR framework that introduced prior knowledge about X-ray imaging by including modules for 1) X-ray attenuation, 2) scatter estimation, and 3) noise generation. They showed that with this DeepDRR framework they were able to generate images more similar to clinical X-ray images. Machine learning models trained using DeepDRR images showed improved performance than using DRR images. Song et al. [68] proposed to introduce oral curvature information as prior to reconstruct 3D oral cavity from panoramic X-ray image. Unlike the other single- or few-image tomography solutions, they did not directly reconstruct 3D CBCT images since it was ill-posed via panoramic X-ray. Instead, they chose to reconstruct the flattened 3D oral structure which has less ambiguity when reconstructing from panoramic X-ray. To recover the curved shape of oral cavity, they extracted dental arch from an intraoral photo and used it as a prior to deform the flattened 3D oral structure which gave the final oral cavity. Shen et al. [66] proposed to introduce geometry information for ultrasparse 3D tomographic reconstruction. Instead of relying on convolutional layers to address the transition from 2D to 3D, they introduced a geometric backprojection operator to unfold 2D projections to 3D space. This operator preserved the geometry information via backprojection, and hence its outputs made it easier for the later 3D network to generate CT images. Li et al. [46] leveraged medical knowledge graphs to better output diagnostic information for medical report generation. Specifically, they proposed to generate abnormality graph as the intermediate output after obtaining the visual features. Then, medical reports could be generated by decoding from the abnormality graph.

9.2 Case study: novel radiography view synthesis

Radiography, widely used for visualizing the internal human anatomy, applies high-energy radiation, or X-ray, to pass through the body, and measures the remaining radiation energy on a planar detector. Since different organs attenuate X-ray to various degrees, the detected energy is visualized as a 2D image or a radiograph, that reveals the internal structure of the body and provides valuable diagnostic information.

Radiography is fast and economical. However, when scanned with high energy radiation, it can cause adverse health effects. Conventionally, only a single, frontal view radiograph is acquired per session, e.g., for chest radiography. While physicians can intuitively relate the different organs on a 2D radiograph in 3D space, such intuition is implicit and varies in accuracy. As such, a radiograph view synthesis algorithm can help provide additional information to assist in understanding a patient's internal structure.

The ability to understand radiographs in a 3D context is also essential beyond providing more visual information. For example, since every pixel on a radiograph represents an X-ray traversing in 3D, it is principally ambiguous to label a pixel as a

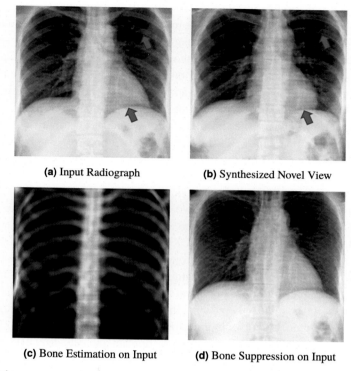

(a) Input Radiograph

(b) Synthesized Novel View

(c) Bone Estimation on Input

(d) Bone Suppression on Input

FIGURE 9.1

From a *real* radiograph (a), XraySyn synthesizes a radiograph of novel view (b). As the view point rotate clockwise in azimuth angle, observe that the heart and the rib bones, as the blue arrows indicate, change accordingly. Additionally, XraySyn obtains the bone structure (c) across all views and can be used to perform bone suppression (d). Both synthesized views and bone estimate are generated without direct supervision.

specific anatomical structure, as X-rays inevitably pass through multiple structures. By exploring 3D context, we can disentangle a pixel into values that represent different structures, and lead to improved analysis algorithms. Particularly, bone extraction on *real* radiographs is difficult, but has been used in fracture analysis [10], lesion detection [47], etc. In this work, we tackle radiograph understanding in 3D, specifically through the tasks of novel view synthesis and bone extraction. Transforming 2D images to 3D objects is by nature ill-posed. In the natural image domain, deep learning-based methods have shown impressive results in addressing such a problem. Radiograph view synthesis, however, poses several unique challenges. Firstly, there is no multiview dataset for radiographs due to privacy and radiation concerns, which prohibits the use of supervised learning. Secondly, there is no *differentiable* algorithm that ensures geometrically consistent transformations between radiographs and the 3D space. Lastly, unlike visible light, X-rays can penetrate objects, therefore to invert the X-ray projection one should take into account both the surface and internal 3D structure, making the problem even more ill-posed than for natural images and thus poses challenges to unsupervised methods.

While inverse graphics is a daunting task to be solved directly on real radiographs, some attempts have been made to address it through Digitally Reconstructed Radiographs (DRRs) [79,28]. DRRs [55] are simulated radiographs from Computed Tomography (CT) volumes, which are abundantly available. This approach addresses the data scarcity for learning a 2D–3D transformation; however, significant differences remain between real radiographs and DRRs. The generation of DRRs also cannot be incorporated into a learning-based algorithm, and either is done offline [28] or has severe limitations in available view angles [79].

In this work, we introduce a novel, two-stage algorithm called *XraySyn* to estimate the 3D context from a radiograph and use it for novel view synthesis and bone extraction (see Fig. 9.1). The first stage of XraySyn, called 3D PriorNet (3DPN), incorporates a pair of differentiable backprojection and forward projection operators to learn the radiograph-to-CT transformation under a simulated setting. These operators ensure the transformations between radiograph and CT to be geometrically consistent, therefore significantly reducing the complexity of learning. We further incorporate the differentiable forward projector into a modified DeepDRR [72], which simulates realistic radiographs, to minimize the domain gap between DRRs and real radiographs.

The second stage of XraySyn, called 2D RefineNet (2DRN), further enhances the projected radiograph from its estimated 3D CT. By using a Generative Adversarial Network (GAN) and residual connections, 2DRN produces high-quality radiographic views and their respective bone structure. In summary, our contributions can be described in four parts:

- We propose a differentiable forward projection operator and incorporate it within a modified DeepDRR, forming a pipeline called CT2Xray that simulates realistic radiographs from a CT, propagates gradients, and runs fast.
- We propose a 3D PriorNet (3DPN), which incorporates CT2Xray and generates the 3D context from a single radiograph through learning from the paired relationships between simulated radiographs and their CT volumes.
- We propose a 2D RefineNet (2DRN), which refines the 2D radiographs projected from 3DPN's output. By leveraging the availability of CT labels and the CT2Xray pipeline, the 2D RefineNet can synthesize not only novel radiograph views, but also the corresponding bone structure.
- We evaluate XraySyn, comprising 3DPN and 2DRN, on real radiographs and find the performance of view synthesis and bone extraction visually accurate, despite the lack of direct supervision in the radiograph domain.

9.2.1 Background

9.2.1.1 View synthesis from a single image

There is a long history of research in natural image view synthesis. For relevancy and brevity, we focus on recent advances in view synthesis based on a single image and with the use of CNN. One approach to tackling such a task is to generate the new view in an image-to-image fashion. Some methods [12,43] propose to generate a disentangled space where the image can be projected to and modified from to synthesize new views, while others [58,69,70,84] rely on GANs to generate the information that is occluded from the original view. In general, the image-to-image approach is based on sufficient pixel correspondence between views, which provide understanding for recovery in either the image space or latent space. Such pixel correspondence is much weaker between X-ray views. In spirit, our method is more similar to the 3D shape generation approaches [20,13,50,77,21,24] that concern the generation of 3D surfaces, which are less ill-posed than generating 3D volumes.

9.2.1.2 Radiograph simulation and transformation to CT

Due to the lack of multiview radiographs and the difficulties in correctly labeling them, data-driven methods that require large number of radiographs often turn to CT-based radiograph simulations. While Monte Carlo (MC) methods based on imaging physics [5,67,65] can lead to highly realistic radiograph simulations, they are time consuming and not scalable. Many works [47,23,79,1,8] use DRRs, which are less realistic but computationally inexpensive radiograph simulations, to perform tasks such as bone enhancement, bone suppression, disease identification, CT reconstruction, etc. In particular, Ying [79] addresses the discrepancy between DRRs and real radiographs by training an additional domain adaptation network. Henzler [28] uses real cranial X-ray images acquired in a controlled setting to recover the 3D bone structure. Song [68] uses a single Panoramic X-ray with a photo of the patient's mouth to reconstruct the 3D structure. As clinical evidence supports that bone suppression on radiograph can improve diagnostic accuracy [44], Li [47] proposes to achieve bone suppression by learning a bone segmentation network based on DRRs, and apply the network on real radiographs with handcrafted postprocesses. Recently, DeepDRR [72] was proposed to model DRR generation more accurately by replicating similar procedures from the MC simulation counterpart, and showed that CNN models trained on such simulations are able to generalize better on real radiographs.

9.2.2 Methodology

The main goal of this work is to synthesize novel views from a frontal view radiograph, which requires a degree of 3D knowledge. As multiview dataset is not readily available for real radiographs, our proposed method, XraySyn, composes of two stages. The first stage learns to estimate 3D knowledge under a simulated setting by using CT volumes. The second stage transfers such learning to generate real radiographs.

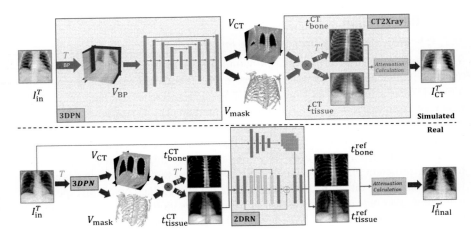

FIGURE 9.2

The proposed two-stage network structure of XraySyn. In the first stage (top), *simulated* radiographs are backprojected (BP) from view T, and refined through 3DPN to obtain their CT and bone mask estimates, V_{CT} and V_{mask}. Through CT2Xray, V_{CT} and V_{mask} are forward projected (FP) from view T' to calculate the tissue and bone content t_{bone}^{CT} and t_{tissue}^{CT}, which are used to simulate the novel view radiograph. In the second stage (bottom), t_{bone}^{CT} and t_{tissue}^{CT} are generated from *real* radiographs through a trained 3DPN, refined through 2DRN, and used to generate the novel view.

The challenge underlying this approach is how to best address the transformation from simulated radiographs to CT volumes, while ensuring the input radiograph can be reproduced from such volume. We first explain the proposed operators that enable learning such a transformation, CT2Xray and Single Image Backprojector. We then introduce XraySyn, which incorporates the two operators for a radiograph-to-CT-to-radiograph algorithm.

9.2.2.1 CT2Xray

CT2Xray, as shown in Fig. 9.2, has two parts: (i) the differentiable forward projection and (ii) attenuation-based radiograph simulation, which, along with the first part, forms CT2Xray and transforms a CT volume into a realistic radiograph. To the best of our knowledge, CT2Xray is *the first algorithm* that can generate realistic radiographs from CT volumes with gradient propagation along arbitrary viewpoint.

Differentiable forward projector (FP). Let V_{CT} denote a CT image, FP generates a 2D projection of V_{CT} by

$$I(x) = \text{FP}(V_{CT}, T) = \int V_{CT}(T^{-1}p)dl(x) \approx \sum_{p \in l(x)} V_{CT}(T^{-1}p)\Delta p, \qquad (9.7)$$

where T is a homogeneous matrix that controls the rotation and translation of the view point and $l(x)$ is a line segment connecting the simulated X-ray source and detector at x. For backpropagation, the gradients of I with regard to V_{CT} can be written as

$$\frac{\partial I(x)}{\partial V_{CT}(y)} = \begin{cases} \Delta p, & \text{if } Ty \in l(x), \\ 0, & \text{otherwise.} \end{cases} \tag{9.8}$$

Equations for (9.7) and (9.8) can be implemented through massive parallelism with GPUs, where every line integral over the volume is a stand-alone operation; as such this implementation can be used in online training.

CT2Xray. Forward projecting CT volumes generates DRRs, which are poor simulations of X-ray images due to the inaccurate assumption that different tissues attenuate the X-ray similarly. DeepDRR [72] produces a better simulation by avoiding this assumption, but it is not differentiable and hence not amenable for end-to-end learning. We contribute a *differentiable X-ray simulation* pipeline, called CT2Xray, which incorporates the differentiable forward projector and produces more realistic radiographs. In [72], a realistic X-ray attenuation I_{atten} is modeled as

$$I_{\text{atten}} = \sum_{E} I_0 \exp(-\sum_{m} \mu(m, E)t_m) + \text{SE} + \text{noise}, \tag{9.9}$$

where $\mu(m, E)$ is the linear attenuation coefficient of material m at energy state E and is measured and known [31], t_m is the material thickness. SE is the scatter estimation term, I_0 is the source X-ray intensity. Along with noise, SE and I_0 are omitted for simplicity.

CT2Xray considers only the bone and tissue materials. With the aid of a bone mask V_{mask} and using the differentiable forward projector FP, it calculates the material thickness $t_m^{\text{CT}}(T), m \in \{\text{bone,tissue}\}$ with regard to the projection parameter T as

$$\begin{aligned} t_{\text{bone}}^{\text{CT}}(T) &= \text{FP}(V_{CT} \odot V_{\text{mask}}, T), \\ t_{\text{tissue}}^{\text{CT}}(T) &= \text{FP}(V_{CT} \odot (1 - V_{\text{mask}}), T). \end{aligned} \tag{9.10}$$

Radiographs are typically stored and viewed as inverted versions of the measured attenuation. Therefore, CT2Xray can be expressed as

$$\text{CT2Xray}(V_{CT}, V_{\text{mask}}, T) = \max(I_{\text{atten}}^T) - I_{\text{atten}}^T, \tag{9.11}$$

with

$$I_{\text{atten}}^T = \sum_{E} \exp(-\sum_{m} \mu(m, E)t_m^{\text{CT}}(T)). \tag{9.12}$$

9.2.2.2 XraySyn

XraySyn is trained in two stages, as shown in Fig. 9.2. The simulation stage trains a radiograph-to-CT transformation network, called 3D PriorNet (3DPN), and with help of CT2Xray generate radiographic views from the estimated CT. The real-radiograph stage, which trains a 2D RefineNet (2DRN), then further closes the domain gap between simulated and real radiographs. Due to the need for calculating the material-dependent attenuation, we also gain the ability to transfer labels from the CT domain to the radiograph domain, in our case with CT bone labels, and achieve bone extraction on real radiographs.

Single image backprojector (BP).   While CT2Xray generates radiographs from CT volumes, an inverse function is needed to transform radiographs back to the respective CT volumes. Such a transformation is clearly ill-posed. However, we can formulate an inverse function of the forward projector to properly place the input X-ray image in 3D. We call such an inverse function the *single image backprojector*. Following a similar formulation from general backprojection algorithm, which reconstructs CBCT from multiview radiographs as described in [41], the single image backprojector (BP) is expressed as follows:

$$V_{\text{BP}}^T(y) = \text{BP}(I(x), T) = \begin{cases} \frac{I(x)}{|I(x)|\Delta p}, & \text{if } Ty \in I(x), \\ 0, & \text{otherwise.} \end{cases} \tag{9.13}$$

By substituting V_{BP}^T in (9.13) into V_{CT} in (9.7), the same I is recovered under view T, hence we denote V_{BP}^T obtained in this way as the backprojection of I at view T. While the same image-wise consistency does not generally apply to CT2Xray, i.e., substituting (9.13) into (9.11) does not recover I. We show that by using a CNN to complement the single image backprojector, such consistency can be better approximated due to geometric consistency.

3D PriorNet (3DPN).   Under the simulated setting, Single Image Backprojector BP produces V_{BP}^T from input view radiograph I^T, and CT2Xray produces a desired view radiograph $I^{T'}$ from V_{CT} and V_{mask}. To complete the end-to-end radiograph-to-CT generation, we train a generator $\mathcal{G}$ to recover V_{CT} and V_{mask} from V_{BP}^T. Mathematically, the generation process between radiograph and CT can be expressed as:

$$\begin{aligned} \{V_{\text{CT}}, V_{\text{mask}}\} &= 3\text{DPN}(I_{in}^T, T) = \mathcal{G}(\text{BP}(I_{in}^T, T); \theta), \\ I_{\text{CT}}^{T'} &= \text{CT2Xray}(V_{\text{CT}}, V_{\text{mask}}, T'), \end{aligned} \tag{9.14}$$

where θ represents the parameters in $\mathcal{G}$. We use a 3D U-Net [15] structure for $\mathcal{G}$. The loss functions for training $\mathcal{G}$ need to ensure consistency both in CT and radiograph domains, and are defined as

$$\mathcal{L}_G = \lambda_{\text{CT}}\mathcal{L}_{\text{CT}} + \lambda_{\text{mask}}\mathcal{L}_{\text{mask}} + \lambda_{\text{xray}}(\mathcal{L}_{\text{xray}}^T + \mathcal{L}_{\text{xray}}^{T'}), \tag{9.15}$$

where λ_{CT}, λ_{mask}, and λ_{xray}^T are loss weights; $\mathcal{L}_{\text{CT}}$, $\mathcal{L}_{\text{mask}}$, and $\mathcal{L}_{\text{xray}}^T$ are defined as:

$$\mathcal{L}_{\text{CT}} = \|V_{\text{CT}} - V_{\text{gt}}\|_1, \quad \mathcal{L}_{\text{mask}} = \text{CE}(V_{\text{mask}}, V_{\text{mask}}^{\text{gt}}),$$
$$\mathcal{L}_{\text{xray}}^T = \|I_{\text{CT}}^T - I_{\text{in}}^T\|_1 + \sum_m \|t_{\text{m}}^{\text{CT}}(T) - t_{\text{m}}^{\text{gt}}(T)\|_1, \tag{9.16}$$

where CE refers to the cross-entropy loss and $\mathcal{L}_{\text{xray}}^{T'}$ is defined similarly as $\mathcal{L}_{\text{xray}}^T$.

2D RefineNet (2DRN).   While 3DPN estimates a degree of 3D context from a radiograph, such estimation is both coarse in quality, due to the ill-posed nature, and in resolution, due to memory constraint. Furthermore, there exists a domain gap between real and simulated radiograph. To address these issues, we introduce a second stage, called 2DRN, which has two goals: (i) to generate realistic radiographs from the output of 3DPN with higher resolution, and (ii) to do so with small refinements on t_m^{CT} such that we can still obtain the material decomposition of the output radiograph. Conceptually, 2DRN can be understood as a part of an augmented, learnable CT2Xray. 2DRN is constructed in two parts. The main refinement network $\mathcal{F}$ is based on Residual Dense Network (RDN) [83]. Additionally, a fully convolutional network $\mathcal{M}$ is used to generate certain convolutional layer parameters in $\mathcal{F}$ directly from the input I_{in}^T. The purpose of $\mathcal{M}$ is to shuttle high level information that may be lost during the process of 3DPN. Overall, the refinement on t_m^{CT} is expressed as

$$t_m^{\text{ref}}(T) = 2\text{DRN}(t_m^{\text{CT}}(T), I_{\text{in}}^T) = t_m^{\text{CT}}(T) + \mathcal{F}(t_m^{\text{CT}}; \phi, \mathcal{M}(I_{\text{in}}^T)), \tag{9.17}$$

where ϕ and $\mathcal{M}(I_{\text{in}}^T)$ represent the parameters in $\mathcal{F}$. Replacing t_m^{CT} in (9.11) with t_m^{ref} yields an augmented CT2Xray,

$$\text{CT2Xray}_{\text{aug}}(V_{\text{CT}}, V_{\text{mask}}, T) = \max(I_{\text{ref}}^T) - I_{\text{ref}}^T, \tag{9.18}$$

where $I_{\text{ref}}^T = \sum_E \exp(-\sum_m \mu(m, E) t_m^{\text{ref}})$. Similarly, the final view synthesis results are defined as $I_{\text{final}}^{T'} = \text{CT2Xray}_{\text{aug}}(V_{\text{CT}}, V_{\text{mask}}, T')$. A Least-Squares GAN (LSGAN) is used to ensure $I_{\text{final}}^{T'}$ is statistically similar to I_{in}^T when T' and T are relatively close. The overall loss function for 2DRN is described as

$$\mathcal{L}_{\text{2DRN}} = \lambda_{\text{recon}} \|I_{\text{final}}^T - I_{\text{in}}^T\|_1 + \lambda_{\text{GAN}} \mathcal{L}_{\text{LSGAN}}(I_{\text{final}}^{T'}, I_{\text{in}}^T). \tag{9.19}$$

$\mathcal{L}_{\text{LSGAN}}$ is defined as

$$\mathcal{L}_{\text{LSGAN}}^{\mathcal{D}}(I_{\text{final}}^{T'}, I_{\text{in}}^T) = \mathbb{E}[\mathcal{D}(I_{\text{im}}^T - 1)^2)] + \mathbb{E}[\mathcal{D}(I_{\text{final}}^{T'} - 0)^2],$$
$$\mathcal{L}_{\text{LSGAN}}^{\mathcal{F} \circ \mathcal{M}}(I_{\text{final}}^{T'}) = \mathbb{E}[\mathcal{D}(I_{\text{final}}^{T'} - 1)^2], \tag{9.20}$$

where $\mathcal{D}$ indicates the discriminator. The LSGAN plays a adversarial game. When training $\mathcal{D}$, it aims to have $\mathcal{D}$ distinguish between the real radiograph I_{im}^T and the generated radiograph $I_{\text{final}}^{T'}$; and output 1 when the input is I_{im}^T and 0 when the input is $I_{\text{final}}^{T'}$. When training $\mathcal{F} \circ \mathcal{M}$, i.e., (9.17), it aims to have 2DRN output $I_{\text{final}}^{T'}$ as realistic as possible so that $\mathcal{D}$ cannot tell it from real radiographs and output 1 on $I_{\text{final}}^{T'}$.

9.2.3 Experiments

9.2.3.1 Implementation details

The two stages of XraySyn are trained separately. To train 3DPN, a CT volume V_{gt} and its bone mask V_{mask}^{gt} is used to simulate the ground-truth radiographs I_{in}^{T} and $I_{gt}^{T'}$; T and T' are sampled randomly from $-18°$ to $18°$ in azimuth and elevation angles. During the training of 2DRN, real radiographs are used as I_{in}^{T} in place of simulated radiographs, and the 3DPN's parameters are frozen. Furthermore, the input is first downsampled through average pooling as real radiographs are of higher resolution. As view angles are not available for real radiographs, we sample T and T' randomly in similar fashion as for 3DPN training. For testing on real radiograph, T is assumed to be the canonical frontal view, T' are twenty view angles uniformly spaced from $-9°$ to $9°$ in azimuth. Due to the discretization of the voxel-based representation, the ray tracing process used in forward and backprojection needs to approximate points in space when those points are not on the coordinate grid. We use trilinear interpolation for such an approximation. The networks are implemented with Pytorch, and trained using four Nvidia P6000 GPUs for five days.

9.2.3.2 Dataset

Both CT and radiograph datasets are needed for training XraySyn. To train the 3DPN, we use the LIDC-IDRI dataset [4], which contains 1018 chest CT volumes. We discards all volumes that have a between-slices resolution higher than 2.5 mm. This leads to 780 CT volumes, from which we randomly select 700 for training, 10 for evaluation, and 70 for testing. To preprocess the data, we tightly crop the CT volumes to eliminate excess empty space, and reshape the volumes into resolution of $128 \times 128 \times 128$. To train 2DRN with real radiographs, we use the TBX11K dataset [51]. Specifically, to avoid the excessive interference of foreign objects and abnormal anatomy, we manually select 3000 images under the healthy category within TBX11K and crop those images to have similar field-of-view as the CT simulation. The images are then reshaped to resolution of 256×256. We randomly select 2600 for training, 100 for evaluation, and 300 for testing.

9.2.3.3 Evaluation metrics

Evaluation of novel view synthesis on real radiograph can be challenging, as there is no ground truth. Therefore, we first provide the results of evaluation on simulated radiographs. Peak Signal-to-Noise Ratio (PSNR) and Structured Similarity Index (SSIM) [74] are used to measure the quality of synthesized novel views and material decomposition. For real radiographs, we use PSNR and SSIM to measure the quality of reconstruction for the input view T and Fréchet Inception Distance (FID) [29] to measure the realism of the novel view radiograph in comparison to the input view radiograph. Since radiographs are grayscale images, we do the following to adapt to the ImageNet-trained InceptionV3 model: 1) we repeat the grayscale values across the RGB channels, and 2) use the middle layer features from InceptionV3, specifically the 768-channel layer before InceptionV3's last auxiliary classifier, for better generalizability.

Table 9.1 Ablation study of our proposed methods against alternative implementations. Note that 3DPN-DRR and 2D Refiner do not use CT2Xray, therefore are without metrics for t_{bone}, t_{tissue}. Also I_{CT}^T for 2D Refiner is trivially generated as I_{in}^T. PSNR/SSIM metrics are provided when ground truth is available, otherwise FID score is reported. The best performing metrics are bold.

| Method | View | | | | | | | |
| | Simulated | | | | | | Real | |
	I_{CT}^T	t_{bone}^T	t_{tissue}^T	$I_{CT}^{T'}$	$t_{bone}^{T'}$	$t_{tissue}^{T'}$	I_{final}^T	$I_{final}^{T'}$ (FID)
2D Refiner	–	–	–	21.1/0.80	–	–	–	–
X2CT	20.4/0.76	16.0/0.45	19.6/0.71	20.2/0.75	16.1/0.45	19.4/0.70	–	–
3DPN-DRR	21.1/0.93	–	–	19.8/0.87	–	–	–	–
3DPN	**29.5/0.96**	**22.3/0.81**	**24.4/0.87**	**27.2/0.93**	**21.63/0.78**	**24.3/0.86**	22.8/0.82	1.090
XraySyn$^{no}\mathcal{M}$	–	–	–	–	–	–	28.4/0.86	0.375
XraySyn	–	–	–	–	–	–	**30.3/0.87**	**0.319**

9.2.3.4 Ablation study

We evaluate the effectiveness of XraySyn against alternative 2D or 3D methods. Firstly, comparisons against 3DPN are made under the simulated setting as described below:

- 2D Refiner: An image-to-image method by synthesizing new views from input $FP(BP(I_{in}^T, T), T')$ through a 2D DenseNet structure. The training is constrained by an L1 loss between the generated X-ray and its ground truth.
- X2CT: Proposed by Ying et al. [79] to transform DRRs into CT volumes. We made the following adaptations: (i) instead of DRRs, the inputs are X-rays generated by CT2Xray, and (ii) the training losses are consistent with Eq. (9.15).
- 3DPN-DRR: An alternative 3DPN that directly uses forward projection to simulate radiographs, i.e., DRRs. Note that no material decomposition is involved in DRR.

Comparisons against the overall XraySyn method are then made for generating real radiographs. These include:

- 3DPN: A direct use of 3DPN trained on simulated data.
- XraySyn$^{no}\mathcal{M}$: An alternative XraySyn where the 2DRN stage does not have $\mathcal{M}$.

Table 9.1 summarizes the performance of different implementations over various view angles, and visualization of the results are provided in Fig. 9.3. Image-to-image approach like 2D Refiner synthesizes mostly a blurry version of the input view. The lack of an explicit 3D loss forces the network to overly smooth the output for the best PSNR. The implementation of X2CT-CNN copies the 2D features along a third axis to achieve the initial upsampling from 2D to 3D, which is geometrically incorrect for arbitrary view angles. While CNN's strong learning ability still helps X2CT-CNN produce a coarse 3D estimation, it has difficulty in learning the geometric transformation that maps the input image to the correct view. Consequently, the

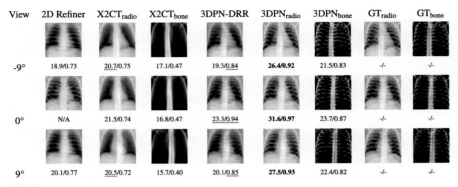

View	2D Refiner	X2CT$_{radio}$	X2CT$_{bone}$	3DPN-DRR	3DPN$_{radio}$	3DPN$_{bone}$	GT$_{radio}$	GT$_{bone}$
-9°	18.9/0.73	20.7/0.75	17.1/0.47	19.3/0.84	**26.4/0.92**	21.5/0.83	-/-	-/-
0°	N/A	21.5/0.74	16.8/0.47	23.3/0.94	**31.6/0.97**	23.7/0.87	-/-	-/-
9°	20.1/0.77	20.5/0.72	15.7/0.40	20.1/0.85	**27.5/0.93**	22.4/0.82	-/-	-/-

FIGURE 9.3

Visual comparisons of novel view radiographs generated by different methods based on simulated radiographs as inputs. View angle change is measured azimuthally. For each non-ground-truth image, PSNR/SSIM are provided as metrics. Note that the input view for 2D Refiner is trivially generated as I_{in}^T. Methods that involve the use of CT2Xray are displayed with both the bone t_{bone}^{CT} and radiograph outputs. The best radiograph generation metrics are bold, the second best is underlined.

synthesized views are reliant on a poorly estimated 3D structure and lack significant details, specifically over the rib cage area.

By using the geometrically consistent backprojection and forward projection, 3DPN-DRR and 3DPN perform much better at preserving the input radiograph during the 2D-to-3D transformation. The main issue of DRR is its assumption that the rays attenuate over bone and tissue similarly, when in fact bone attenuates X-rays much better and therefore has better contrast on real radiographs. The results show that when 3DPN-DRR is used on more realistically simulated radiographs, bone appears much softer. While this impacts PSNR significantly, 3DPN-DRR results have much better SSIM scores compared to X2CT and 2D Refiner due to the superior 3D estimation. Finally, 3DPN, which includes all proposed components, performs much better than other methods (6–7 dB more than the second best method in terms of PSNR) at capturing the 3D anatomy from a single radiograph. As 2D-to-3D transformation is still ill-posed, the metrics worsen when the novel view is further from the input view.

Using 3DPN to perform view synthesis on real radiographs involves additional challenges. Specifically, 3DPN is limited in the available resolution and cannot generate sufficient details, e.g., as shown in Fig. 9.4, 3DPN-generated bone structure is less visible on the rib cage area, as those bones are small and hard to be accurately estimated in 3D. Furthermore, simulation does not address complex imaging conditions. As a result, views synthesized through 3DPN are blurry and constrained to have a certain image style due to the formulation of CT2Xray. 2DRN is proposed to address these problems by performing refinement on $t_m^{CT}(T')$ to preserve the material decomposition information.

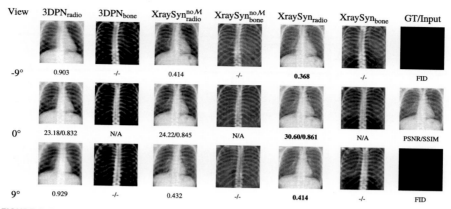

FIGURE 9.4

Visual comparisons of novel view radiographs generated by different methods based on real radiographs as inputs. View angle change is measured azimuthally. PSNR/SSIM metrics are provided for input radiograph reconstruction, FID is provided for novel view synthesis with respect to input radiographs. The best metrics are bold.

After refining the 3DPN results in $\text{XraySyn}^{\text{no}\mathcal{M}}$, the novel views are much improved in both low-level details and overall realism, along with the corresponding bone map $t_{\text{bone}}^{\text{ref}}$. However, some information is inevitably lost during 3DPN. The input in Fig. 9.4 is grayish in the lung area, as opposed to the typical dark color from simulation. This information is not captured in 3DPN, thus the subsequent refinement network is also limited in its recovery performance. Also $\mathcal{M}$ is designed to shuffle information directly from the input radiograph. To prevent 2DRN from learning an identity transform of the input radiograph, $\mathcal{M}$ generates convolutional filter parameters to constrict the information flow. The complete XraySyn, which includes $\mathcal{M}$ in 2DRN, improves the overall performance by almost 1 dB with little additional computational cost. While 2DRN does not explicitly guarantee overall 3D consistency, we observe that the novel views are fairly consistent with each other due to the residual learning on the 3D-consistent 3DPN results. As the refinement on t_m^{CT} is not directly supervised, we observe a slight amount of background noise despite training the network with a residual connection. However, this can be addressed through post-processing steps. It is worth noting that due to the lack of alternative-view radiograph dataset, synthesized novel views beyond a limited range from the frontal view may lead to unfaithful results as compared to real circumstances.

9.2.3.5 Bone suppression

A natural application of XraySyn is on radiograph bone suppression, which seeks to reduce bone attenuation and better reveal the underlying tissues. To best preserve the tissue information from input radiograph I_{in}^T, we find $t_{\text{bone}}^{\text{ref}}$ and $t_{\text{tissue}}^{\text{recon}}$ so that they losslessly reconstruct I_{in}^T, through reversing the CT2Xray operation as shown

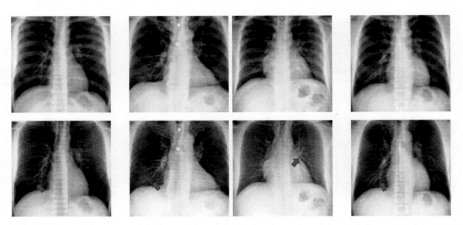

FIGURE 9.5

Bone-suppressed radiographs obtained by postprocessing the results from XraySyn: (top) Input radiographs from TBX11K [51] and (bottom) the bone-suppressed results. Note that the arteries, as indicated with blue arrows, are more visible after bone suppression.

in Eq. (9.12). In Fig. 9.5, we show that our approach suppresses most of the rib cage bones while preserving the tissue content.

9.2.4 Discussion

We proposed a two-stage radiograph view synthesis method, XraySyn. This method estimates a coarse 3D CT from a 2D radiograph, simulates a novel view from the estimated volume, and finally refines the views to be visually consistent with real radiographs. The learning process of XraySyn is enabled by our proposed differentiable forward projector and backprojector. Furthermore, by incorporating the CT bone labels in CT2Xray that is inspired by DeepDRR and implemented with our differentiable forward projector, we not only achieve realistic simulation for training the radiograph-to-CT transformation, but also gain the ability to transfer bone labels from CT to radiograph. We carefully evaluate our method both on simulated and real radiographs, and find that XraySyn generates highly realistic and consistent novel view radiographs. To the best of our knowledge, this is the first work on radiograph view synthesis, which can give practitioners a more precise understanding of the patient's 3D anatomy. XraySyn also opens up possibilities for many downstream processes on radiograph, such as lesion detection, organ segmentation, and sparse-view CT reconstruction. Currently, XraySyn is limited in resolution due to memory constraint of 3DPN. We plan to address this limitation through a more efficient network design. In addition, we will conduct a study to assess the effect of bone suppression for clinical diagnosis.

9.3 Summary

We have introduced deep learning-based approaches to medical data synthesis. We covered two forms of syntheses, unconditional and conditional, and introduced design principles for these two forms. For unconditional synthesis, we focused on solutions with generative adversarial networks (GANs) [22], which have been widely adopted to address medical data synthesis problems. We began by introducing the vanilla GAN and how to train GAN models for image synthesis. Then, we presented different GAN architectures and objective functions on improving the synthesis quality. Finally, we showed how these improvements of GANs can be applied to address the unconditional synthesis of medical images.

We identified two categories of conditional synthesis approaches, homogeneous and heterogeneous domain synthesis. For homogeneous domain synthesis, we highlighted its connection with image-to-image translation and showed how to train deep image-to-image networks for the translation between two homogeneous domains. We then gave examples of applying image-to-image translation models to address the translation between two medical imaging modalities. For heterogeneous domain synthesis, we noted the heterogeneous nature of the source and target domains. Therefore, we focused on solutions that close such domain gaps. In particular, we positioned this challenge under various medical problems requiring heterogeneous domain synthesis, and presented methods that introduce specialized network architectures or prior knowledge to address this challenge.

To exemplify the design principles, we provided a case study on novel radiography view synthesis. We proposed a model called XraySyn that has specialized modules for the heterogeneous domain synthesis between X-ray and CT images and thus facilitates the generation of novel radiography views. Moreover, we introduced prior knowledge of CT imaging and X-ray projection to close the domain gap between CT and radiography. We showed that it not only improves the quality of radiography image synthesis but also can be leveraged to suppress bones from radiography.

References

[1] Shadi Albarqouni, Javad Fotouhi, Nassir Navab, X-ray in-depth decomposition: revealing the latent structures, in: International Conference on Medical Image Computing and Computer-Assisted Intervention, Springer, 2017, pp. 444–452.

[2] Martin Arjovsky, Léon Bottou, Towards principled methods for training generative adversarial networks, arXiv preprint, arXiv:1701.04862, 2017.

[3] Martín Arjovsky, Soumith Chintala, Léon Bottou, Wasserstein GAN, CoRR, arXiv:1701.07875 [abs], 2017.

[4] Samuel G. Armato III, Geoffrey McLennan, Luc Bidaut, Michael F. McNitt-Gray, Charles R. Meyer, Anthony P. Reeves, Binsheng Zhao, Denise R. Aberle, Claudia I. Henschke, Eric A. Hoffman, et al., The lung image database consortium (LIDC) and image

database resource initiative (IDRI): a completed reference database of lung nodules on CT scans, Medical Physics 38 (2) (2011) 915–931.

[5] Andreu Badal, Aldo Badano, Accelerating Monte Carlo simulations of photon transport in a voxelized geometry using a massively parallel graphics processing unit, Medical Physics 36 (11) (2009) 4878–4880.

[6] Christopher Bowles, Liang Chen, Ricardo Guerrero, Paul Bentley, Roger Gunn, Alexander Hammers, David Alexander Dickie, Maria Valdés Hernández, Joanna Wardlaw, Daniel Rueckert, GAN augmentation: augmenting training data using generative adversarial networks, arXiv preprint, arXiv:1810.10863, 2018.

[7] Andrew Brock, Jeff Donahue, Karen Simonyan, Large scale GAN training for high fidelity natural image synthesis, arXiv preprint, arXiv:1809.11096, 2018.

[8] Mónica Iturrioz Campo, Javier Pascau, Raúl San José Estépar, Emphysema quantification on simulated X-rays through deep learning techniques, in: 2018 IEEE 15th International Symposium on Biomedical Imaging (ISBI 2018), IEEE, 2018, pp. 273–276.

[9] Agisilaos Chartsias, Thomas Joyce, Mario Valerio Giuffrida, Sotirios A. Tsaftaris, Multimodal MR synthesis via modality-invariant latent representation, IEEE Transactions on Medical Imaging 37 (3) (2018) 803–814.

[10] Haomin Chen, Yirui Wang, Kang Zheng, Weijian Li, Chi-Tung Cheng, Adam P. Harrison, Jing Xiao, Gregory D. Hager, Le Lu, Chien-Hung Liao, Shun Miao, Anatomy-aware Siamese network: exploiting semantic asymmetry for accurate pelvic fracture detection in X-ray images, CoRR, arXiv:2007.01464 [abs], 2020.

[11] Jieneng Chen, Yongyi Lu, Qihang Yu, Xiangde Luo, Ehsan Adeli, Yan Wang, Le Lu, Alan L. Yuille, Yuyin Zhou, TransUNet: transformers make strong encoders for medical image segmentation, arXiv preprint, arXiv:2102.04306, 2021.

[12] Xi Chen, Yan Duan, Rein Houthooft, John Schulman, Ilya Sutskever, Pieter Abbeel, InfoGAN: interpretable representation learning by information maximizing generative adversarial nets, in: Daniel D. Lee, Masashi Sugiyama, Ulrike von Luxburg, Isabelle Guyon, Roman Garnett (Eds.), Advances in Neural Information Processing Systems 29: Annual Conference on Neural Information Processing Systems 2016, December 5–10, 2016, Barcelona, Spain, 2016, pp. 2172–2180, http://papers.nips.cc/paper/6399-infogan-interpretable-representation-learning-by-information-maximizing-generative-adversarial-nets.

[13] Christopher B. Choy, Danfei Xu, JunYoung Gwak, Kevin Chen, Silvio Savarese, 3D-R2N2: a unified approach for single and multi-view 3D object reconstruction, in: Bastian Leibe, Jiri Matas, Nicu Sebe, Max Welling (Eds.), Computer Vision – ECCV 2016 – 14th European Conference, Amsterdam, the Netherlands, October 11–14, 2016, Proceedings, Part VIII, in: Lecture Notes in Computer Science, vol. 9912, Springer, 2016, pp. 628–644.

[14] Maria J.M. Chuquicusma, Sarfaraz Hussein, Jeremy Burt, Ulas Bagci, How to fool radiologists with generative adversarial networks? A visual Turing test for lung cancer diagnosis, in: 2018 IEEE 15th International Symposium on Biomedical Imaging (ISBI 2018), IEEE, 2018, pp. 240–244.

[15] Özgün Çiçek, Ahmed Abdulkadir, Soeren S. Lienkamp, Thomas Brox, Olaf Ronneberger, 3D U-Net: learning dense volumetric segmentation from sparse annotation, in: Sébastien Ourselin, Leo Joskowicz, Mert R. Sabuncu, Gözde B. Ünal, William Wells (Eds.), Medical Image Computing and Computer-Assisted Intervention – MICCAI 2016 – 19th International Conference, Athens, Greece, October 17–21, 2016, Proceedings, Part II, in: Lecture Notes in Computer Science, vol. 9901, 2016, pp. 424–432.

[16] Salman U.H. Dar, Mahmut Yurt, Levent Karacan, Aykut Erdem, Erkut Erdem, Tolga Çukur, Image synthesis in multi-contrast MRI with conditional generative adversarial networks, IEEE Transactions on Medical Imaging 38 (10) (2019) 2375–2388.

[17] Laurent Dinh, David Krueger, Yoshua Bengio, Nice: non-linear independent components estimation, arXiv preprint, arXiv:1410.8516, 2014.

[18] Lukas Fetty, Mikael Bylund, Peter Kuess, Gerd Heilemann, Tufve Nyholm, Dietmar Georg, Tommy Löfstedt, Latent space manipulation for high-resolution medical image synthesis via the StyleGAN, Zeitschrift für medizinische Physik 30 (4) (2020) 305–314.

[19] Maayan Frid-Adar, Idit Diamant, Eyal Klang, Michal Amitai, Jacob Goldberger, Hayit Greenspan, GAN-based synthetic medical image augmentation for increased CNN performance in liver lesion classification, Neurocomputing 321 (2018) 321–331, https://doi.org/10.1016/j.neucom.2018.09.013.

[20] Rohit Girdhar, David F. Fouhey, Mikel Rodriguez, Abhinav Gupta, Learning a predictable and generative vector representation for objects, in: Bastian Leibe, Jiri Matas, Nicu Sebe, Max Welling (Eds.), Computer Vision – ECCV 2016 – 14th European Conference, Amsterdam, the Netherlands, October 11–14, 2016, Proceedings, Part VI, in: Lecture Notes in Computer Science, vol. 9910, Springer, 2016, pp. 484–499.

[21] Georgia Gkioxari, Justin Johnson, Jitendra Malik, Mesh R-CNN, in: 2019 IEEE/CVF International Conference on Computer Vision, ICCV 2019, Seoul, Korea (South), October 27 – November 2, 2019, 2019, pp. 9784–9794.

[22] Ian Goodfellow, Jean Pouget-Abadie, Mehdi Mirza, Bing Xu, David Warde-Farley, Sherjil Ozair, Aaron Courville, Yoshua Bengio, Generative adversarial nets, in: Advances in Neural Information Processing Systems, 2014.

[23] Ophir Gozes, Hayit Greenspan, Lung structures enhancement in chest radiographs via CT based FCNN training, in: Image Analysis for Moving Organ, Breast, and Thoracic Images – Third International Workshop, RAMBO 2018, Fourth International Workshop, BIA 2018, and First International Workshop, TIA 2018, Held in Conjunction with MICCAI 2018, Granada, Spain, September 16 and 20, 2018, Proceedings, in: Lecture Notes in Computer Science, vol. 11040, Springer, 2018, pp. 147–158.

[24] Thibault Groueix, Matthew Fisher, Vladimir G. Kim, Bryan C. Russell, Mathieu Aubry, AtlasNet: a papier-mâché approach to learning 3D surface generation, CoRR, arXiv:1802.05384 [abs], 2018.

[25] Ishaan Gulrajani, Faruk Ahmed, Martin Arjovsky, Vincent Dumoulin, Aaron Courville, Improved training of Wasserstein GANs, in: Proceedings of the 31st International Conference on Neural Information Processing Systems, 2017, pp. 5769–5779.

[26] Changhee Han, Hideaki Hayashi, Leonardo Rundo, Ryosuke Araki, Wataru Shimoda, Shinichi Muramatsu, Yujiro Furukawa, Giancarlo Mauri, Hideki Nakayama, GAN-based synthetic brain MR image generation, in: 2018 IEEE 15th International Symposium on Biomedical Imaging (ISBI 2018), IEEE, 2018, pp. 734–738.

[27] Xiao Han, MR-based synthetic CT generation using a deep convolutional neural network method, Medical Physics 44 (4) (2017) 1408–1419.

[28] Philipp Henzler, Volker Rasche, Timo Ropinski, Tobias Ritschel, Single-image tomography: 3D volumes from 2D cranial X-rays, Computer Graphics Forum 37 (2) (2018) 377–388.

[29] Martin Heusel, Hubert Ramsauer, Thomas Unterthiner, Bernhard Nessler, Sepp Hochreiter, GANs trained by a two time-scale update rule converge to a local Nash equilibrium, in: Isabelle Guyon, Ulrike von Luxburg, Samy Bengio, Hanna M. Wallach, Rob Fergus,

S.V.N. Vishwanathan, Roman Garnett (Eds.), Advances in Neural Information Processing Systems 30: Annual Conference on Neural Information Processing Systems 2017, 4–9 December 2017, Long Beach, CA, USA, 2017, pp. 6626–6637.

[30] Sepp Hochreiter, Jürgen Schmidhuber, Long short-term memory, Neural Computation 9 (8) (1997) 1735–1780.

[31] John H. Hubbell, Stephen M. Seltzer, Tables of X-ray mass attenuation coefficients and mass energy-absorption coefficients 1 keV to 20 MeV for elements Z = 1 to 92 and 48 additional substances of dosimetric interest, Technical report, National Inst. of Standards and Technology-PL, Gaithersburg, MD, USA, 1995.

[32] Donghwi Hwang, Kyeong Yun Kim, Seung Kwan Kang, Seongho Seo, Jin Chul Paeng, Dong Soo Lee, Jae Sung Lee, Improving the accuracy of simultaneously reconstructed activity and attenuation maps using deep learning, Journal of Nuclear Medicine 59 (10) (2018) 1624–1629.

[33] Fabian Isensee, Paul F. Jaeger, Simon A.A. Kohl, Jens Petersen, Klaus H. Maier-Hein, nnU-Net: a self-configuring method for deep learning-based biomedical image segmentation, Nature Methods 18 (2) (2021) 203–211.

[34] Baoyu Jing, Pengtao Xie, Eric Xing, On the automatic generation of medical imaging reports, in: Proceedings of the 56th Annual Meeting of the Association for Computational Linguistics (Volume 1: Long Papers), 2018, pp. 2577–2586.

[35] Andrej Karpathy, Li Fei-Fei, Deep visual-semantic alignments for generating image descriptions, in: Proceedings of the IEEE Conference on Computer Vision and Pattern Recognition, 2015, pp. 3128–3137.

[36] Tero Karras, Miika Aittala, Samuli Laine, Erik Härkönen, Janne Hellsten, Jaakko Lehtinen, Timo Aila, Alias-free generative adversarial networks, in: Thirty-Fifth Conference on Neural Information Processing Systems, 2021.

[37] Tero Karras, Samuli Laine, Miika Aittala, Janne Hellsten, Jaakko Lehtinen, Timo Aila, Analyzing and improving the image quality of styleGAN, in: Proceedings of the IEEE/CVF Conference on Computer Vision and Pattern Recognition, 2020, pp. 8110–8119.

[38] Tero Karras, Samuli Laine, Timo Aila, A style-based generator architecture for generative adversarial networks, in: IEEE Conference on Computer Vision and Pattern Recognition, CVPR 2019, Long Beach, CA, USA, June 16–20, 2019, Computer Vision Foundation / IEEE, 2019, pp. 4401–4410.

[39] Tero Karras, Timo Aila, Samuli Laine, Jaakko Lehtinen, Progressive growing of GANs for improved quality, stability, and variation, in: International Conference on Learning Representations, 2018.

[40] Yoni Kasten, Daniel Doktofsky, Ilya Kovler, End-to-end convolutional neural network for 3D reconstruction of knee bones from bi-planar X-ray images, in: International Workshop on Machine Learning for Medical Image Reconstruction, Springer, 2020, pp. 123–133.

[41] Paul E. Kinahan, Michel Defrise, Rolf Clackdoyle, CHAPTER 20 - analytic image reconstruction methods, in: Miles N. Wernick, John N. Aarsvold (Eds.), Emission Tomography, Academic Press, San Diego, 2004, pp. 421–442.

[42] Diederik P. Kingma, Max Welling, Auto-encoding variational Bayes, arXiv preprint, arXiv:1312.6114, 2013.

[43] Tejas D. Kulkarni, William F. Whitney, Pushmeet Kohli, Joshua B. Tenenbaum, Deep convolutional inverse graphics network, in: Corinna Cortes, Neil D. Lawrence, Daniel D. Lee, Masashi Sugiyama, Roman Garnett (Eds.), Advances in Neural Information

Processing Systems 28: Annual Conference on Neural Information Processing Systems 2015, December 7–12, 2015, Montreal, Quebec, Canada, 2015, pp. 2539–2547.

[44] M. Ann Laskey, Dual-energy X-ray absorptiometry and body composition, Nutrition 12 (1) (1996) 45–51.

[45] Dongwook Lee, Won-Jin Moon, Jong Chul Ye, Assessing the importance of magnetic resonance contrasts using collaborative generative adversarial networks, Nature Machine Intelligence 2 (1) (2020) 34–42.

[46] Christy Y. Li, Xiaodan Liang, Zhiting Hu, Eric P. Xing, Knowledge-driven encode, retrieve, paraphrase for medical image report generation, in: Proceedings of the AAAI Conference on Artificial Intelligence, vol. 33, 2019, pp. 6666–6673.

[47] Han Li, Hu Han, Zeju Li, Lei Wang, Zhe Wu, Jingjing Lu, S. Kevin Zhou, High-resolution chest X-ray bone suppression using unpaired CT structural priors, IEEE Transactions on Medical Imaging (2020).

[48] Jae Hyun Lim, Jong Chul Ye, Geometric GAN, arXiv preprint, arXiv:1705.02894, 2017.

[49] Fang Liu, Hyungseok Jang, Richard Kijowski, Tyler Bradshaw, Alan B. McMillan, Deep learning MR imaging–based attenuation correction for PET/MR imaging, Radiology 286 (2) (2018) 676–684.

[50] Shaohui Liu, Yinda Zhang, Songyou Peng, Boxin Shi, Marc Pollefeys, Zhaopeng Cui, DIST: rendering deep implicit signed distance function with differentiable sphere tracing, CoRR, arXiv:1911.13225 [abs], 2019.

[51] Yun Liu, Yu-Huan Wu, Yunfeng Ban, Huifang Wang, Ming-Ming Cheng, Rethinking computer-aided tuberculosis diagnosis, in: 2020 IEEE/CVF Conference on Computer Vision and Pattern Recognition, CVPR 2020, Seattle, WA, USA, June 13–19, 2020, IEEE, 2020, pp. 2643–2652.

[52] Xudong Mao, Qing Li, Haoran Xie, Raymond Y.K. Lau, Zhen Wang, Stephen Paul Smolley, Least squares generative adversarial networks, in: Proceedings of the IEEE International Conference on Computer Vision, 2017, pp. 2794–2802.

[53] Lars Mescheder, Andreas Geiger, Sebastian Nowozin, Which training methods for GANs do actually converge?, in: International Conference on Machine Learning, PMLR, 2018, pp. 3481–3490.

[54] Takeru Miyato, Toshiki Kataoka, Masanori Koyama, Yuichi Yoshida, Spectral normalization for generative adversarial networks, arXiv preprint, arXiv:1802.05957, 2018.

[55] C.S. Moore, G.P. Liney, A.W. Beavis, J.R. Saunderson, A method to produce and validate a digitally reconstructed radiograph-based computer simulation for optimisation of chest radiographs acquired with a computed radiography imaging system, British Journal of Radiology 84 (1006) (2011) 890–902, PMID: 21933979.

[56] Sebastian Nowozin, Botond Cseke, Ryota Tomioka, f-GAN: training generative neural samplers using variational divergence minimization, in: Proceedings of the 30th International Conference on Neural Information Processing Systems, 2016, pp. 271–279.

[57] Augustus Odena, Christopher Olah, Jonathon Shlens, Conditional image synthesis with auxiliary classifier GANs, 2017, pp. 2642–2651.

[58] Eunbyung Park, Jimei Yang, Ersin Yumer, Duygu Ceylan, Alexander C. Berg, Transformation-grounded image generation network for novel 3D view synthesis, in: 2017 IEEE Conference on Computer Vision and Pattern Recognition, CVPR 2017, Honolulu, HI, USA, July 21–26, 2017, IEEE Computer Society, 2017, pp. 702–711.

[59] Cheng Peng, Haofu Liao, Gina Wong, Jiebo Luo, S. Kevin Zhou, Rama Chellappa, XraySyn: realistic view synthesis from a single radiograph through CT priors, in: Thirty-Fifth AAAI Conference on Artificial Intelligence, AAAI 2021, Thirty-Third Conference

on Innovative Applications of Artificial Intelligence, IAAI 2021, the Eleventh Symposium on Educational Advances in Artificial Intelligence, EAAI 2021, Virtual Event, February 2–9, 2021, AAAI Press, 2021, pp. 436–444.

[60] Jerry L. Prince, Aaron Carass, Can Zhao, Blake E. Dewey, Snehashis Roy, Dzung L. Pham, Image synthesis and superresolution in medical imaging, in: Handbook of Medical Image Computing and Computer Assisted Intervention, Elsevier, 2020, pp. 1–24.

[61] Alec Radford, Luke Metz, Soumith Chintala, Unsupervised representation learning with deep convolutional generative adversarial networks, arXiv preprint, arXiv:1511.06434, 2015.

[62] Olaf Ronneberger, Philipp Fischer, Thomas Brox, U-Net: convolutional networks for biomedical image segmentation, in: International Conference on Medical Image Computing and Computer-Assisted Intervention, 2015.

[63] Kevin Roth, Aurelien Lucchi, Sebastian Nowozin, Thomas Hofmann, Stabilizing training of generative adversarial networks through regularization, Advances in Neural Information Processing Systems 30 (2017).

[64] Hojjat Salehinejad, Shahrokh Valaee, Tim Dowdell, Errol Colak, Joseph Barfett, Generalization of deep neural networks for chest pathology classification in X-rays using generative adversarial networks, in: 2018 IEEE International Conference on Acoustics, Speech and Signal Processing (ICASSP), IEEE, 2018, pp. 990–994.

[65] Wilfried Schneider, Thomas Bortfeld, Wolfgang Schlegel, Correlation between CT numbers and tissue parameters needed for Monte Carlo simulations of clinical dose distributions, Physics in Medicine and Biology 45 (2) (2000) 459.

[66] Liyue Shen, Wei Zhao, Dante Capaldi, John Pauly, Lei Xing, A geometry-informed deep learning framework for ultra-sparse 3D tomographic image reconstruction, arXiv preprint, arXiv:2105.11692, 2021.

[67] Alejandro Sisniega, Wojciech Zbijewski, A. Badal, I.S. Kyprianou, Joseph Webster Stayman, Juan José Vaquero, J.H. Siewerdsen, Monte Carlo study of the effects of system geometry and antiscatter grids on cone-beam CT scatter distributions, Medical Physics 40 (5) (2013) 051915.

[68] Weinan Song, Yuan Liang, Jiawei Yang, Kun Wang, Lei He, Oral-3D: reconstructing the 3D structure of oral cavity from panoramic X-ray, in: Thirty-Fifth AAAI Conference on Artificial Intelligence, AAAI 2021, Thirty-Third Conference on Innovative Applications of Artificial Intelligence, IAAI 2021, the Eleventh Symposium on Educational Advances in Artificial Intelligence, EAAI 2021, Virtual Event, February 2–9, 2021, AAAI Press, 2021, pp. 566–573.

[69] Shao-Hua Sun, Minyoung Huh, Yuan-Hong Liao, Ning Zhang, Joseph J. Lim, Multiview to novel view: synthesizing novel views with self-learned confidence, in: Vittorio Ferrari, Martial Hebert, Cristian Sminchisescu, Yair Weiss (Eds.), Computer Vision – ECCV 2018 – 15th European Conference, Munich, Germany, September 8–14, 2018, Proceedings, Part III, in: Lecture Notes in Computer Science, vol. 11207, Springer, 2018, pp. 162–178.

[70] Maxim Tatarchenko, Alexey Dosovitskiy, Thomas Brox, Multi-view 3D models from single images with a convolutional network, in: Bastian Leibe, Jiri Matas, Nicu Sebe, Max Welling (Eds.), Computer Vision – ECCV 2016 – 14th European Conference, Amsterdam, the Netherlands, October 11–14, 2016, Proceedings, Part VII, in: Lecture Notes in Computer Science, vol. 9911, Springer, 2016, pp. 322–337.

[71] Maxim Tatarchenko, Stephan R. Richter, René Ranftl, Zhuwen Li, Vladlen Koltun, Thomas Brox, What do single-view 3d reconstruction networks learn?, in: Proceed-

ings of the IEEE/CVF Conference on Computer Vision and Pattern Recognition, 2019, pp. 3405–3414.

[72] Mathias Unberath, Jan-Nico Zaech, Sing Chun Lee, Bastian Bier, Javad Fotouhi, Mehran Armand, Nassir Navab, DeepDRR – a catalyst for machine learning in fluoroscopy-guided procedures, in: Alejandro F. Frangi, Julia A. Schnabel, Christos Davatzikos, Carlos Alberola-López, Gabor Fichtinger (Eds.), Medical Image Computing and Computer Assisted Intervention – MICCAI 2018 – 21st International Conference, Granada, Spain, September 16–20, 2018, Proceedings, Part IV, in: Lecture Notes in Computer Science, vol. 11073, Springer, 2018, pp. 98–106.

[73] Aaron Van Oord, Nal Kalchbrenner, Koray Kavukcuoglu, Pixel recurrent neural networks, in: International Conference on Machine Learning, PMLR, 2016, pp. 1747–1756.

[74] Zhou Wang, Alan C. Bovik, Hamid R. Sheikh, Eero P. Simoncelli, Image quality assessment: from error visibility to structural similarity, IEEE Transactions on Image Processing 13 (4) (2004) 600–612.

[75] Jelmer M. Wolterink, Anna M. Dinkla, Mark H.F. Savenije, Peter R. Seevinck, Cornelis A.T. van den Berg, Ivana Išgum, Deep MR to CT synthesis using unpaired data, in: International Workshop on Simulation and Synthesis in Medical Imaging, Springer, 2017, pp. 14–23.

[76] Kelvin Xu, Jimmy Ba, Ryan Kiros, Kyunghyun Cho, Aaron C. Courville, Ruslan Salakhutdinov, Richard S. Zemel, Yoshua Bengio, Show, attend and tell: neural image caption generation with visual attention, in: ICML, vol. 14, 2015, pp. 77–81.

[77] Qiangeng Xu, Weiyue Wang, Duygu Ceylan, Radomír Mech, Ulrich Neumann, DISN: deep implicit surface network for high-quality single-view 3D reconstruction, in: Hanna M. Wallach, Hugo Larochelle, Alina Beygelzimer, Florence d'Alché-Buc, Emily B. Fox, Roman Garnett (Eds.), Advances in Neural Information Processing Systems 32: Annual Conference on Neural Information Processing Systems 2019, NeurIPS 2019, 8–14 December 2019, Vancouver, BC, Canada, 2019, pp. 490–500.

[78] Xingyi Yang, Nandiraju Gireesh, Eric Xing, Pengtao Xie, XRayGAN: consistency-preserving generation of X-ray images from radiology reports, arXiv preprint, arXiv:2006.10552, 2020.

[79] Xingde Ying, Heng Guo, Kai Ma, Jian Wu, Zhengxin Weng, Yefeng Zheng, X2CT-GAN: reconstructing CT from biplanar X-rays with generative adversarial networks, in: Proceedings of the IEEE/CVF Conference on Computer Vision and Pattern Recognition, 2019, pp. 10619–10628.

[80] Quanzeng You, Hailin Jin, Zhaowen Wang, Chen Fang, Jiebo Luo, Image captioning with semantic attention, in: Proceedings of the IEEE Conference on Computer Vision and Pattern Recognition, 2016, pp. 4651–4659.

[81] Jianbo Yuan, Haofu Liao, Rui Luo, Jiebo Luo, Automatic radiology report generation based on multi-view image fusion and medical concept enrichment, in: Dinggang Shen, Tianming Liu, Terry M. Peters, Lawrence H. Staib, Caroline Essert, Sean Zhou, Pew-Thian Yap, Ali R. Khan (Eds.), Medical Image Computing and Computer Assisted Intervention – MICCAI 2019 – 22nd International Conference, Shenzhen, China, October 13–17, 2019, Proceedings, Part VI, in: Lecture Notes in Computer Science, vol. 11769, Springer, 2019, pp. 721–729.

[82] Han Zhang, Ian Goodfellow, Dimitris Metaxas, Augustus Odena, Self-attention generative adversarial networks, in: International Conference on Machine Learning, PMLR, 2019, pp. 7354–7363.

[83] Yulun Zhang, Yapeng Tian, Yu Kong, Bineng Zhong, Yun Fu, Residual dense network for image super-resolution, in: The IEEE Conference on Computer Vision and Pattern Recognition (CVPR), 2018.

[84] Tinghui Zhou, Shubham Tulsiani, Weilun Sun, Jitendra Malik, Alexei A. Efros, View synthesis by appearance flow, in: Bastian Leibe, Jiri Matas, Nicu Sebe, Max Welling (Eds.), Computer Vision – ECCV 2016 – 14th European Conference, Amsterdam, the Netherlands, October 11–14, 2016, Proceedings, Part IV, in: Lecture Notes in Computer Science, vol. 9908, Springer, 2016, pp. 286–301.

[85] Zongwei Zhou, Md. Mahfuzur Rahman Siddiquee, Nima Tajbakhsh, Jianming Liang, UNet++: a nested U-Net architecture for medical image segmentation, in: Deep Learning in Medical Image Analysis and Multimodal Learning for Clinical Decision Support, Springer, 2018, pp. 3–11.

[86] Jun-Yan Zhu, Taesung Park, Phillip Isola, Alexei A. Efros, Unpaired image-to-image translation using cycle-consistent adversarial networks, in: International Conference on Computer Vision (ICCV), 2017.

Challenges and future directions

10

CONTENTS

We have covered a broad range of topics in medical image computing. As we have shown, deep learning has been applied to almost all areas of medical image computing and led to unprecedented improvements. In the foreseeable future, we believe the popularity of deep learning will continue, and deep learning related techniques will keep evolving with a fairly rapid pace. So far, deep learning is still the most promising technology that we could use to introduce artificial intelligence into the healthcare industry [7]. However, despite its success and promise, there is still a long way to go to make a significant clinical impact with deep learning or machine learning, in general. In fact, even with the tremendous effort from both academia and industry, we do not see many deep learning related solutions successfully deployed in real clinical workflows. The main reason behind this infeasibility is that deep learning based methods have yet to address the complexity of healthcare delivery and earn trust of healthcare professionals and patients.

As an encouraging sign, healthcare professionals are increasingly aware of and open to the adoption of machine learning and artificial intelligence in the healthcare delivery process. They are more and more willing to work together with machine learning technologists to improve parts or whole of the workflow and outcome.

10.1 Challenges and open issues
10.1.1 Effectiveness in clinical workflows

The existing research of medical image computing mostly involves the abstraction of clinical problems into different computer vision tasks and addresses them individually. It usually does not directly solve the exact problem that healthcare professionals aim to solve. When positioned in a clinical workflow, medical image computing solutions may not facilitate the healthcare delivery in a significant way. In particular, when a method cannot always address a task with high accuracy, it becomes tricky to find its role or value in the clinical workflow. While deep learning based methods have greatly advanced medical image computing research, they still do not have guaranteed high or expert-level performance under the complex clinical conditions. This means they may only work to provide side information to assist the healthcare providers' decision-making. Therefore, it becomes important to find the best way that deep learning based solution may be of great help to the clinical workflow [24]. Unfortunately, the current medical image computing research has largely ignored this requirement, leading to hypes rather than substance.

Comprehensiveness.   In clinical practice, what healthcare professionals need is usually a more comprehensive solution that addresses all or many aspects of the clinical workflow. For example, a deep learning model that recognizes only certain types of skin diseases or disorders does not usually reduce dermatologists' workloads as they may still need to check the image for cases of other abnormalities. The examination may also require describing the morphology such as color, size, location, etc., and may even involve different imaging views, imaging modalities or other measurements such as body temperature, blood pressure, urine test, etc. All of these require a general-purpose solution that can not only take multimodal information as input if necessary, but also provide clinical recommendations in a more versatile form.

Generalizability.   Another limiting factor of applying deep learning based methods is their generalizability, i.e., the ability to work with rare or out-of-distribution samples. Deep learning based methods are data-driven approaches. As a result, they perform well on inputs that are similar to the frequently appearing training data, and the performance drops on rare or out-of-distribution inputs. This property makes deep learning approaches data hungry as they require a significant number of training samples to achieve good performance, in general. On the other hand, medical imaging in clinical practice is complicated. Not only there could be many imaging modalities involved, but even for the same imaging modality there could be many imaging variations due to the differences of individual imaging devices, imaging parameters, and imaging operations. Moreover, the imaging content is also subject to great variety such as the inter- and intrapatient variations, different anatomical locations and positions, anomalies, etc. These variations have made it prohibitive to collect training samples that cover all the different imaging scenarios or patient variations, and hence it is almost impossible to guarantee the performance of deep learning models in clinical practice [14].

Data scarcity.   Even worse, collecting medical imaging data is a demanding task and thus it is challenging to perform data collection at scale. There are several reasons that contribute to this challenge. First, medical data is extremely sensitive. Therefore, unlike natural images where we could source training data from public sources, collecting unlabeled medical images itself is often subject to strict regulations [1,21]. Second, annotating medical image usually demands certain expertise in medicine. This means the annotators have to be either medical professionals or at least have received a significant amount of medical training. This high requirement limits the number of available annotators [41] and hence the amount of labeled medical data. Third, annotating medical image is often time-consuming. Such time consumption, on the one hand, comes from the complexity of the medical problems that slows down the reading of medical images, and, on the other hand, comes from the complexity of medical imaging data, e.g., it is inconvenient to browse through 3D volumes and hence takes time to locate the anatomical regions of interest. All of these have greatly limited the amount of training data we may use to train deep learning models, which, as we have discussed, cannot work well without a large number of training samples.

10.1.2 Responsible AI for healthcare

Healthcare deals closely with people, and the decisions made by healthcare artificial intelligence (AI) systems largely impact people's lives. Therefore, healthcare is one of the most regulated fields so that code of ethics is properly followed in the design of AI systems. With the rapid advances in deep learning research, this becomes increasingly critical as deep learning techniques are imminent to the public, on the one hand, and, on the other hand, the vast majority of deep learning research has ignored this aspect. Specifically, there are challenges in the interpretability, fairness, privacy, security, and safety of deep learning models.

Interpretability.   A major problem that slows down the adoption of deep learning approaches in medicine is their interpretability. Deep learning models are often called blackboxes due to the lack of transparency in their decision-making processes. Given an input, deep neural networks directly output predictions, and this process usually does not provide interpretable information about any intermediate steps or side information that associate the predictions with the inputs. What the deep neural networks can provide is a sequence of extracted features, which, however, cannot be directly understood by human. This, on the one hand, provides flexibility to train deep neural networks end-to-end (which helps improve the performance). But, on the other hand, it results in less confidence in applying deep learning based solutions. Although there is a debate over the necessity of interpretability, the fact is that current deep learning based AI systems have not yet reached a robustness level that healthcare professionals can use with full confidence. Therefore, interpretability becomes important for earning trust from people. Especially when making critical clinical decisions, explicit indicators are often expected so that people can know when the AI systems can be trusted. Given this situation, there are even regulations [20] that require the retraceability of the decisions made by AI systems. At present, interpretability remains hard to come by despite of increasing effort by the machine learning community [12].

Privacy.   Healthcare AI systems are also required to protect patient privacy. In fact, regulations have been made to protect privacy in the collection, use, and sharing of health information [1,21]. This imposes challenges in the training and deployment of healthcare AI systems. In the training stage, it often requires that the training data contains no patient sensitive information, or at least that sensitive information is not directly exposed to model developers. This affects the accessibility of medical data to train deep learning models and thus compromises their performance. In the deployment stage, it requires that the AI systems do not leak patient information in the inference pipeline. First, it is often expected that the trained model should not directly consume patient data but takes input in an encrypted format. Second, it means that the AI models themselves should not leak patient information. In particular, researchers have discovered that deep learning models can memorize training data, and attacks can be made to partially recover sensitive information from deep learning models [9]. In medical image computing, efforts have been made to address the privacy issues involved in the sharing of medical data [23]. However, very few studies have been conducted to address the memorization issue of deep learning models.

Fairness. Another concern is the fairness of AI systems. That is, an AI system should treat different groups of people equally or at least should not discriminate or have bias against underrepresented groups [30]. However, this fairness may not be easily satisfied for deep learning-based approaches. Due to the data-driven nature of deep learning, bias in training data can often be translated into the model's behavior. The major issue comes from the imbalance of training data. It is harder to collect medical data from underrepresented groups [22]. Thus, deep learning models may generalize worse on those groups and result in performance disparity. To address this limitation, one way is to collect more data for underrepresented groups, which, however, may not always be an option. The other way is to design better training strategies to counter the data imbalance, which is nontrivial and requires significant effort in development. Another issue comes from the correlation in data, and deep learning models, however, may learn correlation as causation. For example, if certain skin diseases prominently affect people with darker skin, then models may learn to make decisions based on skin color, not based on skin condition. This kind of bias is more challenging to address since it is a more intrinsic property of the data and requires more dedicated efforts [2,47,50].

Security and safety. An important way of earning trust for AI systems is to make sure they are secure and safe to use. First, they should be robust to malicious actions that aim to compromise the system. For deep learning models, it has been shown that they are vulnerable to deliberate attacks. For example, they can be compromised by privacy attacks and leak sensitive information [9]. Their outputs can also be altered by adversarial attacks [16], which leads to unintentional or damaging predictions. Second, they should be reliable themselves, and the risks of making mistakes should be controllable. This is particularly important for AI systems aimed for the involvement of safety- or life-critical decision-makings. However, due to the performance limitations (e.g., limitations in comprehensiveness and generalizability) and lack of interpretability, almost all current AI systems have yet to improve the safety of their usage and meet the requirements of strict regulations in healthcare.

10.2 **Trends and future directions**

COVID-19 and health.   Starting from 2020, this world has experienced an un-precedented pandemic caused by COVID-19. Ever since its origin, the research community has been studying COVID-19 and seeking solutions to address the disease and control its spread. For medical image computing, we also see a surge in studies on this topic, and most of them have more or less applied deep learning [31]. This dedication has created a great opportunity and testbed to understand the potential of deep learning when addressing real-world problems. In particular, thoracic computed tomography and chest X-ray imaging are the two most studied imaging modalities due to their wide accessibility in COVID-19 diagnosis. Classification and segmentation are the two main tasks involved in these studies for the extraction of lesions and lung lobes, quantification of the corresponding morphological features, and, finally, the diagnosis of COVID-19 [32]. Most of the studies [19,40,26] employ existing deep learning solutions with minor modifications to address COVID-19, which provide insights on how those established models may perform in practice. Some other studies [43,35] propose dedicated solutions to address COVID-19-specific challenges and show promising applications of deep learning in this pandemic crisis. To date, we have not yet seen any signs of the end of COVID-19. We believe COVID-19-related research will continue and drive the future development of medical image computing on certain topics.

Telehealth.   Telehealth is defined as the delivery of health care, health education, and health information services via remote technologies. In the early stage of the COVID-19 pandemic, telehealth usage surged as consumers and providers sought ways to safely access and deliver healthcare. In April 2020, overall telehealth utilization for office visits and outpatient care was reportedly 78 times higher than in February 2020 [6]. This dramatic step-change, out of necessity, was enabled by three factors: 1) increased consumer willingness to use telehealth, 2) increased provider willingness to use telehealth, and 3) regulatory changes enabling greater access and reimbursement. Telehealth offered an alternative bridge to healthcare during such an unprecedented global pandemic. Two years later, while the pandemic is far from being over, the healthcare industry is offered a chance to reinvent virtual and hybrid virtual/in-person care models, with a goal of improved healthcare access, outcomes, and affordability. Against this backdrop, the importance and urgency of incorporating artificial intelligence and machine learning among many enabling technologies, into healthcare, has become more compelling than ever [44].

Federated learning.   Federated learning is a machine learning concept that aims to address the sharing of data and computing resources across multiple parties. It introduces the idea to train machine learning models in a distributed and privacy-preserving way so that only the model related training information is transmitted and shared, and the data is kept locally during training. This fashion of training has several benefits, especially under the healthcare context where there are strict regulations in handling patient information. First, federated learning involves no sharing of medical data which clears the way for data regulations. Second, federated learning makes it possible to include more data sources for the training of machine learning models. This could significantly increase training dataset size which is critical for the success of deep learning based approaches. Third, it provides a way to share computing resources. This could not only reduce the effective training time, but also allow the training of large machine learning models. Due to these benefits, federated learning has been attracting increasing attention from the medical image computing community, and attempts have been made to deploy federated learning solutions for medical image computing approaches [33,36].

Big data and large scale pretraining. Another trend in deep learning is the use of large scale datasets for the pretraining of large models. This effort was originally from the nature language processing (NLP) community where we observed a quantum leap in performance when large scale pretraining is applied. Many researchers see this as a potential future of AI, and hence we start to see even larger models and datasets been used for pretraining. Similar attempts are being made from the computer vision community, and the goal is to replicate the success of language model pretraining for vision models. The focus is to design dedicated architectures and pretraining strategies for images so that vision models can effectively and efficiently learn from a large scale image dataset. Even though the recent approaches [17,11,42,5,18] have shown some benefits from pretraining of vision models, the improvement is still far from the level of language model pretraining. For medical image computing, we also see a trend of large-scale pretraining of models [48,10,34,15], but similar to the observation from natural image pretraining, we have yet to explore the true benefits of pretraining large models for medical images.

Learning with less data. Most machine learning tasks can be summarized as learning a mapping (i.e., function approximation) from a structured input to a structured output, including all the medical image computing tasks covered in this book. Such mappings are often learned on paired training data, where an input sample and its corresponding output are both provided. In medical image computing settings, collecting paired training data often involves high-cost expert annotation, and the scale of paired training data is therefore often limited. As a result, the generalization ability of models trained on paired data is also limited. One way to mitigate such small data challenges in the big data era [37] is learning with unpaired data, which is far less expensive to collect. The challenge of unpaired learning turns into how to align the unpaired data in some fashion. With carefully designed objectives, unpaired learning has achieved remarkable progress on several tasks, including recent successes in a wide variety of computer vision and medical image computing applications [13,45,29]. They motivate the researchers to investigate a unified framework for learning with unpaired data, which would involve some level of explicit disentanglement of compounding factors in addition to cycle consistency [25,49]. Furthermore, it is promising that learning with the combination of large unpaired data and small paired data, via semisupervised learning (SSL) [46] and/or distribution-aware few-shot learning (FSL) [27,52,28,51], could achieve better trade-off between high learning performance and low data cost.

General-purpose models. Together with pretraining we have witnessed the emergence of general-purpose models that are versatile for a wide variety of tasks. One key enabler of general-purpose modeling is the introduction of transformers. They were originally proposed to address NLP problems where they demonstrated the flexibility to handle various NLP problem settings with minor modifications. Moreover, the attention mechanism introduced by transformers makes it very effective in learning the long-range dependencies. This is not only critical in language understanding but is also desirable for other problems, such as image understanding or speech recognition. Therefore, we began to see successful models with transformers in non-NLP tasks, such as image classification [11], object detection [8], speech recognition [3], etc. These successes mean that there exists a uniform architecture that could well address many different tasks and modalities. This unification opens two opportunities. First, it becomes easier to learn from multimodal inputs. This is true even for those modalities with significant differences such as image and text. Second, the pretraining of large models can include tasks and modalities in various forms and thus allow more knowledge to be included in the training process. Due to these benefits, there is recently a momentum along this direction [38,39,4]. For medical image computing, this is also a promising direction to address the comprehensiveness requirement of deploying AI systems in clinical workflows.

References

[1] Accountability Act, Health insurance portability and accountability act of 1996, Public Law 104 (1996) 191.

[2] Mohsan Alvi, Andrew Zisserman, Christoffer Nellåker, Turning a blind eye: explicit removal of biases and variation from deep neural network embeddings, in: Proceedings of the European Conference on Computer Vision (ECCV) Workshops, in: Lecture Notes in Computer Science, vol. 11129, Springer, 2018, pp. 556–572.

[3] Alexei Baevski, Henry Zhou, Abdelrahman Mohamed, Michael Auli, wav2vec 2.0: a framework for self-supervised learning of speech representations, arXiv preprint, arXiv:2006.11477, 2020.

[4] Alexei Baevski, Wei-Ning Hsu, Qiantong Xu, Arun Babu, Jiatao Gu, Michael Auli, data2vec: a general framework for self-supervised learning in speech, vision and language, in: Meta AI, 2022.

[5] Hangbo Bao, Li Dong, Furu Wei, BEiT: BERT pre-training of image transformers, arXiv preprint, arXiv:2106.08254, 2021.

[6] Oleg Bestsennyy, Greg Gilbert, Alex Harris, Jennifer Rost, Telehealth: a quarter-trillion-dollar post-COVID-19 reality?, https://www.mckinsey.com/industries/healthcare-systems-and-services/our-insights/telehealth-a-quarter-trillion-dollar-post-covid-19-reality, 2021.

[7] Adam Bohr, Kaveh Memarzadeh, The rise of artificial intelligence in healthcare applications, in: Artificial Intelligence in Healthcare, Elsevier, 2020, pp. 25–60.

[8] Nicolas Carion, Francisco Massa, Gabriel Synnaeve, Nicolas Usunier, Alexander Kirillov, Sergey Zagoruyko, End-to-end object detection with transformers, in: European Conference on Computer Vision, Springer, 2020, pp. 213–229.

[9] Nicholas Carlini, Florian Tramer, Eric Wallace, Matthew Jagielski, Ariel Herbert-Voss, Katherine Lee, Adam Roberts, Tom Brown, Dawn Song, Ulfar Erlingsson, et al., Extracting training data from large language models, in: 30th USENIX Security Symposium (USENIX Security 21), 2021, pp. 2633–2650.

[10] Liang Chen, Paul Bentley, Kensaku Mori, Kazunari Misawa, Michitaka Fujiwara, Daniel Rueckert, Self-supervised learning for medical image analysis using image context restoration, Medical Image Analysis 58 (2019) 101539.

[11] Alexey Dosovitskiy, Lucas Beyer, Alexander Kolesnikov, Dirk Weissenborn, Xiaohua Zhai, Thomas Unterthiner, Mostafa Dehghani, Matthias Minderer, Georg Heigold, Sylvain Gelly, et al., An image is worth 16×16 words: transformers for image recognition at scale, arXiv preprint, arXiv:2010.11929, 2020.

[12] Mengnan Du, Ninghao Liu, Xia Hu, Techniques for interpretable machine learning, Communications of the ACM 63 (1) (2020) 68–77.

[13] Yang Feng, Lin Ma, Wei Liu, Jiebo Luo, Unsupervised image captioning, in: IEEE Conference on Computer Vision and Pattern Recognition, CVPR 2019, Long Beach, CA, USA, June 16–20, 2019, Computer Vision Foundation / IEEE, 2019, pp. 4125–4134.

[14] Joseph Futoma, Morgan Simons, Trishan Panch, Finale Doshi-Velez, Leo Anthony Celi, The myth of generalisability in clinical research and machine learning in health care, The Lancet Digital Health 2 (9) (2020) e489–e492.

[15] Florin C. Ghesu, Bogdan Georgescu, Awais Mansoor, Youngjin Yoo, Dominik Neumann, Pragneshkumar Patel, R.S. Vishwanath, James M. Balter, Yue Cao, Sasa Grbic, et al., Self-supervised learning from 100 million medical images, arXiv preprint, arXiv:2201.01283, 2022.

[16] Ian J. Goodfellow, Jonathon Shlens, Christian Szegedy, Explaining and harnessing adversarial examples, arXiv preprint, arXiv:1412.6572, 2014.

[17] Kaiming He, Haoqi Fan, Yuxin Wu, Saining Xie, Ross Girshick, Momentum contrast for unsupervised visual representation learning, in: Proceedings of the IEEE/CVF Conference on Computer Vision and Pattern Recognition, 2020, pp. 9729–9738.

[18] Kaiming He, Xinlei Chen, Saining Xie, Yanghao Li, Piotr Dollár, Ross Girshick, Masked autoencoders are scalable vision learners, arXiv preprint, arXiv:2111.06377, 2021.

[19] Ezz El-Din Hemdan, Marwa A. Shouman, Mohamed Esmail Karar, COVIDX-Net: a framework of deep learning classifiers to diagnose COVID-19 in X-ray images, arXiv preprint, arXiv:2003.11055, 2020.

[20] Andreas Holzinger, Chris Biemann, Constantinos S. Pattichis, Douglas B. Kell, What do we need to build explainable AI systems for the medical domain?, arXiv preprint, arXiv:1712.09923, 2017.

[21] Chris Jay Hoofnagle, Bart van der Sloot, Frederik Zuiderveen Borgesius, The European Union general data protection regulation: what it is and what it means, Information & Communications Technology Law 28 (1) (2019) 65–98.

[22] Hussein Ibrahim, Xiaoxuan Liu, Nevine Zariffa, Andrew D. Morris, Alastair K. Denniston, Health data poverty: an assailable barrier to equitable digital health care, The Lancet Digital Health 3 (4) (2021) e260–e265.

[23] Bach Ngoc Kim, Jose Dolz, Christian Desrosiers, Pierre-Marc Jodoin, Privacy preserving for medical image analysis via non-linear deformation proxy, arXiv preprint, arXiv:2011.12835, 2020.

[24] Elmar Kotter, Erik Ranschaert, Challenges and solutions for introducing artificial intelligence (AI) in daily clinical workflow, 2021.

[25] Guillaume Lample, Alexis Conneau, Ludovic Denoyer, Marc'Aurelio Ranzato, Unsupervised machine translation using monolingual corpora only, in: 6th International Conference on Learning Representations, ICLR 2018, Vancouver, BC, Canada, April 30 – May 3, 2018, Conference Track Proceedings, 2018.

[26] Lin Li, Lixin Qin, Zeguo Xu, Youbing Yin, Xin Wang, Bin Kong, Junjie Bai, Yi Lu, Zhenghan Fang, Qi Song, et al., Artificial intelligence distinguishes COVID-19 from community acquired pneumonia on chest CT, Radiology (2020).

[27] Wenbin Li, Jinglin Xu, Jing Huo, Lei Wang, Yang Gao, Jiebo Luo, Distribution consistency based covariance metric networks for few-shot learning, in: The Thirty-Third AAAI Conference on Artificial Intelligence, AAAI 2019, Honolulu, Hawaii, USA, January 27 – February 1, 2019, AAAI Press, 2019, pp. 8642–8649.

[28] Wenbin Li, Lei Wang, Jing Huo, Yinghuan Shi, Yang Gao, Jiebo Luo, Asymmetric distribution measure for few-shot learning, in: Christian Bessiere (Ed.), Proceedings of the Twenty-Ninth International Joint Conference on Artificial Intelligence (IJCAI), 2020, pp. 2957–2963.

[29] Haofu Liao, Wei-An Lin, S. Kevin Zhou, Jiebo Luo, ADN: artifact disentanglement network for unsupervised metal artifact reduction, IEEE Transactions on Medical Imaging 39 (3) (2020) 634–643.

[30] Ninareh Mehrabi, Fred Morstatter, Nripsuta Ani Saxena, Kristina Lerman, A.G. Galstyan, A survey on bias and fairness in machine learning, ACM Computing Surveys 54 (2021) 1–35.

[31] Shahabedin Nabavi, Azar Ejmalian, Mohsen Ebrahimi Moghaddam, Ahmad Ali Abin, Alejandro F. Frangi, Mohammad Mohammadi, Hamidreza Saligheh Rad, Medical imaging and computational image analysis in COVID-19 diagnosis: a review, Computers in Biology and Medicine (2021) 104605.

[32] Francesco Napolitano, Xiaopeng Xu, Xin Gao, Impact of computational approaches in the fight against COVID-19: an AI guided review of 17 000 studies, Briefings in Bioinformatics 23 (1) (2022) bbab456.

[33] Dianwen Ng, Xiang Lan, Melissa Min-Szu Yao, Wing P. Chan, Mengling Feng, Federated learning: a collaborative effort to achieve better medical imaging models for individual sites that have small labelled datasets, Quantitative Imaging in Medicine and Surgery 11 (2) (2021) 852.

[34] Xuan-Bac Nguyen, Guee Sang Lee, Soo Hyung Kim, Hyung Jeong Yang, Self-supervised learning based on spatial awareness for medical image analysis, IEEE Access 8 (2020) 162973–162981.

[35] Yujin Oh, Sangjoon Park, Jong Chul Ye, Deep learning COVID-19 features on CXR using limited training data sets, IEEE Transactions on Medical Imaging 39 (8) (2020) 2688–2700.

[36] Bjarne Pfitzner, Nico Steckhan, Bert Arnrich, Federated learning in a medical context: a systematic literature review, ACM Transactions on Internet Technology 21 (2) (2021) 1–31.

[37] Guo-Jun Qi, Jiebo Luo, Small data challenges in big data era: a survey of recent progress on unsupervised and semi-supervised methods, IEEE Transactions on Pattern Analysis and Machine Intelligence (2020).

[38] Alec Radford, Jong Wook Kim, Chris Hallacy, Aditya Ramesh, Gabriel Goh, Sandhini Agarwal, Girish Sastry, Amanda Askell, Pamela Mishkin, Jack Clark, et al., Learning

transferable visual models from natural language supervision, arXiv preprint, arXiv: 2103.00020, 2021.

[39] Aditya Ramesh, Mikhail Pavlov, Gabriel Goh, Scott Gray, Chelsea Voss, Alec Radford, Mark Chen, Ilya Sutskever, Zero-shot text-to-image generation, arXiv preprint, arXiv: 2102.12092, 2021.

[40] Robbie Sadre, Baskaran Sundaram, Sharmila Majumdar, Daniela Ushizima, Validating deep learning inference during chest X-ray classification for COVID-19 screening, Scientific Reports 11 (1) (2021) 1–10.

[41] The Medical Futurist, Data annotators: the unsung heroes of artificial intelligence development, https://medicalfuturist.com/data-annotation/, 2020.

[42] Hugo Touvron, Matthieu Cord, Matthijs Douze, Francisco Massa, Alexandre Sablayrolles, Hervé Jégou, Training data-efficient image transformers & distillation through attention, in: International Conference on Machine Learning, PMLR, 2021, pp. 10347–10357.

[43] Linda Wang, Zhong Qiu Lin, Alexander Wong, COVID-Net: a tailored deep convolutional neural network design for detection of COVID-19 cases from chest X-ray images, Scientific Reports 10 (1) (2020) 1–12.

[44] Zhenxing Xu, Chang Su, Yunyu Xiao, Fei Wang, Artificial intelligence for COVID-19: battling the pandemic with computational intelligence, Intelligent Medicine (2021).

[45] Xitong Yang, Zheng Xu, Jiebo Luo, Towards perceptual image dehazing by physics-based disentanglement and adversarial training, in: Sheila A. McIlraith, Kilian Q. Weinberger (Eds.), Proceedings of the Thirty-Second AAAI Conference on Artificial Intelligence, (AAAI-18), New Orleans, Louisiana, USA, February 2–7, 2018, AAAI Press, 2018, pp. 7485–7492.

[46] Zhongjie Yu, Lin Chen, Zhongwei Cheng, Jiebo Luo, TransMatch: a transfer-learning scheme for semi-supervised few-shot learning, in: 2020 IEEE/CVF Conference on Computer Vision and Pattern Recognition, CVPR 2020, Seattle, WA, USA, June 13–19, 2020, Computer Vision Foundation / IEEE, 2020, pp. 12853–12861.

[47] Mikhail Yurochkin, Amanda Bower, Yuekai Sun, Training individually fair ML models with sensitive subspace robustness, in: International Conference on Learning Representations, 2019.

[48] Zongwei Zhou, Vatsal Sodha, Md. Mahfuzur Rahman Siddiquee, Ruibin Feng, Nima Tajbakhsh, Michael B. Gotway, Jianming Liang, Models genesis: generic autodidactic models for 3D medical image analysis, in: International Conference on Medical Image Computing and Computer-Assisted Intervention, Springer, 2019, pp. 384–393.

[49] Jun-Yan Zhu, Taesung Park, Phillip Isola, Alexei A. Efros, Unpaired image-to-image translation using cycle-consistent adversarial networks, CoRR, arXiv:1703.10593 [abs], 2017.

[50] Wei Zhu, Haitian Zheng, Haofu Liao, Weijian Li, Jiebo Luo, Learning bias-invariant representation by cross-sample mutual information minimization, in: Proceedings of the IEEE/CVF International Conference on Computer Vision, 2021, pp. 15002–15012.

[51] Wei Zhu, Haofu Liao, Wenbin Li, Weijian Li, Jiebo Luo, Alleviating the incompatibility between cross entropy loss and episode training for few-shot skin disease classification, in: Medical Image Computing and Computer Assisted Intervention (MICCAI), Springer, 2020.

[52] Wei Zhu, Wenbin Li, Haofu Liao, Jiebo Luo, Temperature network for few-shot learning with distribution-aware large-margin metric, Pattern Recognition 112 (2021) 107797.

Index

Printed in the United States
by Baker & Taylor Publisher Services